TAMERLANE

TIMUR ON HIS THRONE
(BY BIHZAD)

Zafar Nama
From a MS. dated A.D. 1467

TAMERLANE

THE LIFE OF THE GREAT AMIR

BY

AHMAD IBN 'ARABSHAH

TRANSLATED BY

J.H. SANDERS

INTRODUCTION BY

R.D. McCHESNEY

I.B. TAURIS
LONDON · NEW YORK

New edition published in 2018 by
I.B.Tauris & Co Ltd
London • New York
www.ibtauris.com

First published by Luzac & Co. in 1936 as *Tamerlane or Timur the Great Amir*

ISBN: 978 1 78453 170 6

A full CIP record for this book is available from the British Library
A full CIP record is available from the Library of Congress

Library of Congress Catalog Card Number: available

Printed and bound by CPI Group (UK) Ltd, Croydon, CR0 4YY

FSC
www.fsc.org **MIX** Paper from responsible sources **FSC® C013604**

CONTENTS

CONTENTS

XV

INTRODUCTION
by R.D. McChesney

In the late summer of 1405, when the body of the great Central Asian conqueror, Amir Timur, was returned to his capital, Samarkand, for burial, one
of the residents of the city was a 16-year-old Syrian boy from Damascus
named Ahmad, better known to his later colleagues, and to us today, as Ibn
'Arabshah.[1] Some three decades later, he would take reed in hand and begin
to write what became a world-famous history of Timur, *'Aja'ib al-maqdur fi
nawa'ib Timur* [The Wonders of Destiny Concerning the Calamities Wrought
by Timur]. It is unquestionably one of the most important sources not just
for Timur's life but for the history of the events immediately following his
death (approximately one-third of the book is devoted to the period after
1405). Written in an elegantly literary and very difficult style (referred to by
some as florid and verbose), its fame outside the Arab world has in large
part been generated by the present 1936 translation of it by a gifted but
now-obscure amateur Arabist, J. H. Sanders of the India Civil Service.

While the Sanders translation has been of enormous influence on the
study of Timur in modern times, Ibn 'Arabshah's own life, about which the
translator actually had little to say, has remained relatively unknown. The few
accounts of it found in Western encyclopaedias[2] are abbreviated and do
little to provide any understanding of Ibn 'Arabshah's nearly pathological
distaste for his subject, Amir Timur.

Ibn 'Arabshah's Life

The sources for Ibn 'Arabshah's life are quite rich, in part because he became
a renowned figure and in part because of his connections to three of the
greatest biographers of the fifteenth century writing in Arabic: al-Maqrizi
(1364–1442), Ibn Taghribirdi (1411–69), and al-Sakhawi (al-Sakhawi
(1427–97).

Al-Maqrizi died eight years before Ibn 'Arabshah and so only knew his subject at a certain point in his life but they met several times and on at least one of those occasions Ibn 'Arabshah read to al-Maqrizi from his biography of Timur, which al-Maqrizi says he called *"Umur Timur"* [The Affairs of Timur], a title far from the elaborate one that Ibn 'Arabshah would eventually give it, indicating that the biography of Timur was still a work in progress. Al-Maqrizi's biographical entry for Ibn 'Arabshah focuses on the latter's command of rhetoric rather than his skill as a historian, suggesting that he heard the work that was read to him as an example of Ibn 'Arabshah's rhetorical competence and not as history or biography.[3]

al-Sakhawi and Ibn Taghribirdi, both much younger than al-Maqrizi, outlived Ibn 'Arabshah and so had the advantage of being able to view his entire career. As a consequence they both provide long and comparatively detailed biographies of him, which naturally overlap in many places but also complement one another.[4] The bulk of Ibn Taghribirdi's biographical entry for Ibn 'Arabshah is actually the latter's autobiography, a first-person account presented to the Egyptian scholar in writing in the form of an *ijaza*, a certificate or license giving Ibn Taghribirdi the authority to teach and transmit all of Ibn 'Arabshah's works. The *ijaza* was signed and dated by Ibn 'Arabshah on 15 January 1450, a little more than seven months before his death.[5]

al-Sakhawi's entry on Ibn 'Arabshah, on the other hand, is a third-person account, although he does tell the reader that he met Ibn 'Arabshah in Cairo in 850/1446 at a *khanqah*, or hostel, restricted to Sufi visitors to the capital.[6] al-Sakhawi's sources, besides Ibn 'Arabshah himself, include al-Maqrizi, whom he cites, and "others" (*ba'duhum*) whom he does not specifically name but who probably included Taj al-Din 'Abd al-Wahhab (d. 1495), Ibn 'Arabshah's son.

Ibn 'Arabshah also provides information about his own life in his history of Timur. Although he makes only a few direct references to himself, there are numerous indirect references that may be understood as autobiographical, thanks to information given in these other three sources.

Finally, Ibn 'Arabshah's son, Taj al-Din, a noted scholar in his own right, wrote a biography of his father, *Tarjamat walidihi sahib Fakihat al-khulafa* [Biography of the Author of *Fakihat al-khulafa*], which, however, does not seem to have survived but may have been one of al-Sakhawi's sources.[7]

Ibn 'Arabshah's Life and Career

Ibn 'Arabshah was born in Damascus on 15 November 1389 and, after an adventure-filled life, died a highly respected scholar in Cairo in late August 1450.[8] Other than the date of his birth, we have very little information about his childhood. This is not surprising given the tendency in biographical literature to focus on the accomplishments of the adult years. We know that he grew up in Damascus and studied the Koran there under a Koran-reciter named al-Zayn 'Umar b. al-Labban.[9] Perhaps Ibn 'Arabshah's father was a businessman or skilled artisan – someone who could afford to send his son to a *maktab* to study the Koran or perhaps even hire al-Zayn 'Umar as a private tutor.

When Ibn 'Arabshah was just 11 years old his world was turned upside down. In the late fall of 1400, Damascus fell victim to Timur, who besieged the city and the Mamluk garrison defending it. A Mamluk army sent to confront the Central Asians withdrew without a fight, leaving the garrison on its own. As Ibn 'Arabshah tells the story, the garrison only surrendered after obtaining guarantees of security "forty-three days" after Timur first entered Damascus. However, no security was actually given and, after its surrender and execution, the whole city was turned over to Timur's troops for the traditional three days of rape, plunder, and murder (*qatl-i 'amm*):

> And they took matrons prisoners, uncovered the veils of veiled women, made the unveiled suns descend from the orbits of palaces and the moons of beauty from the sky of dalliance, afflicting great and small alike with every torture … and men fled from their brothers, mothers, fathers, friends and children … and I call God to witness that those days were a sign among the signs of the last day. And this general plunder lasted three days.[10]

This is somewhat rhetorical to be sure, yet one cannot help but feel there was a good deal of Ibn 'Arabshah's own experience being described here. Matrons taken prisoner and men fleeing their children, sounds like what might have been happening to his own family. When Timur and his troops finally withdrew, among the spoils of war was the 11-year-old Ibn 'Arabshah, his mother and sister, and, according to al-Sakhawi, his sister's son. In his *ijaza* to Ibn Taghribirdi, Ibn 'Arabshah only briefly mentions this event, which at his age must have been extremely traumatic. The trauma comes through more clearly in the lengthy account he gives to the siege and its aftermath in *'Aja'ib al-maqdur*. In the *ijaza*, after relating the precise time of his birth, he launches rather laconically into this apparently first memorable event of his life:

> It happened that I made my way to Samarkand with [my] sister and [my] mother as a result of the disaster which happened in 803 [1401] at the hand of the God-forsaken Timurlank.[11]

He does not say here 'we were taken as captives' but that was the story he told al-Maqrizi, for the latter writes, "he was among those who were taken prisoner and transported with the Timurid army (*al-Timuriyya*) to Samarkand."[12] Ibn 'Arabshah probably told the story of his capture and transportation from Damascus in late winter 1401 to many different people but when it came time to write out the *ijaza* for Ibn Taghribirdi, perhaps because he realized his end was near, he omitted things that he did not consider relevant to the *ijaza* or, more likely, that he did not want people to remember about him.

The Timurid army, its size now swollen with booty and prisoners, including women like Ibn 'Arabshah's mother and sister, who were probably taken for the sexual pleasure of the troops, now left Damascus. A more positive interpretation often placed on Timur's transportation of captured populations to Central Asia is that he wanted to have access to their artisans, artists, and scholars and that the women and children transported were presumably the families of the artisans. There is nothing to suggest that this was the case with Ibn 'Arabshah and his family. Sexual slavery would seem to have been the fate of many Syrian women, including "maidens and brides" taken in Homs and Hama.[13]

However, a few of those involuntarily returning with Timur did go as honored guests. Ibn 'Arabshah mentions two: 'Abd al-Malik Tikriti and Yalbugha "al-Majnun" (the demented one) being later appointed governors in Central Asia. Of the people whom Timur hoped would bring lustre to his capital, Samarkand, were:

> learned men and craftsmen and all who excelled in any art, the most skilled weavers, tailors, gem-cutters, carpenters, makers of head coverings, farriers, painters, bow-makers, falconers, in short, craftsmen of every kind ... Likewise all his amirs and lords took an infinite multitude of theologians, of men who knew the Koran from memory, and learned men, craftsmen, slaves, women, boys and girls....[14]

But the horde of displaced persons was, as one would expect, not so fortunate – desperate, miserable, and fearful of what lay ahead. Timur could have had no inkling that in this mass of humanity there was a young boy who would return to his native land one day and devote himself to blackening Timur's name forever in the Arabic–reading world.

At Hama, the force turned east, striking out across what was mostly desert, to reach the banks of the Tigris almost 120 miles away. There they crossed in boats, perhaps near present-day al-Raqqa, then continued on in a north-easterly direction reaching Mardin, another 130 miles away on the 10th Ramadan (24 April 1401). This must have been a trip from hell for Ibn 'Arabshah and his family – and more was to come.

At this point, Timur's army and captives had covered at least 360 miles in perhaps a little more than fifty days. At Mardin the captives had a chance to rest as Timur mounted a month-long (ultimately unsuccessful) siege of Mardin's citadel. When he lifted the siege, he turned his eyes on Baghdad. Before he marched down the Euphrates, however, he dispatched many of the captives to Samarkand under the command of Allahdad Bahadur, one of Timur's generals and a man for whom Ibn 'Arabshah later showed considerable respect in his book.

The group that was sent on to Samarkand almost certainly included Ibn 'Arabshah, and probably his mother, sister and nephew as well. We can make this assumption for a number of reasons. First, he provides a fairly detailed itinerary of the group's march to Samarkand, with a plausible account of the speed with which it moved. Second, he names one of the notable individuals sent with this group as if he was familiar with him. Third, when he returns to his account of Timur's 1401 attack on Baghdad, he indicates that he was not with the army, telling the reader that he was later briefed about the Baghdad attack and its bloody aftermath by Qadi Taj al-Din Ahmad al-Nu'mani, the Hanafi governor of Baghdad at the time of the assault.[15] So it seems most likely that Ibn 'Arabshah was in the group that was sent off to Samarkand shortly after the siege of Mardin ended. Here is Ibn 'Arabshah's account as given in the translation:

> Then he [Timur] descended to Bagdad [sic] with troops countless like ants, moths, and locusts, and sent a company to Samarkand with Allahdad and they reached the city of Sur, where there was no high-built house; then came to Khalat and Abduljauz, which are populous cities of the Kurds, well built and first among those submitting to his authority in the provinces of Tabriz and Azerbaijan; and the company kept that holy day of Ramzan [sic, presumably the 'Id al-Fitr, 14–15 May 1401] at Abduljauz.
>
> Then they entered the province of Tabriz, then Sultania and then the territories of Khorasan. And now the winter was ending and spring adorning herself and approaching ... And that company continued its journey day and night, not like the pilgrims of Mecca, who daily complete the day's journey and rest each night; then they reached Nisabur, then Jam, then they crossed the deserts of Bavard and Makhan, then came to Andkhui, then to the river Oxus, which they crossed in skiffs, and proceeded on their journey like a piercing star, and at length came to Samarkand on the thirteenth day of Muharram and the third day of the week in the year 804 [23 August 1401]. There were among them many Syrians, of whom the chief was Qazi Shahabuddin Ahmad, son of the martyr Vazir, while the rest were farriers, dyers and silkworkers. And this was the first spoil which he had brought from Syria and the first fruits of prisoners and wealth, which he had plucked, to reach Samarkand.[16]

All told, Ibn 'Arabshah's party spent about a hundred days on the road from 'Abd al-Jawz (somewhere just west of Tabriz) to Samarkand.

We can never know for certain why Ibn 'Arabshah and his mother, sister and nephew were taken to Samarkand. His experiences in Timur's capital, where he would stay for the next eight years, indicate that he was not a slave, although he may have been kept for his sexual attractiveness until he reached puberty. He was apparently free to pursue an education and he might have had a sponsor in doing that since one did not sit at the feet of the masters with whom he studied without paying a fee or perhaps working off the tuition. Conceivably, Ibn 'Arabshah's including "silkworkers" among the group brought to Samarkand could have included his mother and sister but there is no real evidence. One would hardly expect that the fate of his mother and sister would ever have been explicitly stated had it been to serve the sexual needs of Timur's troops, and in some ways it is surprising to find it even alluded to. Perhaps it is a measure of how traumatized the boy had been that in writing and telling about it years later he would mention things that the reader or listener who knew the context would understand as happening to him or his family.

It is difficult not to conclude that it was this moment in his life – the kidnapping of his family from Damascus – that sowed the seeds of his antipathy for Timur. To be wrenched from Arabic-speaking Damascus by foreigners whose tongue was completely alien to him, and to be forced to make the long march to Samarkand and a very uncertain future, could hardly have left the young man with feelings of respect and warmth for Timur. And there is also the unknown fate of his father. Neither Ibn Taghribirdi nor al-Sakhawi seems to mention him, which suggests that he had no distinction as a scholar. Ibn 'Arabshah's silence on the subject suggests his father was dead or had vanished and may indicate a lack of close attachment to his father. His own rhetoric in describing the havoc wreaked in Damascus by Timur's troops – "men fled from their brothers, mothers, fathers, friends and children" – is also suggestive of the fate of his father.

The education of Ibn 'Arabshah in Samarkand (1401–9)

Ibn 'Arabshah would stay in Samarkand for some eight years. He arrived at a most extraordinary moment, when some of the greatest figures in fifteenth-century scholarship were gathered there – many against their will. But for Ibn 'Arabshah the moment was brief. Although Ibn 'Arabshah stayed in Samarkand for eight years, Timur died only a little more than three years after his arrival and with Timur's death there was a mass departure of scholars to other more welcoming places. We do not know how quickly these men departed Samarkand after Timur's death but we know that they did leave. It is probably safe to say that Ibn 'Arabshah would have had four or five years to take advantage of the presence of some of the greatest figures in Islamic scholarship, men known even in their own time as great, and elevated to the status of intellectual legends after their deaths. One of the greatest of these, Sa'd al-Din Mas'ud al-Taftazani, had already passed from the scene when Ibn 'Arabshah found himself in Samarkand but 'Ali b. Muhammad al-Jurjani, known as al-Sayyid al-Sharif, al-Taftazani's successor as dean of the city's intellectuals, was at the peak of his powers and influence.

Another great figure who arrived in Samarkand about a year after Ibn 'Arabshah was a fellow Damascene, Shams al-Din Muhammad b. Muhammad al-Jazari, in his early fifties when Ibn 'Arabshah first met him. Al-Jazari was renowned for his scholarship in the Islamic subjects of jurisprudence, the variant readings of the Koran, and in the Traditions (*hadiths*) of the Prophet Muhammad. He wrote an enormously popular work of selected *hadiths* used in prayer called *al-Hisn al-hasin* [The Mighty Fortress] that was a staple in the library of any Sunni who had one. He was a well established scholar in the Arab lands and in Anatolia, where he had, from his standpoint at least, the misfortune to be serving the Ottoman sultan, Bayazid I (r. 1389–1402) at the time of the latter's defeat at Ankara by Timur on 20 July 1402. Forcibly taken back to Central Asia, first to Kash and then to Samarkand, al-Jazari made the best of it for the approximately two years he spent in Samarkand before Timur died. He was ensconced at the Bagh-i Khuda,[17] one of the garden residences for which the city was famous and from this fact, and from the reputation he already had, we know Timur treated him well. One can imagine that Ibn 'Arabshah might have offered al-Jazari his help in getting acclimated to Samarkand and the latter might well have been grateful for the help of this young man from his own home town.

It is not unreasonable to think that al-Jazari and Ibn 'Arabshah, despite the nearly forty-year difference in their ages, were in some sense kindred spirits. Both were originally from Damascus and both had been forced against their will to leave their homes and move to Samarkand. Also, Ibn 'Arabshah was already well trained in Arabic, the only language that al-Jazari ever wrote in or probably ever really knew.

The second great scholar that Ibn 'Arabshah claims to have studied with in his early teenage years in Samarkand was the dean of Samarkand scholars: 'Ali al-Jurjani (1339–1413), "al-Sayyid al-Sharif" (the Noble Sayyid). Like al-Jazari and Ibn 'Arabshah, al-Jurjani had been forcibly brought to Samarkand after Timur captured Shiraz in south-western Iran in 1387.

Al-Jurjani was a prolific and well known scholar by the time he arrived in Samarkand as a privileged captive. Using the commentary form as the medium of choice for his works, he wrote on jurisprudence, logic, law, Arabic grammar, theology and lexicography. In Samarkand, al-Jurjani's base was the Idigu (Edige?) Timur Madrasa[18] and it was here that Ibn 'Arabshah attended his lectures.

A third very influential figure with whom he had at least enough of an acquaintance to include him in his *ijaza* was a man he calls simply Mawlana Muhammad al-Bukhari al-Zahid ("our master Muhammad from Bukhara, the ascetic") who, he says, wrote a "one hundred volume commentary on the Koran." Muhammad al-Bukhari "the Ascetic" was far better known later in Naqshbandi Sufi circles by the name Khwaja Muhammad Parsa (d. 1420).

Although the list of Ibn 'Arabshah's teachers is illustrious, nothing suggests that they were particularly kind to him. He appears to have suffered, as many students did, from overbearing and sometimes even sadistic teachers.

There is a section in the 'Aja'ib where Ibn 'Arabshah seems to be reflecting on his experiences as a student under a harsh mentor:

> But some [teachers], along with poverty of estate and subtlety of the faculties and abundant learning and elegance had a heart harder than rock and by their deeds wounded more vehemently than the blows of the sharpest sword, speaking with the words of the most excellent of creatures [i.e. the Prophet] but bending away from religion as the arrow bends the bow. When any Muslim fell into their talons or a stranger was afflicted by their torture, that wise searcher of truth and subtle doctor in extorting wealth devised tortures and torments of diverse sorts and employed books and questions as means of torture and composed speeches and dissertations in the science of accusation, but when that wretched one was scorched with pain and lamented and with impatient wrath implored the aid of God and His miracles and besought the intercession of all those in earth and sky, angels, prophets, friends and helpers, that elegant one would smile and show his skill and turn proudly this way and that, flatter, recite witty verses and employ the refinement of rare sentiments and histories; sometimes he would be kindled with anger and would weep and groan at the torture which he inflicted and grieve vehemently and do as some judges of Islam, who having seized the goods of orphans and lament, while by their deeds they wound the hearts of Muslims.[19]

One would like to know which of his teachers might have inspired such resentful feelings.

Samarkand to Astrakhan, 1409–11

Now begins a peripatetic period for Ibn 'Arabshah. He did not immediately leave Samarkand, as many scholars did on Timur's death, but remained four more years, his departure coinciding apparently with the time when Timur's youngest son, Shahrukh, took Samarkand in 811/1409 and ended the struggle to succeed Timur.

Despite the departure of his teachers, there were many factors that might have kept Ibn 'Arabshah from following his mentors west any earlier than 1409 – for example, his age (he was just 16 when Timur died but 20 when he quit Samarkand), and possible family obligations.

One important skill he gained at Samarkand and polished subsequently was linguistic. "I acquired the ability to speak Persian (al-lisan al-farisi) and to write 'Mongol' (al-khatt al-mughuli)," he notes in the ijaza.[20] Spoken Persian would certainly have been extremely important to him in Samarkand. All his formal studies with al-Jazari and al-Jurjani would have been in written Arabic and, certainly with al-Jazari at least and probably with al-Jurjani, any lectures and discussions would have been in Arabic. But with the people he had to deal with daily in Samarkand – shopkeepers, officials, and service people – Persian would have been the language to speak. What he meant by 'Mongol' is probably what his Spanish contemporary, Ruy Gonzalez de Clavijo, meant by it – i.e. Chaghatay Turkish.[21] If we imagine the career prospects of a literate young man in the Timurid capital, it is not hard to understand why written Chaghatay would have been useful to know.

By the time he left Samarkand Ibn 'Arabshah had lived through momentous times. He was there when news came of the victory of Timur over the Ottoman sultan Bayazid I at Ankara on 27th of Dhu'l-Hijja 804/28 (28 July 1402);[22] he was present when Ruy Gonzalez de Clavijo, ambassador of King Henry III of Castile and Leon, accompanied by an ambassador of the Mamluk sultan, al-Malik al-Nasir Faraj, arrived in the city in 1404;[23] and he was there for the great feast that was held that same year to celebrate the marriages of some of Timur's sons and grandsons (although he was probably not invited). He probably witnessed the construction work on Timur's huge congregational mosque and work done on Muhammad Sultan's (Timur's grandson's) *madrasa*-tomb complex, where Timur himself would eventually be buried. Yet he gives no signs either in his *ijaza* or *'Aja'ib al-maqdur* that he was aware of any of these at the time they were happening. If he was, he left no record of them as far as we know. He was in Samarkand when Timur set out on his final campaign and was there when Timur's body was brought back and buried beside his grandson. When he records this and other events thirty years later, he does so in a manner that distances himself as bystander, observer, or participant in any of them. How aware he was of them as they happened cannot be answered.

After a brief sojourn in the east, Ibn 'Arabshah turned around and headed for Khwarazm. By this point he was almost certainly married for he switches from the first person singular, used up to this point in the *ijaza,* to the plural ("then we made our way to Khwarazm"). In Khwarazm (probably meaning here the city of Urganj) Ibn 'Arabshah says he studied with "Mawlana Nur Allah and Mawlana Ahmad al-Wa'iz al-Sara'i the son of Shams al-A'imma." Ibn 'Arabshah describes the latter thus: "He is called the king of eloquence (*malik al-kalam*) in Persian, Turkish and Arabic."[24]

His stay in Khwarazm must have been brief – a year at most. From Urganj he set off across the desert for Saray. At this time Saray, on the lower Volga River, was still an attractive destination despite Timur's sacking and burning of it in 1395. It remained the capital of the Golden Horde, or the remnants of that once mighty western Mongol power. The politics of the place probably mattered little to Ibn 'Arabshah. To all appearances he was prompted to head for the lower Volga region by the reputation of the people he hoped to study with there, despite the difficulties posed by travel conditions.

His comments in *'Aja'ib al-maqdur* emphasize the challenge, even in settled times, of crossing the desert that flanks the northern and eastern sides of the Caspian Sea, let alone the parlous times in which he lived. He imagined that conditions for the caravans that had in the past routinely made the journey from Khwarazm to what is now south-west Russia and the southernmost part of the Ukraine were far better than those he experienced. In the *'Aja'ib*, he blames Timur's devastating 1395 campaign for the changed conditions.

> There used to advance convoys from Khwarazm, making the journey in wag-
> ons, securely without terror or fear, as far as Crimea – a journey of about three
> months; in width there is a sea of sands as broad as seven seas through which
> the most skilful guide could not show the way nor the most crafty of experi-
> enced men make the journey and those convoys did not take supplies or fodder
> or join to themselves companions – this because of the multitude of the people,
> and the abundance of security, food and drink among the inhabitants, and did
> not set out except tribe by tribe or turn aside except to one who would receive
> his guest generously, so that they were well described by that verse:
>
> > All the people of Mecca go round the hill of Okaz
> > And their sons shout: "There comes a guest."
>
> But now through those places from Khwarazm to the Crimea of those people
> and their followers none moves or rests and nothing ranges there but ante-
> lopes and camels.[25]

In other words in pre-Timurid times the hospitality and generosity of people on the route ensured the safe and speedy passage of anyone who traveled it. Nonetheless he himself did not hesitate to set off, although we have to assume that it took him a good deal longer than the three months he says caravans previously took in traveling all the way to the Crimea.

After a short stay in Saray, Ibn 'Arabshah went to Astrakhan, where he became the student of one of the most famous of Hanafi legal scholars of his age, Mawlana Hafiz al-Din Muhammad, the son of Nasir al-Din Muhammad al-Bazzazi al-Kardari. "I stayed with him about four years," he writes, "and from him learned legal reasoning (*fiqh*) and its principles."[26]

Astrakhan to Aleppo, 1411–21

After Astrakhan, Ibn 'Arabshah moved to Old Qirim on the easternmost tip of the Crimean peninsula, near present-day Kerch, where he attended sessions with two scholars: Mawlana Ahmad Bayruq and Mawlana Sharaf al-Din b. Kamal al-Qirimi. His association with Mawlana Sharaf al-Din shows his continuing interest in acquiring credentials in jurisprudence, although, as mentioned above, his own writings do not reflect that interest at all. One strongly suspects that these credentials were intended to serve the more practical purpose of landing a job, as in fact they eventually did.

From the port of Kefe in the Crimea, Ibn 'Arabshah took ship sometime in or after 1413 for the western shores of the Black Sea, probably disem-
barking at Sozopolis, the nearest Black Sea port to Edirne (Adrianople), at this time the Ottoman capital. In 1413 Muhammad b. Bayazid, known as Mehmed I, succeeded in establishing himself in Edirne as sultan of much

of the former Ottoman state, at least the part that lay in the Balkans and Rumeli. It seems likely that Ibn 'Arabshah went to Edirne at this particular moment to seek Mehmed's patronage. It would have seemed like an auspicious moment. As an outsider he had the advantage of not having been a partisan of any of the other princely or non-princely factions that Mehmed had to overcome. Thanks to his background, or perhaps thanks to the intervention of an old friend, he was soon working as a *munshi* (drafter of correspondence) for the sultan and as an interpreter and translator. The friend was al-Jazari's son, Shaykh Abu al-Khayr, and it is reasonable to imagine that he provided Ibn 'Arabshah with an entree to the court. In the *ijaza*, Ibn 'Arabshah describes this period and what he was doing:

> Then I crossed the Black Sea (*Bahr al-Rum*) to the land of the Ottomans where I stayed for about ten [*sic* probably no more than eight] years. There, for al-Malik Ghiyath al-Din Abu'l-Fath Muhammad [Mehmed] b. Abi Yazid Murad b. Adar Khan b. Uthman – May God Most High have mercy on his soul – I translated from Persian into Turkish *Kitab Jami al-hikayat wa lami' al-riwayat* [A Collection of Stories and a Luster of Narratives] in some six volumes, [from Arabic] into Turkish, Abu al-Layth al-Samarkandi's commentary on the Koran, and [translated into Turkish] and versified the *Ta'bir al-Qadiri* [al-Qadiri's Dream Interpretation]. After this I worked for him [Mehmed I] as a writer of formal correspondence (*insha'*) during which I wrote on his behalf to foreign kings in Arabic, Persian, and Turkish. I also read *al-Miftah* with Mawlana Burhan al-Din Haydarat [sic] al-Khwafi.[27]

This suggests that the focus of his working life in Edirne was government work and perhaps less on engagement with the intellectuals who had gathered under Mehmed's patronage. We should keep in mind that he was only in his early twenties when he arrived in Edirne and there is no sign that others saw him as academically qualified to recite works and have his own students. Quite the contrary: it was he who was consistently seeking out others to instruct him. This would seem to have been the case throughout his time at Edirne and well after he returned to Syria.

In 1421, probably due to Mehmed I's death, Ibn 'Arabshah returned to Syria, but he does not give this as a reason for moving on. Certainly he must have been curious about, if not homesick for, Damascus. Stopping first in Aleppo and finding himself back on his native soil for the first time since his kidnapping twenty years earlier, he affectionately refers to it as "the old homeland" (*al-watan al-qadim*). "I stayed there [in Aleppo] for about four months then made my way to Damascus entering it in Rabi' al-Akhira 825 (March–April 1422).[28]

Damascus and Cairo, 1422–50

Ibn 'Arabshah would settle in Damascus and spend the rest of his life there, though he made frequent and prolonged trips to Cairo. He lived fairly modestly according to his *ijaza*, without entree to the governor's court or to any other source of patronage, at least for a time. In the obituary for him in *al-Nujum al-zahira*, Ibn Taghribirdi says, "he had held a number of religious offices, including that of Cadi (qadi) of Hama on occasions."[29] But it would take him awhile to establish himself. As he would later recall: "I did not try to make contact with anyone and wrapped the foot of effort in the hem of frugality,"[30] by which I understand him to mean he had to find real work (as distinct from a government appointment) to keep himself alive. This is not surprising: whatever patronage he enjoyed under Mehmed I was not transferable to Damascus. Although scholars could and did pass back and forth between the Ottoman and Mamluk territories, they were either clients of the patronage system of one or the other and it would have been highly unusual to carry a letter of introduction from an Ottoman patron to a prospective Mamluk one.

In any case Ibn 'Arabshah's Ottoman patron, if one can call the relationship a patronage one, was dead and there is little to suggest Ibn 'Arabshah yet had a reputation that would have solicited such an invitation from a Mamluk patron. As he told the story to al-Maqrizi and al-Sakhawi, although in somewhat different terms, he had to earn his living in Damascus working in an unprestigious profession. When he met al-Maqrizi in Cairo in 840/1436-7 he told him that when he first arrived back in Damascus "he earned his living as a professional notary [*shahid* pl. *shuhud*] in the stalls of the notaries."[31] Ten years later, when he met al-Sakhawi for the first time, he appears to have revised this somewhat in a way that suggests he felt the work was unworthy of him: "He [Ibn 'Arabshah] sat in the stall of the Qasab Mosque with its (other) notaries where most of the time it was easy to stay clear of the common herd."[32]

It is not surprising that he might have wanted to gloss over his work as a notary. After serving as the Ottoman sultan's amanuensis, or so depicting himself, being a mere notary among the hundreds that must have populated Damascus at the time might have seemed an embarrassing plunge in status. A man of his apparent – though we should remember mostly self-reported – skills (linguistic, diplomatic, and literary) might be expected to have an entree to the governor's court or at least the household of a wealthy merchant or religious figure, but for reasons unknown Ibn 'Arabshah either did not seek employment on his return to Damascus or, as seems more likely, simply had to make a virtue of necessity, not finding a market for his particular talents.

This situation may have lasted about seven or eight years. In his mind the turning point of his return to Damascus came during the last days of Muharram 832/early November 1428, with the arrival in Damascus of Mawlana Abu 'Abd Allah Muhammad b. Muhammad al-Bukhari, a man better known to his contemporaries than to posterity and not to be confused with Khwaja Muhammad Parsa.

al-Bukhari clearly became Ibn 'Arabshah's most important mentor. Not only did he work with him for nine years – by far the longest contact he had had with any other scholar – but the attributes he accords him are far more extensive than those he accords any other scholar – "accomplished, consummate, and excellent, pearl of the age, phoenix of time, wisest of men, teacher of the world … pole star of his time, guide of the age…."[33]

Writing Timur's biography

By the time of his return to Damascus, the idea of a book about Timur must have been percolating in Ibn 'Arabshah's head. One of the oral sources whom he cites in Aja'ib is Mawlana Jamal al-Din Ahmad al-Khwarazmi. The story that Ibn 'Arabshah proceeds to narrate from al-Khwarazmi makes it clear that the interview could not have taken place in Samarkand because the story relates to events that happened after al-Khwarazmi left the city following Timur's death. The last months of 824/1421, when Ibn 'Arabshah was on his way out of Ottoman territory, seem the most likely time for their meeting. What is most interesting about al-Khwarazmi's story, is that it is not about an event or deed related to Timur particularly but rather is al-Khwarazmi's mea culpa for having served Timur. In the story, he tells of an encounter with some warriors of Timur, who speak bitterly and regretfully of the atrocities they have been forced to commit as obedient soldiers. They profess wonder that someone of al-Khwarazmi's apparent learning and moral stature would willingly choose to serve such wickedness. Al-Khwarazmi berates himself in the story for having done so and says how this reminder of his sins has added "affliction to my affliction and trouble to my troubles." The story is quite long, taking up six pages (pp. 324–30) in the Sanders translation and its moral point is never in doubt. It is not unthinkable that part of the inspiration for writing the kind of history that Ibn 'Arabshah undertook came from this self-flagellating tale of al-Khwarazmi. Or at least, perhaps, the story served to focus Ibn 'Arabshah's own sense of moral outrage.

Whatever the time and significance of his interview with al-Khwarazmi, one can at least say that by 831/1427–8 Ibn 'Arabshah had formulated the idea of writing a history of Timur and was beginning his research, dredging his own memory and mining the recollections of others who had lived and worked in Samarkand. Some considerable part of the intellectual activity of the next nine years of his life would be devoted to interviewing sources and organizing and writing the history.[34]

From the interview that took place 833/1429–30, Ibn 'Arabshah learned that after the people of Sistan returned to their cities following Timur's withdrawal from the region, they wanted to perform the Friday prayer but they no longer knew when Friday was and someone had to be sent from Kerman to tell them.[35] From the interview of 836/(28 August 1432), this one with his Damascus mentor al-Bukhari, he was told that Timur killed his arch-rival Sultan (or Amir) Husayn in Sha'ban 771 (March 1370), the point from which Timur's reign as ruler of the former Chaghatayid lands of Central Asia is conventionally dated.[36]

His career progresses

The years after 830/1426–7 were highly productive for Ibn 'Arabshah, with more than just research for the book on Timur. He was beginning to make a name for himself with other works of rhetoric as well. In 836/1432–3 al-Sakhawi writes that Ibn 'Arabshah met Ibn Hajar al-'Asqalani, arguably the most famous living scholar in the Mamluk realm, and recited his *Mir'at al-adab* [Mirror of Etiquette] to him, a 2,000-verse work in *ghazal* format on rhetoric. Ibn Hajar al-'Asqalani was said to be impressed.[37] It would appear, then, that by the mid-830s/early 1430s Ibn 'Arabshah was becoming known in fairly rarefied scholarly circles as a capable and noteworthy rhetorician. It was at this time that he must have realized he would need to go to Cairo and try to see the Mamluk sultan, if his reputation had become well known enough to warrant an official appointment and thus a respectable income.

The first record we have that Ibn 'Arabshah visited Cairo comes in 840 (the year began 16 July 1436), when he met al-Maqrizi for the first time. This year was also important, for it is the year cited in *'Aja'ib* as the "current year", i.e. the year in which he was writing the history of Timur.

But after this visit, and for another ten years, we know almost nothing of Ibn 'Arabshah's life. It is possible that he stayed the whole period in Cairo hoping for some office. Ibn Taghribirdi is alone in saying that Ibn 'Arabshah received appointment as qadi of Hama, but he does not indicate the year or the length of tenure. Fierce competition for such patronage positions was common among the ulama and it may have resulted in a premature death for Ibn 'Arabshah.[38]

On the first of Dhu'l-Hijja 854/15 January 1450, Ibn Taghribirdi came to see Ibn 'Arabshah at the Sa'd al-Su'ada hostel (*khanqah*) in Cairo and asked him for an *ijaza*, a license to transmit his "poetry and prose, whether heard or written." Ibn 'Arabshah wrote one out—in effect the autobiography referred to above—and signed and dated it. Eight months later, at the age of "sixty-two (Hijri) years, six months and twenty days"[39] he passed away at the *khanqah*, "far from his family and home."[40]

Conclusion

As a product of the time, the *'Aja'ib al-maqdur fi nawa'ib Timur* is most remarkable for the uncompromising hostility that it shows for its subject. Even the book's end, where its author, Ibn 'Arabshah, sums up what we might call the accomplishments of Timur's career, suggests at best a very grudging regard for the man, and includes information that could only have

been considered defamatory.[41] In general, major political figures, however loathsome their deeds, were almost always treated in writing with a
degree of respect. Not only does Ibn 'Arabshah fail to attach even the most
innocuous verbal marks of regard to Timur's name but he never hesitates to
modify that name with adjectives like "the vile" (*makhdhul*) and "accursed"
(*mal'un*), or simply to refer to him as "the deceiver"(*al-ghaddar*) or "the
coward" (*al-kharab*).[42] At the outset of his book Ibn 'Arabshah calls on God
to banish Timur from Paradise and, when he gets to recording Timur's death,
he praises God for His mercy in relieving mankind of Timur's wickedness.
Given the intellectual status that Ibn 'Arabshah achieved within his life-
time, and the mature age at which he wrote his account of Timur, the level
of calumny and bitterness seems even more unusual. Undoubtedly, there
were political considerations based on the time and place where he wrote
the work and which affected the tone, but even these are not sufficient to
explain the level of vituperation. No doubt there exist works with literary
and historical pretensions that rise to the same degree of obloquy as this
one in denigrating a contemporary historical figure but I am hard pressed to
think of one. Ibn Taghribirdi, who borrowed heavily from Ibn 'Arabshah, his
teacher, in his own biography of Timur offers a "May God damn him" here
and there in reference to Timur[43] – but these seem mild compared with the
scathing excoriations of Ibn 'Arabshah.

On the other hand, the great historian of Iran, V. M. Minorsky, in his review
of the translation pointed out that along with "the opprobrious epithets
which he heaps on Timur's head" Ibn 'Arabshah also "very keenly appraises
Timur's natural gifts and talents."[44]

Ibn 'Arabshah's legacy as a rhetorician, if not jurisprudent, would long
survive in the Perso-Turkish-Arab world that had shaped him and in turn
been shaped by him. In comparison with his peers he was extraordinarily
accomplished in terms of his multilingualism and command of rhetoric. He
is also remarkable for having left an autobiographical legacy, both explicitly
in the *ijaza* given to Ibn Taghribirdi, and implicitly in the many direct
and indirect observations about his own life made throughout the *'Aja'ib
al-maqdur*. From the standpoint of his wide travels and his network of
acquaintances he was not, however, unusual for his time. This was a period
of great mobility for scholars, helped immensely by an extensive network of
financial and institutional support for them.

Outside Islamdom, it was Ibn 'Arabshah's role as recorder of the life and
times of Timur, the *'Aja'ib al-maqdur*, and as a compiler of animal fables, the
Fakihat al-khulafa', that define him down the ages. The former work was first
published and translated in the seventeenth century and there have been
many editions since, with translations into Latin, French, Turkish and English.

Ibn 'Arabshah's life and career provide the means to understand the subjects, tone and perspective of his published writings. The emphatically hostile
tone of the *'Aja'ib al-maqdur* is understandable when we view his own life,

especially his childhood and adolescence, and when we consider the political conditions under which he would write it. His life is also symbolic of the larger world of Muslim scholarship in the fifteenth century, its dynamism and its ecumenical, transnational and social qualities. It was a special time, perhaps not unique but certainly noteworthy, for the relative freedom with which scholars could move from one political jurisdiction to another. The Ottoman state was enriched by the migration of Central Asian and Iranian scholars to and through it, and Cairo, with the rich institutional support provided by the *khanqahs* and *madrasas*, was a powerful magnet for qualified individuals.

Appraising the translation

The reception of Sanders' 1936 translation was decidedly mixed. As Minorsky made clear in his review, the translation would have been greatly improved had Sanders been aware and made use of two later editions of Ibn 'Arabshah's *'Aja'ib al-maqdur*. Sanders also omitted both the 13-page introduction and the conclusion in the edition he did use. Moreover, alluding to Sanders' amateur status in the field of orientalism, Minorsky mildly bemoans the disconnect between the important work done by amateurs like Sanders and the professional scholars of whose work the amateurs, no matter how gifted linguistically, often fail to show any awareness. This is most noticeable in Sanders' strange renderings of names and places ("it would be well-nigh impossible to enumerate all the single misspellings"), his mistakes in converting dates, his misidentifications of places and his outright mistranslations. Two other reviewers, R. Hartmann and Gustave von Grunebaum were somewhat less kind than Minorsky in their criticism. Von Grunebaum's review really consists in little more than a list of the mistakes he found.[45]

Nonetheless, despite its many failings, both Hartmann and Minorsky considered the translation an important contribution to the history of Timur for its bringing scholarly attention to the value of the original work by one of the few contemporaries of Timur to leave an independent record. Minorsky, in fact, admitted that the translation inspired in him a fresh interest in Ibn 'Arabshah and his work. Much recent scholarship on the Timurid century would be decidedly less rich had the Sanders translation not drawn scholars to Ibn 'Arabshah's biography of Timur.

Acknowledgement

This introduction is a much abbreviated but somewhat updated version of my "A Note on the Life and Works of Ibn 'Arabshāh" in Judith Pfeiffer & Sholeh A. Quinn, eds, *History and Historiography of Post-Mongol Central Asia and the Middle East: Studies in Honor of John E. Woods*, Wiesbaden, Harrasowitz, 2006, pp. 205–49.

Notes

1. His given name was Ahmad the son of Muhammad and his lineage went back five generations to a man named 'Arabshah, hence the family name Ibn 'Arabshah. The Egyptian historian, al-Maqrizi, writing sometime between 840/1437, when he first met Ibn 'Arabshah, and 845/1442 when he himself died, said he was known as "the Persian, the Hanafi." *Durar al-'uqud al-farida fi tarajim al-a'yan al-mufida* [The Unique Strung Pearls of Biographies of Noteworthy and Instructive People] (henceforth *al-Durar*) (Beirut, 2002), 4 vols, vol. 2, p. 26. To the Egyptian biographer al-Sakhawi, he was "known as al-'Ajami [the Persian] and as Ibn 'Arab Shah and this is most common." *al-Daw' al-lami' li-ahl al-qarn al tasi'* [The Bright Light Cast on the People of the Ninth/Fifteenth Century] (henceforth *al-Daw'*) (Cairo, 1394 H), vol. 2, p. 126. A modern Turkish source (Abdulkadir Yuvalı, "Ibn Arabshah, Sehabeddin," *Türkiye Diyanet Vakfı Islam Ansiklopedisi*, vol. 19 (1999), pp. 314–15 says he was called "al-Rumi" because he spent time under Ottoman aegis (p. 314).
2. Ibrahim Kafesoğlu, "Ibn Arabşah," *Islam Ansiklopedisi*, vol. 5 [1950], p. 698–701; J. Pedersen, "Ibn 'Arabshāh, "*Encyclopaedia of Islam, New Edition*, vol. 3 (1971), pp. 711–12; John E. Woods, "Ebn 'Arabsāh," *Encyclopaedia Iranica*, vol. 7 (1996), p. 670; Abdulkadir Yuvalı, "Ibn Arabşah, Şehabeddin," *Türkiye Diyanet Vakfı Islâm Ansiklopedisi*, vol. 19 (1999), pp. 314a–15c.
3. *al-Durar*, vol. 2, pp. 26–7.
4. Yusuf Ibn Taghribirdi, *al-Manhal al-safi wa al-mustawfi ba'd al-Wafi* [The Limpid and Satiating Spring after the Adequate One (the latter referring to *al-Wafi bi al-wafayat* of al-Safadi (d. 1363), a major biographical dictionary of the 14th century)] ed. Muhammad Muhammad Amin (Cairo, 1984), vol. 2, pp. 131–44 (henceforth *al-Manhal*) and *al-Daw'*, vol. 2, pp. 126–31.
5. *al-Manhal*, vol. 2, p. 144.
6. *al-Daw'*, vol. 2, p. 129.
7. C. Brockelmann, *Geschichte der arabischen Litteratur [GAL]* (Leiden, 1938), Suppl. II, pp. 13, 25.
8. His birth date as found in non-Arabic sources has frequently been given in the wrong Common Era years. All sources, Arabic and non-Arabic, agree on the Hijri date that Ibn 'Arabshah himself gave to al-Maqrizi and Ibn Taghribirdi: "Friday night, the 15th of Dhu'l-Qa'da, 791." (al-Sakhawi says "the middle of Dhu'l-Qa'da.") Brockelmann may not have been the first to equate this incorrectly to 1392 (i.e. "6.11.1392" [6 November 1392] see *GAL* 2, p. 29/36) rather than 15 November 1389 but his error has proven durable, making its way through both editions of the *Encyclopaedia of Islam* and into work by otherwise careful scholars. It is worth noting, however, that neither Kafesoğlu nor Woods repeats the error.
9. *al-Durar*, vol. 2, p. 26; *al-Daw'*, vol. 2, p. 126.
10. *Tamerlane or Timur the Great Amir*, translated by J.H. Sanders (London, 1936), p. 157. Henceforth referred to as *Tamerlane* (Sanders).
11. *al-Manhal*, vol. 2, p. 140.
12. *al-Durar*, vol. 2, p. 26.
13. *Tamerlane* (Sanders), p. 163.
14. Ibid., pp. 161–2.
15. Ibid., p. 168.

16. Ibid., pp. 165–6.
17. The Bagh-i Khuda is not one of the bagh-garden estates listed in the authoritative work of Lisa Golombek and Donald Wilber, *The Timurid Architecture of Iran and Turan*, 2 vols (Princeton, 1988), vol. 1, p. 174. but there were probably many such that predated the Timurid era of garden-residence building but were occupied by the Timurids.
18. There are two significant military figures with the name Idaku (Edige?). The one most likely to have founded the *madrasa* in Samarkand was Idaku Timur, one of the first members of Timur's band in Kash and a lifelong devoted follower. See Kafesoğlu, "Ibn Arabşah"; and Ibn 'Arabshah, '*Aja'ib al-maqdur* (al-Himsi edition, Beirut, 1986), p. 42, *Tamerlane* (Sanders), p. 2.
19. *Tamerlane* (Sanders), pp. 322–3.
20. *al-Manhal*, vol. 2, p. 141.
21. See Guy Le Strange's introduction to Ruy Gonzalez de Clavijo, *Embassy to Tamerlane 1403-1406*, translated by Guy le Strange (London, 1928), p. 12.
22. Ibn 'Arabshah's own date, *Tamerlane* (Sanders), p. 184. (20 July 1402 according to F. Taeschner, "Ankara," *Encyclopaedia of Islam, New Edition*, vol. 1 (1960), p. 510b.)
23. *Tamerlane* (Sanders), p. 220.
24. *al-Manhal*, vol. 2, p. 141.
25. *Tamerlane* (Sanders), p. 77.
26. *al-Manhal*, vol. 2, p. 141.
27. Ibid., pp. 142–3.
28. *al-Manhal*, vol. 2, p. 143. The Qudsi edition of *al-Daw'* says he stayed three years (sic!) in Aleppo.
29. Ibn Taghribirdi, *History of Egypt, 1382–1469 AD Part V 1438-1453 AD*, trans. William Popper (Berkeley and Los Angeles, 1958), vol. 19, p. 224.
30. *al-Manhal*, vol. 2, p. 143.
31. *al-Durar*, vol. 2, pp. 26–7.
32. *al-Daw'*, vol. 2, p. 127.
33. *Tamerlane* (Sanders), pp. 5–6.
34. He dates interviews to 833/1429-30, 834/1430–1, and 836/1432–3 (*Tamerlane* (Sanders), pp. 23, 168, 5–6 respectively). He explicitly dates the writing of his work internally to 840/1436–7 (*Tamerlane* (Sanders), p. 78), a year confirmed by al-Maqrizi (*al-Durar*, p. 27), although the latter indicates that Ibn 'Arabshah had yet to come up with the final title, so the work may still have been in progress in 1436–7 albeit substantially completed. Ibn 'Arabshah also indirectly confirms 840 as the date of composition when he speaks of his mentor in Damascus, al-Bukhari, as being alive (*Tamerlane* (Sanders), pp. 5–6) and in his *ijaza* (*al-Manhal*, vol. 2, pp. 143–4) gives the date of al-Bukhari's death as Ramadan 8, 841 (5 March 1438).
35. *Tamerlane* (Sanders), p. 23; al-Himsi ed.,'*Aja'ib al-maqdur*, pp. 72–3.
36. *Tamerlane* (Sanders), pp. 5–6.
37. *al-Daw'*, vol. 2, p. 128.
38. See R. D. McChesney, "A Note on the Life and Works of Ibn 'Arabshah," pp. 241, 243.
39. *al-Manhal*, vol. 2, p. 145.
40. *al-Daw'*, vol. 2, 128. "*ghariban 'an ahlihi wa watanihi*" and in the abbreviated obituary found in Ibn Taghribirdi's *Hawadith al-duhurfi mada al-ayyam wa*

al-shuhur (Beirut, 1990), 2 vols, vol. 1, p. 308. Popper, in his translation of the same author's al-Nujum al-zahira, vol. 19, p. 224, says "far from his wife and children." The Arabic version in al-Nujum al-zahira is indeed "ghariban 'an ahlihi wa awladihi" as Popper translated.

41. *Tamerlane* (Sanders), p. 311, where he charges Timur's daughter with lesbianism.

42. Sanders chooses to translate the word as "bastard." Unvowelled, the word has a number of possible meanings, including the (presumably derogatory) "anus" (al-khurb) but no dictionary of my acquaintance translates it as "bastard." However, to rhyme with its consort al-'Arab it must be al-kharab, universally translated (Lane, Dozy, Hava) as "the male bustard, hence coward." Presumably, Sanders – or his editor – misread "bustard."

43. *al-Manhal*, vol. 4, pp. 103–38.

44. V. Minorsky, Review of *Tamerlane or Timur, the Great Amir, Bulletin of the School of Oriental and African Studies*, University of London, vol. 9, (1937), pp. 237–8 (quotation on p. 238).

45. Minorsky's review appeared in *Bulletin of the School of Oriental and African Studies*, University of London, vol. 9, no. 1 (1937), pp. 237–8; Hartmann's in *Historische Zeitschrft*, Bd. 157 (1938), pp. 172–4; and von Grunebaum's in *Wiener Zeitschrift für die Kunde des Morgenlandes*, vol. 45 (1938), pp. 148–9.

INTRODUCTION

TAMERLANE is now scarcely more than a name. Though his career inspired a play by Marlowe and occupied nearly a chapter of Gibbon's Decline and Fall of the Roman Empire, most educated people to-day would be at a loss to give him a date or his place in history.

Yet he is one of the world's great conquerors, of the same class as Jenghizkhan, Alexander, Attila and Napoleon; in short, a scourge of humanity. It would be difficult to maintain that any benefits which he conferred on his subjects or their posterity were equal to the evils which he inflicted. " The ground," says Gibbon, " which had been occupied by flourishing cities was often marked by his abominable trophies, by columns, or pyramids of human heads. Astracan, Carizme, Delhi, Ispahan, Bagdad, Aleppo, Damascus, Boursa, Smyrna and a thousand others, were sacked, or burnt, or utterly destroyed, in his presence and by his troops : and perhaps his conscience would have been startled if a priest or philosopher had dared to number the millions of victims whom he had sacrificed to the establishment of peace and order." Gibbon flatters Timur's conscience. There is nothing to suggest that he had a conscience of that sort. He seems to have put even children to the sword without pity. Clemency to the conquered was with him the exception. A man of learning like Ibn Khaldun might save his life with the help of flattery. An opponent worthy of his steel, like Bayezid, was treated with ignominy and ingenious refinement of cruelty. Dangerous rivals were liable to be entrapped by a show of friendship and murdered under the guise of hospitality.

Though Tamerlane had no greatness except his military genius and that is one of the lowest kinds of greatness, yet his bigness is unquestionable. He ranged over the Middle East like a roaring lion, seeking whom he might devour. He conquered from the Levant and Hellespont to the borders of China ; in the north he dominated at least for a time Southern Russia and parts of Siberia and southwards he carried his banners to victory over Northern India. From his victories he brought back to Samarkand the loot of many cities and not a few men of learning, artists and craftsmen.

The life by Ahmed Ibn Arabshah, formerly secretary of Sultan Ahmed of Bagdad, has never before been translated into English. It is one of the chief authorities for the career of Tamerlane or Timur and the period from his death to the accession of his youngest son Shah Rukh, written soon after the events described. The author, who wrote as a good Moslem, is sometimes charged with bias against " the great amir," but I find no injustice in the account, except in the first few pages where he vaguely depreciates Timur's origin. The book is especially important for the later and principal years of the reign and for the description of Timur's character and appearance in Chapter XCVI of Volume 2. The style is florid but often eloquent and adorned with beautiful passages both in prose and verse ; crammed too with phrases from the Koran and quotations from the poets, which retain their charm even for a Western ear.

To clear up the facts of Timur's birth it should be said here that he was born in A.D. 1336 at Kesh in Transoxiana (called in Arabic Mawaralnahr), roughly fifty miles south of Samarkand and was the son of Teragai, the head of the Berlas tribe of Turks and the great grandson of Karachar Nevian, who was commander-in-chief under Jagatai, the son of Jenghizkhan.

On the death of Jenghizkhan his empire had been divided among his sons and the middle portion had been allotted to Jagatai. Hence the inhabitants of this area came to be called Jagatais in addition to their own tribal names. This area too was subdivided and at this time the western Jagatais were ruled by Kazan, who was overthrown by Kurgan. The latter deputed Timur to invade Khorasan and he succeeded in this and other military operations. Kurgan was murdered and the succession was disputed. Toghluk Timur of Kashgar invaded the country and Timur was made governor of Mawaralnahr, then displaced in favour of a son of Toghluk, whom Timur however defeated. Toghluk died and Timur with Hussein (Hosain), his brother-in-law, reconquered Mawaralnahr and gained some additional territories. In 1369 Hussein was murdered and Timur became sole ruler and was enthroned at Samarkand. He ruled until his death in A.D. 1405 and the thirty-six years were spent chiefly in conquest : the following is a brief summary of his chief expeditions :

A.D.	
1370.	Invasions of Jat country.
1371–2	Invasions of Khwarizm.
1374.	Invasion of Jat country.
1375.	Invasion of Khwarizm, Jat country and Kipchak.
	Timur sets up Toktamish against Uruskhan.
	Timur defeats the army of Uruskhan.
1376.	Toktamish enthroned at Saganak.
1377.	Birth of Shah Rukh, youngest son of Timur.
	Toktamish defeats Timur Malik of Kipchak, son of Uruskhan, and becomes Khan of Kipchak.
1378–9	Conquest of Khwarizm.
1380–1	Conquest of Khorasan.
1382.	Conquests in Persia.
1383.	Invasion of Jat country and of Sistan.
	Taking of Kandahar.
1384–5.	Conquest of Mazanderan and Sultania.
1386.	Conquest of Azarbaijan (incl. Tabriz) and Georgia.
1387.	Defeat of the army of Toktamish Khan of Kipchak, who had revolted against Timur.
	Defeat of the Black Sheep Turkomans.
	Submission of Erzinjan.
	Seizure of Ispahan and Shiraz.
1388.	Return to Samarkand to repulse Toktamish, who had invaded Transoxiana.
	Reconquest of Khwarizm.
1388–9.	Campaigns against Toktamish.
1389.	Invasion of the Jat country incl. part of Mongolia.
1391.	Invasion of Kipchak. Flight of Toktamish.
1392–3.	Invasion of Iran (Persia) to suppress revolts.
1393–4.	Invasion of Iraq.
	Capture of Bagdad, Avenik, Erzinjan, etc.
	Invasion of Georgia.
1395.	Defeat of Toktamish in Kipchak.
	Invasion of parts of Russia: Sharifuddin says that his troops reached the Dnieper and that he himself went to Moscow, and plundered it.
	Invasion of Kuban (Circassia).
	Destruction of Astrakhan and Serai.
1396.	Conquests in South Persia.
1398–9.	Invasion of India. Occupation of Multan, Delhi, Jammu, etc.

A.D.

1399–1400.	Invasion of Georgia.
1400.	Invasion of Rum (Anatolia) and Syria.
1401.	Taking of Damascus, Bagdad and other cities.
1402.	Battle of Angora. Defeat and capture of Bayezid, Ottoman Sultan.
	Capture of Smyrna.
1403.	Death of Bayezid.
	Expedition in Georgia.
1405.	Expedition against China sets out.
	Death of Timur at Otrar.

For this summary I have drawn on Sharifuddin's *History of Timur Bec"* in the English version, a good though too eulogistic account: somewhat long however and not easily obtained. Throughout I have used freely Manger's annotated Latin version of Ibn Arabshah.

After Timur's death his issue strove for power and before long Shah Rukh gained the empire. He ruled with success until A.D. 1447, when he died and was succeeded by his son, Ulugh Beg, who was murdered two years later. However he had already achieved fame as a patron of architecture and astronomy. After his death the dynasty declined, though another line descended from Timur gained power in India.

Samarkand is now the capital of the Uzbek Soviet Republic and a town of some activity. The Muslim city is still beautified by colleges and other buildings of the time of Timur and his successors, but his own tomb is half in ruins.

. . . I have to acknowledge help received from and my debt to the Encyclopædia Britannica (14th edition), Rodwell's Translation of the Koran in Everyman's Library and *Tamerlane, the Earth Shaker* by Harold Lamb (Thornton Butterworth), which contains a good bibliography and a lively account of Timur's life.

Moscow

Sketch

Rus (Russia)

Dasht Kipchak (Golden Horde)

R. Ural

R. Dnieper

R. Volga

Sarai

R. Don

Astrakhan

Crimea

R. Kuban

Circassia

Caucasus Mountains

R. Terek

Caspian Sea

Derbend

Black Sea

Adrianople
Istanbul
Sea of Marmara
Gallipoli

Sinope Samsun

Georgia Tiflis

Azerbaijan
Shirvan

Brusa R. Sakaria
Rum Angora
Kastamuni
Amasia Tokat
Mangasha
Trebizond

Armenia
Erzinjan Erzerum
Karabagh Tabriz

Smyrna

Akshahr
Kaiseri Siwas

Van
Vastan
Bitlis Kurds
Mardin

Sultaniyeh
Kasvin Mazanderan
Hamadan Rei

Karaman
Malatia
Bire Arbil
Urfa
Mosul
R. Tigris
Asker Malwan Burujird
Luristan

Crete Candia

Aleppo
(Halab)
Hama
Tripoli Homs
Beit Syria
Damascus
Safad

Tikrit
R. Euphrates

Iraq
Bagdad

Irak Ajmi
Isphahan

Mediterranean Sea

Levant

Gaza Mamelukes

Persia
(Iran)
Khuzistan

Basra

Egypt

Cairo

R. Nile

Hejaz

Medina

Arabia

Red Sea

Persian Gulf

Shiraz

Mecca

Map illustrating
campaigns of Timur

Sibir
(Siberia)

Lake Balkash

Jat Country   Mongols

Lake
Aral   Otrar   Issyk Kul

Khwarizm   Tashkend   Khakas
                  Khojend   • Kashgar
          Samarkand Feraghan   E. Turkistan
          • kesh   (Andekan)
       Bokhara Transoxiana
       Qars hj (Mawarulnahr)
                  Andakhoi
                  Balkh

-abad
-ar, Nishapur (Nisabur)
Khorasan
          Herat
       Sabzuar   • Ghazni

-zd,
-kova   • Kandahar   Jamma
  • Kerman   Seistan   • Multan
-rs
-a Hormuz I.   Sind   • Delhi
                                     Hind
                                     (Hindustan)

                                     (India)

Arabian Sea

R. Indus

Amu Jama (Oxus)
Syr Jaxartes (Sihun)

VOLUME I

CHAPTER I

OF HIS ORIGIN AND THE WAY IN WHICH HE GRADUALLY SUBDUED KINGDOMS TO HIMSELF

HIS name was Timur; it is pronounced in this way and so also the form of the name implies; but foreign words are turned in a circle like a ball by the sporting cudgel of the Arabic tongue and revolve at pleasure in the field of speech; so they say sometimes Tamur, sometimes Tamarlang—which is not wrong; and *Tamar* in Turkish means iron, but *lang* means lame.

He was the son of Taragai, son of Abgai. The birthplace of this deceiver was a village of a lord named Ilgar in the territory of Kesh—may Allah remove him from the garden of Paradise!

And Kesh is one of the cities of Transoxiana, about two days distant from Samarkand.

They say that on the night on which he was born something like a helmet appeared, seemed to flutter in the air, then fell into the middle of the plain and finally was scattered over the ground; thence also live coals flew about like glowing ashes and collected so that they filled the plain and the city: they also say that when that evil man saw the light, his palms were full of freshly shed blood.

They consulted the augurs and diviners about these portents and referred to seers and soothsayers about their meaning, of whom some replied that he would be a guardsman; others that he would grow up a brigand, while others said a blood-thirsty butcher, others finally that he would be an executioner, these opinions contending with each other, until events decided the issue.

He and his father were shepherds, belonging to a mixed horde, lacking either reason or religion; others say that both belonged to a tribe accustomed to travel hither and thither, and courageous, who lived in Transoxiana and wintered within its borders. Others again say that his father was a poor smith, but that he himself from his youth excelled in keenness of intellect and strength ; but because of poverty began to commit acts of brigandage and in the course of these exploits was wounded and mutilated ; for when he wanted to carry off a sheep, which he had stolen one night, the shepherd cleft his shoulder with an arrow and maimed it, and shooting a second arrow at his hip, damaged the hip. So mutilation was added to his poverty and a blemish to his wickedness and fury, with which he went about with his hand against every man.

Then he sought men like and equal to himself and neglected God, and collected Satanic companions, such as Abbas, Jahanshah, Qamari, Suliman Shah, Idaku Timur, Jaku and Seifuddin, about forty men without resources or religion.

But however powerless he was and however meagre his resources and equipment, and however weak his physique and bodily condition, without property or troops, yet he used to tell them that he aimed at royal rank and would attack the kings of this world with fatal onset ; and they jested together about these professions, most counting him a lunatic and imbecile ; and they went to him and met him to make him the object of laughter and ridicule.

" Truly when fortune aids him and makes the weak strong, he will forward his purpose, with fate directing and providence guiding."

" By no means despair of glory, from which you are far removed : for the path to it is made by stages and degrees.

Truly the reed, which you see rising high, grows and swells joint by joint."

Now there was in the city of Kesh an old man named Shamsuddin Fakhri, of the greatest authority in those parts, consulted by all in affairs of state and religion. They say that Timur, when poor and weak and between his imagined greatness and actual wretchedness, he had nothing but a cotton garment, sold it and with the price of it got himself a she-goat from the flock, with which he went to pay respect to the Sheikh and entrusted his plan to the Sheikh's honour. Now he had fastened one end of a rope to the goat's neck and with the other bound his own neck and so, leaning on a staff taken from a branch of a palm, he advanced with slow step, until he came to the worthy Sheikh, whom he found engaged with fakirs in remembrance of divine things and plunged in the deepest meditation. Accordingly he waited until they had come back to themselves and rested from their conversation. As soon as the Sheikh turned his eyes towards him, he at once kissed his hands and threw himself at his feet. Then the other, reflecting for a little, raised his head to the company and said : " This man spends his self and pelf that he may ask our aid in seeking that which Allah Almighty reckons of less worth than the wing of a fly. Let us see therefore that we help him and do not curse or repel him."

Accordingly they assisted him with prayers, by which they aided his desire ; and so he acted the part of a fox ; then he came back from the Sheikh's presence and advancing climbed gradually, lame though he was, to his desired eminence.

It is related, too, that when he was engaged upon a certain robbery and appeared to be missing his way—in fact, he wandered so much from the right path that he almost died of thirst and hunger—when he had spent a week in this plight, he came on the Sultan's horses, whose keeper received him with courtesy and kindness.

Now Timur was one of those who know the points of a horse and can distinguish at a glance by the outward shape between good and bad stock. Accordingly, when the keeper of the horses had sounded him and learned this science thoroughly from him, his affection for him grew and he sought his constant society. He also took him before the Sultan with horses which he had collected, showing the Sultan Timur's skill and what he himself had seen of his capacities. The Sultan therefore received him with favour, and dismissed him after commending him to the keeper of the horse. When the keeper died soon afterwards, Timur was appointed to his place and did not cease to insinuate himself in a higher degree into the Sultan's favour, until he married the Sultan's full sister.

This lady afterwards was annoyed by his conversation and reproached him with his original condition and status ; whereupon he drew his sword and threatened her so that she fled from his hands. But when she paid no heed to him he slew her with a blow and gave her body to burial.

Then he had no course but sedition, rebellion, ferocity and outrage until he achieved his destiny.

This Sultan was called Hussein, and was of royal blood,

with power of life and death ; his capital was Balkh, in the country of Khorasan, but the seas of his commands flowed through the territory of Transoxiana right up to the borders of Turkistan.

Others say that his father was an Amir under the said Sultan, renowned among his comrades for strength and courage. But these differing traditions can be reconciled by a consideration of different times and the change which alterations and accidents of fortune bring.

The sounder opinion is that his father, the above-mentioned Taragai, was among the magnates of the Sultan's court. And I have seen, in the appendix of the Persian Chronicle called Muntakhab, which is brought down from the creation to the times of Timur with truly admirable effort, the genealogy of Timur traced without a break to Jenghizkhan through females, snares of Satan.

But after conquering Transoxiana and rising above his companions, he married princesses and therefore they gave him the surname Kurkan, which in the Mogul language means Son-in-law, since he had gained affinity with kings, and enjoyed the highest authority in their courts.

He was one of four Viziers of the said Sultan, with whom was the hinge of evil and good, since they were the eyes of the kingdoms, and by their advice affairs were directed. The Turks forsooth have tribes and a race, like the Arab tribes, and each of these Viziers was to his own tribe a tall wick for the lamp of its counsels in the houses of its habitation.

One of these tribes is called Arlat, the second Jalabar, the third Qavjin, the fourth Barlas. Timur, however, sprang from the fourth ; as a youth he grew up brave, great-hearted, active, strong, urbane, and won the friendship of the Viziers' sons of his own age and entered into company with his contemporaries among the young Amirs to such a degree, that when one night they had gathered in a lonely place and were enjoying familiarity and hilarity among themselves, having removed the curtains of secrecy and spread the carpet for cheerful intercourse, he said to them, " My grandmother, who was skilled in augury and divination, saw in sleep a vision, which she expounded as foreshadowing to her one among her sons and grandsons, who would conquer territories and bring men into subjection and be Lord of the Stars and master of the Kings of the age. And I am that man and now the fit time is at hand and has come near. Pledge yourselves therefore to be my back, arms, flank and hands and never to desert me."

They assented and promised to aid him whenever summoned and swore that they would be with him in prosperity and adversity and never against him.

Nor did they cease to carry these conversations everywhere with them and stir hither and thither the flood of the pool of this treachery without shame or secrecy, until every inhabitant of Egypt and Syria saw his lightning and all who had long been absent from their own country, from the least to the greatest, had in talk followed his new enterprise.

The Sultan well knowing this, for his rebellion was open, wished to outstrip his treachery in its beginning and to keep the world quiet from his villainy and protect his subjects and territories from Timur's wickedness and havoc, and did according to the words of the poet :

" The apex of a height will not be safe from injury unless its sides are drenched in blood."

But Timur, informed of this plan by an honest adviser, revolted and fell safely to the abyss of rebellion, nay, in this way climbed higher. It may be that at this time and while affairs stood thus, he visited the Sheikh Shamsuddin, already mentioned, and implored his help, as just now described, for executing the object which he had revealed to him, for he was wont to say: "Whatever empire I have gained and whatever forts I have stormed, are due to the intercession of Sheikh Shamsuddin Fakhri and the zeal of Sheikh Zeinuddin Khwafi, and I have not won success except by the aid of Said Barka " ; and the tale of Zeinuddin and Barka will be told hereafter.

Timur further said, " Not open to me were the gates of happiness and fortune, nor did victories over the world smile upon me like a bride until after the arrows of Seistan and from that very time, when that damage befell me, right to this day I have won continuous gains."

For it is agreed that the beginning of his exploits and rebellion fell at that time, which is between the years 760 and 770.* And my master, the learned Imam, accomplished, consummate and excellent, pearl of the age, phœnix of his time, wisest of men, teacher of the world, glory of religion, teacher of those who rightly and subtly study philosophy, polestar of his time, guide of the age, Abu Abdallah Mahomed,

* A.D. 1358 and A.D. 1368.

5

son of Mahomed, son of Mahomed Bukhari, citizen of Damascus, (May Allah Almighty make eternal the days of his life and increase Islam and the Muslims through his fortunate bene- dictions!), said during the year 836 that Timur killed the said Sultan Hussein in the month of Shaban, in the year 771,* and was raised to royal rank from that moment, and that his death fell in the month of Shaban, in the year 807,† as will be told later.

The period of his complete dominion was therefore thirty-six years, and that without reckoning the time from his sedition and brigandage up to his gaining the throne. For after he had rebelled, he and his companions were ravaging the territories of Transoxiana with hostile and violent assaults on the people. Therefore all moved to drive them out and closed to them those habitations and places.

Accordingly, they crossed the Oxus, and when that tract was exhausted by brigandage, turned to the territory of Khorasan and particularly the borders of Seistan, nor could their raids in the huge deserts of Bavard and Makhan be counted.

But setting out one night, when want pressed his men, and the flame of hunger scorched them, he entered one of the enclosures of Seistan, into which a shepherd had taken his sheep, and when he had carried off one sheep the shepherd saw him making off, and following him out of the enclosure pierced him with two arrows, one of which penetrated his thigh, the other his shoulder, so that by the will of Allah he was maimed in half his body through that justly weighed blow.

Then he seized and brought him and carried him before the Sultan of Herat, by name Malik Hussein, who ordered him to be whipped and then crucified.

Now the Sultan had an unwise son named Malik Ghayatuddin, who interceded for him and sought to have him from his father, and his father replied: " Nothing proceeds from you to show that you are acting aright and to reflect a fortunate disposition and destiny ; for if this Jagatai brigand, cancer of corruption, is left alive, he will be the bane of peoples and lands."

But his son answered: " That half-man already over- whelmed by dire calamity can achieve nothing. The end of his life is already without doubt at hand. Do not then be the

* A.D. 1369.   † A.D. 1405.

cause of his death." Accordingly the Sultan gave him up to his son, who entrusted him to a doctor, that his wounds might heal and his scars be cured. Afterwards he was among the slaves of the son of the Sultan of Herat, a most sage and valuable servant. In his household his dignity grew, and his rank was advanced and all that he said was obeyed.

And when a Nawab of the Sultan's rebelled, the Governor of Seistan, Timur sought the opportunity of opposing him, and the Sultan trusted him and granted his wish and gave him a military force. And when he reached Seistan, he seized the Governor, who was continuing in rebellion, and after exhausting the resources of that country and taking the troops which followed him, he began an open revolt and crossed into Transoxiana with his men.

Others, however, say that he remained in the service of the son of the Sultan until his father had died and passed away and the son had attained full power. Then, they say, Timur fled into Transoxiana, and his forces were strengthened. For already his companions were joining him and his fellow-bandits and friends were again collecting round him.

Then, indeed, Ghayatuddin sent men to pursue them from the rear, exerting himself to keep the Moslems safe from their assaults and attacks. But, alas ! the sword had already eluded his grasp and they came after the feast.

CHAPTER II

OF HIS TUMULTUOUS AND MARVELLOUS CROSSING OF THE OXUS

AND Timur and his company reached the Oxus, which then—like them—was swelling beyond its bounds, and they could not delay, because their pursuers, like themselves, were ruthless. Timur therefore bade his men with all speed hurl themselves into the water, each holding the bridle and mane of his horse ; and they arranged a place among themselves. He added, " Cross without delay and everyone who does not come to the appointed place will know that it is finished with him." Then they threw themselves and their horses into those roaring waters and swelling waves, like moths flying towards a lamp. Nor did one care for another's plight or the man in front watch the fate of the man behind, and they endured the tortures of death and saw openly the terrors of destruction.

They emerged however, and without even a man lost collected at the place agreed ; but as soon as the country was free of anxiety about them and each man was quietly attending to all his business, they began to spy out everything and make war upon Allah and His Prophet and harass His worshippers and break His laws. Nor did he cease to rage hither and thither in that manner, until he came to the city of Qarshi.

CHAPTER III

OF THE DANGER WHICH HE CONFRONTED IN THE ATTACK ON
THE CITY OF QARSHI AND HIS ESCAPE FROM THAT DIFFICULTY

TIMUR said one day to his comrades, when fate was already driving and spurring him to evil, and bringing abundant booty in the place of their brigandage and blossoming finely : " Near us is the city of Nakhshab, the city of Abi Tarab the Nakhshabi (on whom be the mercy of Allah !), well fortified and strong. If we seize it, it will be a protection to us, a fortress, refuge and place of escape, and its ruler is Musa. If we surprise him, take his wealth, and slay him, his horses and means will be a strength to us and we shall win escape after difficulty. And I know a narrow street into which one can easily climb by means of water which runs through it." Accordingly, they girded their loins and leaving their horses in a certain place, gave the night to execution of their plans, and entering the city canal, eagerly sought the house of the Amir and they raised their hands and withdrew them. And the Amir was in a suburban garden. Then they seized all that they found of his arms and supplies, and mounting his horses, slew by surprise the leading men that they encountered.

But the townsmen gathered against them and summoned the Amir, who following them with a large force, heaped damage upon them there and from all sides, until they had no resource, but to commend themselves to the help of Allah.

And when Timur's friends said to him, " Now in truth we have rashly hurled ourselves to certain destruction," he replied,

" This does not become you, for in such fields of battle a man is tried and proved. Therefore summon your devices, then attack in mass, and rush upon the gate of the city, breaking in with united hand and breaking through the enemy without sloth or delay. And I think nothing will resist you or stand before you."

And hearing his words they raised a shout and made for the gate, meeting the floods of death, and rushed on the enemy with the charge of a lion and poured out with far more force than a bursting cloud. And they had the gate open by the will of the supreme Arbiter. Nor did one man succour another against them. Nor did the great strength of the enemy avail him anything. Then they came back safe to their position, and none the less in this condition of affairs they ceased not to move from place to place carrying havoc.

And assembling their comrades and combining with those who were equally committed to brigandage, they reached a number of about three hundred, collecting a horde of scoundrels.

And the Sultan sent an army against them which they overthrew, while it regarded them as of little account, and they seized one of the forts, which they made a safe place for all their booty.

I have said :

> " Weigh not lightly any act and trick of a foe ;
> For sometimes the fox has overthrown lions."

It is said also that " the gnat wounds the eye of the lion " ; or in other words, " The King sometimes is checkmated by a wretched pawn."

CHAPTER IV

RELATES WHO WERE HELD BOUND BY THE ATTACK OF THAT
DESPOT AND WHAT NOBLE PRINCES HE WISHED TO BE ENSLAVED
TO HIM

TIMUR sent to the prefecture of Balkhshan, governed by two brothers holding absolute power received from their father. But when the Sultan had torn it from their grasp, presently he confirmed them in it on condition that they should be under his sway, wishing that their sons should be hostages with him, whereby they became slaves of his rule.

And Timur demanding their submission, they assented and placed themselves under his dominion.

CHAPTER V

HOW WHEN THE MOGULS ROSE AGAINST THE SULTAN HIS POWER WAS BROKEN

THEN the Moguls rose on the East against Sultan Hussein, who equipped an army against them and crossed the Oxus and battle was joined between the two sides. Then the Sultan being put to flight, that demon (Timur) also sent an envoy to them, and their leader was called Qamaruddin Khan. And they assented to his petition and followed his wishes. And they set him against the Sultan, that he might drag his territories from his hand, promising him a matrimonial alliance and supporting him by their help.

And they returned to their own country, leaving him the control of his own affairs. His power, therefore, grew strong by these means and fear of him filled men's hearts.

Therefore the Sultan could not but exert his zeal and power to destroy him completely with all his followers. Accordingly, attacking him, he proceeded against him with an army which gave forth a roar like a raging sea, until he came to a place called Qaghalghar. In that place is a double tract of mountains, between the jaws of which a large road, by which it is crossed, goes for an hour's distance, in the midst of which is a narrow pass; and when this is closed and defended, nothing is so inaccessible.

Mountains surround it, each of which rises to a lofty ridge, while the foot stands fixed and immersed in abysmal depths, so much that it may truly be said of them " Nose in the sky and rump in the water.".

And the army occupied the entrance of that pass from the direction of Samarkand, while Timur held the other side, where he was, as it were, in a defile and besieged.

CHAPTER VI

TIMUR'S CRAFTY DESIGNING AND THE DEVICE WHICH HE
PLANNED

THEN Timur said to his friends : " I know that somewhere here is a hidden way with most difficult paths,
which footsteps have never trodden and through which even
the *sandgrouse* birds would not offer themselves as guides. Come,
then, let us go by night and leading our horses let us come on
them from the rear while they suspect no harm ; for if we
come upon them by night we are safe." And when they had
approved this, they presently strove to climb these hilly and
difficult paths.

And all night they advanced, but when, the sun rising and
the dawn coming upon them, they had not yet reached the
enemy, the earth was narrowed for them for all its breadth
and they were thrown into the greatest anxiety. Nor could
they go back, since the sun was already rising, when they came
near the army, which, with baggage packed, was already
prepared for the march.

His comrades therefore said : " We have formed a ruinous
plan ; we have come into the power of the enemy and now
we have fallen into a trap and have with our own hands hurled
ourselves to destruction." But Timur replied : " There is
no danger ; turn towards the enemy and in their sight dismount
from your horses and send them to graze, and complete the
span of sleep and rest which you have lost during your night
march."

Then they dismounted from their horses and threw themselves down and loosened their horses to graze.

" When the eyes of safety guard thee, sleep ; and every
kind of horror will be security itself ; and chase the griffin
with security's aid and it will be like a net : lead the sheep with
her favour and it will be in place of a halter."

The army passed them, thinking they were comrades in
arms, until having taken their rest they mounted their horses,
and with a shout drew their swords against the enemy and
riding on their shoulders from behind dealt them swift
destruction and left them wounded and prostrate.

And general was the awful slaughter and none knew the disaster how it befell.

And when the Sultan heard the news and no chance of recovery remained, he fled to Balkh and put on a foul hide instead of the royal robe torn from him.

But Timur was active in plunder, pillage and spoliation, and gathered supplies and collected resources and won to his side the common people and the leaders alike, who obeyed him whether they wished or not.

So he gained the realms of Transoxiana and subdued the population by force and compulsion. And he began to establish forces and armies and seize forts and castles.

The Governor of Samarkand in the name of the Sultan was one of the magnates, called Ali Shir, to whom Timur wrote that they should divide the power between them and that he should stand on his side against Sultan Hussein. Then Ali Shir agreed, and dividing with him the provinces and kingdoms and coming to him, stood in his presence and was active in showing him every kind of honour and omitted nothing by which he might honour him.

CHAPTER VII

TIMUR PROCEEDS TO BALKHSHAN, RECEIVING AID AGAINST THE
SULTAN FROM THOSE WHO WERE HOLDING THAT CITY

THEN Timur, dismissing Ali Shir and confident of his loyalty, proceeded to Balkhshan, whose two Princes went to meet him, showing him reverence, and presented him with gifts and helped him with soldiers and followers.

They themselves went with him and advanced from Balkhshan, from which place they continued to Balkh to besiege the Sultan, whom they surrounded on all sides, while he was equipping himself against them. Accordingly, he produced the sons of both of them, whom he held as hostages—and cut off their heads in their fathers' sight, showing them no pity or mercy. Then his condition weakened and his cavalry and infantry were broken and fell away from him, and he surrendered and gave himself up to destiny and Providence, resting in the decision, whether sweet or bitter, of the Divine decree. Then, when he had been cast into bonds, Timur seized power. Then, sending the Princes of Balkhshan to that place with honour, he advanced to Samarkand, taking Sultan Hussein with him ; and this was in the month Shaban, of the year of the Hegira 771.*

And when he reached Samarkand, he made it his capital and, laying the foundations of empire, he placed the city in the cord and bond of his rule.

Then, after slaying the Sultan, he appointed deputy in his own name one Shiur Ghatmish of the seed of Jinkizkhan. And only men of the tribe of Jinkizkhan claim the title Khan and Sultan, since they are the Koreish of the Turks, of whom no one can take precedence or pluck that nobility from their hands ; for if anyone could have done it, it would certainly have been Timur, who conquered kingdoms and dared everything.

However, he set up Shiur Ghatmish to repel the calumnies of detractors and cut off the piercing point of every tongue.

And he was only entitled Timur, the Great Amir, although under his sway were ruler and subject alike ; and the Khan was in his bondage, like a centipede in mud, and he was like the Khalifs at this time in the regard of the Sultans.

And he continued Ali Shir in the Governorship of Samarkand, and honoured him, seeking advice from him in his business, and kept him in the chief position.

CHAPTER VIII

DESCRIBES THE EXPEDITION OF TOQTAMISH KHAN, SULTAN OF
DASHT AND TURKISTAN

THEN, when Toqtamish Khan, Sultan of Dasht and of the Tatars, saw what had occurred between Timur and Sultan Hussein, his heart's blood boiled and raged—and that because they were kinsmen and neighbours—and enrolling a numerous army and plentiful forces, he advanced against Timur's camp from the side of Saghnaq and Atrar. Timur coming out against him from Samarkand, they met in the parts of Turkistan, near the river of Khajend, which is the Jaxartes (Sihun) ; and

* A.D. 1369.

Samarkand is between the rivers Jaxartes (Sihun) and Oxus (Jihun). Then, between the two armies seethed the traffic of battle and nothing was sold there between them but the trade of mutual blows and the millstone of war did not cease to turn until Timur's army was being crushed to pieces ; and when his army was already broken and the bond of his hosts dissolved, lo, a man came, called Said Barka.   To whom Timur in this utmost crisis said : " My Lord Said ! My troops are being put to flight."   To him the Said replied, " Fear not ! "   Then the Said, dismounting from his horse and halting, seized a handful of gravel, and mounting his ash-coloured steed, hurled the gravel in the face of the enemy, who were fighting with the utmost vigour, shouting at the top of his voice, " The brigand is in flight."   And Timur echoed the cry in a terrific voice, following the valiant old man and shouting like a man calling a thirsty camel to the water.

Then the army turned like cattle around their young and began to fight with the enemy and those like unto themselves and there was none in the army but shouted in a great voice, " That brigand is in flight."   Then with united force they again charged, with well-combined courage and zeal in mutual aid.   And the forces of Toqtamish, driven to flight, turned and retired with back turned.   Then Timur's army, falling upon them with the sword, through these openings poured out for them goblets of death ; and they seized the supplies and beasts of burden and took prisoners of every rank.   Then Timur returned to Samarkand, having already subdued Turkistan and the territories of the River Jaxartes.

And he conferred great authority at his court on Said Barka and made him Governor throughout his dominions and kingdom.

About this Said accounts differ.

Some say that he came from the West and had been a surgeon in Egypt, then went to Samarkand, where raised to the rank of Said, he obtained higher power and authority.

But others say that he came of the people of Medina Al Sharifat, others, on the other hand, that he came of the people of Mecca Al Munifat.   Whatever the truth, he was certainly among the great magnates of the provinces of Transoxiana and Khorasan ; especially, after he aided Timur so actively and snatched him from that danger, his cunning coinciding with destiny and Providence.

And Timur said to him : " Ask of me and use your right with me." And he replied : " My Lord and Amir, there are several fiefs in the provinces of Mecca and Medina, and particularly that of Andakhoi, in the territory of Khorasan, to which benefit I and my sons among all are entitled. And let the basis of this be openly fixed and the whole produce of it be ascertained. And let the estates and properties and income be assigned, lest my portion and my sons' in this town be slighter than a reed in this valley ; therefore, allot that to me."

Timur therefore allotted it to him with its territories, estates and villages, and his grandsons, descendants and kin have held it right to this day.

CHAPTER IX

CONCERNING THE QUARREL AND EVIL THINGS WHICH AROSE BETWEEN ALI SHIR AND TIMUR

THEN a quarrel arose between Timur and Ali Shir, and both had their partisans, but Timur suddenly took him by surprise. Then, after he had been seized and put to death, the kingdoms and territories were subdued to Timur with some tranquillity, all the magnates hastening to do homage to him, who had hitherto haughtily declined.

CHAPTER X

WHAT TIMUR DID WITH THE ROGUES AND VILLAINS OF SAMARKAND AND HOW HE SENT THEM TO HELL

AT Samarkand there was a crowd of rogues of different sorts, among them wrestlers, swordsmen, boxers and mountebanks. And there were two factions among them like Qais and Yemen, which constantly practised mutual enmity and hostility and both sides had their leaders, supporters, helpers and partisans.

Timur feared them despite his power, when he saw their obstinacy and hostilities. And when he wished to leave the place, he used to appoint a deputy at Samarkand. And as soon as he had left the city, they used to break into revolt and depose the deputy or form a faction with him and declare open rebellion. And Timur did not return until the string of pearls was broken and everything in confusion; consequently he was compelled to restore, make smooth, destroy and build, putting some to death and removing some from office, wooing others with presents and rewards. Then he betook himself elsewhere to arrange and strengthen the affairs of his kingdom, but they soon would return to their own filth and recur to their deceit and craftiness. And this story was repeated about nine times. Accordingly Timur, finding force in vain against those rogues and villains, sought by cunning to destroy them and to restrain the injuries they inflicted and root them up completely. He therefore arranged a feast, to which he invited men of every kind and divided them into sections and placed each workman under his overseer together; but he placed those rogues separately with their leaders, in the manner in which Anushirvan, the son of Kaikobad, dealt with the infidels.

And he placed on one side in ambush guards, with whom he arranged that they should do away with anyone whom he removed to them and this removal was a signal to kill.

Then calling the chief persons to him he extended a goblet with his own hand and clothed them in splendid raiment and when the turn of those vagabonds came, he gave each a cup to drink and presented each with a mantle, at the same time giving a signal that having put it on he should go towards the men in ambush. And when he reached them, they stripped off his mantle—nay, rather the garment of life—and tore it to shreds, pouring the gold of its pattern into the bowl of destruction and melting it, until all were destroyed.

And when they were utterly destroyed and all trace of them wiped out and when their fire was quenched, the springs of water flowed for him and his kingdom was cleared of enemies and rebels, for none was left in Transoxiana disobedient to him or ready to resist him.

CHAPTER XI

THE TERRITORIES OF SAMARKAND ARE DESCRIBED AND ALSO
THOSE WHICH LIE BETWEEN THE RIVERS OF BALKHSHAN AND
KHAJEND*

SAMARKAND, with its provinces, has seven *tumans*, and
Andekan (or Feraghan) with its districts has nine *tumans;*
and tuman is the common name for a population that produces
ten thousand soldiers. Among the more notable cities and
famous places of Transoxiana is Samarkand, the walls of which
formerly, according to popular account, were of twelve
parasangs in length and that from the time of Sultan Jalaluddin
before Jenghizkhan.

I saw at the end of the wall on the west a town built by
Timur, called Damashq, half a day's journey from Samarkand—
where to this day they dig up remains of old Samarkand and
discover drachmas and obols inscribed in the Cufic character,
by melting which they obtain fine silver.

There is also a city of Transoxiana called Marghinan,
which was once a capital in which the Ilek Khan resided, and
from which came the famous and wise Sheikh, Burhanuddin of
Marghinan, author of the " Hidaya." May God Almighty
have mercy upon him !

Besides there is Khajend, which is on the Jaxartes ; and
Tarmaz on the bank of the Oxus ; Nakhshab, otherwise called
Qarshi, which I have already mentioned, Kesh, Bokhara and
Andekan, which are famous places. Further among the
provinces of Balkhshan are the territories of Khwarizm and
the regions of Saghainan and other spacious countries and
far-flung domains. And that part which lies beyond the Oxus
on the East is commonly called Turan and the part on this
side the Oxus on the west, Iran. For when Kaikaus and
Afrasiab were dividing provinces between themselves, Turan
went to Afrasiab and to Kaikaus, son of Kaikobad, Iran and
Irak on the West of Iran.

* i.e. the Oxus and Jaxartes.

CHAPTER XII

OF THE BEGINNING OF HIS TYRANNY AFTER HE HAD SUBDUED THE PROVINCES OF TRANSOXIANA

AFTER the provinces of Transoxiana were reduced to absolute submission and those had accepted his sway, who had long proudly resisted, Timur eager to win territory for himself and to reduce men to servitude, began with fingers of cunning to weave nets and snares, that with them he might catch kings of countries and lords of lands.

Accordingly, he first made an alliance by marriage with the Moguls, and gained their friendship and brought them to peace and tranquillity, taking as wife the daughter of their king, Qamaruddin, and became safe from their onslaughts and attacks ; for they were his neighbours on the east. And they were not torn or divided among themselves, since there was a double reason, first race, affinity and neighbourhood, and second, their religion, which is called the law of Jenghiz Khan and was spread through the whole of both states ; he was therefore safe from their enmity and repelled their wiles and power to injure.

CHAPTER XIII

TIMUR PLANS TO INVADE COUNTRIES AND FIRST THE TERRITORIES OF KHWARIZM

THEN Timur, secure from their arts and having blocked their boundary by pacification, planned to invade the territories of Khwarizm, which bordered his own on the west on the left side, but differed from him in maintaining the principles of Islam ; the capital of those territories is Jurjan, a very large city. And this kingdom contains large cities and great provinces. The capital is a place in which gather men of distinction, a place of meeting for the learned, a home for men of culture and poets, a resort of the refined and great, a centre of the sect of Mutazalites and a fountain of a multitude searching for truth following right and wrong paths. The city abounds in luxury and excellent plenty, and its beauties make a fine show; the name of the Sultan was Hussein Sufi, who followed untrue doctrines.

The cities of Transoxiana almost resemble each other, for all are built of brick and tile on earth. And the people of Khwarizm equal those of Samarkand in subtlety, but excel them in magnificence and elegance, being devoted to poetry and humane learning, admirable in various kinds of fine arts and accomplishments, especially in the science of music and tone, which is practised equally by the nobles and commons. In truth, it is commonly said of them that their children in the cradle when they cry or shout " Ah ! " do it in harmony.

When Timur came to Khwarizm, Hussein Sufi was absent and he laid waste the country round and all that his hand obtained thence ; but he made little effort over the city which he could not take and made little of it. Then collecting his followers he went back to his own kingdom.

CHAPTER XIV

THE SECOND INVASION OF KHWARIZM

THEN tightening the belt of resolution, Timur invaded Khwarizm a second time, equipped with every requirement and a large army, while the Sultan was still absent, as before ; and to the beautiful virgin (city) he sent in a suitor and besieged her and reduced her to the utmost distress, tightening the garments of the throat at the neck of her approaches, so that his nails were almost fixed in her lappets.

Therefore a man went out to him, one of the chief citizens, a merchant, who had won much merit with the Sultan, and who was named Hasan Surbaj, praying him to free them from that confusion and offering him what he might demand in place of the expected gain from captives and booty.

Then Timur demanded from him that a weight of silver coin, such as two hundred mules could carry, should be conveyed to his treasury. Nor did he cease to persuade and cajole him and steadfastly refuse, until he agreed with him for a quarter of the sum demanded, and he performed that undertaking, weighing out that sum immediately to him from his own resources and private means.

Timur accordingly betook himself on his way, prohibiting the devils of his army from plunder, and sought to return to Samarkand.

CHAPTER XV

TIMUR SENDS A LETTER TO MALIK GHAYATUDDIN, SULTAN OF HERAT, WHO SNATCHED HIM FROM THE CROSS, AND ON HIS ACCOUNT OPPOSED HIS OWN FATHER

TIMUR then wrote a letter to the Sultan of Herat, Malik Ghayatuddin, who was really his helper, beginning it with a saying (of Mahomed), " God has written concerning every wicked soul," and praying him to submit to his sway and demanding a consignment of slaves and a contribution in proportion to his strength ; adding that if he refused, he would attack his cities and destroy him.

But Malik Ghayatuddin replied : " I swear by the allies of the Prophet ! You were my slave and I did good to you, and spread over you the mantle of my kindness and favour, but you have deceived and slain, destroyed unawares and given over to slaughter, acted guilefully and accomplished the crime which you have accomplished, although I rescued you from blows and the cross ; but if you refuse to be a man who recognizes kindnesses, be like a dog." Then he crossed the Oxus and advanced against him, but when Ghayatuddin had not strength to meet him in open battle, his followers and townsmen at his command had assembled with their beasts around Herat and he dug round the gardens a ditch, which surrounded the wretched cowards and weaklings ; but he shut himself in the fortress, thinking that in this way he would be inaccessible—because of the weakness of his counsel and the stupidity and folly, by which his mind and the condition of his state was overthrown and confounded.

I have said :

> Him whose rule is not aided by fortune,
> Ruin assails, though he govern well.

Timur however did not think it worth while to fight with him and make a siege, but the army surrounded him on every

20

side, Timur holding a safe and secure position, while his enemy had exchanged open spaces for confinement. For, meantime, the nobles and commons were troubled and the cattle and beasts moved this way and that, and the town was choked with a dense mob, gentle and simple perished, disease consumed them and hunger destroyed them and wailing and murmuring arose.

Accordingly, the Sultan sent to him, seeking security, and informing him that because of him he had been brought into the greatest stress and that he had helped him previously and cared for him, and reminded him of his former kindness and the web of good service he had woven for him, and sought from him security confirmed by oath.

And Timur swore to him that he would preserve for him his ancient rights and would not shed his blood or break his skin. So he went out to him, and approaching him submitted to him; then Timur entered the city and climbed the fort and the Sultan with him, with the troops and guards of Herat surrounding him; then one of the brave men, the governor of Herat, gave a sign to the Sultan that he would slay Timur and that he was ready to sacrifice his life on his behalf and spoke to him in this wise : " I will ransom the Muslims at the risk of my life and wealth, and will kill this cripple, caring naught." But he did not consent to his intimation, and trusted to the decree of Almighty God and His will, and said : " Almighty God has supreme power over his servants and the arrow of His will cannot fail to go through them, nor can be escaped or avoided the decree, which God Almighty has made and decreed."

> When any destined thing ought to befall you, while you
>   flee from it, you will approach the nearer to it.
> Nor can this mystery of Providence fail of its issue ;
> Nor can man dispute the truth of its behests.
> He who struggles with Fate, is conquered
> And he that resists Fortune is dragged along.
> Who opposes the floods of Destiny is drowned
> And he that slothfully enjoys the resorts of pleasure is
>   choked.

Then he remembered what his father had said to him and marked its truth, but the arrow once shot could not be brought back.

CHAPTER XVI

HOW THAT TYRANT VISITED THE VENERABLE ZAINUDDIN ABU BAKR OF KHAWAF

WHEN at length Timur came into Khorasan, he heard that in a town called Khawaf there was a man, to whom God Almighty had granted excellent gifts, a man of learning and action, born in noble station, endowed with excellent understanding, remarkable for pure virtue and wonderful holiness, ready and brilliant in daily conversation, but his deliberate speech in the assemblies excelled much more ; in doctrine he was faithful, in dealing with God always true, and was called Sheikh Zainuddin Abu Bakr, who with the wings of his zeal occupied a lofty nest in the chief place in Paradise.

Timur, therefore, anxious to see him, hastened to him and his company. And when they said to the old man, "Timur comes to you desiring to see you and hoping for your blessing," the old man did not reply even a word or raise his eyes ; and when Timur came to him, he dismounted from his horse and went in to him. But the old man sat occupied in his accustomed posture meditating on the carpet of adoration. But when he reached him, the old man rose, but Timur bent with his face bowed towards his own feet and the old man put his hands on his back. Timur said : " If the old man had not quickly removed his hand from my back, I should have thought it was broken ; and I truly thought the sky had fallen on the earth, and that I was to be broken between the two with a mighty breaking."

Then he sat in the presence of that incomparable one ready to receive instruction and said to him courteously in conversation as though greedy to learn but not disputing : " Venerable master ! Do you teach nothing to your kings concerning justice and equity and warn them not to turn to violence and tyranny ? " And the old man replied to him : " We teach that in truth and for that reason we visit them ; but they do not suffer themselves to be taught, and so we have appointed you Lord over them."

But as soon as he went out from the old man, his hump stood erect and he said : " I am Lord of the World by the

Lord of the Kaaba ! " And this old man is he about whom a promise was made before to speak.

Then Timur throwing into bonds the King of Herat resolved to guard his gains, and to hold all his territories in allegiance, appointed in each a deputy, and returned to Samarkand with his booty.

But the Sultan he held prisoner in the city and forbade him to go out and entrusted him for being guarded to the citizens, to whom he joined his lions as guards, stark and staunch watchmen, because of his oath not to shed his blood and to maintain his rights ; therefore he did not indeed shed his blood, but slew him in prison with hunger and thirst.

CHAPTER XVII

TIMUR RETURNS TO KHORASAN AND LAYS WASTE THE PROVINCES OF SEISTAN

THEN Timur returned to Khorasan with a fixed purpose of taking revenge on Seistan, whose inhabitants went out to him asking for peace and agreement, which he granted them on condition that they should hand over their arms to him, of which they produced the whole equipment which they had, hoping in this way to escape from their extremity ; and he put them on oath and ordered them to swear plainly that no further weapons of theirs were left in the city.

And as soon as they had given this guarantee, he drew the sword against them and billeted upon them all the armies of death. Then he laid the city waste, leaving in it not a tree or a wall and destroyed it utterly, no mark or trace of it remaining.

And when he went away, no one was left alive in the city ; and he dealt in this manner with them only because he had first been injured by them.

An old man, skilled in the law, Zainuddin Abdul Latif, son of Mahomed, son of Abil Fatah of Kerman, a Hanifi, living at Damascus in the college of Jakmak, told me in the year 833 that those of the citizens of Seistan, who had escaped slaughter by flight, either by aid of darkness or by the special grace of God Almighty and Generous, when they had gone back to the city after the departure of Timur and wished there to hold sacred assemblies, forgot the day of assembly and did not learn it until a messenger sent to Kerman showed it to them.

CHAPTER XVIII

THAT DECEITFUL ONE ADVANCES TO THE TERRITORIES OF SABZUAR, WHICH SUBMIT TO HIM AND WHOSE PRINCE COMES TO MEET HIM

THEN Timur, after taking that revenge on Seistan, advanced with an army to the city Sabzuar, whose Governor, named Hassan Jauri, who had seized power and was a Rafizite,* was obliged to submit to him and offer him gifts and slaves to the extent of his power ; he accordingly confirmed him in his governorship, nay, increased his authority.

It was Timur's habit and care at the beginning of his rule, that when he was a guest with anyone, he questioned him about his descent, and noted his name and stock and said to him : " When you perceive that I have attained power and have been raised to dominion, come to me with this token and I will repay you generously."

Accordingly, as soon as his renown was spread abroad and his power published, and his exploits became known in the world, men hastened to him, bringing those tokens and all those at a distance came to him, and he placed each in his station and allotted to each his rank.

CHAPTER XIX

THE ACTS OF THAT VILLAIN IN THE CITY OF SABZUAR WITH SHARIF MAHOMED, THE HEAD OF A BAND OF VILLAINS

IN the city of Sabzuar there was a noble among the rebels, by name Said Mahomed Sarbazal, and his followers were all rogues called Sarbazalis or insurgents. And this Said was a man famous for remarkable gifts and renowned for especial

* i.e. a Shiah.

virtues. Timur therefore said : " Bring him to me ; I have come only because of him, for already I have desired to see him and have burned with desire to observe his gifts more closely." Accordingly, they sent for him, and Timur rose when he entered and embracing his neck received him with outstretched and smiling face and honoured him and took him nearer to himself and spoke to him briefly in this way : " My Lord Said ! Tell me how I shall gain the kingdoms of Khorasan and occupy them and how I shall win its near and distant territories ; and what must be done that I may accomplish this business and climb this steep and rough path ? "

Then the Said replied to him : " O Lord and Amir ! I am a poor man, even if of the seed of the Prophet ; why such prominence for me ? Indeed, though I am called Sharif, I am a man powerless, weak and unequal to deadly campaigns ; and who am I to discern regarding the ordering of the kingdom ? For he who mixes in the affairs of kings, either by opposing or by jesting, is like one who swims in the confluence of two seas or who sits between the butting of two goats ; and he who uses a tongue other than his own errs, and there is a great difference between Mamun* and a miller."

Then Timur said to him : " It is necessary that you should show me this way and point out to me the right path to arrive here ; in truth had I not observed this concerning you and divined that kingdoms follow your counsel and had you not been suited to this knowledge, I would not have spoken a word to you or sought aid from you like poor men from rich ; for in skill in physiognomy I am like Iyas and all my judgments are conclusive."

Then the counsellor replied : " O Amir ! Will you comply with my opinion in this thing, and follow my counsel ? " Timur, however, replied : " I have not consulted you, except to follow you, or met you, except to walk with you." Then the other said : " If you desire for yourself a clear spring of water and the occupation of kingdoms without wearying yourself, you need Khwaja Ali Ibn Muid Tusi, who is the hub of the wheel of these realms and the centre of the circle of these paths, and if he joins you outwardly, he will not inwardly be anything but your ally, but if he turns his face from you, no one else will help or profit you. Be, therefore, resolutely eager to conciliate him and attract him. For he is a staunch man,

* One of the Abbaside Khalifs.

the same without and within, on whose allegiance hangs the allegiance of the rest, by whose counsel the acts of all are bound, who do what he does, stand if he stands and go if he goes." This man just mentioned, to wit, Khwaja Ali Shia, was a follower of Ali in continuous series, from father to son, who minted money in the name of the twelve Imams and at the beginning of the assembly prayed in their names and he was fearless and expert in weighty business.

Then the Said said : " O Amir, summon Khwaji Ali, and if he obeys your summons and appears before you, you should omit no kind of respect and honour, nothing honorific and splendid, which you can show to him ; for that will serve you and amply repay you ; and set him in the rank of great kings, exalting, honouring and venerating him ; and do not omit towards him anything which befits your honour, for all that will redound to your majesty and greatness."

Then the Said left Timur and sent a messenger to the said Khwaja Ali, to say that Timur was entrusting all affairs to him ; if then that messenger came to him, he should not hesitate to obey or delay a moment in presenting himself before him and should be cheerful and without fear of violence to his condition and estate.

Accordingly, Khwaja Ali prepared for the coming of the messenger and the presence of the envoy and made ready gifts, offerings and beasts of burden and struck gold and silver coins engraved with his name and his Governor's, and spoke in their names in the mosques of the chief cities, and applied himself devotedly to furthering his business and held himself ready and equipped for accomplishing whatever was desired ; and then came Timur's messenger with a letter, in which he openly summoned him, using flattery and harlotry of language, and with the fullest indication of honour and favour. Accordingly, he rose, declaring himself ready for allegiance, and did not delay more than was needed for traversing the way, and came full of abundant hope and with firm confidence.

When his arrival had been announced to Timur, he sent to meet him the generals of his army, manifesting the greatest pleasure, and behaving like one who had newly become King. And when he came near, he offered him valuable gifts, precious offerings, excellent riches of princes and royal treasures, and showed him the highest honour and in the most courteous manner conferred favours upon him, and abundantly threw

LIFE OF TIMUR

upon the height of his hope the flowing skirts of the mantles of his own generosity and confirmed him in his province and heaped favours and honours upon him. Then there remained in Khorasan no Amir of a city, Governor of a fortress or counsellor, but came to Timur, and joined his side, chief of whom were Amir Mahomed, Lord of Bavard, and the Amir, Lord of Sarkhas.

And the fear of him spread through the further countries and dread of him reached to Mazanderan, Gilan, and the Provinces of Rai and Irak and hearts and ears were filled with his fame and terror of him seized neighbours and distant people, but above all Shah Shujah.

And all this happened in a little time and a few days—about two years, after he had killed Sultan Hussein.

CHAPTER XX

A LETTER OF THAT INTREPID ONE TO THE SULTAN OF PERSIAN IRAK, ABUL FUARIS SHAH SHUJAH

WHEN the provinces of Khorasan were completely subdued and the whole population near and distant submissive to his authority, Timur sent a letter to Shah Shujah, Sultan of Shiraz and Persian Irak, demanding from him homage and obedience, and that he should send goods and slaves ; and this letter was briefly in this wise :

" God Almighty has appointed me Lord over you and over unjust Princes and despotic Kings, and has raised me above my enemies and aided me against my adversaries, as you have seen and heard ; therefore if you obey and compose yourself to it, you will have done well ; if not, know that three things go before me, devastation, barrenness and pestilence ; all which evil will come back upon you and be imputed to you."

And Shah Shujah had no choice but to appease and conciliate him, undertaking a marriage alliance and friendship, and gave his daughter to Timur's son ; however these joys were not fulfilled because of a new onset of misfortunes and that happiness after being arranged was scattered, becoming a matchmaker of destruction, a compeller of accusation and

27

a tirewoman of desolation. Whereon I have improvised these verses :

> If you have chosen the noblest of women to negotiate
> Beware none the less her misfortunes and be wary in consideration of your business.
> And know that human nature is based
> On cunning, deceit and fraud.
> Trust yourself therefore to no female matchmaker
> But without delay yourself manage your transaction.
> He is indeed a man without compare and unique,
> Who leans on no one in this world.

But to loosen the reins of speech upon this topic would take us too far from our mark ; meanwhile however the gardens of love were blooming and the bed of affection was frequented and the caravans of intercourse and friendship came and went hither and thither, and in this wise they continued without dispute until the death of Shah Shujah. This Shah Shujah was a learned and excellent man and expounded the Kashaf* with orthodox and sound interpretation, also a charming poet and excelling in culture, of whose Arabic poetry this is a sample :

> " If my life were spent in love
> And the cause of my long suffering ceased not to delay,
> Would I not keep her love, whenever the rising sun scatters its beams anew,
> Though wasting destroy me ?
> He who has not tasted the pure sweetness of love in youth,
> Truly I know that he is utterly a fool."

And of his Persian verse :

> " O thou who art peerless beauty to the taste of lovers,
> If ever I choose another in thy stead
> Or neglect thy memory, may my life be accursed !
> And if by thy cruelty I die and my life-blood flows,
> Let all see to my affairs,
> We will commit them to the Best Protector."

This Shah Shujah was son of Mahomed, the son of Muzaffar and his father, an excellent and pious man, lived in the plains

---

* A commentary on the Koran.

of Yezd and Abarkova, noted for great courage, feared and dreaded by neighbours and those dwelling afar.

And there had arisen between Yezd and Shiraz an Arab brigand of the family of Khafaja, by name Hamaluk, who had blocked the straight course to travellers and used to rob the rich and slay the poor, reckless of small numbers or great and careless of gleaming darts, when stars were strewn above his head, and who slew many husbandmen and destroyed fields and men. But God loves not outrage.

Then the father of Shujah laid an ambush for him in a certain valley or plain, where attacking him face to face and engaging him in close combat he overthrew him, and cut off his head, which he offered to the Sultan, who set him over the whole army and presented him with many places and gave him private audience, planning to use his aid in every difficulty. He had many children, relatives and grandsons, all princes practised in submission and his sons were Shah Muzaffar, Shah Mahmud and Shah Shujah, each of whom had gained great authority and power ; but the Sultan had no son to succeed to the throne or hold dominion. And when the shepherd of death approached him, he assented to him and turned himself back and did not kick back, since the pegs of Mahomed, son of Muzaffar, were firmly fixed ; and in the Sultanate he was preferred to his comrades and he became absolute king in the realms of Persian Irak and was raised without sedition or dispute and according to his will exercised dominion, with the mantle of which God Himself had clothed him. " O God, Lord of the kingdom ! Thou grantest the kingdom to whom Thou wilt ! "

And while he was still alive, his son Shah Muzaffar already mentioned died, leaving a son Shah Mansur. But after there had arisen between Shah Shujah and his father a quarrel and extreme evil, he seized and held his father and plucking out his eyes, blinded him and seized the Sultanate and was confirmed in it.

But he was so torn by faintness that he could not endure fasting either at home or abroad, and often prayed God the Forgiver to raise no dispute between himself and Timur. When, however, he was close to his destined goal and the valet of death folded up and removed from him the carpet of hope, he summoned his relatives and sons and divided the kingdoms and countries between them and bequeathed to

29

his own son Zain Abadin Shiraz, the capital and centre of chief men of the kingdom, and to his brother, Sultan Ahmed, gave the provinces of Kerman ; but to his brother's son, Shah Yahia, he gave Yezd, and to his brother's son, Shah Mansur, Isfahan, and of this will he appointed Timur executor, and he confirmed that by open document making all who were present witnesses to that transaction, like one who adds wind to a storm.

And when death had marked with a border the garment of the life of Shah Shujah, shreds of dissension and dispute unfolded between his kindred, and Shah Mansur attacked Zain Abadin, and taking him, obtained Shiraz and took out his eyes, and opposing his uncle's wish, broke the bond of his will and dealt with his son, as his father had dealt with the grandfather of Zain Abadin. But the extended thread of this tale, and the task of its loosening and twisting would lead me from my purpose.

But Timur, seized by grief, restrained and held down his anger, but nevertheless waited in that matter for an opportunity which he might seize.

CHAPTER XXI

THE THIRD EXPEDITION OF TIMUR INTO KHWARIZM WITH ARMIES RAVAGING AND DESTROYING

THEN Timur, renewing his zeal and strengthening his purpose of invading Khwarizm, moved towards those parts from Khorasan along the road of Asterabad, wishing, while the Sultan was still absent, to set over them a deputy in his own name. But Hassan, already mentioned, met him and sought to appease him, and gained from him injury and insult and said to him : " O Lord and Amir ! We are all your slaves ; but when in the absence of our Sultan, a deputy is set over us in your name and the Sultan returns to us, without doubt enmity will arise between them, and if this happens, trouble will thereby easily be made for me, and this will be the cause of establishing hostility, so that annoyance and distress would increase between you and your rage would be poured upon Muslims and destruction would come upon them ; and Allah

loves not destroyers. Proclaim therefore that Hussein Sufi
is truly your deputy, for all men are bound to maintain your
service and your side and your purpose is foremost and it is
best to obey your command."

Then Timur hearing his speech and calmly receiving his
words, moved his tents.

And that Hassan had a son, who was reckless and wicked;
and when he had violated one of the concubines of the Sultan,
the crime began to be made known and its odour to be carried
to the noses of the world; but Hassan recked little of that
shameful crime, saying : " The Sultan owes me far the greatest
thanks, since I have protected his country from every wicked
man and infidel and have poured out in that business my wealth
and dignity three times, and no doubt he will pay for this
pacification by pardon and connivance in my son's crime."
But when the Sultan returned home from his journey and
learned the truth of all that affair, he put Hassan and his son
in chains and slew them, and threw them into the grip of the
lion of his might, who devoured them and laid waste their
houses and transferred all their goods to the treasury.

Then, shortly afterwards, when Hussein Sufi died, his son,
Yusuf Sufi, succeeded him. But Timur aided them before
and gave them resources and support against their enemies,
and gave to his son, Jehangir, as wife a maiden from them of
the highest rank and greatest wealth, sprung of distinguished
stock, of brilliant beauty, more beautiful than Shirin and more
graceful than Waladah; who, although she was a daughter
of kings, was called Khanzada, and she bore to him Mahomed
Sultan, who was a manifest prodigy in his noble nature and
vigour. And when Timur saw in his nature signs of singular
good fortune and that in the excellence of his talents he
surpassed the rest of his sons and grandsons, he disregarded
all of them and turned his mind to this one and appointed him
his heir, while so many of his uncles were alive; but fate
resisted that despot and he died before Timur himself at
Ak-Shahr in the territory of Rum—which will be told in the
proper place.

CHAPTER XXII

THE FOURTH EXPEDITION OF THIS WANDERER INTO KHWARIZM

BUT when Timur heard the misfortunes which had befallen Hassan, seized with anger, he resolutely discharged the cavalry of his wrath against Khwarizm, and captured it and killed the Sultan, pulled down its fortifications, laid waste the buildings, and set up over the remnants of it a deputy in his own name, and carried away everything movable from there to the realms of Samarkand. And the era dating from the spoiling of Khwarizm is called Azab, as that from the spoiling of Damascus is called Kharab.

CHAPTER XXIII

THE THREATS UTTERED BY THAT DEMON AGAINST SHAH WALI, THE AMIR OF MAZANDERAN

THEN after he had come to Khorasan, he sent a letter to Shah Wali, the Amir of the territories of Mazanderan, and wrote to the Amirs, who were under his own sway in this region, especially to Iskandar Aljalali, Arshiund and Ibrahim Alqami, summoning them according to his habit ; and under stress of force Ibrahim and Arshiund and Iskandar submitted to him, but Shah Wali, that brave hero, refused, and disregarding his addresses replied roughly to him.

CHAPTER XXIV

OF THE LETTER OF SHAH WALI TO THE SULTANS OF IRAK AND THE DISSENSIONS AND DISCORD WHICH THEN AROSE

THEN Shah Wali sending a letter to Shah Shujah, Sultan of Persian Irak and Kerman, and to Sultan Ahmed, son of Sheikh Avis, ruler of Arabian Irak and of Azerbaijan, imparted to them the dispatches received from Timur and the reply sent by himself and added : " I am your defence ; if my affairs are well contrived, yours will be also ; if disaster befalls me from him, it will also reach your kingdoms ; if you both aid me, I shall suffice to you for averting this trouble ; if not, it will happen to you according to the saying of the poet : ' When the beard of a man's neighbour is shaved, he should water his own beard.' "

As for Shah Shujah, he rejected and completely spurned his advances and as already said made peace with Timur ; but Sultan Ahmed replied ambiguously, saying : " Does this maimed and lame Jagatai assume to achieve anything and how could that lame Jagatai trample upon both Iraks ? For indeed between him and these countries there intervenes a fence of goat's thorn, and even between one place and another ; and he will not come down into Irak, as into Khorasan ; but if he has firmly resolved to invade our countries, he will rush to his own fate and his ambitions will abandon him. For certainly we are a race possessing courage and vigour and equipment and numbers and power and high spirit and it is our habit to hold our heads high and show pride, so much that regarding us Mutanabi seems to have said :

" We are a race, sprung from demons, in human form ;
Above our head is a bird tall like a camel."

When Shah Wali understood this from them, and knew that both of them were careless of him, he said :

" Truly by Allah ! with vigorous purpose and confident spirit I will meet him ; and if I conquer him, I will make you a public example and an example to those that have eyes, and if he conquers me, the fault will not be mine, whatever may reach you both ; therefore upon you would fall over-powering fate and complete disaster."

Then he prepared to meet him and committed himself to the Providence of God Almighty and to His decrees ; but when the armies were in sight of each other and blows of javelins, swords and spears were being dealt indiscriminately, Shah Wali withstood some time his adverse fortune ; then he turned his back after deciding upon withdrawal and flight and in fleeing he followed the tradition concerning flight and made for Rei, since he could not regain Irak.

The absolute Amir of that place was called Mahomed Jaukar, governing these towns and cities with complete power,

33

a prince noble, fearless and of great power; none the less he flattered Timur and obeyed his orders in many things, and fearing his violence and power he put to death Shah Wali, and sent his head to Timur.

CHAPTER XXV

THE CONFLICT OF ABU BAKR OF SHASBAN WITH THIS DESPOT

THERE was in a certain province of Mazanderan, a man called Abu Bakr, from a village called Shasban, who in battles was like a fierce lion and had destroyed and overthrown many nobles and commoners alike among the forces of the Tatars, whom men could not withstand, when he came into the field of battle, and when he laid down his turban, he caused among them a Day of Judgment, and he ceased not to lie in ambush between hills and mountains and overcome soldiers and warriors, so that proverbs were coined about him and men's shoulders shook in fear of him, even in a dream. Nay some of them would say to their beasts, when they gave them fodder or water and the beast drew back from the water or jumped back from the sack of food: " It is as though Abu Bakr of Shasban were in the water or the beast saw him among the food."

And it is said that the army of Timur received no harm in the whole period of his rule in all his battles, fights and expeditions, except from three men, who inflicted great disasters on him and his armies, and drove many of them to the abodes of hell, of whom the first was Abu Bakr of Shasban, the second my Lord Ali Kurd, and the third Amma Turkoman.

As for Abu Bakr, they say that in a certain narrow place in Mazanderan, when Timur was overcoming him on all sides and they had blocked the way of escape against him and tightened the noose of the hunting-net and had driven him to a height, opposite which was another height, and between the two a space of eight cubits, the bottom of it deep like a well or like the bottom of Gehenna: that Abu Bakr dismounted from his swift horse and jumped down from one height to the other with his arms and helmet and escaped without suffering any harm from them, as Taäbata Shara escaped; then he came to the followers of Timur, whom he overcame and among

34

them transferred to the millstone of perdition those whose threshing and harvesting he had completed.

But I do not know what afterwards befell him and what changes he experienced.

But my Lord Ali Kurd was Amir in the country of the Kurds, and had a troop of excellent horses and men by no means beardless, in rough mountains and impassable and precipitous places, from which he came out with his comrades and those who were entirely in submission to him and leaving men whom he trusted at the entrance of the pass, he used to make raids in different directions on the forces of Timur and on behalf of the Muslims wreaked vengeance upon them many times over, cutting off the extremities of his armies and seizing whatever he could of the beasts.   Then he would return to his caves, having fulfilled his purpose, and he did not give up raids of this sort, as long as Timur was alive and after Timur's death, until death overtook him and he met his end.

Finally Amma Turkoman was one of the Turkomans of Karabagh and he had two sons, each of whom put on the heart of Timur a blister which burnt grievously, between whom and Amiran Shah and the armies of Timur there were continuous fights and engagements and of their armies they destroyed a countless multitude and endless host, until the treachery of one of their followers, who took advantage of their carelessness and led the soldiers of Amiran Shah to them ; who attacked them by night and shed their blood like a torrent.   And by martyrdom these three were honoured in the way of Allah.   May Allah be merciful to them !   I have said :

" It is a terrible trial to be consecrated to death by dire enemies, but more terrible to be betrayed by friends."

And the poet says :

" The wrong done by kinsmen is a heavier blow to a man than the stroke of an Indian sword."

And from another poet :

" If it be so done to neighbours, what kindness shall be felt towards strangers ? "

35

CHAPTER XXVI

HOW TIMUR INVADED PERSIAN IRAK AND SHAH MANSUR WENT
UNDER THE FLOODS OF THAT SEA WHICH DEVOURED WITH
OPEN MOUTH

AFTER the death of Shah Shujah there arose discord among
his family, as I have said, while the rule of Persian Irak
remained with Shah Mansur and the provinces and territories
of Mazanderan passed to Timur, whom he had appointed
guardian of his son Zain Abadin and of all his interests as
already recorded ; and Timur found an opportunity of attacking Shah Mansur in the crime, which he had committeed
against Zain Abadin his uncle's son ; because of which he
arraigned him and advanced against him.

Shah Mansur therefore sought aid from his neighbours, but
they were all his enemies and carried on feuds and were un-
friendly to him, one and all being set on the defence of their
own borders. He therefore prepared alone to meet Timur
with about two thousand mail-clad cavalry, after he had fortified the city and strengthened it with warlike equipment,
distributing the cavalry and infantry and rousing the citizens
to endurance and resolution ; but the great leaders and the
heads of the state said to him : " Undoubtedly through you
we are exposed to the gravest danger and the web of war is
being woven and we have shut out Timur from approach to us
and even driven him back from raiding us and perchance
should have overthrown his troops and held in check brave men
of his army. But what more will you do with two thousand
cavalry against this thick and solid cloud ? When your necklace is broken and your army overthrown, you will think in
the struggle that no counsel is so wise for you as to seek escape
and flight and you will leave us, like meat on a butcher's pole,
after our foot is entangled in battle with them, and belated
repentance will not help us after establishing our enmity,
nor will this fracture then be repaired by us unless by slaughter,
rapine and chains."

But Shah Mansur with his hand on his battle-axe swore :
" These thousand men are a match for six thousand of those,
who have fled from Timur ; as for me, I shall fight ; but if my

men betray me, I will carry on the fight alone and spend all my energy and vigour upon it, and will make difficult for him my persistent effort and exertion ; but if I come out victorious, I will complete my undertaking ; if I fail, I shall not be to blame by those who survive me ; and it is as though I had been present and had observed by the mind of the poet, when he says :

' When he does this, he fixes the mark with his eyes ;
And he turns away from thought of evils to follow.' "

And it is said Shah Mansur distributed his troops among his forts, wishing in this way to defend the cities, but he suffered loss in the country ; then summoning the governors and troops of Shiraz and its citizens and his own children, he said :

" This enemy is grievous, who, though a heretic, has entered our territories ; therefore my counsel is not to be shut in a place with him or to attack by sword or spear, but I will move in all directions and with my followers assail him from every side and we will cleave their shoulders and cut off their flanks ; by day we shall cling persistently to him and by night keep a watch on him and we shall use against him so far as may be the power and pressure of cavalry and whenever we catch him off his guard, we shall break his neck and front ; at one time we shall strike with the horn, at another we shall reach out with our heels : at one moment we shall drive him, at another wound him ; we shall rob him of rest and prevent him from going back ; we shall block the passes for him and stop up for him nocturnal approaches and paths, in addition to your activities.

" But you, lovers of liberty and leopards of the desert and eagles of the desert, will defend with vigour the walls and will not neglect them during the hours of night or early or late in the day. But so long as I live separated from you, none of them shall attack you at close range : but if they besiege you, you will be sufficient to yourselves ; and I commend you to Allah, whose protection is best ; and there will be an end to the time, during which you shall be in this distress, as God Almighty promised by his prophet Moses. By Allah ! this plan is the soundest and the face of this purpose the most beautiful."

He then hurriedly went out and departed.

CHAPTER XXVII

OF THE SUBTLE PLAN WHICH WAS UNCOVERED AND HOW THAT WHICH SHAH MANSUR WOVE WAS UNRAVELLED

BUT while he was going out of the gate of the city, an old vampire and witch saw him and assailed him with abuse and rent him with curses, shouting in a loud voice in Persian : " There goes the son of a whore ! He has devoured our resources and usurped the right of life and death over us ; now he deserts us in the enemy's grip, when we need him most. May Allah turn to evil his warfare and grant no success to his purpose and promote not his desire ! "

Then the tinder of his wrath was lit and his heart wounded and the fires of his anger were kindled and the heart of his flame shook the summit of his purpose and his spirit rose to indignation and the fury of the Age of Ignorance seized him, until the understanding of this prudent man failed and wandered, and evening came and he clung to his error and doubled the reins of his purpose and set the teeth of persistence and swore that he would not leave his army or rest on the field of battle from constant struggle and that he would make this his aim morning, evening and night, until Allah gave the victory to whom He willed.

Then he went to the battle-front and after deploying his troops gave battle ; however in Shah Mansur's army there was present the Amir of Khorasan, a secret friend of Timur, named Mahomed son of Zainuddin, a villainous rebel, and with him was the chief part of the army, and he went over to Timur and the greater part of the soldiers followed him, and scarcely a thousand of them remained, but none of them refused battle and Shah Mansur persisted, though his affairs were overthrown and the bulls of war did not cease to attack each other with their horns and the tinder of battle to give out fire when struck, and the sparks of arrows to fly and the harvest of heads to be gathered and scattered with swords for scythes, until the army of night approached and the forces of day girded themselves for flight, when all of them returned to their nests and Shah Mansur laboured to devise a stratagem.

CHAPTER XXVIII

OF THE BATTLE AND DESTRUCTION WHICH SHAH MANSUR
INFLICTED ON THE ARMY OF TIMUR UNDER THE WING OF NIGHT

THEREFORE he made use of a bucking horse, more
impetuous and untamable than time and he led it to the
army of the enemy, when night was already far advanced :
then he bound to the tail of the horse a bronze cauldron rolled
in a piece of rag, which he fastened with a firmly-tied knot
and turned its head towards the enemy and urged it forwards ;
and the horse wandered through the camp, and men, overthrown and confounded by it, engaged in combat, and swords,
like streams, poured through the channels of their throats and
spread far and wide, as though it were the dread hour of the
last judgment, or the sky with shining stars had fallen upon
them and the earth had been shaken and swollen ; and Shah
Mansur persistently, like a falcon hovering over them, slew
each and every foe and destroyed all who took to flight, as it
is said :

" The night was dark and the Rams struggled fiercely
with each other : I did not see them make peace :
" If one stood, another sank ; another fell prone ; he
who escaped with his head, could count it gain."

They say that they fought so among themselves that about
ten thousand were destroyed. But when night had struck
its tents, and the day had raised its standards, they understood
how that disaster had befallen them and would that night had
not removed their defence ! Then Shah Mansur at dawn, his
men now reduced to few and his allies having scattered, chose
from his army a troop of about five hundred and rushed against
the enemy with the onset of a lion and with them entered the
eddies of death, and no one stood against them and turning to
left and right he shouted continually, " I am Shah Mansur, the
staunch, who is a host in himself ! " and before them they
seemed like frightened asses, who fly from lions, and when he
approached the place of Timur, the latter fled from him and
withdrew among the women and hid among them and lay concealed under the quilts ; but they hastened to him and said :

" We are women " and they showed a squadron of the army engaged in combat saying : " There is what you seek and among them is what you want." Then he returned and left them being deceived and went away in the direction they showed, and there the squadrons of soldiers again gathered around him and closed the ring, as I have written on the spur of the moment :

> " None but the women cut the throats of men ; and what hardship is there that they do not devise ?
> " And however many fires of evil have burnt the hearts of men, yet none was more consuming than their deceit."

And Shah Mansur riding a noble horse with two-edged sword fought right and left and with him his swift horse striking and biting any who came near in that struggle ; and it was as though Mansur remembered the sense of that which I said in the " Mirror of Ethics ":

> " The hand of God strengthens me, but both hands of *them* are bound :
> " Therefore this my hand with two-edged sword smites blows upon them."

Whenever therefore he attacked a troop, they scattered before him right and left, though all were people of the left or North.

> " When the help of Allah does not succour a man,
>   Then is what confronts him greatest, and his zeal most intense."

At length, his strength exhausted by battle and his hands weakened by stabs and blows, his cavalry and infantry overthrown and slain and his position in every way desperate and his roads blocked and the passes closed, his vigorous shouts became silent amid the destruction of his cavalry and his thunderbolts were extinguished while his infantry faltered and his good fortune waned, his wings were clipped and his vigour worn down and he was burdened by wounds and his roaring subsided and his bellowing ended and he was cut off from his men, being now heavily smitten and overborne by wounds ; in which flux of fortune only two men remained with him, one named Tokal, the other Muhutar Fakhiruddin ; and he began to be daunted and thirst conquered him and dust and heat dried up his liver and he sought for drink and found it not ; had he found it, whereby he would have wetted his saliva, no one could have stood in his way.

Therefore seeing it was best to throw himself among the slain, he fell among them, casting away his weapons and loosing his horse. And Tokal was slain, but Fakhiruddin escaped and after receiving seventy wounds, has yet lived to his ninetieth year, and was a doughty and gallant fighter.

Then Timur's army reformed and assembled and rose again after reaching the portals of death, and after innumerable hosts of them had been slain and during the night and day a vast and infinite multitude had been destroyed.

But Timur was in continual restlessness, anxiety and insomnia, since Shah Mansur was missing and knowledge lacking of the state of that ravening lion, whether he was still among the living and his cunning to be feared or whether he was already carried to the house of death and he himself could be safe from his devices ; and therefore he ordered searches among the wounded and inquiry about him among the dead and fallen, until the sun was about to hide himself with a curtain and place his glittering sword in the sheath of darkness: and when the white shilling (of the sun) had hidden under a cloak the wealth of light and the weaver of Providence had spread in the free air the mantle of all-shadowing night and scattered over its surface of transparent glass the glittering silver coins of his stars, and darkness was scattered and fixed far and wide, then one of the Jagatais lighted upon Shah Mansur, when he was about to breathe his last and Shah Mansur caught that man, or rather devil and traitor, and shouted to him : " Spare me, spare me ! I am Shah Mansur ; but hide this matter and accept from me these gems ; and conceal my fate and reveal it not ; and let it be as though I had not seen you or you me, and I had not known you or you me ; but if you hide my place and lead me to my brothers and supporters, you will be as one who freed me after buying me and recalled me to life when already dead and you will see reward from me and instead of booty you will take back my sincere friendship."

Then he offered to him gems which would have sufficed him and his descendants until the last day ; but in his history and his trouble he was like one who prays for help from life even in the hour of mourning ! and the other stayed not from leaping upon Shah Mansur and cutting off his head, which he offered to Timur, telling him what he had done and the story of the attempted ransom. But he believed him not nor confided in his words, but ordered the tribesmen and kinsmen of Shah Mansur to be brought, who had knowledge of him and they recognized him by a mole with which his face was marked.

But when Timur knew that it was really Shah Mansur, he distinguished the truthfulness of that man from falsehood; but stirred by indignation and anger he grew hot over the murder of Shah Mansur and was grieved. Then he asked that man about his origin and father and children and his tribe and master and teacher and when he had explored his affairs and learned his family and home, he sent a command to the Governor of that tribe, and slew his household, children, supporters, friends, neighbours, grandsons, relatives and kinsmen and killed him with cruel torture and destroyed all trace of him and treated his master evilly and put him to death and laid waste his lands. Then he sent to his most distant provinces letters, in which he set out the manner of those struggles and conflicts and what had been seen concerning the assaults of Shah Mansur and his steadfastness and his rush into the floods of war and his blows and what happened in the battle among the ranks of horsemen and how the vanguard trembled, and the women wailed when their apartments were opened, with terrifying descriptions and words turning in the field of eloquence and fluency; and these letters were read in assemblies and meeting-places and read out to those who came and went, and learned men took material from them and teachers and boys in school strove to commit them to memory and write them down.

I saw in the accounts of one of the learned, that in the month of Shawal of the year 95* there came an envoy of the Lord of Bastan, who informed the Sultan of Egypt, that Timur slew Shah Mansur and after subduing Shiraz and the remaining towns, sent his head to the Governor of Bagdad and demanded obedience from him and from those whom he had with him, sending him a robe of honour and ordered him to coin money inscribed with his name and to hold assembly in his name on the day of prayer, and he, putting on the robe, obeyed, following all his commands, and fixed to the wall the head of Shah Mansur after it had been carried round. But I doubt the truth of this account.

* 795, i.e., A.D. 1393.

CHAPTER XXIX

OF THE EVENTS AND DISASTERS WHICH BEFELL AFTER THE OVERTHROW OF SHAH MANSUR

ACCORDINGLY when the Kingdoms of Fars and the land of Persian Irak had been subdued by Timur, he wrote to the kinsmen of Shah Shujah and neighbouring Kings and conciliated them and freed the people of the plains and towns from fear and departed and entered the city of Shiraz, and strengthened its condition and placed on it a guard of horse and foot and pledging his honour he summoned men from a distance and those that were scattered ; and the Kings of countries obeyed the summons, for, not being a match for him, they had no choice but to obey and submit.

Then came to him Sultan Ahmed from Kerman and Shah Yahia from Yezd ; but Sultan Abu Isaak in Shirjan resisted ; and he received kindly and presented with robes of honour those who obeyed and submitted and did not confront those who defied him, or break a lance between himself and his enemies, honouring only those who respected his authority, that he might in this way attract the recalcitrant ; and he conferred security upon Shiraz and the other cities and appointed a deputy everywhere in his own name, then setting out for Ispahan he treated with kindness Zain Abadin whose guardian he had been appointed by his father and assigned to him gifts and presents which would suffice for him and his people.

CHAPTER XXX

OF THE EFFICACY OF THE TIME OF HIS ENTRY INTO ISPAHAN

WHEN he came to Ispahan, which is a great city, full of excellent men and teeming with nobles, there flourished there a doctor of Islam and learned teacher, who had reached the apex of erudition ; and was perfect in the practice and study of religion, by his deeds acceptable to Allah and renowned for his wonderful works and famed for his talents ; his merits were written on the forehead of the days and he was a pillar of Muslims, by name Hamamuddin ; and when the people of Ispahan mentioned Timur to him and said how they dreaded his tyranny, he replied : " So long as I survive among you, his cunning will not cause you any injury, but when the end of my life comes, then beware of harm from him."

And it happened that when Timur came, the Sheikh died and Ispahan was turned into darkness, darkness upon darkness, after it had been light upon light and their sighing was doubled and one disaster followed another and they fell into stupor, so that what Abu Harira—on whom be the favour of Allah— once said, suited them :

" Other men have one care only ; I to-day have two ;
The loss of my wallet and the loss of Sheikh Othman."

Then they went out to him, making peace with him, after offering a load of wealth and to collect it he sent men to them ; and they dispersed their resources and laid the burden on villages and parts of the city, and the collectors of tribute were divided among them, and advanced against them to do injury, treating them proudly and dealing with them as slaves, nay even laying hands on holy things ; and they were afflicted by them with the heaviest affliction and the people of Ispahan raised complaints to their Governor, but their indignation was increased the more because they were a spirited people and they said : that death was better in such a state than life under this tyranny. Then the Governor replied to them : " When evening comes, I will beat a drum, but not at the end of the night and when you hear that the drum has been beaten and that I have carried out what I said, let each of you seize on a stranger and judge according to his discretion, whether strong or weak."

And they accepted this perverse counsel and vain command under an evil star and the hands of their futile counsel availed not to accomplish this feeble project.

And when the air was stripped of the garment of light and the sky had changed ermine for sable and part of the night had passed, the Governor beat a drum and soon lamentation came on the tax-gatherers of whom they slew about six thousand and with the first light they planted in the orchard of rebellion the saplings of sedition, which bore as fruit for them want after plenty. And ruin confronted them and in the morning they arose most miserable among this destruction.

But when the dawn had drawn her sword and the day had stripped off his covering, Timur perceived that evil crime; and Satan puffed up his nostrils and he forthwith moved his camp and drew the sword of his wrath and took arrows from the quiver of his tyranny and advanced to the city, roaring, overthrowing, like a dog or lion or leopard; and when he came in sight of the city, he ordered bloodshed and sacrilege, slaughter and plunder, devastation, burning of crops, women's breasts to be cut off, infants to be destroyed, bodies dismembered, honour to be insulted, dependents to be betrayed and abandoned, the carpet of pity to be folded up and the blanket of revenge to be unfolded; nor did he pity the aged for his age, or the infant for his infancy, or honour the learned for his learning, or the educated for his excellence, or the noble for his blood, or the eminent for his dignity or the stranger for his strangeness, the kinsman for his kinship and propinquity, or the Moslem for his faith, the dependent for his dependence, the weak for his weakness, the obtuse for the weakness ot his judgment and his obtuseness; altogether he showed pity to none of the townspeople.

And the citizens knew there was no room for resistance, much less for assault and attack, rather that it would be absurd to put forward excuses and that they would not rescue their wealth or their sons from destined doom nor would their offers be accepted in that hour, and that ransom or entreaty would gain nothing for them; therefore, they armed themselves with the bows of patience, and put on the corselets of precedents and received the arrows of destiny from the hiding-places of Fate with the shield of submission to the Will of Allah, and bore the blows of Providence from death-dealing swords with necks of surrender and obedience; then he loosened the reins of the cutting sword in the fields of their necks and made their graves in the bellies of wolves and hyenas and the crops of birds; and the whirlwinds of destruction did not cease sweeping them from the trees of existence, until they counted the number of the dead, who were six times more than the people of Nineveh.

And one of the wise men implored the aid of one of the chief Amirs and said: " Spare, I pray, the remainder and show pity on the wretched multitude ! "

And to this suppliant fakir that Amir replied :

" Collect some infants on the hills, that he may be a little softened by the sight of them—as by chance may happen."

And following this counsel they placed in his path a company of children.

Then that Amir riding with Timur came with him to those babes and said as he went past : " Behold, my Lord, with the eye of pity, as God beholds him, who needs pity," and when Timur asked, " Who are those poor, abandoned creatures ? " he replied : " They are innocent babes and a company needing pity and inviolable ; death has snatched away their parents and the wrath of our lord and Amir has fallen on high and low, but now they beseech pity through your royal mercy and their own weakness, and pray you because of their worthlessness, feebleness, bereavement, poverty and distress to pity their worthlessness and spare the remnant."

He made no reply and uttered no speech, but urged his horse into them, as though he had not seen them, and likewise with him his troops and army, until he came upon all without exception, and he gave them up to the horses' hooves and ground them beneath the horses' feet. Then collecting wealth and baggage and placing goods on the baggage animals he returned with his booty to Samarkand.

But the calamities and hardships which happened amid these affairs and misfortunes and the histories, raising of squadrons and appointments and removals from office and the merriment he produced in the guise of seriousness and seriousness in the guise of jest, how much he built and destroyed, hindered and abandoned, how many places that were laid waste he settled and how many that were settled he laid waste, how many he debased and honoured and made to bear changes of fortune or supported and his consultations with the learned and disputes with magnates, the raising of the lowly and debasing of the noble, the passing of laws of state, collection of goods from far and removal of goods at hand and promulgation of edicts among all men near and distant, beside other things of this sort, are so many that they could scarcely be recounted or contained in book or tome.

CHAPTER XXXI

OF THE MILITARY STATIONS WHICH HE IMPOSED ON THE MOGULS
AND JATAS AND HIS EXPLOITS IN THOSE PARTS

WHEN he came to Samarkand, he sent his grandson, Mahomed Sultan, son of Jahangir, with Saifuddin, the Amir, to the furthest borders of his rule and empire, that is beyond the Jaxartes into the East up to the confines of the kingdoms of the Moguls, Jatas and Khatas, a journey of about a month from the kingdoms of Transoxiana ; and there levelling valleys and low-lying places they built several forts, of which the most distant was a city called Ashbara, in which they built an impregnable citadel, equipped for purposes of plunder and devastation. And he sought a second queen among the daughters of kings. His first queen was called the Queen major and the second the Queen minor. And their King consented, obediently and humbly conceding to his request what he desired of him.

And the fear of him spread through the countries of the Moguls and Khatas, especially when they had marked the deeds of violence which he had committed everywhere and that he was extirpating the faith of Islam in all countries and making himself master ; and the messenger in that matter was his grandson and the aforementioned Saifuddin, the same who plundered the wealth of Damascus after being received in the house of Ibn Maskur.

Timur also ordered a city to be built on the near bank of the Jaxartes and joined to it a bridge over the river with anchors and skiffs, which city he called Shah Rukhia, and it was placed in open country. The reason why he had distinguished his son by this name, Shah Rukh, and also this city, was that when he was engaged according to his habit in playing chess with one of his attendants and had already ordered that this city should be built on this bank of the river, and one of his concubines was present with him in a state of pregnancy, he attacked his opponent with the Shah Rukh and by this move his opponent was weakened and unnerved ; and while he was defeated, two messengers appeared, one of whom announced that a son had been born to him and the other that the building of the city was finished ; and therefore he called both by this name and distinguished them by this mark.

E

CHAPTER XXXII

THEN, after he had settled the countries and made laws for the kingdoms of Turkistan, he went back to the territories of Khorasan and there went out to meet him the kings and armies and sultans and viziers and both infantry and cavalry hastened to him from every side, obeying his summons and fearing his terrible power, thinking it a triumph to show obedience to him, and they surrendered to him high places and low, mountains and deserts, towns and their citizens and camps with their inhabitants and fortified citadels, and bound every forelock with the fringe of his authority, complying with his commands and anxiously avoiding those things which he forbade ; binding the girdle of his service with fingers of sincere submission, following the lead of his will on camels of subjection and homage and among them all those whom I have mentioned as having subjected themselves and those who had defended themselves among inaccessible mountains, and especially Iskandar Jalali, one of the Chiefs of Mazanderan, Arshiund Fariskuhi, that angry lion, lord of the mountains and of peaks with impregnable summits and also Ibrahim Al Qami, lord of courage, ready for any danger ; and Sultan Abu Isaak of Shirjan did homage to him ; and seventeen men among the Chiefs of Persian Irak assembled before him, all Sultans or sons of Sultans or sons of brothers of Sultans, each of whom enjoyed royal authority in his own realm : namely, Sultan Ahmed, brother of Shah Shujah, and Shah Yahia, son of the brother of Shah Shujah, besides the chiefs of Mazanderan and Arshiund and Ibrahim and the chiefs of Khorasan.

And when Sultan Abu Isaak went to render homage in the same manner as his kinsmen and acted in the same way, he appointed a deputy in his city Shirjan, by name Kudran.

And on a certain day it happened that while these great kings were with Timur and indeed in his tent, where he was alone among them, one of them made a sign to Shah Yahia, an opportunity having arisen, that he should slay him and remove from the world this suffocating evil; and some assented, others opposed; and to those who were approving Ahmed, one of the Sultans who disagreed, said: " If you do not restrain yourselves and refrain from this talk, I will reveal this saying to him and inform him of this matter." So they were driven from this firm counsel and prudent purpose by their disagreement, and did not cease from disputation; but he divined their attitude or knew their conversation by their faces, but he concealed it in his mind and did not reveal it to them.

Then after some days had passed he administered justice in public clad in a red robe, and summoned these same seventeen Princes, all of whom at once he ordered to be violently put to death. And after their destruction he seized their territories, collected their wealth, new and ancestral, slew their sons and set over their kingdoms his own sons, Amirs, relatives, grandsons and soldiers. And the reason why he put to death and crushed these kings and rent and tore the curtain of their life was, that the territories of the Persians were not lacking in great kings and men who held kingship and Sultanate by continuous succession : indeed, this kingdom is of wide extent, its borders are widespread, cities abundant, towns numerous, the bases of its mountains fixed deep and their jutting peaks raised to the sky and the virgin citadels raised on high, the treasures of its hidden places and mines not apparent, its Khosrus mighty to destroy and the wings of its vultures outstretched to threaten and its bandits leaping like leopards, its brigands like victorious tigers, its warriors like basilisks conspicuous in the rivers of battle and its rulers like crocodiles strong in seas of war : therefore, Timur saw with the eye of perspicacity in the mirror of his contemplation and wisdom, that the rose of its cheek would not be free from the thorn of a rival or the taste of its sweet mouth free from the touch of an enemy and that in establishing these kingdoms he would lack a solid foundation and that in the garden of its kingdoms no pleasant shoot would sprout for him. But his purpose was to let its buildings remain and to extend his authority there, in the manner that the religion of Jengizkhan required.

But he could not cultivate his Sultanate in its wide extent or cause to flow far and wide through the tracts of the kingdoms the rivers of his commands without plucking out the brambles of its nobility and breaking the embroidery of the dignity of its

Khosrus; therefore he strove to pluck them out root and branch and made every effort to destroy them utterly, nor did he see even the smallest bud sprouting from them in the ground of kinship without plucking it out; or smell the odour of a flower still folded by the calix without plucking it.

It is said that he held an assembly at which Iskandar Jalali was present and that when the talk grew lively and the assembly merry and free, he asked Iskandar: "If fate resolves to destroy my building, who, do you think, will oppose my sons and my issue?" And Iskandar replied (for he was drunk and his brain already affected and from drunkenness he had put the candle of judgment on the ground) "I am the first man, who will oppose your misshapen sons, then Arshiund and Ibrahim; if any of them escapes my claws, he will certainly not escape the teeth of that lion Ibrahim; but if any of them evades that trap, he will find no way out of the net of Arshiund."

But since Arshiund and Ibrahim were then absent, Timur held it not worth the trouble to injure Iskandar or reprove him, planning in preserving him to destroy him along with his two friends; and when Iskandar had slept off his drunkenness, and was blamed for his words, he replied: "What Allah has decreed cannot be avoided or resisted and no blame falls on me for what Allah made me say, who has given a voice to all things."

Then when Iskandar and Ibrahim had taken to flight, he seized Arshiund and threw him to destroying angels and there came to him the message of death and violated the shrine of his life, when he made him swallow the terrors in the beginning of the chapter entitled "Thunder" and bade him read the ends of the chapters "Noah" and "Saba."

Then no trace was found of Iskandar and nothing was heard of him up to our time; and his head was high and he was tall in stature and when he walked, projected among men like a standard, so that it was said that this Colossus filled the measure of three ells and a half in iron. And Ibrahim Al Qami escaped by rapid flight and at length died on his bed. And that was the cause of his destroying those Princes and their sons.

CHAPTER XXXIII

KUDRAN however resisted Timur in the fort of Shirjan, saying " My master, Shah Mansur, is still alive " and this saying was spread everywhere. And Kudran expected that he would appear and in that hope spent his years and months, but Timur besieged the fort of Shirjan and no chance of seizing it appeared to him and he moved to it the armies of Shiraz, Yezd, Abarqoa and Kerman, and joined to them the troops of Seistan, after he had surrounded the place of habitation, and in the siege Shah Abul Fatah took the lead for him ; and they kept it besieged for about ten years, now withdrawing from the place and now persisting. The place was like a maiden, who did not open the gate to her suitor, and a severe maiden from whom the suitor could not gain even a reply.

But Timur set over Kerman a man named Idaku, one of the brothers of the Sultan mentioned above, a man of great authority in the army.

And when Kudran learned of the death of Mansur and that he himself was deprived of any assistance, he fled and Abul Fatah continuously sent messages to him and on his behalf pleaded with Timur ; then he submitted to terms, employing the services of Abul Fatah for that purpose and surrendered, throwing himself at their feet, and handed over the fort to them.

But Idaku, becoming enraged with him, because the knot of this peace had not been untied on his own hand, slew him immediately, heedless of Abul Fatah and his entreaties. Then Timur hearing of it from Abul Fatah, while he was staying in a certain province, blazed with furious anger against Idaku, but there was no remedy.

CHAPTER XXXIV

THERE is a story about this Idaku, the Governor of Kerman: his Sultan Ahmed, brother of Shah Shujah, had two little sons, one of whom was called Sultan Mahdi, the other Suliman Khan. Suliman Khan was of consummate beauty and charm, possessing the virtues of elegance and ability, full of perfection, abounding in good humour ; his words were pleasing, his eyes penetrated like a dart, people were seized with love of him, and even wise men were devoted to him ; his movements sank into men's hearts and the sight of him bewitched them, as it is said :

> " The scent of the crocus in running water
> And the reflection of light on the surface of the air."

He was then in his sixth year ; but because on his account the nobles and commons were bewitched, Idaku resolved to remove both and gather them to their fathers and did not ward off disaster from this pearl, because he was at once most precious and an orphan, or pity his mother, whose territories were laid waste, though she was virtuous and noble, and there was no one to check him and defend them ; he therefore sought an assassin to whom he might entrust the task, but no one wished to do violence to the boy and meanwhile some time passed and many were anxious and troubled because of this, until they found a black slave, in whom misfortunes resided as in a watch tower, and who was served by devils and afrits were his soldiers and attendants ; from the warp of his blackness a night-garment of savagery was woven and a root of the tree, whose branches are like heads of devils, sprouted and rose from the seed of his heart ; compared to the grating of his voice the lowing of bulls would give pleasure and compared with the appearance of his form the sight of spectres would seem beautiful. I have said :

> " The angels of the lower world shun his face
> And seeing him seek hell as a refuge."

Certainly Allah removed pity from his heart and implanted an evil spirit in his breast ; him therefore they bade destroy those two by deceit ; however Suliman Khan was suffering in the eyes and was resting in the lap of his nurse, when that evil man, when opportunity arose, came upon him and attacking him suddenly while he slept, pierced his side with a dagger penetrating his other side and there rose shouting and wailing and clamour and confusion and the same crime overtook the affrighted mother with her household and men grieved and mourned therefor.

And it was plain that these things were done at a sign from Timur nor was the army of this infidel despot lacking in evil deeds of that sort and evil men and if anyone was not equally wicked, he yet so became by familiarity and association.

STORY

When he departed from Syria with his abundant army, one soldier had with him a woman captive, whose veil of modesty had been uncovered by the hands of misfortune, and her face buffeted. She was carrying on her arm her sucking child, which she weaned ; and when the army came near Hama and the child began to cry loudly, and because of some pain, was much troubled and wept, there was present a camel-driver of Bagdad, given up to violence, abandoned to harshness, formed for roughness and hardness, compounded of inhumanity and stupidity, full of baseness, packed with vice, in whose heart Allah Almighty had implanted no pity, that could be extracted nor given his tongue any goodness that could be heard. But he took that small girl from its mother, who supposed that was done to assuage its discomfort and sat on the camel ; then he went away from the baggage for a while, and at length returned empty-handed and laughing loudly ; then the mother asked about the state of the child and he said : " What is she to me ? " and she bereft of her senses and confounded threw herself down from the camel and reaching out towards the child took it away and turning back took it with her and mounted the camel.

However he took it from its mother a second time on condition that he would do it no harm, then leaving it and returning, he did as before ; then the mother again threw herself down and went off to the child a second time and came when she was already drained of strength and in the agony of death and riding on the camel, took the child away and placed it on her belly, whence she had given it birth. But he raging with violence, took it away a third time, and swore to her falsely that he would carry it without harm and he carried it for a while, but soon leaving the highway hurled it into a marsh and committed the same crime against it, as the Jew did against the slave girl distinguished for her charity, then came ; and his hand crushing its skull was full of crime but carried no child ; so he robbed it and took the spoils to the mother,

53

who fell before him weeping and wished to return to her daughter, but he said to her: "Do not weary yourself; I will give you enough of trouble; therefore return and ride away"; then she wept, shouting, lamenting and wailing, and relapsed into grief, though she had become calm for a while.

> "Men truly walk according to the character of their kings,
> Walking in their ways."

CHAPTER XXXV

THE CAUSE OF HIS INVADING ARABIAN IRAK, THOUGH HIS TYRANNY NEEDED NO REASON OR CAUSE

THEREFORE when all the Persian kingdoms had submitted entirely to Timur and kings and peoples had surrendered to him, and his rule had reached the borders of Arabian Irak, Sultan Ahmed, lord of Bagdad, becoming angry and disturbed, equipped a powerful army, over which he put in command a brave general, by name Sabtani, and the army confronted the forces of Timur; and when the report and knowledge of this reached Timur, his heart rejoiced over it and his breast was cheered and he made it the occasion of interfering and attacking the King of Irak and falling upon him and he sent a fierce army, nay a swollen and tempestuous sea; and they joined battle with vehement determination near the city Sultania and fell on each other with violent blows, with spear-points, and arrows of mutual slaughter, turned towards the throats of the enemy and the sea of the Jagatais rose with the abundance of its waves and collided and the lances of the army of Sabtani were broken in its surging dust, and that army being driven to flight, all betook themselves to Bagdad and were scattered over the country.

But Sultan Ahmed ordered Sabtani to be led through Bagdad clad in a woman's veil after being scourged and tortured.

And Timur refrained from further violence and returned, marching to his own country.

CHAPTER XXXVI

THE REST AFTER THAT FIERCE STORM AND THE CALMING OF THAT
TROUBLED SEA, THAT IT MIGHT BREAK AT WILL THE SURROUND-
ING COASTS, FREED FROM FEAR OF IT, AND MAKE UNTOWARD
HAPPENINGS BEFALL THERE

THEN Timur setting forth from Samarkand to its further
regions, traversed them on every side and built towns
everywhere, which he called after great cities and capitals.
And Samarkand was now transferred to him in absolute
obedience along with its provinces, and the realms of Transoxiana with their territories, Turkistan with its countries,
over which Khudaidad ruled in his name, and Khwarizm,
which he had suddenly overthrown and brought under his
tyranny—Kashgar in the sea of the kingdoms of the Khatas
and Balkhshan—which kingdoms are far from the realms of
Samarkand ; moreover the lands of Khorasan and the greater
part of the territories of Mazanderan—and Rustamdar and
Zulistan, Tabaristan and Rei and Ghazni and Astarabad and
Sultania and the rest of those countries and the inaccessible
mountains of Ghor and Persian Irak and Fars the mountainous
—and all that without any enemy disputing or restraining
him ; and he had through the whole empire of these realms,
either son, grandson or deputy in whom he trusted.

CHAPTER XXXVII

AN EXAMPLE OF THE WAY IN WHICH THAT FAITHLESS DESPOT
PLUNGED INTO THE SEAS OF HIS ARMY, AND DIVED INTO AFFAIRS,
THEN ADVANCED WITH THE SURGE OF CALAMITIES ; AND
PARTICULARLY HIS PLUNGES INTO TRANSOXIANA AND HIS
COMING FORTH FROM THE COUNTRY OF LUR*

THEN although his kingdom was widespread and fear of
him was spread abroad and all men everywhere smitten
by fear of him and his equipment so large that no expedition
or movement of his could be hidden, yet he ran to the ends

* Luristan.

of the earth, as Satan runs from the son of Adam and crept through countries as poison creeps through bodies.

I have said :

" Aiming right he struck left
And threatening the brow he attacked the neck."

Meantime while in the eastern districts he had the standards of armies, lo! in the west darted forth thunderbolts of disaster —and while the sound of his drums and the blows of his drumsticks fell as he besieged Irak, Ispahan and Shiraz, behold the twanging of his strings and the blasts of his trumpets were heard in the dominions of Rum and the assembly of Ruha (Edessa) and the convoy of the Hejaz.

So he remained some time at Samarkand, occupied in planting gardens and building forts, until the countries were free from terror of him and the borders feared naught. But as soon as his affairs were finished and his buildings completed, he ordered his troops to be ready at Samarkand, then commanded them to make for themselves felt caps, which he himself had devised and invented of a certain design and to march covered with these so that while it should not appear whither they were proceeding, these caps should be signs to them ; and he had already collected squadrons and disposed them through all quarters of his kingdom.

Then setting forth from Samarkand he gave out that he was proceeding towards Khajend and the countries of the Turks and Jand,* then hid himself in the whirlpool of his army and was submerged as though he had sunk into an abyss of the sea, none knowing whither he was making his way and whence he purposed plunder and he continued to march by day and night and traverse countries and run with the speed of a rider and travel like the stars, driving the sluggish and wearying the noble beasts until he appeared in the country of Lur, observed by none.

This country is well tilled, abounding in good things, rich in fruits ; its fort is called Burujird, and was ruled by Azuddin Abbasi ; and that fort, although placed on low ground, yet by its strength could rival forts of the firm-based mountains, being set in the neighbourhood of Hamadan and opposite Irak of the Arabs, like Azerbaijan.

Then Timur surrounded this fort and its territory and

* A town in Turkistan.

besieged its ruler and governor, but since the lord of the place was without troops, equipment and aid, like a man who is secure and self-sufficient, disaster befell him whence he had expected not—and nothing was left him but to seek safety and do homage to Timur and submit ; so he surrendered and entrusted himself to Timur's will, who cast him in chains and seized his country, then sent him to Samarkand, where he held him in prison and treated him most hardly, but at length taking an oath from him, set him free from his misfortune and made peace with him, after exacting tribute of horses and mules and sent him away to his own country over which he appointed him in his name.

But after that infidel had plundered the provinces of these districts, he immediately made his way to Hamadan and reached the place, its citizens acting with negligence, and disaster befell it by night, the citizens sleeping at midday.

And there went out to him a noble, by name Mujtabi, a confidant and friend of kings, who interceded for the citizens and won favour on condition that they should pay the tribute of safety and redeem their souls and bodies which he would grant them with their wealth, and they accepted the terms and executed them and they apportioned this tribute among themselves and after collecting it brought it to his treasury.

And when that persecutor strove a second time to impose tribute upon them, this true man approached him and stood supplicating with the mien of an abject wretch and he accepted his entreaty and granted everything to him.

Then he stayed and remained where he was, until his army joined him and assembled.

CHAPTER XXXVIII

THIS BASTARD BEGINS TO LAY WASTE AZERBAIJAN AND THE KINGDOMS OF ARABIAN IRAK

HOWEVER when Sultan Ahmed son of Sheikh Avis learnt what this wolf did in the flock of his neighbours the people of Lur and Hamadan, he knew that without doubt he would invade his kingdom and country, since he had shown enmity openly against him and had sent sparks flying against his wickedness ; and he knew that his army was like a flowing torrent and that he could not resist its sea and its waves, for when the river of Allah comes, the river of Isa stops ; nor can Pharoah's magic resist the staff of Moses.

I have said in verse :
" The torrent overflowing roots up the trees in its path and
carries them away among the mountains, and rocks
are split by it.
Until it reaches the abyss of the sea ; then you see it has
disappeared and no trace of it remains."

So he prepared for disasters before they came upon him and looked forward for himself before they befell him, and girded himself for flight, knowing that a safe return is equal to plunder ; and reducing to brief compass his full knowledge of fighting and combat, he quickly deserted the realms of Bagdad, Irak and Tabriz, saying to himself " Fly ! Fly ! " And he sent his dearest possessions with his son Sultan Zahir to the fort Al Naja and sent to Timur verses and satire, from which I have translated these lines :

" Although my hand is palsied in war,
Yet my foot is not lame in flight."

Then he made for Syria, and it happened in the year 795,* when there was living Al Malik Az Zahir Abu Said Barkuk,† upon whom be the mercy of Allah the Almighty !

And Timur reached Tabriz, where robbing humble and powerful alike, he sent armies to the fort Al Naja, which was the place of refuge of Sultan Ahmed where he had placed his son, wife and treasures ; but he himself marching to Bagdad plundered the place for he did not lay it waste but despoiled it.

The Governor of Al Naja was a man brave and bold, by name Altun, whom Sultan Ahmed greatly trusted and relied on him and he had a force of brave, daring and gallant men, about three hundred in number, with whom Altun used to descend upon the enemy, when the quiet of night fell and from all sides send plunderers into that army and into the camp while it was at rest and harassed the leader of the army.

And when this news was brought to Timur, he sent to their help about forty thousand famous soldiers with four

* A.D. 1393.   † Sultan of Egypt.

Amirs, of whom the chief was called Kablagh Timur and when they approached the fort, Altun was absent, having gone to plunder the surrounding fields ; and while he was returning, dust sprang up and on discovering it, he said : " Where is there a place to flee to ? " But they said : " None ; there is no refuge ; we know that there is no place of refuge from Allah but to Him." Then strengthening his own heart and his comrades and taking courage, he said : " Leaders in a position of this sort are wont to be under standards ; therefore break through the centre of these wretches ; and if you succeed or even if you fall dead on your horses' backs, you will show nobility, since nothing can take you from this disaster but true blows of lance and sword."

I have said :

> " Nobly seek death doomed else to die ignoble.
> By Allah ! after death one has not again to die."

Then they aided each other with true and vigorous courage, believing that Allah Almighty would afford them safety. And already they surrounded them like fish with a net and they were in the midst of them like a spindle in a spinning-wheel but they sought the standard and its bearers and those that followed it and belonged thereto and a favourable constellation aided them, and freed from the unfavourable influence of the stars, they made the red blood of the enemy flow over the white standards and all had the way open to the threshold of victory, and safety shone upon them and a happy issue befell them and they escaped from misfortunes with much rejoicing after they had slain two Amirs of the army, one of whom was Kablagh Timur.

And when this news was brought to Timur, the world seemed to him to grow black, nay the whole universe seemed to be overturned upon him. Then he set out against the fort and pitched his camp beside it with his followers and surrounded it on every side and made his followers swallow the mouths of swords.

CHAPTER XXXIX

THE FORT OF AL NAJA IS DESCRIBED

NOW this fort was more inaccessible than the ridge of a mountain and higher than the very clouds ; its height reached to the stars, its strength rivalled the heavenly orbs ; the sun at its zenith seemed like a golden shield fixed to its white ramparts and the constellation of the Pleiades in its high station a candle hung from its gate; the bird of imagination would not fly to it nor the garter of imagination and thought hang from the stays of its metacarp, still less would a bracelet be bound on its wrist by troops of horsemen.

But Altun, to whom its site was his native soil—and the people of Mecca are the fittest to show its paths—was accustomed, at dead of night, when devilish thieves set their hopeful eyes in ambush, to descend from these hills and walk by night like a ghost, and creep as fat creeps into flesh and water into wood and fire into coal, from the mountain passes, which imagination could not picture, Allah the invisible helping him, so that neither the sentries marked him nor the night-watchmen observed him and ceased not to lull them to sleep as though by a spell and to conceal himself and hide by a sort of magic and go nearer and search until a suitable chance should appear to him ; then he used to kill, rob and plunder and finally withdraw by flight and return unhurt and laden with spoils to his camp ; and this manner of things continued, until he had reduced Timur and his men to impotence.

Accordingly Timur thought it best to retire because of the narrowness of the plain and difficulty of the place and so left the fort, after he had established a military post to besiege it—and this siege lasted long, Fate saying to him, " Persist, for it will not cheat you."

It is said to have remained under siege for twelve years. And this was the cause of its capture.

Altun, whom I have mentioned, had a brother notorious for wantonness, between whom and the mother of Sultan Zahir an illicit intimacy arose, which made both liable to the punishment which is due to the adulterer, and when Zahir, son of Sultan Ahmed, learnt this, he seized both of them and put them to death, observing that praiseworthy opinion. However at that time Altun was absent from the fort, having gone out to drive booty, but when Altun returned, they shut the gate of the fort to him and hurled his brother down from the wall to him and explained to him what had happened and all his evil fate.

But he said : " May Allah render the best reward and magnify your fortune with excellent wealth ! If I had known his crime or had been present with him, I would have dealt with him according to his deserts and inflicted on him the punishment, which is due to his crime and instead of fortune misfortunes would have befallen him and in him I would have shown an example to you and given him as a guilty person to be seen of men and through the public crier would have announced against him that this is the reward of the man who has committed treachery against a good master."

Then he sought to be admitted, but they refused to let him in and he said : " Truly my brother, since he committed a crime, has tasted the fruit, which he gathered for himself ; but I lately strove with all my heart to fulfil even to death the faith pledged to you nor will I cease to show myself an ally to your friends and an enemy to your foes ; but if you drive me out, whither shall I fly and if you rebuff my affection for you, on whom shall I bestow it ? "

But they replied: " Perchance indigation and the love of kindred will touch you ; then you will remember your brother and will think of hardness after softness and will take fierce vengeance and show yourself perverse after behaving rightly and will disturb the calm ; and the story of the two brothers and the woman called Zat Alsafa will suit you."

I have said in verse :

" A rope that has been cut can be joined, but yet there will remain in it the knot that binds it."

Then he swore that his words and promises were faithful, but they replied to him : " Do not prolong it, for while you live, you will have no place to take sleep with us at noon or night ; therefore return whence you came ; we have no longer anything in common with you, whether it displeases or pleases you."

Then he began to revile his fortune and to bite his hand with remorse and grief, since he had spent his life in the service

of one who did not know his worth ; then he again tried bland-
ishments, but being repelled departed with a gloomy face,
abandoning his wealth and leaving his cavalry and infantry.

And since he had no place of refuge except the fort of Al
Naja, but it had betrayed him, and he had set fire to his own
liver, he dissembled where among men he would go.

Then he kindled his purpose to betake himself to the city
Marand,* which was under the sway of Timur and subject to his
rule ; so he sought this city and came to its governor wearing a
blanket, leaving his wealth and children. And when this was
told to the governor, he was beset by cowardice and languor
and, smitten with apprehension, he trembled and being
excited, confounded and seized with terror wished to fly, but
when it was said that he was alone without followers or arms,
his mind was restored and Altun entered ; whom he questioned
about his affairs, then cut off his head and sent it to Timur,
who because of that blazed with anger and sorrowed much and
for his sake was overcome by grief and wept ; and sending an
order to the murderer, removed him from his office and then
beat him and put him to death.

After this, Sultan Zahir, when these things had become
public and he had defiled himself with this impurity, could not
remain there longer and accordingly announced his departure
and led his assembly in migration, because the matrons of the
fort were disobedient to him and he was unequal to guarding
its defences, enduring hardships from the violation of its
maidens and matrons, his forces being broken and diminished ;
and he took thence his goods and offspring. Then the haughty
defenders submitted to Timur, and the gate was opened to
him without a struggle and he set over it a guard on which he
relied, entrusting that on account of neighbourhood to Sheikh
Ibrahim, governor of Shirvan.

Then he turned the reins of violence against Bagdad with an
army—but Sultan Ahmed, as already said, had escaped into
Syria—and this was in the month Shawal of the year 795,† and
he came to that city on the eleventh day, which was the Sabbath
day, and smote it and the surrounding lands and fully subdued
it.

* Near Tabriz.   † A.D. 1393.

62

CHAPTER XL

THE STORY OF THE LORD OF BAGDAD, THE NAMES OF HIS FATHERS AND ANCESTORS AND HOW HE CAME TO THIS COUNTRY

THIS Sultan Ahmed Mughituddin, son of Sheikh Avis, son of Sheikh Hassan, son of Hussein, son of Akbuga, son of Idkhan, was lord of Bagdad and Azerbaijan and the parts of the provinces and realms of Ilkhan and Idkhan which belong to Azerbaijan; his ancestor was son of Ilkhan, and was the great and brave Sharafuddin, grandson of Ilkhan Argun, son of Abu Said.

His father Sheikh Avis was a religious and upright man, a just king, a brave leader, an excellent man, refined, victorious, brave, beloved, of few faults, abounding in piety. His appearance was as pleasing as his character. He reigned nineteen years, a friend of poor religious men, companion of the learned and great; but when he had seen in sleep that death was coming to him, he with his relatives left the province of Bagdad, making for Diar-Bakr and Erzinjan and he prepared for the coming of death and marking the approach of his end he abdicated his rule, which he gave to his son Hussein— the eldest—who excelled the rest of his family; and giving up meaner things he turned to worship of his Lord whom he prayed to be favourable to him and forgive all that was past and he was constant in prayers, fasts, charities and worship of Allah and ceased not to pray and fast until the appointed time of death overtook him; then he opened his hidden secret and read: "When their end shall have come, they shall not put it off for an hour nor go before it."

And when he had maintained this way of piety and clung to it for more than thirty years, his moon was eclipsed to the west of Tabriz. And this news came to Syria in the year 776* and in his place was confirmed his son Jalaluddin Hussein, who made his goodness and beneficence abound towards his subjects and possessed a noble nature, great in virtues, full of courage, excellent in generosity and wished to follow the example of his father and recall to life the obliterated traces of his footprints and his precepts, but the fates thwarted him and misfortunes confounded his pure endeavours.

* A.D. 1374.

Now in the year 783* several ambassadors of his came to Syria, to wit Qazi Zainuddin Ali, son of Jalaluddin Abdullah son of Najamuddin Suliman Alsiafi, the Shafeite, Qazi of Bagdad and Tabriz : Sahib Sharafuddin son of Haji Azuddin Hussein Al Vasiti, Vazir of the Sultan, and others.

Then in the month Jumadi (the latter half) in the same year Sultan Ahmed, attacking his brother mentioned above, killed him and resolving to aid the kingdom and religion in his stead turned from him and filled the eyelids of his life with the sleep of death, when he was over twenty years of age.

But Sultan Ahmed obtaining the Kingdom of Irak stretched out the hand of wickedness and contracted the wing of piety and courtesy and was constant in injustice in himself and towards his subjects and spent days and nights in profligacy and wickedness, then exceeded the bounds in wickedness and crimes displaying his sins and showing his evilness and took the shedding of blood as a ladder to despoil sacred things and rend dignity ; therefore the people of Bagdad are said to have spewed him out and called Timur to aid ; but† they were aided by water, which like lees of oil or molten pitch scorches the face and Ahmed did not observe until the Tatars overwhelmed him and the armies of the Jagatais, horse and foot, broke him, on the Sabbath mentioned above of the said month.

And they overthrew his cavalry and attacked the walls, the river (Tigris) checking them naught nor the arrows shot against them by the townsmen and Ahmed knew that nothing would help him to safety but flight ; therefore he departed with those whom he trusted, heading for Syria, but mean hordes of Jagatais pursued him, whom he attacked, but soon avoiding them and fleeing from them he thereby roused their ardour more and there was a bitter conflict between them and great numbers were slain on both sides, until he reached Hilla, where the river Tigris passed through a bridge ; and when this was broken he escaped the danger of capture, for the Tatars continuing to follow him, their leading men had almost overtaken his rear, but coming to the bridge they found it broken, therefore they threw themselves into the water and advanced from the further bank and continued to pursue without abatement, but he slipped from them and came to the sepulchre of the Imam which is three days' journey from Bagdad.

CHAPTER XLI

OF THE TRICKERY AND FRAUD WHICH HE COMMITTED IN THE
COUNTRY OF ERZINJAN AND DIAR-BAKR

HE then invaded Diar-Bakr and conquered it and dragged
it out of the hands of its governors; but when the Fort of
Tikrit resisted him, he sent against it all the afrits of his armies
—on the third day of the week, the 14th of Zulhaja—
the country being now seized with incredible fear of him;
and besieging the place he took it in the month of Safar,
giving a promise of security, and the governor, Hassan, son of
Bulimur, came down to him, wearing muslin in token of
mourning and carrying his small children at his bosom and
neck, and his household bade him farewell and his horse
and foot left him, after Timur had promised him that he would
not shed his blood, but he sent him to a wall and hurling it
upon him crushed him, and slew the men who were in the
fort, and made the women captives, and the children prisoners
and began to devastate, utterly destroy and ravage continuously, until he pitched his camp at Mosul, on the day of
assembly, the 21st of the month Safar in the year 796*; and after
laying waste and destroying that place, he proceeded to Rasain,†
and after despoiling it and taking the inhabitants prisoners,
he moved to Urfa and entering it on the first day of the week
the 10th of the first half of the month Rabia, he was active
in damage and violence and imitated the vehemence of
Thamud and Ad; and he left that city on the first day of the
week, the 12th of the same month.

Then he chose from his people vultures to fly in all directions
seeking for blood, accustomed to slaying Muslims, and taking
them he made an attack and plunged into the kingdom of
Diar-Bakr, where they continuously did damage, ravaged
and committed violence, and there is Mardin, whither he
moved with those mighty afrits and continued his march,
and came to the place in five days from Tikrit, though the
distance between them, even with the greatest diligence, is at
least twelve days.

And the Sultan Azzahir, assured that he would not harm

* A.D. 1394.   † Raselain.

one who fled to him, went to him clad in the garb of obedience for he could not but cling to the hem of his protection and put himself in the rope of his service.

CHAPTER XLII

CONCERNING THE CALAMITY AND HARDSHIP WHICH THAT TREACHEROUS IMPOSTOR BROUGHT UPON THE SULTAN OF MARDIN, ISA MALIK AZZAHIR

BUT when he feared Timur's attack, he assembled his whole household and his friends and said :

" I depart to this man, to offer my submission to him ; if he sends me away, as I wish, I have what I want ; but if he demands the fort from me, it will be your part to drive him back and repel him haughtily, and beware of handing it over to him or relying on his words ; but if the matter turns between surrender of the fort and my death, preserve the fort and look to your own advantage by my death ; for if you surrender the fort to him, you will give up all you have, you will all be massacred to a man, you will lose all and will be cheated of your lives and homes ; since that is so, I will give my life to save you, and avert your calamity at the risk of my life ; for one evil is lighter than another ; and look, I will feel his pulse for you."

Then he sought that grim and wicked tyrant and first appointing in his own place his nephew, son of his brother Al Malik Al Sala Shahabuddin, by name Ahmed Al Malik Al Said Iskandar son of Al Malik Al Sala Al Shahid,* he went down on the fourth day of the week, the 25th day of the month Rabia (the former) in the year 796† and came to Timur about the end of the month in a place called Halalit, but he received him foully and laying hands on him demanded from him the surrender of the fort, but he replied : " The fort is with its possessors and in the power of its guards, but I possess nothing except my own life, which I offer you and have brought to you ; do not therefore compel me to that to which I am unequal or force me to that which I cannot perform."

Then he brought him to the fort, demanding it from them,

---

* i.e., The Martyr.   † A.D. 1394.

and when they rejected the demand, he proposed to them that he should be put to death or saved by them, but they refused; he therefore demanded from him for the purchase of his safety a hundred tumans of silver drachmas, each tuman being worth sixty thousand, besides all that he had already offered him. Then he closed every gate to him and held him hard and fast, to take from him all his strength and power, and girt his loins to ravage and ordered that rest be afforded to his infantry and refreshments for his cavalry and drank one after another cups of rapine and raged against the servants of Allah and His countries, and continued in this way neither to come to himself nor emerge from drunkenness and wavered to and fro between Firdaus and Rasmal, Nisibin, and old Mosul. Then he ordered his troops in the second month of Jumadi to make for Mardin by a forced march; then they outpaced the birds and continuing their march crossed rivers by day and torrents by night and cut through the ribs of deserts like an Indian sword and in crossing those mountains and hills did what Alkandi said, to wit :

" I climbed to it while its people slept, as bubbles of water climb one after another."

And they came upon Mardin unawares and hastened into the place forthwith, when, on the third day of the week, which was the 12th of the month, the dawn had drawn the sword of its rising and the crow of darkness had flown from its nest and they surrounded the walls on all sides and made destruction a guest in these places and gradually they covered the walls on all sides and dragged them down and overthrew them by shaking and by beating crushed them with violent disturbance and clung to the very edges of the walls and climbed with the help of ladders from earth to sky : and their climbing was from the South and the slow-stepping West and the enlivening East and they took the city by force and violence and filled it with outrages and impiety and the citizens were driven to ascend the fort—though none else would not desire a higher place and elevation ; and in trembling flight like fowls they made for its ramparts and projections and they drove them from the fort with arrows and cross-bows ; then Timur's men slew all whom they seized, men and women, small and great—not content with the booty gained there or the prisoners they had made ; some therefore boldly resisted them, hoping thereby that their zeal would attain to martyrdom ; and the fight did not cease to be waged against them until the city was filled with wounded and dead and it lasted from before sunrise beyond the evening ; but when the two sides of the face of night had fallen on both faces of the world and these men, measuring unjustly, had exacted the full measurement of their injustice and excess, and when the fish of darkness was hastening to swallow the Jonah of the sun, there came after these commotions calm and they retired and the army pitched camp opposite Arbun and countless hosts were slain of both armies, but more among the citizens.

But by night they prepared and made ready their weapons, waiting for the dawn which they thought slow to come, till when night had rent its hidden bosom and darkness had revealed the secret of its hidden mystery and Nature had enjoined the face of day to strike the sides of the horizon with the edges of its whiteness, then in the morning they were active as crows, and hastened to battle and rapine and pressed the citizens and closely surrounded the city and overthrew it with its walls at midday and destroyed its traces about evening ; then they gave themselves to iniquities and now darkness spread like their wickedness.

CHAPTER XLIII

HIS HIDDEN DESIGNS BECOME CLEAR AND THOSE EVIL PLANS ARE IN VAIN

AFTER he had spent the night in frustration of purpose and could not gain the fort by inspiring fear, he sharpened his mind and used fresh cunning and instead of rudeness turned to pacification, and on that fifth day restrained that army and sent one to them to tell the contents of a letter, with an envoy : " Let the people of the fort of Mardin know : they are weak and powerless, destitute and thirsty ; we grant pardon to them and give them security concerning their lives and blood ; so let them be free of anxiety and redouble their supplications to us "—and this message I have rendered as I found it ; but his guile did not succeed nor did he gain his mark, because the guardians of the fort were by no means givers, and its demon defenders were intractable like death ;

therefore on the morning of the Sabbath that plague departed to Basharia and sent troops against Amid under an Amir called Sultan Mahmud, who moved against the place a large army, and when he had besieged it for five days, asked for help to be sent him against it; then he himself moved to the place and humbled it so that they sought peace, and he promised safety to the gatekeeper who opened the gate to him; then entering the town through the gate he put all to the sword, and destroyed them all whether they resisted or submitted; and he put the children in chains, violated the purdahs and the women behind the purdahs, and made men wear the garment of misery, and when some had fled to the mosque, they slew about two thousand of them while engaged in prayer and bowed in devotion.

Then after violating the mosque they departed and left the city desolate, then the Devil led him to the fort of Arjis; then hastening further he descended to the fort of Avenik, held by Misar, son of Qara Mahomed, Amir of the Turkomans, and after besieging it, took it, giving a promise of safety—which happened in the year 796,* after the feast of Ramzan; then he put to death all the soldiers of the garrison and sent Misar to Samarkand.

CHAPTER XLIV

THEN with evil purpose he took with him Al Malik Azzahir, and departed on the seventh day of Zulkada in the year 796,† and kept him in prison in the city Sultania and with him of the Amirs Amir Rukanuddin and Azuddin Turkoman and Astabugha and Ziauddin, and held him in such strict custody that his household could not receive news of him and no one knew aught of his condition. Then after he had weakened him by harsh imprisonment, he decided to proceed to Dasht Kipchak, and inflicted calamities upon it, establishing them on a firm footing, while Al Malik Azzahir remained for a year in that condition that naught was known of him whether awake or asleep.

Then the senior queen coming to Sultania assuaged his distress and hardship and gave him freedom to write letters

* A.D. 1394.   † A.D. 1394.

to his household and urged him to seek admission to the favour and homage of Timur, pretending that she was his true friend and sought his good. But this was a plot of Timur's and according to his counsel.

Then Timur, returning from Dasht* in the month Shaban in the year 798,† halted at Sultania thirteen days, then made for Hamadan and halted there until the thirteenth of Ramzan, then with honour and kindness called from Sultania to himself Al Malik Azzahir, who when his fetters and the fetters of his companions had been loosed and he and his treated with the greatest honours, went to Timur on the fifth day of the week, which was the fifteenth, and came to him on the Sabbath day, the seventeenth, and he received him magnificently and embraced him and dispelled his fear and trepidation and kissed him often on the face, and openly sought from him pardon for what he had done to him and said to him : " Certainly you are a friend of Allah and of high dignity, like Abu Bakr and Ali," and he excused himself to him for the offence which he had committed against his dignity and entertained him for six days and clothed him with the cloak of great kings and assigned him a beautiful house and gave him many gifts, especially one hundred horses, ten mules, sixty thousand Kubakia dinars, six camels, a cloak embroidered with gold, adorned with gems, and many other gifts without number and a royal standard to wave above his head and sixty-five open diplomas, each with the governship of a city, lest anyone should resist him therein, from Urfa to the furthest limit of Diar-Bakr to the borders of Azerbaijan and Armenia ; and all that out of craft and cunning and so that all the rulers of those countries should be reckoned under his power and all his subjects and the people should bring to him tribute and gifts and should not dare even to put a foot forward except at his orders ; so much that each of his neighbours, along with the booty which Allah had given into his hand, would be given to him and nothing would come to Timur or any other.

And this, though in appearance it seemed honourable, yet in the end was harm to him and keenness of vengeance and in all this there was something as you will afterwards see and he put enmity between him and his neighbours and contrived that he should flee to him and rely on him in all his affairs and before the multitude of his enemies seek his protection and so

* The Kipchak country north of the Caucasus.   † A.D. 1396.

70

hold his fort. Then he agreed with him that whenever he sent
for him, he should come to him ; then he embraced him and
sent him away and ordered his Amirs to conduct him.

Accordingly he passed from distress to freedom on the
23rd of Ramzan, on the day of assembly, in the year 798* and
came to Sultania, spending a pleasant life and enjoying
elegance and splendour ; then he went to Tabriz with an
exquisite and splendid retinue and met Amiran Shah,† who
heaped upon him honours and gifts and conducted him with a
fine procession and the greatest security and he came to Vastan
and Bitlis and Arzan,‡ right up to Sur ; but when the news
reached his tribes and households, men rejoiced on that
account and instruments of joy were struck and townsmen and
nobles went to meet him as he approached on the day of
assembly, the eleventh of the month Shawal, his deputy
Al Malik Al Salah going in front ; and entering the city with a
fortunate omen and signs of prosperity he approached the
school of Husamuddin and visited the tombs of his father
and his dead ancestors and wished to leave his noble capital
and visit the holy Hejaz, but the nobles and people refused to
let him go, throwing themselves before him and kissing his
feet ; therefore he occupied his palace and remained quiet on
his throne ; these things will be more fully declared in turn
and the things which happened, when Timur came and his
base soldiers occupied Mardin, after they had laid waste the
kingdoms of Syria.

It is said that Al Malik Azzahir, when he had become
established in his kingdom, called assemblies of learned men
whom he knew, and that when he urged them to compose
verses forthwith on that event, first Badruddin Hassan, son
of Tifur, said :

" His sea has been stirred and has overflowed and utterly
torn men up with its violence.

" And his mortal sins are spread over both sides of the
horizon.

" Truly his iniquity has grown to the limit ; now we
rejoice while it wanes :

" For when a tyrant comes to the end of his insolence, the
adversities of fortune turn against him."

Then Ruknuddin Hussein, son of Alasafar, one of the
public readers, said :

* A.D. 1396.　　　† Third son of Timur.　　　‡ Perhaps Erzinjan.

" You are one of those, who when anything hard and grave befalls them

" Entrust their affairs to God, and are content with that gain,

" And when they have seen dangers, commit business to Allah the Almighty and after that, escape unharmed."

Third spoke Qazi Sadaruddin, son of Zahiruddin Hanifi of Samarkand :

" He is long-lived, like the day at dawn,
Whose glory does not grow beyond bounds ;
And doubtless all increase has its decrease ;
And the Mighty in power will deliver His servant."

Then fourth spoke Alauddin, son of Zainuddin Hasani, one of the public readers, in double rhythm :

" Be not sad, for what Allah has decreed will be.

" And a thing entrusted to the Divine command already comes to pass :

" Between the twinkling of an eye and its ceasing

" The present condition has ended and that matter goes forward."

And he marvelled thereat, and ordered a gift of 5,000 drachmas to be counted out to him : but Allah knows.

CHAPTER XLV

TIMUR RETURNS FROM DIAR-BAKR AND IRAK, AND TURNS
TOWARDS THE DESERTS OF KIPCHAK,* WHOSE KINGS AND
KINGDOMS ARE DESCRIBED, WITH AN ACCOUNT OF ITS
PLAINS AND WAYS

THEN he returned from Arabian and Persian Irak in
which countries he had already firmly planted his foot-
mark, and that after Sheikh Ibrahim had come over to him
and handed to him the keys of his dominions, who placing on
his neck the yoke of his servitude and transferring himself
to his sway, put himself among his slaves, but was treated
by him like a son; soon, however, we shall relate how he
went to him and in what way he gained his favour.

Then Timur made for the desert of Kipchak with great eagerness and haste.

This great kingdom contains vast deserts, whose Sultan
was Toqtamish, the same who was the leader of the Sultans
who fought against Timur, indeed the first who showed
hostility to him, and met him in the regions of Turkistan and
came against him and joined battle and there Said Barka
overcame him as was told before.

The country is called Dasht Kipchak and Dasht Barka and
" Dasht " in the Persian language is the word for desert and
the special name of it Barka,† who was the first Sultan, who
after embracing Islam unfolded its standards through that
country; for they were worshippers of idols and given to
polytheism, ignorant of Islam and the true faith and the most
of them have remained idolaters to this day.

He set out for these regions by way of Derbend, which
was under the sway of Sheikh Ibrahim, Sultan of the Kingdom
of Shirvan, whose family goes back to King Khosru Anushirvan;
and he had a Qazi by name Abu Yazid, who of all the pillars of
the state was in close touch with him and this Yazid was a
minister of the kingdom and the first in the sultanate; and
when he consulted him about the matter of Timur and the
action required of himself—whether he should submit to him
or make preparations against him, whether he should take to
flight or engage with him—Yazid replied: " In my opinion

* The country of the Golden Horde.   † Grandson of Jenghizkhan.

it is best to fly, and I think the safest and finest plan is to fortify yourself in the highest mountains."

The Sultan, however, said : " This does not seem to me well advised, that I should escape, but desert my subjects in time of danger, and what should I reply to Allah on the day of resurrection when I have directed their affairs and destroyed my subjects ? Therefore I do not choose to attack him or engage with him, but as quickly as may be I shall hasten to him and make myself compliant to him, obeying his command, but if he restores me to my throne and confirms me in my kingdom, that is the very thing which I wish and the cul- mination of my prayers ; but if he treats me ill or removes me from my province or throws me into bondage or kills me, at least my subjects will be defended from the evil of slaughter and rapine and captivity, and he will then set over them and over the kingdom whom he wishes."

Then he ordered that supplies should be collected and gave leave to the soldiers, who scattered and withdrew, and ordered that the cities of his territories should be decorated and beautified and that their inhabitants should carry on their work secure by land and sea and devote themselves to it and that orators should recite his name from platforms and that gold and silver money should be marked with his name and sign.

Then taking gifts and presents he started to meet him with good will and firm foot. And when he came near to him and stood in obeisance before him, he offered the gifts and presents and various rare and choice things. Now the custom of the Jagatais in offering gifts of homage was to give nine of whatever kind that in this way they might gain honours and higher dignity with the receiver ; therefore Sheikh Ibrahim offered nine of every sort of various gifts, but of slaves eight ; but when the men who received those gifts said to him " Where is the ninth slave ? " he replied, " I myself am the ninth," and Timur admired this saying, by which he won a place in his heart and said to him : " Nay, you shall be my son and my deputy in this country and the support on which I shall lean," and he clad him in a precious mantle and restored him to his kingdom glad that he had gained his wish. And the supplies were divided and the fruits and foods distributed, out of which parts like mountains were left over by that army, which was itself in number like gravel and sand.

Then after dismissing Sheikh Ibrahim, Timur set out to the countries of the north and of the Tatars. But the other reason of invading that kingdom, though he needed it not, was Amir Idaku, who was one of the chief leaders of Toqtamish on the left wing, and one of the ministers employed to ward off disasters and a counsellor, whose tribe was called Qomkomat ; for the Turks have different tribes and names—like the Arabs.

But when Idaku saw that the mind of his master was altered, he feared for himself from him, since Toqtamish was a man of stern violence ; so being afraid that some day he might encounter it, he did not cease to be ware of him and to be ready to take to flight, when he saw that it was necessary for that reason, and he watched him constantly and acted prudently with him and accompanied him constantly and soothed him with flattery ; but on a festive night, when the glasses like stars were revolving in the orbits of hilarity and wine was lording it over the captive judgment, Toqtamish began to say to Idaku (when the light of his prudence was being quenched and he was becoming heated) " A day will come for me and you, which will bring you to hunger and remove you from tables piled with food to a wandering life and the eye of your life will be filled with the sleep of death." But Idaku put him off and flattered him, saying : " Let not my Lord and Khakhan* foster wrath against a slave who has not done wrong and let him not destroy a sapling which he himself has planted or overthrow a foundation which he has laid ! "

Then he took the guise of a suppliant, humility, obedience and submission and certain of what he had thought before, he exercised his mind to find a way of escape and used cleverness and cunning for that purpose, knowing that if he neglected his threats or allowed them time, it would not be long before the Sultan would attend to their performance : then he slipped out from amidst the attendants and guards, and went out suddenly as though to answer a natural call and came hurriedly but not without determination to the stable of Toqtamish and took a horse ready saddled, of the best breed and very swift, which stood ready for any emergency and said to one of his followers, who was a loyal sharer of his secret :

" Whoever wishes to come to me, will find me with Timur ;

* Emperor.

75

but do not reveal this secret, until it is certain that I have crossed the deserts."

Then he left him and set off, no one observing him, unless when he had already gone a great way, and riding steadily he wove long threads in the web of his journey—and they could not follow his tracks or even reach the dust which he raised ; and he came to Timur and kissing his hands told his story and unfolded to him his misfortunes and said : " You are seeking places far distant and rough pathless places and for that reason you charge into dangers and cut the backbones of deserts and enter upon long journeys ; but this is an easy prize in front of your eyes, which you will gain—rich and fine —with the greatest convenience ; and why should there be delay, somnolence, hesitation and postponement ? Rise therefore with firm purpose and I give security that there will be no fort to repel you or fortification to check you or sword to restrain you or weapons to drive you back or soldier to attack you ; for they are naught but a mixed and confused rabble of the lowest sort of men and resources collected at random and treasures as it were coming of themselves." And he ceased not to urge him to it and entreat him and in every way make him pliant, just as Othman Qara Iluk did with him, when he came to Tabriz, with wicked instigation and incited him to invade Syria after killing Sultan Burhanuddin Ahmed and besieging Siwas, as will afterwards be related.

Then Timur prepared with the greatest haste to win for himself Dasht Barka, which is the proper country of the Tatars, filled with cattle of different kinds and tribes of Turks ; fortified on the borders, it has well-tilled parts and wide tracts, healthy in water and air ; its people nomads ; its soldiers expert archers, most eloquent of speech among the Turks, pure in disposition, of charming features and perfect in beauty ; their women seem suns, their men full moons ; the kings are heads, the great men like chests ; neither falsehood has place with them nor fraud, nor does cunning obtain among them nor sycophancy; it is the custom among them to move from place to place securely on wagons, where they are placed beyond fear ; their cities are few and their settlements far apart.

Dasht is bounded on the south by the Caspian Sea, violent and dangerous, and the Black Sea, which turns thither from the countries of Rum, and these two seas almost touch each other, but that the Jirkas Mountains (Caucasus)

put a space between them to prevent their joining. On the
east it has for boundaries the Kingdoms of Khwarizm, Atrar
and Sighnaq and other countries and tracts extending to
Turkistan and the countries of the Jatas, going up to the
borders of the Sin (Chinese), under the sway of the Moguls* and
Khatas. On the north is Abir and Shabir (Siberia) and wastes,
deserts and hills of sand like mountains; for how many
deserts are there, where birds and beasts roam! And it is,
like the favour of the great, an end which cannot be reached
and a limit which cannot be attained; on the west it borders
on Russia and Bulgaria and the country of the Christians, and
its confines extend to the dominions of the son of Othman,
Ruler of Rum.

There used to advance convoys of travellers from Khwarizm
making the journey in wagons, securely without terror or fear,
as far as the Crimea—a journey of about three months; in
width there is a sea of sand as broad as seven seas, through
which the most skilful guide could not show the way nor the
most crafty of experienced men make the journey and those
convoys did not take supplies or fodder or join to themselves
companions—this because of the multitude of the people, and
the abundance of security, food and drink among the inhabitants, and did not set out except tribe by tribe or turn aside
except to one who would receive his guest generously, so
that they were well described by that verse:

" All the people of Mecca go round the hill of Okaz
    And their sons shout : ' There comes a guest ! ' "

But now through those places from Khwarizm to the
Crimea of those peoples and their followers none moves or
rests and nothing ranges there but antelopes and camels.

The capital of Dasht is Serai, a city devoted to Islam and
beautifully built, which I shall describe. It was founded by
Sultan Barka (on whom be the mercy of Allah !) when he
became a Muslim, and he made it his capital and chose it and
drove in and invited the people of Dasht so that they might
enter the protection of Islam, which faith having been received,
the place became a resort of all good and happiness and was
called Barka having before been named after Kipchak.

Maulana, the venerable Khwaja Asamuddin, son of the
blessed Maulana the venerable Khwaja Abdul Malik, who is of

* or Mongols.

77

the sons of the great Sheikh Burhanuddin Marghinani on whom be the mercy of Allah, when he had returned from the Hejaz in the year 814* and in our time, that is in the year 840,† had come to the governorship of Samarkand, recited to me in Haji Turkhan,‡ one of the cities of Dasht, this verse : (and in the pass of Dasht he had endured various troubles) :

> " When I had lately heard that there was prosperity
> In the deserts, which are called after their Sultan Barka,
> I caused the camel of my migration to halt in that country,
> But saw no happiness§ there."

And the same man referring to Maulana the venerable and revered Hafizuddin Mahomed, son of Nasiruddin Mahomed Kurdi Bazazi, whom Allah Almighty protect with His mercy ! at the same time and place recited this also to me :

> " When the citizens committed their affairs into the hands
>   of a Hafiz,¶
> Their Hafiz became their Sultan, and the Sultan was no
>   longer a Hafiz."

And when Barka Khan had been exalted by the royal garb of Islam and had raised the standards of the religion of Hanifa in the country of Dasht, he called learned men from every side and doctors, to teach the people the doctrines of their religion and show them the ways of their profession of the Unity of God and the truth of the Faith, and he paid great rewards to them and poured forth on those who assembled seas of generosity and brought reverence to the Faith and the teachers and magnified the laws of Allah Almighty and the institutes of the Prophet and he had with him at that time and after- wards Uzbeg and Janibeg Khan, Maulana Qutbuddin, the learned, of the city of Rei, and Sheikh Saduddin Taftazani and Said Jalal, Commentator of the Hajabia, and other doctors of the sects of Hanifis and Shafeites ; afterwards these were followed by Maulana Hafizuddin Bazazi and Maulana Ahmed of Khajend on whom be the favour of Allah !

And thanks to these famous men Serai became a meeting- place of learning and a home of every sort of prosperity and in a short time there gathered there of learned men and doctors and

---

* A.D. 1411. † A.D. 1436. ‡ Astrakan.
§ The Arabic for happiness is " barka " making a play on words.
¶ i.e., protector.

the cultured and able, all the most excellent, eminent, brilliant and charming, and never a great city and its suburbs held so many.

Between the building of Serai and its devastation there passed sixty-three years, and it was among the greatest cities in extent and abounding in population.

They say that a slave of one of the magnates of this city fled and fixed his abode in a place by the side of the road and opened a shop where he supported himself by trade, and that base fellow remained for about ten years—but his master never met him or found him or saw him, because of the size of the city and the multitude of its people.

This city was placed on the bank of a river derived from the river Atal (Volga), about which it is agreed by travellers, historians and those who cross waters, that among rivers and waters which are fresh and growing in size none is greater than this; it rises from Russia, and is not useful, but carries off life, and flows into the Caspian Sea, like the Oxus and the other rivers of Persia, though that sea is shut off on all sides and is surrounded by several Persian provinces such as Gilan, Mazanderan, Asterabad and Shirwan.

The name of the river of Serai is Sankila and up to now it is crossed only by skiffs and neither footman nor horseman sets foot in it and how many arms divide from this great, long and broad river which are separately greater than the Euphrates and Nile!

But after Janibeg Khan became ruler of Dasht [lacuna].*

CHAPTER XLVI

THAT FLOOD COMES AND SWEEPS OVER THE PEOPLES OF DASHT AFTER BREAKING TOQTAMISH

THEN Timur came into those parts with a great army, nay, a turbid sea, whose soldiers carried flying arrows, sharp swords and quivering spears and were ravening lions and furious leopards, all of warlike spirit, which takes vengeance on the enemy, stoutly defends its own flag and its allies and homes and its prey and its lairs and covers with the sea of war him who opposes its waves and breakers.

* There is a gap in the MSS.

G

Therefore Toqtamish sent to the lords of his subjects and the magnates of his peoples and the dwellers in sandy places and inhabitants of the borders and chiefs who were his kinsmen and leaders of the right and left of his army, whom he summoned and called to meet the enemy and wage war and they came clad in the long robe of obedience and hastening from every high mountain ; and there assembled hosts and tribes of horse and foot and swordsmen and javelin-throwers and archers and attackers and defenders and warriors and slayers with the sabre and skilled archers and wielders of spears, who would not miss the mark compared with the sons of Tual, skilled spearmen. When they take their weapon and aim at what they need, they strike the mark whether sitting or flying.

Then Toqtamish rose to fight, ready for onslaught and battle, with an army numerous like the sands and heavy like the mountains.

CHAPTER XLVII

CONCERNING THE CONTENTION THAT AROSE IN THE ARMY OF TOQTAMISH AT THE TIME OF BATTLE

AND when they were within sight one of another and the two fronts were engaged, from the army of Toqtamish advanced a leader of the right wing who wished to take vengeance on one of the Amirs and he asked Toqtamish for him and for leave to kill him ; and Toqtamish said to him " Be of good heart, truly I will grant your request :

But you shall see a thing new to men and what happens.

Therefore wait until, when the battle is over and according to our prayers we have survived, I shall grant you your debtor and hand over to you your enemy ; then I will exact your vengeance from him and satisfy you."

He replied : " No, but forthwith ; else I will not be loyal to you or obey you." But Toqtamish said : " We are in grave trouble, which harasses us more than your purpose, and in a dark business, which torments more than your distress ; therefore be patient and do not hasten, and be confident and fear not, for no one shall be deprived of justice nor shall what is due be lost ; do not fly to a blind precipice or be one of those who worship Allah for gain ; now you are in the night of

distress, which has already passed, and in the dawn of prosperity, which has already grown light ; therefore keep your
place and face your foes and do not turn your back, but show
the loyalty which you owe."

Then that leader took with him a great multitude and
there followed him every rebel and rogue and his whole tribe
called Aktav and he went away towards the kingdoms of
Rum and arrived with his followers in the country of Adrianople
and remained in those parts. And thereby the army of
Toqtamish was damaged and the arrows of his purposes missed
their mark, but when he saw that the attack could not be
avoided and that the place was settled, he strengthened his
spirit and the spirit of his army and put aside heaviness and
levity and placed in the front line the bolder of his followers
and arrayed his horse and foot and strengthened the centre
and wing and made ready arrows and swords.

SECTION

But Timur's army was not wanting in these things, since
what each one had to do was decided and explored and where
to fight and where to stand was inscribed on the front of its
standards. Then both armies, when they came in sight one of
the other, were kindled and mingling with each other became
hot with the fire of war and they joined battle and necks were
extended for sword-blows and throats outstretched for spear
thrusts and faces were drawn with sternness and fouled with
dust, the wolves of war set their teeth and fierce leopards
mingled and charged and the lions of the armies rushed upon
each other and men's skins bristled, clad with the feathers of
arrows and the brows of the leaders drooped and the heads of
the heads* bent in the devotion of war and fell forward and
the dust was thickened and stood black and the leaders and
common soldiers alike plunged into seas of blood and arrows
became in the darkness of black dust like stars placed to
destroy the Princes of Satan, while swords glittering like
fulminating stars in clouds of dust rushed on kings and sultans
nor did the horses of death cease to pass through and revolve
and race against the squadrons which charged straight ahead or
the dust of hooves to be borne into the air or the blood of swords
to flow over the plain, until the earth was rent and the heavens

* i.e., captains.

like the eight seas; and this struggle and conflict lasted about three days; then dust appeared from the stricken army of Toqtamish, who turned his back, and his armies took to flight, but the soldiers of Timur were sent hither and thither in the kingdoms of Dasht and were stationed there, whose tribes he subdued and subjected all without exception to his will and collected cattle which he distributed and gold and silver, which he stored, and took booty and divided it, and let his men despoil and make prisoners and gave leave to use force and violence and wiped out their tribes and overturned their forts and changed the whole condition and took away with him all he could of wealth, prisoners and goods ; and his vanguard reached right to Azaq and laid waste Serai, and Seraijuq and Haji Turkhan and those parts ; and the dignity of Idaku became great with him ;   then he set out towards his Samarkand, taking Idaku with him, whom he asked to follow him.

CHAPTER XLVIII

OF THE CUNNING OF IDAKU AND HOW HE DECEIVED TIMUR AND CAJOLED HIM

THEN Idaku sent a message to his kinsmen and neighbours and the tribes of the right hand, all of whom were his allies—without the knowledge of Timur—to leave their places, and set out in haste from their country and journey to its side and the intervening parts, where the roads are difficult and there are many precipices, and not to stay two days in the same halting-place and to accomplish it ; for if Timur overtook them, he would scatter them all and destroy them all.

Then doing what Idaku had advised, they departed without delay. When Idaku learnt that his people had gone forth and that his followers had escaped Timur, he said to him: " My Lord and Amir, I have of kinsmen and followers a great multitude, nobles and commons, who are my strength and protection, and if they live well and prosper it is well for me also ; but they are not safe, if ever they should fall after me into the oppression and tyranny of Toqtamish, nay, without doubt he will destroy them and wipe them out to a man ; and while my side is shielded from him by the dignity of your august threshold, he in his malice will take revenge on my followers and kinsmen, since I have woven the web of these conflicts and driven him headlong into the straits of affliction and despair ; and in any case, I shall not be able to be content, if they live near him, and how will my life be pleasant, if my best friends are placed in his neighbourhood ? If then in your august judgment it seems good to send a messenger to those places and numerous tribes with a gracious command and high and eminent mandate to conciliate their minds and entice the hearts of the tribes and their households, and with an edict that they should change their place and condition, we shall all be under a noble shade in gardens of delight and blooming pastures and the people of Dasht will be freed from this desert and the past life will be ended and we shall spend the time that remains in gardens under which rivers flow ; but the august judgment is best and to obey what it resolves concerning its slaves, is the first duty."

And Timur replied to him : " You are a man on whose counsel your people rely and from it they may gain advantage, since you are most experienced in these ways."

Then Idaku said : " All mortals are your slaves and subject to your will and are your followers and to one whom you think fit for anything every difficulty is easy." And Timur replied : " Nay, you are the originator of this plan : therefore undertake it yourself ; since you are lord in the city." And Idaku said : " Join to me one of the Amirs to be in place of vazirs over them with your noble commands according to your august judgment."

And Timur consented and granting his desire, added to him whom he wished ; accordingly both, having completed and accomplished their necessary affairs, prepared to carry out their purpose.

But as soon as Idaku left Timur, Timur comprehended his headlong error and knew that Idaku had rent his mind and led him into error ; therefore he sent a messenger to him and ordered him to return on account of a matter which had arisen and a plan which had occurred to him ; but when this messenger came to him and brought to him his instructions, Idaku said to him and to the Amir who accompanied him, prohibiting both from proceeding, " See to your necessary affairs and go to your master and place yourselves before him and tell him that the goal of our association is ended here ; and I am free of him, since I fear Allah ! "

83

But they could not treat him roughly and in that difficult pass they could not but deal gently with him ; therefore they let him go and departed without delay.

And when Timur learnt this, he was excited and kindled with anger and seized with disgust and annoyance and ground his teeth against him with indignation and repented when there was no room for repentance and almost slew himself in anger against Idaku and drank the cup of death ; " on that day the wicked shall bite his hands."

And since he could not cure him, he made no move concerning him, and returning to his own kingdom, then to Samarkand, paid no heed to him ; this therefore was the end of his expedition into Dasht Barka, so that it was said that no one deceived and injured Timur and cheated him alike by word and deed and misled him, except Idaku, about whom I have told ; and except the Qazi of Qazis, Waliuddin Abdur Rahman, son of Khaldun Al Maliki, whose story will follow.

CHAPTER XLIX

OF THE FIGHTS AND BATTLES BETWEEN TOQTAMISH AND IDAKU FOUGHT IN NORTHERN PARTS, UNTIL THE CONDITION OF THOSE PARTS WAS UTTERLY CHANGED

AND when Timur departed with his booty and after returning rested in his own kingdom, Idaku reached his followers and cheered by his friends and allies began to inquire into the affairs of Toqtamish and took precautions against him and earnest care for his own safety and stood ready and prepared to oppose him, since he could not repair his friendship once severed or mend it after it was once torn ; also he could not take the title of Sultan, for if that could have been done, Timur would have claimed that title, being King of Kings ; therefore he set up a Sultan on his behalf and in the house of the kingdom raised a Khan to whom he called the heads of the left side and the chief men of its tribes, who, obeying his summons, came to him, since they were more powerful than the rest, safe from the injury and havoc of the Jagatais ; and in this way the Sultan was strengthened and the Khan equipped with armies and his foundations in that house of the kingdom became strong and his pillars high.

But Toqtamish, when he had recovered from fear and reason had regained its place in his brain, and his enemy Timur had gone and his quiet was restored, collected his armies and entreated the help of his people, who came to his aid. And diverse battles and clashes of war ceased not to happen between him and Idaku and the eyes of tranquillity, like eyelids of blind fortune, slept from conciliation, until they had fought fifteen times—now one victorious, now the other. And by these frequent battles the affairs of the tribes of Dasht began to be ruined and scattered and since there were few places of refuge and forts, they became dispersed, all the more because the two lions attacked them in turn and two oppressors came upon them from either side, nay, even before, the greater part of them was driven away by Timur and in distress, constrained by his rule and held in his strict custody ; and from them separated a horde, which could not be numbered or counted or contained in any reckoning or list, and betook itself to Rum and Rus,* and that through ill fortune and loss of prosperity, and amid Christians, who add companions to God, and Muslim captives, became like Jabala, son of Ghasan—which horde was called Qara Boghdan.†

Therefore from these causes the cultivated part of Dasht became a desert and waste, the inhabitants scattered, dispersed, routed and destroyed, so that if anyone went through it without a guide and scout, he would certainly perish losing the way, even in summer ; since winds, lifting and scattering sands, hide the way, passing over it, and wipe it out ; but in winter, since snow falling there collects on the road and covers it, for the ground is desert without marks of a road and its halting places are thrown into confusion, its stages and watering-places are fearful wastes and the roads utterly deadly and difficult.

At last in the fifteenth battle Idaku was conquered and scattered, put to flight, dispersed, a solitary wanderer, and plunged into a sea of sands with about five hundred of his companions, where none knew him.

Toqtamish therefore remained unrivalled in his kingdom and Dasht Barka was clear for him ; yet with that he strongly desired news concerning Idaku and his condition and he expected to be informed how he had perished in the sands ; and meanwhile about half a year passed and all trace of him

* i.e. Russia.   † In what is now Moldavia.

went from men's eyes and mention of him from men's tongues ; but Idaku was expert in those sandhills and one who with his own feet had cut the surface of those barren sands and hard lands ; and waited, watching with meditation and attention, according to these verses of mine :

" Watch business rightly and expect joy and seize its fit
    time, if it comes,
  And join patience to industry ; thereby the mulberry
    leaf turns to silk."

When it was certain that Toqtamish thought him despaired of and torn by the lion of death, he began to inquire into his affairs and follow and explore his footprints and watch until he was informed that he was living in a place of pleasure, apart from his army. Therefore riding on the wing of a horse and with the night watches for his coverlet, he continued his journey by night and bartered sleep for wakefulness, climbing mountains as bubbles ascend and descending from heights as the dew falls, until he came upon him unexpectedly and rushed on him like a fate firmly knotted and he did not come to himself, until already disasters were driving him into the nets like a beast at bay and the lions of death were seizing him, and spears biting him like snakes and arrows like vipers ; and he resisted them for a while and long wandered around them, then fell slain ; and this sixteenth combat was the seal of mutual attack and the judgment of separation ; therefore the rule of Dasht remained with the governor, Idaku, to whose orders submitted distant and near, great and small ; but the sons of Toqtamish fled hither and thither, Jalaluddin and Karim Bardi to Rus ; and Kubal and the other brothers to Sighnaq.*

And men's affairs were governed according to the laws of Idaku, who gave the place of Sultan to whom he wished and deposed the same man at will ; he ordered and none opposed him ; he forbade and none transgressed the mark which he had fixed ; but of those whom he made Sultans were Qubaligh Timur Khan and his brother Rashadibeg Khan ; then Fulad Khan, son of Tuligh Timur, then his brother Timur Khan, in whose time troubles arose, when he would not let himself be ruled by Idaku, saying :

" He is neither great in skill nor birth ; I am a ram to be

* Near Tiflis.

obeyed ; how then should I obey ? and a bull, whom it is right to follow ; how then shall I become a follower ? " Thus the web of discord was woven between the two and from hatred was kindled animosity and there flowed evils, afflictions, battles and enmities and meanwhile the darkness of troubles was woven and the stars of misfortunes were enveloped in the thick fogs of Dasht between the two factions and when the prosperity of the rule of Jalal was in full brilliance, behold, from the East rose resplendent the offspring of Toqtamish and gained height in the country of Rus on the opposite side.

And this event happened during the year 814.*

Then affairs worsening and misfortunes increasing and the state of Idaku being weakened, Timur (Khan) slew him and rivalry and discord endured between the kings of the Kingdom of Kipchak, until Idaku died, overwhelmed and wounded, and they drew him out of the river Jaxartes on to the dry land of Huq and cast him away abandoned, may Allah have mercy !

And marvellous things are told of him and his achievements and wonderful excellence ; arrows of attack well-aimed against his enemies ; his thoughts ambushes ; his battles hunters' nets ; and he had in the principles of political science a gold-mine of wealth pure and base, out of whose product he drew what he wished.

He was almost black in complexion, exceedingly dark, of middle height, strong in body, high-spirited, generous, polished, cheerful, in judgment keen and shrewd, a lover of the learned and able, genial to the good and fakirs, jesting with them, with subtle wit and clever suggestion, keeping fasts, rising at night (for prayer), holding the lappets of the law, putting the Koran and the traditions and the opinions of the learned to intercede between himself and God Almighty.

He had twenty sons, each holding princely authority, with their own vilayets, armies and followers.

He led the people of Dasht for twenty years and his days are a white star on the brow of the age and the nights of his reign like curls on the face of that time.

* A.D. 1411.

CHAPTER L

RETURNING TO THE STORY OF THE DEEDS OF TIMUR AND HIS OPPRESSIONS

WHEN Timur reached Azerbaijan and his army poured into the kingdoms of Sultania and Hamadan, he sent for Malik Azzahir, Sultan of Mardin, whom he set at liberty and treated kindly, as stated already, and confirmed him in the kingdom and entrusted to him the governorship of the countries between Syria and Irak and kept those kingdoms under his rule with as much deceit and simulation as he could.

But he could not remain in Persia, because he was taking with him many prisoners from Dasht; so he made for the kingdoms of his Samarkand, where he shook his bags and emptied his pouch of the booty from Dasht.

Then he advanced without further delay and crossed the Oxus with an army like a flood and reached Khorasan, whence he continued to Azerbaijan; and Zahartan, Governor of Erzinjan, came to him, receiving the collar of his commands with the rope of obedience and submission.

However he neglected the business of Mardin, which he wished to appear to have forgotten, and did not attack any cities or villages dependent on it.

CHAPTER LI

HE BEGINS TO INVADE THE TERRITORIES OF SYRIA

THEN he made for Urfa, seeking the spoil of it, but there went out to him one of the chief men and heads of the citizens, by name Al Haj Ottoman, son of Al Sakshak, who placated him and redeemed the city with a load of wealth, which he brought to him and paid over; then he sent to Qazi Burhanuddin Abul Abbas Ahmad, Lord of Kaisaria and Toqat and Siwas, several envoys and violent despatches, in which he lightened and thundered and foamed and raged like the sea and conveyed arrogant meanings; and the whole meaning and purport came above all to this, that the name of Mahmud Khan* or Sabur Ghatmish Khan† and his own should be said in public prayers and money minted in the form and stamp, which he himself used.

And when his envoy gave this message to him with a letter, neither on account of his envoy nor on account of his letter did the Sultan believe him, or think him worthy of a reply to his message; nay, he cut off the heads of the heads of the envoys and hanging them to the necks of the rest, ordered the latter to be led around through his country. Then he cut them in the middle and having divided them in two, sent them in the two directions, that is, to Sultan Malik Azzahir Abu Said Barkuk (of Egypt) one segment of them, and the other to Sultan Aba Yazid,‡ son of Murad, son of Aurkhan, son of Ottoman, Lord of the kingdoms of Rum, and showed them plainly what he had done and the speech which he had received from the hated Timur and that he had replied with silence and slain his messengers with outrage; and he did not exaggerate this story, but behaved exactly thus with his envoys and messengers, because he thought nothing of him and resented his crimes against the servants of Allah and His countries.

And the Qazi added " You must know that I am your neighbour and that my country is yours also and that I am a particle of your dust and a drop of your seas and I have not committed this against him with the weakness of my condition and smallness of my resources and narrowness of my sphere and country and meagreness of my following newly gained or inherited, but in reliance on your aid and confidence in gaining help from you, and in order to raise the standards of the majesty of your rule and unfold the flag of fear of your power; for I am the defence of your mouth and protection of your throat, the herald of your armies and comrade of your legions; the watch-tower of your scouts and the scout of your battles; otherwise how should I be equal to resisting him and in what way would a conflict with him go well for me ?

" You have already heard his deeds and perceived his public acts—how many armies he has broken—how many kings he has taken captive, how many kingdoms he has seized—how many rulers he has destroyed—how many curtains he has torn—how many souls he has slain—how many defences he

* Khan of the Jagatais.   † Raised by Timur to the place of Sultan Hussein.
‡ Bayezid I.

has stormed and given over to plunder—how much wealth he has carried away, how many powerful men he has despoiled and humbled the proud—how many disasters he has inflicted—how he has restrained the fierce—seduced the wise ; put horsemen to flight—overthrown foundations—how many prayers he has rejected—how many plots he has checked—how many hills he has made low—how many infants he has tortured—how many heads he has crushed—how many backs he has broken—how many pacts he has torn up—how many fires he has kindled—how many winds he has made to blow and how many waters to boil over—how many dust-storms he has stirred up—how many hearts he has scorched—how many breasts he has burned—how many necks he has broken—how many eyes he has blinded—how many ears he has stopped—how then was I to resist the flood of Arim and the charge of that raging elephant ?

" If you bring me aid, you will restore me, but if you deprive me of help, you will betray me and you will have enough terror and fame and attain glory and victory, since there are slaves in front of you to repel what threatens you ; and if harm strikes me, which Allah forfend, and a spark from the coals of that evil flies to my realm, perchance in the turn of affairs that action will pass to another to endure and to a second and then to a third.

" I have written a poem on the cause of disasters :
' Evil, like fire, leaps forth, when you seek to quench it,
  One little spark, if you check it, is extinguished.
  But if slackly you shirk crushing it,
  It kindles the peoples and burns heart and liver,
  And if all the nations of the earth were gathered,
  Never would it help you to extinguish it.'

" But I have disregarded his speech and put off a reply, that you may arrange, and I will follow ; and you may prescribe and it will suffice for me ; and you may lay the foundations and I will build on them and you may reply and he will receive the same reply from me."

CHAPTER LII

OF THE REPLY WHICH SULTAN ABA YAZID GAVE TO QAZI
BURHANUDDIN ABUL ABBAS, SULTAN OF THE TERRITORIES OF
SIWAS

SULTAN ABA YAZID, son of Ottoman, pleased with
this action and moved by the beauty of this address,
praised this decision of the Qazi and approved it and sent
back a message to him saying, that if Timur refrained and was
prevented, it would be well; but if not, he would lead an
army against him, which he would not resist, and would gladly
engage with him and resist him with the greatest zeal and
sincere good faith; and would not fear his great army, for
how often a small band has conquered a great host! Nay, if
good counsel and auspicious decisions required that he should
himself advance against Timur and meet him with brave
troops, he would raise his standards and carry out his orders
and be a hand for his sword and an arm for his side.

Then having sent his letter, he waited for the reply.

But as for Malik Azzahir, I have not seen his letter or found
out with certainty, what reply he gave him, but it is probable
that the reply of Malik Azzahir Abu Said was like that of Sultan
Mughazi Aba Yazid, since their actions and speech used
secretly and openly to reflect their mutual benevolence.

I saw afterwards a document which contained a despatch
and a reply: the despatch was attributed to that deceiver
(Timur) and the reply to Malik Azzahir and the letters of
both were not distinguished with any yellow or bright colour;
and the manner of the despatch was of this sort: " Say, O
Allah, Founder of the heavens and the earth, knower of the
secret and the open! Thou shalt judge between thy servants
concerning that in which they were at variance. You should
know that I am the soldier of Allah, created out of His wrath,
to whom dominion is entrusted against those who merit His
wrath; I am not moved with tenderness towards him who
weeps nor do I pity the tear of him who wails; in truth Allah
has taken pity from my heart. Woe then, woe to him, who
has not submitted to my rule! For I am he who has already
wasted countries and destroyed men and spread rapine over

the earth ; the centres of our armies are like mountains and our numbers like the sand ; our horses victors, our spears piercing ; our kingdoms not subject to invasion and our allies invincible. If you accept my terms and obey my rule, whatever is for me will be for you and whatever is against me will be against you ; but if you show yourselves hostile to me and haughty and persist in your insolence, throw the blame on none but yourselves ; forts will not defend you from me and armies will not avert or repel my attack ; nor will your prayers against me be answered or heard, for you eat what is forbidden and neglect the assembly for prayer ; therefore show submission and fear.   This day you will receive the punishment of humiliation.

" You hold me to be an infidel, but it is settled with me that you are wicked ; and Allah has granted me dominion over you. His commands are mighty and His edicts powerful. Your greatest numbers are few to me, and he who is most excellent to you is base to me. I possess the earth from east to west, and seize by force every ship therein.

" I have sent this letter to you ; reply to it quickly, before the covering is withdrawn and not even the slightest remnants are left you and the Herald proclaims destruction upon you ; (as is written in the Koran) canst thou find even one of them or canst thou hear a whisper from them ?

" I have acted justly with you in sending a letter to you and scattering upon you the gems of this conversation and peace."

And this is the form of the reply and its author is said to be Qazi Alauddin, son of Fazalallah, but this I do not believe :

" In the name of Allah the Compassionate and Merciful !

" Say, O Allah, King of the Kingdom ! Thou grantest the kingdom to whom Thou wilt and takest it from whom Thou wilt ; and raisest whom Thou wilt and bringest low whom Thou wilt ; in Thy hand is good, for Thou art powerful over everything ! I have received the letter sent by His Majesty the Ilkhan from the mighty, potent Court of the Sultan, saying, ' We are created from His wrath ; we are appointed the lords of those on whom His wrath falls ; we are not moved by tenderness towards him who laments nor do we pity the tears of him who wails ! ' Verily Allah has taken pity from your hearts and this is your greatest crime and the worst fault, which you attribute to yourselves. But this exhortation will suffice to you, if you will heed it :   Say, O unbelievers ! I will not worship what you worship ! '

"But in your whole letter you show and in the whole disgraceful writing declare and proclaim that you are unbelievers, but the curse of Allah is on unbelievers, who cling to the roots (of Islam) but do not care for the branches. But we are the faithful, among whom no fault obtains and nothing doubtful is allowed. The Koran sent down to us from heaven follows us with constant pity ; common to us is the blessing of its interpretation and special to us is the excellence of its prohibition and permission.

"But for you and your skins is created the fire of hell, to be kindled when the sky shall have been split. But it is a wonder of wonders that cowards should frighten lions and hyenas frighten wild beasts and common soldiers men clad in mail.

"Our horses are Arabs to which we devote the greatest care and our spears that strike vehemently are famed throughout the east and west. If we slay you, there is excellent gain ! But if we are slain by you, there is but a moment between us and Paradise (as is written in the Koran), ' Think not those dead, who are slain in the way of Allah, nay, they live and are cherished in the presence of their Lord.'

"You say : ' The centres of my armies are like mountains and my numbers are like the sand ' ; but the butcher does not care for the number of the cattle and a few brands are enough to burn many logs ; how often a little band has scattered a great army by the will of Allah ! And Allah is with the patient ; misfortunes are not avoided. Death we strongly desire ; if we live, we shall live happy ; but if we fall, we shall die martyrs, but verily those who are the sect of Allah shall be victors. The commander of the faithful and deputy of the Lord of the world rejects the obedience which you demand from us ; there is no obedience to you and no subjection.

"You demand also that we should declare our position to you, but all this conversation is made up of madness and futility ; is the heart revealed before the revelation ? Or is anyone accused of impiety after profession of the true faith ? Have you submitted to a second Lord ? Now truly you have brought forward a stupendous thing, on account of which the heavens might almost be rent and the earth cleft asunder and the mountains be shaken and fall. Say to your scribe who

93

devised the letter and composed the despatch : ' The meaning of the letter is like the creaking of a gate or the buzzing of a fly.' But we will write down what he says, and will lengthen his punishment. And we have nothing for you except a sword in the strength of Allah Almighty."

Then I found in writing, whose ink the lapse of years has destroyed with antiquity and whose blackness age has whitened with the whiteness on the face of time, a copy of this letter and the form of this despatch, which was composed by Nasiruddin Tusi in the name of Hulagu* Tatar, who sent it to the Sultan of Egypt. And the copy of his reply is in the very style of someone, who lived at that time.

And when Timur learned what Sultan Burhanuddin had done with his envoys, he was wroth and poised himself on the wings of anger and his heart's blood boiled and was disturbed and he was seized by such anger that he was almost suffocated by its vehemence ; nevertheless when he knew what was hidden in secret places and that the soldiers and brave men of Islam and the lions among the Muslims still lived in the lair of the Faith and that there were opposed to him ravening lions and fierce beasts of prey, for a time he showed patience and withdrew, waiting for the turn of their fortune.

CHAPTER LIII

OF THE EXPEDITION OF THE ARMIES OF SYRIA TO REPEL THAT DANGER

WHEN Tanam, Lord of the Amirs of Syria, had led forth the armies to Erzinjan, he withdrew and counted his return as a success, and they did not then feel damage and Allah repelled those who were unbelievers after they had gained no profit by their fury ; but of the army of Islam there returned every ravening lion and they took from Durak men like themselves and what came their way : " light upon light."

* Grandson of Jenghizkhan and first Ilkhan of Persia.

94

CHAPTER LIV

OF THE RETURN OF THAT COVETOUS ONE (TIMUR) AND HIS PLAN OF SUBDUING THE COUNTRIES OF INDIA

WHEN Timur learnt that the Sultan of India, Firoz Shah, had been carried out of the trouble of this world to the mercy of Allah, with no son surviving to succeed him, he strove that by the decree of death and fortune he might succeed to that office.

For the Indians after the death of their lord became equal among themselves without a leader, and the rule of India was loosened and stirred by swelling waves and all began to mingle in disputes, some gaining power, others being debased. Then it was agreed among them that a Vazir should be appointed, by name Malu, who restored the shattered state, and raised men who were worthy of honours, but put down the unworthy; but his brother, Sharnak Khan, Governor of the city of Multan, opposed him, and when this struggle arose between them, the people of India also was divided into parties and factions; and their discords greatly helped Timur and afforded him aid and assistance. I have said:

"The discord of enemies in their plans joins closer the minds of friends."

And when Malu* reached Multan, Sharnak Khan opposed him; therefore he besieged the city and wearied it; and his forces were very abundant and his black squadrons as dark as night, so that it is said that in the sum of that mighty army there were eight hundred elephants, since all the Amirs of Hind and the chiefs of the regions of Sind had already gathered their following and assembled their infantry and horse and packed their baggage with what was needful and equipped their elephants for their uses, and this struggle and contest lasted for about two-thirds of a year, until he stormed the city and took it from the hand of Sharnak Khan.

SECTION

But when Malu had obtained power and the rule of India had been established in his hands and he had learned that

* The text says " Timur " but this seems to be a slip.

H

Timur was advancing against him, he prepared armies and arms with diligence and equipped aids and supports and poured out abundant wealth, thinking that no one would overcome him, and scattered wealth and assembled horse and foot and collected all the elephants in his kingdom ; then he fortified cities and strengthened ambushes and raised war-towers upon the elephants and spared no expense in the struggle.

But Timur marched with such vigour that he almost overtook the birds, since there was none to check him in entering on that inheritance nor in the armies of the Sultan of Hind anyone to come near him. But when with his men he reached the Indians, they led out their army against him, the elephants going in front to terrify the horses ; and they built on all the elephants towers armed with shields and filled each tower with soldiers proved in desperate enterprises and bold, after strengthening the towers with strong coverings, and they hung from them bells and fearsome gongs, which might call to flight the fiercest foe, and fastened to their trunks the finest swords, which are called swords of Hind. The brightness of their flame drew men's heads, which fell before them, as though in adoration, so that their flame could be called the fire of Sind and this besides the tusks of the elephants used in war, like pikes, which in paying their debt take nothing from the sum, and the arrows, which aimed at the throats of foes break every arrow and spear ; and those elephants seemed in the line of battle like a forest walking with its lions or like castles running with their soldiers and mountains passing with their leopards or seas with their hosts of waves going back and coming or like thick clouds falling with their thunderbolts or nights of separation marching with their black vicissitudes. And behind them came the war-horses of the Indians and brave soldiers with lance and sword, black lions, and smooth-skinned wolves and spotted lynxes with spears of Khat* and Indian swords and arrows of the khalanj tree, with breasts afire and brave hearts and firm purpose and calm endurance.

* A city in Arabia.

CHAPTER LV

OF THE STRATAGEM OF THAT DECEIVER IN PUTTING THE ELEPHANTS TO FLIGHT

WHEN Timur had explored this condition and learned that the web of the Indian army was woven on this loom, he used cunning to unravel the net and stew them in their juice thicker than broth and first planned a device to avert the craft of the elephants and used keen thought in fashioning spikes of iron, with three extremities of new design, recalling by their horrid shape the dogma of the Trinity or the triangle of the geometricians ; and they made for him many thousands of them ; and he marking the places where the elephants would stand in lines scattered the spikes by night and so prepared for them and the men with them slaughter and lamentation and set a limit and prevented that work from going beyond.

Then he arranged his eager warriors, and drew up his lions and lions' whelps, and disposed his cavalry and ordered his infantry and set part of his army to the right and the left in ambush against the enemy ; and when the Sultan of the planets* had loosened his cavalry in the zones of the sky and the army of darkness had gathered the infantry of its stars and lifted its train for flight, his army slowly advanced to that limit until it reached it ; and when both armies had come in sight of each other, he suddenly turned and veered with his cavalry from the path of the elephants, wherefore they, thinking that his horses were routed and that the sun of his victory was suffering eclipse and that the stars of his army had set, drew from their place the fortress-like elephants ; and the elephants rushed forth, like torrents, and they drove them steadily behind his army over those spikes thrown in the way, the Indian infantry and cavalry following the elephants ; but when the torrents of elephants reached the limits of the scattered spikes and those spikes seized in their embrace the fore feet and hind feet of the elephants and their hooves clung to the spikes and they felt their feet checked by them, they suddenly withdrew, nay, turned their backs, bereft of sense,

* i.e. the sun.

and the drivers chided them and checked them from flight, but the check and chiding were in vain and in the advance against the enemy they did as the elephant of Abraha ; and when the spikes in the hard ground hurt them, they could not but turn from the battle and take to flight ; and the elephants trampled on infantry and horsemen, so that the slain became like mountains and in the valleys thereof blood flowed like torrents and men in ambush went forth against them from the left and right, who routed the survivors and destroyed all to a man.

And they say that, since the country of the Indians has no camels and the sight of them terrifies elephants, so that they fly to a distance, therefore Timur ordered that five hundred swift camels should be got and their saddles and carts stuffed with dried reeds and cotton soaked with oil and that they be driven in front of the cavalry, until the two armies came in sight of each other and when they were drawn up for battle, and nothing remained but slaughter, those bundles and loads should be set on fire and they should be driven against the frightened elephants, and when the camels felt the heat of the fires, then they cried out and leapt and rushed against the elephants, and it happened as is said :

> " As though you were among the camels of the sons of
>   Aqish,
> Between whose feet straw crackles."

And when the elephants saw the fires and heard the cry of the camels and saw their form and presence, while they groaned and leapt and thudded with the strokes of their hooves, in fear they turned against their drivers and trampled on them and against their riders and mutilated them and trod down the cavalry and broke the infantry, and the infidels read the verse (of the Koran) concerning aid against the masters of the elephants and their foes sent against them arrows like birds in flocks and they got no use from the elephants, nay, the elephants destroyed most of the cavalry and infantry ; then the armies of Hind and their brave cavalry withdrew and the squadrons assembled and the legions were set in order. Then they refitted themselves and collected and joining closely together bore themselves actively, some Magi,* some Muslims, and warriors famous and noted for valour, all black of the

* Zoroastrians or here probably Hindus.

colour of iron, like the depth of the dark night. Then they advanced against the Tatars and joined battle and after shooting arrows attacked with spears, then smote with swords, then seizing their opponents' throats leaped on each other and hurled one another from the backs of the horses, and in that dust day was confounded with night, and they ceased not to exchange blows and hurl attacks and press fierce charges, until the tongue of Fate and Providence recited " In the succession of night and day there are signs."

Then the battle was ended and the tumult scattered and the judgment declared that the rage of the army of Hind be calmed and the black army being driven to flight, ruin came upon the Indians and Allah destroyed the standards of night.

And when the Indians were scattered and put to flight and dissolved—the bond of their warlike labour being ended—and the nobles had withdrawn and their Sultan, Malu, had fled, Timur established his rule in Hind, as he had in Samarkand, and assembled its kings and maintained its elephants and set his hands on its affairs and did not fail to seize everything which pertained to it and the master of the elephants surrendered them.

Then he advanced against its capital, the city of Dehla (Delhi), which is a great city, where various arts and men skilled in them are gathered, a home of merchants, a mine of gems and scents—which city when he could not besiege, he surrounded that vast region with a countless multitude of his armies and of peoples and tribes which he had with him.

They say, too, that these armies and peoples, however great and abundant, could not surround it on account of the greatness of its circuit and when he had taken it on one side which had been besieged, the other still resisted and held out for three days, no one in the captured part knowing what was happening in the other by reason of distance and the abundance of the population.

CHAPTER LVI

THAT WICKED ONE RECEIVES NEWS OF THE DEATH OF KINGS—
ABUL ABBAS AHMAD AND MALIK AZZAHIR BARKUK

MEANWHILE, when he had seized the throne of Hind and had brought under his power its cities and territories and borders and his commands had reached its most distant mountains and valleys and his forces were scattered through its provinces smooth and rugged and subjects had felt their violence on land and sea, he received from Syria the joyful news " that Qazi Burhanuddin Ahmad Siwasi and Malik Azzahir Abu Said Barkuk had been translated to Paradise," whereby his heart was mightily cheered and he was almost flying to Syria for joy.

Therefore quickly settling the affairs of Hind, he transferred to his own kingdom his forces and the army, which was there, along with booty he had seized and precious things, and distributed the multitude of that captive army through the boundaries and borders of the parts of Transoxiana and appointed in India a Nawab* from whom he had nothing to fear.

Then, leaving Samarkand, he hastened to Syria, taking with him the leaders of the army of India and its chief ministers and the Sultan of its Princes and the elephants of its Sultan, and delighted with that great company, journeyed in the beginning of the year 802,† and poured with that deluge from the Oxus into Khorasan, after first appointing his son Amiranshah, King of Tabriz and its territories, and already Sultan Ahmad, that opportunist fugitive, had returned to Bagdad ; and the reason of his expedition into Syria (though he was at other times constant in destroying the offspring of kings) was the crime of Qazi Burhanuddin, lord of Siwas, against his barbarian envoys ; nevertheless he wished that his aim should be doubtful and to conceal from men his setting out and position.

I have improvised these verses :

" How can the splendour of the sun be withdrawn from the eyes, when the day is already bright ?

* Deputy.   † A.D. 1399.

> And how shall be hidden the fragrance of musk, which
> fills the nostrils of men on a warm day ?
> And how shall the sound of a drum at the time of flight
> be concealed from the ear ? "

And since his march was distant and long, needing much
equipment, and he shunned imitating the Tabuk expedition,*
he put forward a pretext, by which he might hide his purpose,
out of craft and cunning, and revealed and published it and
with it men's hearts and ears were filled.

Here is shown the substance of a letter, which he received
while in India, and they say his son Amiranshah sent it to
him ; that is his said son Amiranshah wrote to him and advised
him among other things :

" Certainly through your advanced age and weak constitution and infirmity you are now unequal to raising the standards
of empire and sustaining the burdens of leadership and government and above all things it would befit your condition to sit
as a devotee in a corner of the mosque and worship your Lord,
until death came to you ; there are now men among your sons
and grandsons, who would suffice to you for ruling your subjects
and armies and undertake to guard your kingdom and territory ;
but to what purpose are countries to you, who are shortly
to die ?

" But if your eye is clear and your vision keen in penetrating
things, dismiss worldly affairs and give constant care to the
life to come ; if you possessed the kingdom of Shadad and
there came to you the power of Amalek and Ad and victory
and fortune so aided you, that you attained the position of
Haman and Pharaoh and a quarter of the earth paid tribute to
you, so that you surpassed Qarun† in multitude of riches and
in ravaging countries became a second Nebuchadnezzar, to
whom Allah Almighty granted great power, but soon rendered
him powerless ; in a word, if your rule reached to the furthest
borders and you gained the sum of your worldly prayers and
your life in this world became the longest of all and in it the
greatest kings served you and your army conquered Cæsar
and utterly broke Khosru and Tuba Al Najashi obeyed you and
the foremost kings and princes came to you as slaves and
attendants and Faghfur‡ knelt before you on his callous knees

---

* The last expedition of Mahomed, when he openly declared his objective.
† Or Korah.   ‡ The Emperor of China.

and you raised your tent over Khan and Khakhan and every Shah cast himself down on the floor of your bedchamber, and the Pharaoh of Egypt and its Sultan submitted to you and Iran and Turan were devoted to you and your power reached so far that all the inhabitants of the climes of the world were yours, will not the end of the greatness you have seized be at length impotence and the goal of your perfection destruction and of your life death and of your habitation the tomb? I have said :

> " ' Live, while you wish, in the world, and obtain
> In it all the fame and renown you desire.
> Life's thread is woven and joined with a break,
> And the chain of age knotted by death.'

" It is also said :

> " ' A shirt of cotton for covering.
> And a draught of clear water and food
> Which a man receives, in place of what he has hoped,
> These are generally his, who is to die.'

" But where are you, if you are compared with Noah and his mourning over his family and his good service and piety and with Lokman, who admonished his son and fed his vulture until old age, and with David, who had a great kingdom and yet was constant in full observance of the Divine commands and worship and praise of God Almighty and with Solomon, his successor, and his dominion over men and jinns and birds and beasts and winds, and with Alexander, who ruled the whole East and reached the West, and built a barrier between two mountains and subdued countries and brought men under his sway? And what are you compared with the chief of the prophets and seal of messengers, most elect of the elect, messenger by Divine mercy to His creatures, prophet, when Adam was still between water and clay, Mahomed Mustafa Ahmed the Chosen, to whom turn the countries of the East and West, and whom present and absent alike revere; to whom His secrets have been revealed and His open and hidden things have offered themselves for scrutiny; whose armies were honoured angels; on whom believed men, jinns, beasts, and reptiles; to whom Allah Almighty gave aid, so that the King of the Mountains submitted to him; and the east wind carried his standards victorious to right and left and he subdued tyrants by terror and force and he was feared by Khosrus and Cæsars a month's march distant; and Allah strengthened him by His own aid and that of the faithful—both Fugitives and Helpers—and succoured him, when the unbelievers drove him out with another, when ,the two were in a cave; and that venerable one attained such honour that Allah (to Whom be praise) transferred him on a certain night from the mosque of Mecca to the mosque of Jerusalem and his beast was the noble Al Buraq, with which he ascended to the seven storeys of heaven and God joined His glorious name with his and the religion which he founded will last until the day of resurrection without change, according to his definition and law; and for his sake God created the universe and in his sight made created things plain and no other man was placed in the world more noble and excellent than he; and all his sins were forgiven him; and the more wonderful of his miracles are that he filled a great multitude with a cake of barley and gave drink to many from clear water gushing between his fingers, and for him the moon was rent and a tree walked to him and a lizard believed in him and a stone saluted him; can his miracles be recounted and his marvels numbered? And enough for you is his most certain miracle and his eternal sign, lasting through the course of ages, perennial, while night and day revolve, stable while daytime and nighttime move, that is the glorious Koran; and falsity comes not to it from before or behind; a revelation from the Wise, the Praise-worthy; and this place of honour in this world is besides what Allah stored for him in the future, and announced to him in that saying: ' Verily the end shall be better for you than the beginning and afterwards your Lord shall give you that wherewith you may be content '; besides that Allah Almighty made a covenant concerning the true faith with the prophets by his help and aid. And if they had lived in his time, they could not but have obeyed him and followed his command. And there is the calling of Abraham, the Friend of God, and Moses the intercessor and the doctors of the children of Israel and concerning his coming the tongue of Jesus brought glad news in the gospel; and he bears the standard of the praise of God on the day of judgment, when Adam and all his descendants shall be under his banners; and is Lord of the lake that is drunk from and speaks with God in the place of intercession and abode of praise.

" And this is the meaning of what I said out of great love and devotion : speak, you shall be heard : beseech, you shall be accepted : seek, you shall receive and shall put on a new embroidered robe of honour and you should obtain for yourself my benefits and look to those princes, mines of goodness and keys of happiness ; did they seek earthly things 'and put trust in them ? Or did they regard them except with the eye of contempt ? Did they not seek to exalt the cause of Allah and show pity towards the creatures of Allah ? But enough for you are the Khalifs of the true faith and especially Abu Bakr and Umar who were in this sect like two moons, and add to them the just Khalifs and perfect kings and excellent sultans, who cared for and observed the statutes of Allah Almighty concerning His servants and keenly defended the worshippers of Allah from oppression in their countries and laid the foundations of goodness and in the royal road of justice and equity made a noble journey and so walked that their foot-prints endure and even after death their prosperous times and achievements are as it were recalled to life and who thus surpassed the example of the ancients and left behind them a true message among their successors for those who strive to imitate what they hear.

" May his memory become a noble example !

" For truly men are examples.

" But you govern men, nay also you still administer justice, but unjustly ; you feed, but it is on their wealth and corn ; you act the defender, but by burning their hearts and ribs ; you lay foundations, but foundations of afflictions ; you go forward, but on a crooked road. But if you climbed above the seven solid heavens, you could not obtain the rank of Pharaoh and Shadad and if you raised your palaces above the highest mountains, you would not equal Iram furnished with pillars, the like of which have not been made on earth.

" Turn your mind therefore to those who restrained and warned and then passed away ; but turn it away from the overbearing and abandoned, and the wicked and unbelievers. And let this address suffice you for a reply and yield the bow to its claimant and the house to its builder to live in ; and show yourself the friend of Allah and the Prophet and the faithful. But since you have been of those who labour to lay waste the earth that they may ravage it, I in the same way will meet you and restrain you and prevent you from your

zeal for laying waste, that I may teach you to walk aright."
And besides there was much insolence and utterance of
reproaches.

When Timur received this letter, he set out for Tabriz ;
Amiranshah however had with him a company of evil men, such
as range the earth corrupting it, and among them Qutb of Mosul,
a wonder of the transient age, a famous master of music and its
modes ; when he played on the pipe, he reduced to silence the
best artists and putting the flute to his mouth he far surpassed
the lyre of Isaac and his father and when he began to sing, he
singly equalled all others, each person saying of his soft air,
" My sadness consoles me " and with fingers outstretched
showing his excellence and saying : " I feast my eyes upon
you " ; when he played on the flute he healed every wounded
heart and brought medicine to every injured spirit and when
he stood up dancing, the zither bowed with bent back because
of the sweetness of that sound, and when his mouth was opened,
because of the delight, which the ears took in his melodies,
with bended neck the lyre gave ear to him, rubbing its ears
with finger-tips of courtesy. He is said to have drawn every
kind of modulation both simple and compound from every
opening of the flute and there are attributed to him books on
musical modes and arguments were held between him and
Master Abdul Qadir Al Maraghi.

Amiranshah being immoderately devoted to him, valued
his society and intimacy ; but Timur, who was not drawn to
admiration by wonderful things or attracted by amusements
and pleasures, said that Qutb had spoiled the mind of Amiranshah, as Abdul Qadir corrupted Ahmed, son of Sheikh Avis,
and perverted him.

And he came on the seventeenth day of the first month
Rabia in the year 802* to Qarabagh, where he made his riding
camels halt and gave rest to his beasts of burden and occupied
the territories of Azerbaijan and put to death those dangerous
men and evildoers, but did not harm Amiranshah, his own
son, whom he had himself reared ; and complex affairs passed
between the two, which none but Allah can unfold.

Then, setting out with that army, on the second day of the
latter month of Jumadi, which was the fifth day of the week,
he took the city of Tiflis and advancing to the countries of the
Karj† laid waste whatever forts and towers he took and drove

* A.D. 1399.   † Georgia.

the people to castles and defended forts and slew all without distinction, who submitted, as well as those who resisted, and cut off their heads and forelocks.

Then he bent the reins of destruction and spurred his insolent soldiery against Bagdad, and Sultan Ahmed escaped from that tumult to Qara Yusuf on the twenty-eighth day of the month Rajab. But Timur checked his attacks and thus reassured those who were watching him and his enemies and loitered on the way and by his changes of behaviour tricked the enemy and wandered and ran hither and thither, pretending negligence.

" I pointed at Saadi instead of Alvi, while I wanted you.
For I did not want Saadi or Alvi."

Therefore on a certain day Sultan Ahmed and Qara Yusuf returned to Bagdad, thinking that he had not left the countries of the ignoble Karj, but when they learned that he was advancing and knew that when he was intent on anything, he did not turn aside, both fled to Rum, abandoning their homes, in which the crow and owl screeched. Then that old vulture departed to the summer pastures of the Turkomans and put his sword in its sheath and stayed himself from destruction and the summer passed.

CHAPTER LVII

OF THE CALAMITIES AND NEW THINGS WHICH BEFELL AND EVILS
AND INJURIES WHICH WERE INFLICTED WHEN THE SWORD WAS
DRAWN AFTER THE DEATH OF THE SULTAN OF SIWAS

IN that turbid state of affairs, a disturbance fell also on the countries of Egypt and Syria and on Siwas ; as for Egypt and Syria, through the death of the Sultan ; but as for Siwas, through the slaying of its Chief, both which deaths happened about the same time, as well as the death of Qara Yusuf and Al Malik Almuid Shaikh and Abul Fata Ghayatuddin Mahomed son of Othman, for the space between the deaths of these great Princes was about half a year and the same also between the deaths of those two Sultans.

CHAPTER LVIII

A FRAGMENT OF THE AFFAIRS OF THE QAZI AND HOW HE BECAME
RULER OF SIWAS AND THOSE LANDS

THE cause of the slaying of Qazi Burhanuddin was the dissension which befell between him and Othman Qara Iluk, the leader of the rebels, of which more in its place. And the father of this Sultan was a Qazi* under Sultan Artata, ruler of Kaisaria and of certain territories of Karaman, and was one of the Amirs and Vazirs of chief position and rank. His son, the said Burhanuddin Ahmed, was in the flower of youth a lover of noble learning and learned men who labour in gaining and getting it : he went therefore to Egypt to learn sciences and grasp them by the double road of reasoning and perception ; and he possessed keen intellect and a fountain of talent and an eye that never slept and therefore in a little time gained much learning.

While he was walking in Egypt, he saw a wretched beggar, who was sitting near the road, to whom he gave something, to cure his want and poverty and affliction ; then that beggar spoke openly to him in clear language and revealed to him a hidden secret, saying to him : " Do not stay in these parts, for you will be Sultan of Rum." And this speech mightily affected him and after arranging necessary matters and cutting short his business, he set forth taking his companions.

And when he reached Siwas, his father and the chief men received him with great joy and a firm fabric was built for him with the people and solid foundations laid and he devoted himself to studies and conversation with chief men and leaders, having lofty spirit, liberal disposition, noble character, pleasant manners and praiseworthy qualities, wholesome writing and exposition perfect in all respects ; approving the talk of learned men and with keen eye testing the opinions of doctors ; his are books on " The Intelligible " and " Witty Tales " ; he would compose charming poetry and reward poetry with great rewards and admire elegant speech, which he repaid with abundant reward, and with this zeal for letters he walked nevertheless decked in military guise and manner and imitated

* Judge.

the life of princes, in riding and hunting, and followed the manner of a sultan and acquired servants and allies—and when the Sultan died, leaving a son under age, they put him on the throne, and with him there were of chief Amirs and head Vazirs Ghaznafar, son of Muzaffar, Faridun, Ibn Al-Muid, Haji Kaldi and Haji Ibrahim and others beside them and the most powerful of them was the father of Qazi Burhanuddin ; and these Amirs and head Vazirs ruled the state and did not disturb what was settled except by common consent.

And when the father of Qazi Burhanuddin died, he was succeeded by his son, who surpassed his father and his own contemporaries in learning and good government ; and the administration of the provinces of those parts was divided between Ibn Al-Muid, Haji Kaldi and Haji Ibrahim, while around Sultan Mahomed there remained Faridun, Ghaznafar and Burhanuddin Ahmed.

Then on the death of Sultan Mahomed, leaving no son, the rule remained among the three like a common heritage ; but seldom do two rivals agree over one husband and live in harmony ; nay, if in earth and heaven there were a God beside Allah, certainly both would be destroyed ; and a hundred beggars roll themselves in one rug, but a great kingdom does not even hold two kings.

Therefore Burhanuddin desiring to acquire the kingdom and absolute authority for himself alone, laid nets of cunning for his associates, since the kingdom was sterile* ; and when he had marked a favourable constellation for this purpose and rightly attended to the stars, he said : " I am sick " and so both his associates thought, " To visit the sick is to serve Allah " and they sought merit by visiting him and when he wished them to repeat the visit, they again visited him, but he was hostile to them ; but in truth they did not fear him, but he feared them and truly did not want them kept alive and he laid an ambush for them and posted against them armed men and slew them both and they fell victims to association and the sultanate of Ahmed was freed of associates, whereby his power was strengthened and the cause of the kingdom was tested by clear argument and proof.

But those who had been his allies opposed him and those of the Nawabs who had been equal and like him resisted him and his enemies and ill wishers openly showed their hidden

* Had no heir.

enmity and said: " His fathers and ancestors did not hold this rank; but we are by origin men of Siwas; whence therefore has he rule over us ? And jealousy in the state is a lousy chain and the rivalry of equals a wound which does not heal."

And among them was Sheikh Najib, the Lord of Tokat, a strong place, and Haji Kaldi, the Naib of Amasia.

And when he was established in the kingdom, he took the title of Sultan at the time when Sultan Alauddin obtained the territories of Karaman. But Sultan Burhanuddin said: " As authors of annals relate and inform us and books of travel assure us, the surrounding countries belong to our sway and are our hereditary possession." Then he strove to gain what belonged to his sultanate and began to make raids upon those, who persevered in rebellion, and by force snatched the fort of Tokat from Sheikh Najib, whom he took with him regardless of his will, and the Tatars of Rum all sought his protection and Othman surnamed Qara Iluk said to him : " I will follow your commands and walk bound by the fetter of obedience to you." And Qara Iluk was among his servants and in the number of the Turkomans and his followers, going with his men winter and summer through the plains surrounding Siwas.

CHAPTER LIX

HOW QARA ILUK OTHMAN DESTROYED THE TRACES OF THE FIRES OF SULTAN BURHANUDDIN, BECAUSE OF HIDDEN ENMITY RAISING OPEN REBELLION AGAINST HIM, AND SEIZED HIM, WHEN FORTUNE BETRAYED AND DECEIVED HIM

THEN rivalry arose between Qara Iluk and the Sultan, which turned to contention and at length issued in mutual insult and abuse and he broke his agreements and obligations as a vassal and refused any longer to send gifts and slaves and fortified himself with the Turkomans and his followers in inaccessible places. But the Sultan troubled not much about him, since he was least of his allies, but resolved meanwhile to make for Amasia, then Erzinjan. And near Siwas was a summer resort; its appearance beautiful, the soil clean, the water clear, the air pleasant; a garden of perennial verdure clothed the extreme borders of its meadows with its green embroidered cloak and Paradise had made water flow between the trees from its river Kauter on to gardens like heavenly pleasaunces and the hill on its brow astonished the eyes and delighted the sight. I have said :

" On it is a grassy and flowery expanse, like cups studded with gems, full of nectar."

But Qara Iluk making for that place with great efforts passed near Siwas, and though Qazi Abul Abbas was there he rode past, not caring about him ; then the heat of his wrath blazed and he almost burst with anger and said : " That dog has gone so far that he enters the lion's den and puts forward the foot of boldness, though I am now moving in this part " ; then he ordered his men to mount their horses and he rushed fiercely against him and anger and levity carried him away, so that in riding he outstripped the army. Therefore several of his companions among the retinue said to him : " If our Lord the Sultan delayed a little, until the army came, it would be more prudent, expedient and better ; and the formidable majesty of our Lord the Sultan, which is strong enough, suffices in itself, nevertheless Qara Iluk Turkoman is a cunning contriver of ambushes."

But the Sultan disregarding this talk did not cease to rush after him, until darkness came on, when Qara Iluk made a charge against him with his company and forthwith seized him ; but the army not knowing his condition, his Amirs and soldiers were scattered hither and thither.

CHAPTER LX

OF THE GOOD COUNSEL WHICH QARA ILUK TOOK, BUT TURNED TO BAD AT THE PROMPTING OF SHEIKH NAJIB

THEN Qara Iluk wished to renew a treaty with him and plucking up the saplings of dissension, to found a structure of sincere friendship and concord and to restore to him his dignity and become as before his defender and ally and he informed the Sultan of it, that is that he would be a faithful friend to him and would not admit concerning him the speech of an informer or secret enemy.

But Sheikh Najib, who had been Governor of the fort of

Tokat and whom the Sultan had besieged and shutting the
roads to him, had driven him to surrender and seizing the fort
had taken him with him against his will, found an opportunity,
which he seized and showed the hatred which was hidden in
his heart and for that reason visited Qara Iluk, to whom in
servile manner he showed honour, and said: "I hate the
teacher of your wisdom, if he slips, and the guide of your
sagacity, if he errs, and your good counsel, if it goes ill; and
your fine judgment, if it is impaired. Lo, Allah has given
power against the enemy, and whence is your quiet and calm-
ness with him ? I have said :

> "The time of fortune is but a moment, which soon ends,
> And in it a man strikes or repents."

"But if you spare him, he will not spare you and if you
look on him with the eye of pity, by Allah ! he will not so look
on you, for he is a fool and filled with every sort of craft and
deceit, one who cannot be led, whom, by your father ! kindness
will not move ; imagine yourself, which Allah forbid ! put
in his place, would he pity you or pardon you ? Perish the
thought : this, by Allah ! is impossible.
"But now a chance has come to you, and it is not every
time that generously supplies what is desired and fortune and
time are only found in certain occasions, since the greater part
is sorrow. Therefore beware ; if the chance should slip, you
will fall into distress and repentance will profit nothing, when
your foot has slipped ; but consider what I have said and draw
a proof of this question from what is agreeable to reason and
maintain your lofty eminence, by shedding his blood and
beautify the curtains of your dignity by crushing his and
remember, O Amir, the history of Qabus son of Vashamgir."
Nor did that devil cease to commend to him counsel concerning the killing of the Sultan, saying : "This plan is the
soundest for you and most expedient, as did Bastam, Amir
of the Kurds, to Qara Yusuf, after he seized Sultan Ahmed."
Therefore Qara Iluk abandoned his opinion, being deceived
and beguiled, and slew the Sultan without delay or postponement. Allah be merciful to him ! (But Qara Yusuf slew
Sultan Ahmed son of Sheikh Avis on the tenth day of the
month Rajab in the year 813.* Which history is well known.)

* A.D. 1410.

This Sultan (Burhanuddin) on whom be the mercy of Allah !
was as I said at the beginning a man learned, excellent,
generous, distinguished, a champion of the truth in argument,
subtle in pursuit of truth, genial though of vehement and fearless disposition, not maintaining a large household, possessed
of good character and culture, an elegant poet, prudent, clever,
beneficent, brave, a great-hearted prince, plundering the
world and in turn giving largesse ; he would give a thousand
things, of which he made no count ; he loved learned men,
with whom he would sit ; he admitted fakirs with whom he was
courteous and generous ; he had assigned the second and fifth
days of the week and days of prayer to learned men and those
who knew the Koran, since beside them no one was admitted
to his presence out of that vast multitude and already before
his death he had abandoned his affairs and turned to Allah
Almighty and returned to him ; he wrote several books,
among them " The Investigation of Proofs " and he had a
companion, guarded because of excellence, by origin a Bagdadi,
named Abdul Aziz, who was a marvel of the time and in the
refinements of prose and verse, in Persian and Arabic, the
flower of the age ; whom he stole from Bagdad from Sultan
Ahmed son of Sheikh Avis to whom he was chief companion
and first among men of excellence and wisdom.

The Qazi (Burhanuddin) used to cherish learned men, seeking from every quarter men of culture and poets ; and men of
excellence and culture sought his court from all sides, until
it became a Ka'ba of pilgrimage not of litigation.

And the manner in which he stole him was this : when he
heard of his gifts, he desired him and wished for his society
and therefore asked for him from his master, but Sultan Ahmed
could not find it in his heart to dismiss his favourite and
fearing because of the Qazi's greed and afraid on account of
his great cunning, that he might escape, he watched him and
held him tightly and placed guards upon him, " a succession of
angels to watch over him behind and before."* But the Qazi
sent a clever envoy, who spoke to him secretly and gave generous gifts to him and made splendid promises to him, making
great distinction between the two Sultans in respect of goodness
and badness, as is the difference between the two seas, the
fresh and the salt, and the two parts of the day, evening and
morning.

* From the Koran.

And he gladly assented to this invitation and promised to make his escape after the return of the envoy. Then he escaped, when the heat was intense and Sultan Ahmed was sleeping in the harem and placing his clothes by the bank of the Tigris, he set his foot in the river on the mud, then after going into the water returned and went forward from another place and joined his companions, among whom he hid, like a fieldmouse in its hole. Therefore Sultan Ahmed ordered him to be sought and they followed his tracks, but he was not found; however seeking him with great diligence, until they found his clothes and saw the prints of his feet in the mud, they did not doubt that the waves had carried him away and he had been drowned and so they checked their zeal in searching for him and troubled no one on his account, but a little later that drowned Bagdadi raised his head at Siwas out of his distress, at the court of Qazi Burhanuddin, who drowned him in the sea of his generosity and spread over him the long cloak of his liberality and beneficence and he was held by him in the chief place, greatly esteemed and honoured.

He composed for him an admirable chronicle, using lofty style and incomparable method, in which he set forth his exploits from the beginning almost up to his death and events and his battles and contests and he adorned it with fine figures and elegant descriptions, pleasing metaphors, eloquent diction, the highest eloquence, acute observations and subtle explanations and gave rein to his words. It is found in the Kingdom of Karaman in four volumes, as I was informed by one who dived in this sea, and gathered its pearls, who saw also a charming history of Yamin* Sultan Mahmud son of Sabaktagin, but he said this (of Abdul Aziz) was written in a more beautiful method and overflowed with more copious and sweet waters; for I have not seen them and could not obtain them because of my poverty.

Then the venerable Abdul Aziz after the blaze of this fire migrated to Cairo and ceased not from trouble and was abandoned to the wine of sadness, until the intoxication of desire overcame him and with a cry he fell from a high roof and perished; and died afflicted by the same death as the author of Alsahah. Allah knows.

* A title of honour.

CHAPTER LXI

OF THE EVILS WHICH THE WORLD AND THE FAITH ENDURED AFTER SULTAN BURHANUDDIN WAS SLAIN BY QARA ILUK

BUT when after the murder of Sultan Burhanuddin there was none among his sons who was fit to rule and wield the authority of the Sultanate and kingdom, Qara Iluk returning to Siwas wished to draw men to his side, but they spurned him and pursued him with curses and abuse ; therefore he began to besiege them and vex them, reduce them to distress and attack them ; accordingly they called to aid against him the Tatars, who brought them assistance and some auxiliary troops of them came, but when these were broken and put to flight by Qara Iluk, they called troops to aid, which came again and attacked with fresh onset and filled the valleys and lowlands. But when Qara Iluk was no match for them, he sought their protection and betook himself to Timur, the sea of whose army was raging in Azerbaijan, and kissing his hands attached himself to him and began to call and urge him to invade this country, just as Amir Idaku did with him, and moved him by flattery so that he consented as Barsisa consented to Satan.

CHAPTER LXII

THE PEOPLE OF SIWAS TAKE COUNSEL HOW THEY SHOULD PROCEED AND WHO SHOULD RULE

THEN the people of Siwas and the chief leaders and the wise men took counsel among themselves, to whom they should hand the reins of their kingdom and entrust their country, whether to the Sultan of Egypt or the Chief of Karaman or to Sultan Mughazi Aba Yazid* son of Othman. Then by a sound opinion they agreed concerning Ildarim Bayazid of blessed memory, to whom they sent an envoy and urged him to come to them and while begging his aid they recited to him this verse :

* Bayezid I.

" How many have I seen beautiful! But above all my choice falls on you."

Therefore he went to them forthwith and brought to them armies and troops and strengthened the state and its supports and set over them his eldest son, Amir Suliman, to whom he added five men among the great Amirs, Yakub, son of Auranis, Hamza, son of Bajar, Quh Ali, Mustafa and Davadar, and won over the minds of the chief men ; then when he was on his way to Erzinjan, Tahartan, mentioned above, fled thence and in his flight betook himself to Timur ; and Bayezid, having seized the city of Erzinjan, captured the wealth of Tahartan and his treasures and harem, which he granted to his generals, sons and servants.

And returning with wealth and baggage, he set himself to besiege Stambul.

But Qara Iluk and Tahartan roused the malice of the sleeping Timur, though he was in himself active enough in constant aggression, until he turned to this country and destroyed countries and men without distinction. And they reached Erzinjan bent on slaughter, and starting thence and devastating they halted at Mardin, where Malik Azzahir resisted him because of the hardships, which he had formerly borne, when he had submitted to that traitor ; therefore Timur repented that he had let him go the first time, like a man who shall repent late on the day of resurrection, when penitence and grief will avail him naught ; and this happened in the year 802.* And now discord arose between the armies of Syria and Egypt which spread to the whole host and their counsels were scattered like the Sabæans, and one was inclined to the West, another to the North and that one to the East and they disregarded the affairs of their subjects and cared not for the evils which beset them. I have said in verse :

" A man who neglects his foes, careless of their plots,
Is like one who sleeps deep, while one who wakes watches him."

And

" The robber has no better guide to the man he seeks than the sleep of the watchman."

* A.D. 1399.

Then Tanam, Lord of the Amirs of divinely protected Syria, slew the principal Amirs and the eminent governors, in the month of Ramzan of the same year, and these matters are written in the Books of Annals.

I have said in verse :

" When the lions of the forest submit, the foxes proclaim
    safe going therein."

CHAPTER LXIII

THAT TRAITOR ATTACKS SIWAS AND ITS TERRITORIES

THEN Timur turned the reins of outrage towards the city of Siwas, which was held, as I have said, by Amir Suliman, son of Bayazid, son of Murad, son of Aurkhan, son of Othman, who sent an envoy and informed his father of this danger, and urged him to render him assistance, while he was engaged in besieging Stambul, but he could not help him, because he himself wanted more troops and the places were far apart. Then he collected from his army his bravest men and fortified the city and citadel and prepared for battle and collected guards to sustain a siege and entrusted a part of the walls to each of his generals and Timur sent out spies from his army to confirm his suspicions, but when Amir Suliman saw the fineness of his army, he fled at the sight of it and decided to take himself to his father, stipulating with his generals and troops that they should guard the city for him, while he looked for forces and supplies and they could not but consent and remain behind and they could not follow him ; but he sought safety for himself and escaped in hasty flight.

But Timur came to the city with his swelling floods of men on the seventeenth day of the month Zulhaja in the year 802* and when he had halted with ill-omened foot at Siwas he said : " I will storm this city on the eighteenth day."

Then he set up while besieging it signs of the last judgment and stormed it on the eighteenth day, after doing damage and havoc, on the fifth day of the week and the fifth of the month Muharram in the year 803,† after swearing to the troops of the garrison, that he would not shed their blood and would protect

---

    * A.D. 1399.   † A.D. 1401.

them and preserve their families and goods ; nevertheless when the storming was ended, when he had the soldiers in his power, he cast them all in chains and ordered a crypt under the earth to be dug for them, and ordered them to be hurled alive into those pits, as the leaders were hurled into the well of Badar. And the number of men hurled into those pits was three thousand. Then he loosened the reins of plunder and caused plunder, captivity and havoc.

And this city was among the finest of great cities, set in a beautiful region, remarkable for public buildings, fortifications, famous qualities and tombs of martyrs renowned among all. Its water is pure, its air healthy for the bodily tempers ; its people modest, lovers of magnificence and pomp and devoted to means of ceremony and reverence. And this city borders on the frontiers of three countries, Syria, Azerbaijan and Rum, but is now quite removed and overturned and its people scattered hither and thither, and is utterly destroyed and laid waste.

CHAPTER LXIV

THE THUNDERSTORMS OF THAT EXCEEDING DISASTER POUR FROM THE CLOUDS OF GREED UPON THE TERRITORIES OF SYRIA

THEREFORE when he had stripped Siwas to the flesh and marrow and had emptied it utterly by reaping and grazing, he aimed the arrow of vengeance to destroy the territories of Syria with his army, which might be likened to locusts scattered wide ; truly the stream of blood flowed from the edges of swords and the points of spears ; or they were like scattered fireflies and truly the fireflies burned when its arrows flew ; or like rain poured forth and truly constant rain was exhausted in laying the dust of that army.

There were men of Turan, warriors of Iran, leopards of Turkistan, tigers of Balkhshan, hawks of Dasht and Khata, Mongol vultures, Jata eagles, vipers of Khajend, basilisks of Andakan, reptiles of Khwarizm, wild beasts of Jurjan, eagles of Zaghanian* and hounds of Hisar Shadman, horsemen of Fars, lions of Khorasan, and hyenas of Jil, lions of Mazanderan,

* The name may be connected with Zigani, i.e. gypsy.

wild beasts of the mountains, crocodiles of Rustamdar and Talqan, asps of the tribes of Khuz and Kerman, wolves of Ispahan, wearing shawls, wolves of Rei and Ghazni and Hamadan, elephants of Hind and Sind and Multan, rams of the provinces of Lur, bulls of the high mountains of Ghor, scorpions of Shahrizor* and serpents of Askar Makram† and Jandisabur.

" A people to which, when evil bares its teeth to them,
    Men fly in hordes and one by one."

To these were added hyena-cubs of slaves and whelps of Turkomans and rabble and followers and ravening dogs of base Arabs, and gnats of Persians, and crowds of idolators and profane Magi ; peoples whom no list could cover and no roll include.

In a word, he was a false prophet, and with him Gog and Magog and barren rushing winds. Wherever he turned, victory led him, fortune was his forager, destiny favoured him, fate aided him, the will of Allah Almighty drove him, and the purpose of Allah, the mighty and great, went before him in destroying men and countries.

But when news of him reached the countries of Syria and came to the regions of Egypt, an august command was brought to the Governor of Syria and the other Governors and Lords and Defenders of the Faith and champions of Islam, that they should go to Haleb and assembling a great army against him, make every effort to repel him and conspire to restrain him.

Therefore exerting every effort, the Governor of Syria, Saidi Sudun, with the Governors and army, moved to Haleb in the year 803,‡ in the month Safar.

But Timur came to Bahasna, and laid waste utterly the surrounding country and took the fort after a siege of twenty-three days ; yet by the grace of Allah destruction was turned away from it.

Then he crushed the city of Malatia and destroyed it and razed its hills. Then he advanced to the fort Arrum, whose Governor was Nasari Mahomed, son of Musa, son of Shahri, of whose dealings with him and the vigour with which he opposed him, the story will afterwards be told fully.

And he halted there one day, but did not take Arrum and did not wish to toil in besieging and attacking it, saying: " This

* The capital of a Kurdish kingdom.   † i.e. Samarra in Irak.
‡ A.D. 1401.

city is easier to me than Tabala Ali Hajaj." And when he looked at it from a distance, he said of it, what the fox said, who could not reach the grapes ; but when he truly saw it, he said : " Allah, when he established it, set it apart and chose it for Himself."

Then that cloud came to Aintab, whose Governor was Arkamas, a brave man, who fortified it and prepared himself and himself entered the battle, in which being left alone, then receiving a wound, he fled to Haleb and none was sent to seek him.

CHAPTER LXV

OF THE LETTER AND BASE DESPATCH, WHICH HE SENT TO THE
GOVERNORS AT HALEB,* WHILE HE WAS AT AINTAB

THEN, while he was at Aintab, he sent a messenger to the governors and with him an order, containing various boastings and diverse threats, of which this was the substance : that they should obey his command and abstain from fighting and hostility and that prayers should be said in the name of Mahmud Khan and the name of the Great Amir Timur Kurkan and that they should send to him Atilamish, who was formerly with him, but accused of treachery and arrested, whom the Turkoman† carried off and sent to Egypt to the Sultan.

Now this Atilamish had as wife the daughter of Timur's sister and had come to Syria before these misfortunes befell and meantime, while amid those affairs he at first lay hid, he soon became prominent and he was at first a prisoner in Egypt and subjected to evil and hardship, but later he was distinguished by honours and authority.

And Timur being enraged with him had that for a pretext and occasion of waging war and began to say, turning round in the course of this letter and raging : " that all men were subject to his rule and that the one whom he appointed was Khalif and Imam ; that it was fitting that he himself should be the Ruler, whom all the other kings of the world should serve and obey ; and whence had another beside himself experience of rule and how did the Circassians know the art of

* Aleppo.   † Apparently Qara Yusuf.

government ? ''—with many threats and excess of words and prolixity ; but he knew that it was impossible that they should obey his request, and that he was seeking from them what he would never obtain, but he wished thus to prepare the way for war and to fashion a cause against them for opening the doors of battle. But they did not reply in words, but by action gave him what he desired, and Saidi Sudun, caring naught for his words, ordered the neck of the envoy to be cut off in public ; and they prepared for conflict and equipped themselves for war.

CHAPTER LXVI

HOW THE GOVERNORS IN HALEB PLOTTED AGAINST TIMUR, WHO WAS AT AINTAB

THEN the Governors and Amirs and the heads of the army and chief men took counsel among themselves, how they should meet him and on what plain they should attack him, and one of them said : '' It seems to me best that we should fortify the city and keep watch on its walls, guarding the towers of its orbs, as the heaven is guarded by its angels ; but if round about it we see one of the demons of the enemy, we will send against him falling stars of arrows and stars of catapults, a well-directed flame.''

And another said : '' This is sheer distress and a sign of weakness and defeat ; rather let us surround the city and drive off the enemy as he approaches it ; thus we shall have a wider field of battle and freer space for the struggle.''

Then each of them unfolded what he thought of the matter and they mingled feeble speech with weighty and noble counsel with base ; and Al Malik Al Muid Sheikh Al Khaski, a man of sound judgment, who was then Governor of Turabulus,* said : '' O Council of Allies, lions of war and warlike knights ! you should know that your business is arduous, since your enemy is an intractable villain, a prodigy of disaster and a dangerous man, his army strong ; his plans forceful and his ravages spread far and wide ; therefore beware of him and use your prudence to repel him skilfully, for prudent counsel can effect

* Tripoli.

more than the sharpest sword. The consultation of wise men is the kindler of prudence and the disputation of learned men leads to clear vision. This sea cannot carry a continent.

" His army is numerous like rain and atoms; and though it is like a cloud that has burst, yet it is hidden, being a foreign army in our country.

" I therefore think it best to fortify the city on all sides and assembling outside on one flank, we should all watch him from an ambush and digging trenches round us, make walls of standards and flashing weapons and send letters flying to the Arabs, Kurds, Turkomans and peoples of countries, that they may attack him from all sides and that all the infantry and cavalry may rush upon him, slaying, destroying, plundering and spoiling ; but if he holds out (but how could that happen ?) he will certainly be in a sad state ; if he comes to us, we will receive him with the arms of spears and the hands of shields and fingers of arrows ; but if he goes back, which is most to be desired, he will go back with his purpose defeated, and we shall have honour and respect from our Sultan ; but if his might presses us, truly (praise to Allah) we also have might and in our might deliverance. And at all events we ought to delay him and beware of his army ; perchance Allah will give victory or some command from Himself."

This plan, which in truth was the best, was formerly used by that lion, Shah Mansur.

But Tamardash, the Governor of the city, said : " These opinions are weak and these plans feeble ; nay, it is better to fight than to delay and to descend into this battlefield before the chance be lost ; and the engagement should be in a place, where it is impossible to leave the battle and there is room everywhere for fighting ; this is a bird in a cage and a spoil taken in hunting ; therefore seize the opportunity, join battle with him and anticipate him with blow of lance and sword, lest he take us for cowards and smell from our idleness the odour of victory. Therefore collect your goods and hasten and do not dispute among yourselves or behave like cowards but be alert, constant and patient ; for you are (praise to Allah) men of courage, vigorous and brave; and each of you is expert in the art of war and excels therein and is a tower in knowledge of shedding the blood of the enemy and has in it sufficiency and method and completion, of which others know only the elements and each of you is a full treasury and a perfect collection and a defence of all Islam ; the law of your swords tends to the wounding of heads and is in expression sound and perfect and your spears fix their teeth in the breastplates of all that do violence with perfect and sound inflection.

" But if we rout him, we shall achieve our aim and Allah will protect the faithful from slaughter and by the favour of Allah we shall have defended the armies of Egypt from harm ; that will be our highest honour and add strength to our valour in victory and will heat and refine the air of our victory ; and to his weeping eye bring tears and harm.

" But if the affair happens otherwise—which Allah forbid ! —the fault will not be ours, since we shall have exerted every effort and furnished ourselves a just excuse and the Lord will exact our revenge and keep alive our fame.

" Therefore commit yourselves to Allah the Great and Mighty and prepare to meet these wicked men and when you meet their attack, do not turn your backs."

And Tamardash ceased not to press on them this futile counsel, until they agreed to it and planned to advance, since he was the lord of the city, and in his words was confidence ; but Tamardash had spoken against all, since secretly he was working with Timur, which was his habit, his nature being disposed to cunning : and he was like a blind sheep or a woman confounded and jealous,* when the two armies met, and he could scarce stand firm in either of them because of fear and cunning, but crossed now this way, now that, though he was a figure without meaning and a voice without sense ; but Timur relied on him and entrusted business to him, as did the armies of Syria and the hosts of Islam.

Then they fortified the city and shut its gates, blocked up its highways and large open spaces and placed soldiers on guard in all the wards and cross-roads, but they opened the gates on the side of his attack, that is the gates called Bab Al Nasar, Bab Al Farj and Bab Al Qanat.

* Or fickle.

CHAPTER LXVII

HOW HE POURED THUNDERS OR SWORDS AND BREASTPLATES
UPON THE ARMIES OF SYRIA, WHEN HE REACHED HALEB

THEN Timur moved his troops and arrived on the seventh day at Haleb from Aintab and halted with that army, on the ninth day of the first month Rabia, the fifth day of the week; and from that army a band of about two thousand advanced to battle, whom about three hundred of the lions of Syria encountered, who broke them with broad swords and scattered them with spears and dispersed and repelled and split them and put them to flight.

Then in the morning of the day of prayer about five thousand of the army of Timur advanced to the field of battle, and were met by another band in squadrons and in scattered order, and when their wings engaged, between the two hosts the fingers of spears were mingled and they pressed each against the other and charged and raged and the spears ceased not, like pens, to draw lines on the tablets of men's breasts and the edges of swords to cut the points of the pens and the arrows, like lancets, to cut off foul sores and the earth to groan under the weight of mountains of slain, until the depth of night had drawn a great fog of darkness and dust, and they withdrew; and Allah granted victory to whom He wished, and made two rivers of the blood of the enemy flow into the river Qoiq, only two men being lost of the armies of Islam.

Then on the morning of the Sabbath day, the eleventh, the hosts of Syria and the armies of Islam and of the Sultan drew up in perfect order, with complete equipment, excellent horses, straight spears and splendid banners. And nothing was wanting to those stalwart soldiers but a particle of divine help and aid, and they advanced against him to force him back and drive him off; and his army went forward to meet them, under the auspices of favourable fortune, with fate his minister and destiny aiding him, with renowned troops and armies loyal and victorious, and in front the lords and the elephants of war.

And now he hid the disaster which he was planning for them, and when night had come on, drew up his armies, which he stretched around them and sent skirmishers against them and opposed the vanguard to them and kept them engaged with his front ranks, while the rest went round them and so came upon them from the rear and the right and the left.

Then he went over them like a razor over hair and ran like locusts over a green crop.

This engagement occurred near the village of Hylan. And when matters were confused and disturbed and the tumult and violence of battle was raging, lions charging against each other and rams butting each the other, the right wing, which Tamardash was leading, took to flight, whereby the army was broken and stunned and because of the shock fear seized brave men and consternation and anguish conquered them and they scarcely held firm for one hour of the day, then turned their backs, which were scored with his spears and they attacked them from the front continuously, while from the rear his army harassed them, as I have said :

" We made their backs in the battle like faces, on which we carved mouths, eyes and brows."

Therefore they made for the city towards the open gate, torn and wounded, while they were being cleft by swords and pierced by spears, so that swamps flowed with their blood and all the eagles and beasts of prey fed freely on their remaining flesh. But as soon as in their rout they reached the gate of the city, they hurled themselves into it with one rush and crowded together and without ceasing one trod down another, until the upper threshold of the gate was levelled with the ground and the gates were so blocked with dead men, that nothing at all could enter through them ; therefore they scattered through the countries and dispersed in the deserts and mountains.

And the foreign slaves breaking the Antioch gate, went out thereby, making for Syria, and some of them reached Damascus in wretched state and their foul semblance told the manner of this battle.

But the governors climbed to the fort of Haleb, and there fortified themselves and the earth though wide became narrow for them. Therefore seeking security, they committed themselves to him, using Tamardash as mediator and now all despaired of their lives.

Then he advanced at his own ease, in keeping with his dignity, majesty and tranquillity, and entered Haleb, and took therein what he wished and seized men and plunder.

And when the Governors had surrendered to him, he laid hands on Saidi Sudun and Shaikh Ali Al Khaski; but clad Tamardash with a mantle; he also laid hands on Tunbagha Othmani, the Governor of Safad, and Umar, son of Tahan, Governor of Gaza, all of whom he put in chains and strove to seize wealth and collect goods and booty; and men's hearts were filled with thoughts of terror of him and the sparks of his tyranny were scattered through the world and he was not content to have destroyed men but even built towers of skulls. The reason of this was that Timur was reminded of the fate of his kinsman Baridi, whom he had sent as envoy to Haleb, but whom the Governor of Syria had beheaded and plundered; he therefore wished to avenge his kinsman at the cost of the people of Haleb and they granted his desire and let him choose from themselves those with whom he would do as he wished; therefore slaying many of them, he built several towers of their skulls.

CHAPTER LXVIII

THIS DISASTER IS MORE FULLY SET FORTH FROM THOSE THINGS WHICH I HAVE TAKEN FROM THE CHRONICLE OF IBN AL SHAHANA

HE said: "Al Hafiz Al Khwarizmi related to me that in the roll of Timur's armies were written 800,000 names; and that Timur attacked the fort of the Muslims, whose Governor was Al Nasari Mahomed son of Musa son of Shahari, who resisted him and repeatedly made sallies." Then he said in his own words:

"He gave much trouble to the hosts of Tamarlang and to his scouts, while he was besieging Bahansa, and slew a multitude of them and sent their heads to Haleb; and overthrew with shameful defeat a tuman* which was sent against him, so that the most of them threw themselves into the Euphrates, and Tamarlang sent a letter to him, in which he used these words:

"'I went forth from the distant country of Samarkand and none stood against me and the other kings of countries came over to me; and you send men to harass my followers and

* Ten thousand.

slay any that they can seize. But now we are leading our armies against you. If therefore you care for yourself and your subjects, come over to us, that you may experience pity and clemency, which we shall not proffer any further; if not, we shall come upon you and lay waste your city; and lo, Allah Almighty said that kings, when they have entered a city, lay it waste and bring low the most powerful of its people; and thus they will do. Therefore prepare for that which will befall you, if you refuse to side with me.'

" But he held the envoy and threw him in chains and cared nothing for Tamarlang's words. Then the first line of his army came against him, and he went forth against it and slew and crushed them.

" And on the second day of the week when Tamarlang came to the fort of the Muslims, he went forth against him and fought fiercely with him and when the battle was at its height, Tamarlang discovered in it his resolute courage and ceased to wage war with him and strove to deceive him by pretence and flattery and sought peace from him and that he should send him horses and supplies, because of his dignity, but he did not suffer himself to be bewitched by him; and when he sank to the point of asking only one slave from him, he did not gain even this, but withdrew foiled; then he attacked Tamarlang's rear and slew and plundered and took prisoners and that after leaving open the gate of his fort, which he did not shut even for one day. And the matter is described in these verses:

" ' This Amir, whose virtues are plain, is a lion of war, whose
        praises are celebrated throughout the world.
    Often Tamarlang retreated, his vanguard broken by him
        and his rear destroyed.'

" Now Ali Nasari had gained this success above other lords and governors of citadels because of his knowledge and religion, and sincerity and piety and because he was of the holy line of Umar, on whom be the favour of Allah !

" But on the fifth day of the week, the ninth of the first Rabia, Tamarlang attacked Haleb, the governor of which was Al Muqar Al Saifi Tamardash and he had armies of the cities of Syria, the army of Damascus with its Governor Saidi Sudun and the army of Turabulus with its Governor Al Muqar Al Saifi Sheikh Al Khaski and the army of Hama with its Governor Al Muqar Al Saifi Daqmaq and the army of Safad and others, and their counsels conflicted, one advising : ' Enter the city and fight from the walls,' another : ' Pitch a camp in tents outside the city.' And when Al Muqar Al Saifi saw their conflict, he let the people of Haleb leave the city empty and betake themselves where they wished ; and this indeed was the best counsel, but they did not agree to it and pitched tents outside the city towards the enemy.

" And when Tamarlang's envoy had come, the Governor of Damascus ordered him to be slain and a slight skirmish happened on the day of prayer between the wings of the armies.

" But on the Sabbath, the eleventh day of the first Rabia, when Tamarlang led out his armies and his people against the enemy, the Muslims retreated towards the city and crowded in the gates and many of them met their death, the enemy slaying them from behind and making prisoners. And Tamarlang took Haleb by force with the sword, but the Governors of the kingdom and the nobles climbed to the fort, in which the people of Haleb had hidden most of their goods.

" And on the third day of the week the fourteenth of the first month Rabia, after giving a promise of safety and an oath he took the fort ; nevertheless the oath was not kept ; and on the next day he climbed the fort and at the close of day summoned its learned men and judges ; and we appeared before him and after he had made us stand a little while, he ordered us to sit and summoned his own learned men and said to the chief of them, whom he had with him, namely Maulvi Abdul Jabar son of Ulama Namanuddin Hanifi, whose father was among the famous Ulamas of Samarkand : ' Tell them that I wish to put a question to them, concerning which I have asked the Ulamas of Samarkand, Bokhara, Herat and all the cities which I have taken, but they have not found the right answer ; but do not be like them, and let none reply to me except your most learned and most eminent man, who knows rightly what he says, for I am intimate with learned men, to whom I am greatly devoted and in whose company I delight and I have the ancient zeal for learning.' And we had already learnt about him, that he troubled learned men by putting a certain question, which he used as a reason to put them to death or torture ; and Qazi Sharafuddin Musa Ansari, the Shafeite, said concerning me* : ' This is our Sheikh and the professor and mufti of these countries—ask him by Allah the Helper ! ' Presently

* That is Ibn Shahana.

Abdul Jabar said to me : ' Our Sultan asks : " Yesterday when some of our men and yours were slain, who were the martyrs, our slain or yours ? " Then everyone was silent because of fear and we said to ourselves : ' This is the very thing, which we have heard of his harassment.' Howbeit Allah, while all kept silence, opened to me a reply ready and apt, and I said : ' This same question was put to our master, the Prophet of Allah, on whom be the favour of Allah and peace ! to which he replied and I reply the same as our master, the Prophet of Allah, on whom be the favour of Allah and peace ! ' My friend, Qazi Sharafuddin Musa Ausari, said to me after this misfortune had been averted : ' By Allah the Great ! When you said this question was put to the Prophet of Allah, on whom be peace ! And he gave a reply to it, and I shall reply accordingly, truly this doctor of ours has lost his reason, for it will not be possible to reply to this question in this place ; ' and something of this sort came to the mind of Abdul Jabar and Tamarlang turned his ear and eye towards me and said to Abdul Jabar, gibing at my speech : ' How was this question put to the Prophet of Allah, on whom be the favour of Allah and peace ! And how did he reply ? '

"I said : 'An Arab came to the prophet of Allah, on whom be the favour of Allah and peace ! and said : " O Prophet of Allah ! One man fights to defend his own, another to show his courage, another to display his power ; which of us will be in the way of Allah ? " And the Prophet of Allah on whom be the favour of Allah and peace !—replied : " He who fights to make strong the word of Allah, which is the highest thing, is a martyr." '

" Then Tamarlang said : ' Good ! Good ! '

" Also Abdul Jabar said : ' How excellently you have spoken ! '

" And the gate of familiarity being opened, Tamarlang said : ' I am half a man and yet I have taken such and such countries ' and he numbered all the kingdoms of Persia and Irak and Hind and all the countries of the Tatars.

" Then I said : ' Give thanks for this fortune by sparing these Imams and slay none.' And he said : ' By Allah ! I slay no one of set purpose, but you bring death on yourselves ; but I, by Allah ! will slay none of you and you will be secure concerning your lives and goods.'

" And he repeatedly put fresh questions, to which we

replied and with eagerness all those present skilled in the law were most ready to reply, and thought they were in a college ; but Qazi Sharafuddin restrained them, saying to them : ' By Allah ! Be silent, that this man may reply, for he knows what he says.'

" And the last question of Tamarlang was : 'What do you say concerning Ali and Muavia and Yazid ? '*

" Then Qazi Sharafuddin, who was at my side, whispered to me : ' You should know how to reply to him, for he is a Shia.'

" Now I had not fully heard his words, when forthwith Qazi Alamuddin Qafsi Al Maliki replied to him, saying : that each of them fought for the faith, on account of which saying Tamarlang seized with violent anger replied : ' Ali was the right successor, Muavia an usurper and Yazid wicked ; but you men of Haleb join with the people of Damascus, who being followers of Yazid, slew Husein.'

" Then I began to soothe him and excuse Al Maliki, because he gave a reply, which he found in a book, not discerning its meaning ; and he almost returned to his former calm.

" Then to Abdul Jabar, who asked about me and Qazi Sharafuddin, he said concerning me : ' This is an excellent doctor ' and concerning Sharafuddin, ' This man is a clear speaker.'

" Then Tamarlang asked me about my age; ' I was born,' I replied, ' in the year 749 and have now reached fifty-four years.'

" Then he said to Qazi Sharafuddin : ' And how old are you ? '

" And he replied : ' I am about one year older than he.'

" ' Therefore,' said Tamarlang, ' You are of the age of my sons ; but I have now reached the age of seventy-five.'†

" Then it was the time of evening prayer, which was said, Abdul Jabar leading us as Imam, and Tamarlang prayed standing at my side, prostrating himself and bowing his head. Then we departed.

" On the next day he broke faith with all, who were in the fort and took all the goods, furniture and utensils therein

* This refers to the controversy concerning the Khalifate. The Shias regard Hasan and Husein, sons of Ali, as the true Khalifs after Ali. The Sunnis recognize Muavia (Moawiya) and his son Yazid as Khalifs. Hasan resigned his claim. Husein resisted Yazid but was defeated and killed.
† In fact his age was about 65.

of which the number cannot be reckoned.   A certain scribe of his told me that in no city did he gain so much booty as in this fort ; and most of the Muslims were subjected to various tortures, whom they kept in the fort, some bound with fetters and chains, some shut in prison or in their own houses.

" At length, leaving the fort, Tamarlang stayed in the house of the Governor and he gave a banquet in the manner of the Moghals, all the rulers and governors serving him, to whom he ordered goblets of wine to be carried; but the Muslims were wretchedly afflicted, despoiled, slain and thrown in chains, their mosques, colleges and houses destroyed, burned and laid waste and overturned up to the end of the first month of Rabia.

" And Tamarlang summoned me and my friend Qazi Sharafuddin and repeated the question concerning Ali and Muavia ; and I replied to him.

" ' Without doubt right is with Ali ; and Muavia is not among the Khalifs, for it is known concerning the Prophet of Allah—on whom be the favour of Allah and peace !—that he said : " The succession of Khalifs will last for thirty years after me."   And these years ended with Ali.'

" Then Tamarlang said : ' Say, Ali is the true Khalif, and Muavia is an usurper.'

" I replied : ' The author of the Hidaya said : that it was permitted that Qazis be appointed even by unjust rulers, for truly many of the friends and followers (of Mahomed) were appointed Qazis by Muavia and the right was with Ali in succession.'

" And delighted with this, he called together the Amirs, whom he had chosen to leave at Haleb and said : ' Both these men will be your guests at Haleb and do you treat them well and their followers and friends and those who belong to them ; let none harm them ; fix pay for them and do not keep them in the fort, but set their place in the college, that is the college of the Sultan, which is opposite the fort.'

" They did accordingly what he had bade them, except that they did not let us out of the fort, and he among them who had been appointed chief Governor of Haleb, namely Amir Musa Bin Haji Taghai, said to us : ' I fear for you, but I have marked this in Tamarlang's habit that when he orders any evil, he does it speedily and there is no turning therefrom, but when he orders anything good, he entrusts that business to another.'

" And on the first day of the second month Rabia, he left the city, making for Damascus and on the second day he summoned the learned men of the city and we went to him in the evening, and the Muslims were in perplexity and their heads were being cut off ; we said therefore ' what is the news ?' and they said that Tamarlang had demanded from his army heads of Muslims according to the habit which he used to follow in the cities which he conquered ; but when we went to him, there came to us one of his learned men, named Maulvi Umar, and we asked him why he was summoning us ; and he said : ' He wishes to consult you about the slaying of the Governor of Damascus, who put to death his envoy.'

" Then I said, ' These heads of Muslims are being cut off and brought to him, without his taking counsel, though he swore that he would kill none of our men except in battle.'

" And when Umar had returned to him, we saw him eating of boiled meat which was placed before him in a dish and he spoke a short time with him ; then someone brought to us a piece of that meat, which we had not eaten, when a din arose and Tamarlang shouted in a loud voice, one running this way, another that way. And the Amir came to us, excusing what had been done and saying: ' Our Sultan did not order heads of Muslims to be brought, but wished only, that the heads of the slain should be cut off to raise a tower thereof in his honour according to his custom. But his purpose was understood differently from what he wished. But he ordered that you should be let go, and so go where you will.'

" Then Tamarlang rode forthwith and marched towards Damascus and we returned to the fort seeing that it was best to remain therein.

And Amir Musa (to whom may Allah show favour !) began to favour us and receive our requests and look after our affairs, so long as he remained at Haleb and in its fort.

" And news was brought to us, that the Sultan of the Muslims, Al Malik Al Nasir Faraj,* had come to Damascus and driven Tamarlang to flight, but soon the opposite was announced, until at length it was clearly known concerning the return of the Sultan to Egypt, after fighting a great battle with Tamarlang, in which Tamarlang was almost defeated and put to flight by him, but one of his† generals was treacherous to

---

* Sultan of Egypt, son and successor of Barkuk.
† That is, the Sultan's.

him, and for that cause he withdrew to secure himself.

" Then Tamarlang entered Damascus, which he plundered and burned and dealt worse with it than with Haleb. But he did not enter Turabulus, but wealth therefrom was offered to him. And he did not cross Palestine, but turned towards Haleb returning, seeking his own country.

" And on the seventeenth of Shaban in the same year Tamarlang, returning from Syria, reached the high mountains of Haleb, but he did not enter, but ordered those who held it for him to lay waste and burn the city, which they did, and Amir Azuddin, who was among his great Amirs, sent for me and said : ' The Amir ordered to let go you and yours ; therefore ask, whom you wish, even many, that I may go with you to the tomb of Husein, and remain with you, until none is left of our soldiers ' ; Qazi Sharafuddin did not leave me ; then we sent for the other Qazis, and with us gathered about two thousand Muslims and we made our way to the tomb of Husein, with that same man as companion, and halting there we saw the fire, with which the whole city blazed, and after three days no one was left in it and when we returned to it, we saw no one therein ; therefore seized with grief, we could not remain there because of the stink and solitude, or, for the same reason, walk through the streets.

" ' As if between Al Hajun and Al Safa there were no human creature.

" And none holding nightly converse in Mecca.'

" And he took the governors of the cities of Syria with him in chains, of whom one after another escaped ; but Sudun died of a disease of the stomach, while prisoner in his hands in the tower Yalbagha. And Tankari Wardi remained in the governorship of Damascus. Allah knows."

This is what I have copied from the words of Ibn Shahana, as I found it.

(End of Volume I)

VOLUME II

CHAPTER I

HOW THE TROUBLOUS NEWS WAS BROUGHT AND ISTANBUGHA
ALDAWADAR AND ABDUL QASAR CAME TO DAMASCUS

THERE came from Haleb, Istanbugha Aldawadar and Al Fatah Al Mahir, whose surname was Abdul Qasar, who said : " O Assembly of Muslims, to fly from evil which cannot be overcome is among the counsels of the prophets ; let him who can fly seek a way of safety and let him who can, gird his loins and not stay a night in Damascus or deceive himself, for rumour is nothing compared with what we have ourselves seen."

Then opinions were divided and desires clashed and the affairs of men flowed violently and the assembly was divided according to their wont. Some accepted the advice and arranged their affairs and fled : but some were angry and grinding their teeth bared them against Istanbugha and Abdul Qasar and wished to stone these advisers and give them the cup of death to drink, saying, " Truly you intend by this advice only to divide men and scatter them from their homes and uproot them and divide their speech and rend their skin, though there is nothing to fear and the Sultan (thanks be to Allah !) is approaching ; and the Governors in Haleb were few and besides lacked prudence and cunning against him ; some beside secretly nursed treachery and the rest lacked zeal in mutual confidence and defence ; and they lost their heads and hence in this question did not conceive the argument rightly. But the armies of Egypt are large and excellently equipped with every requirement, and will give Muslims freedom after distress."

But they said, " We, after enduring every sort of hardship from his wickedness, escaped and we declare nothing but what we know well and each of us has publicly shown his due zeal and by Allah ! in warning Muslims has shown himself a faithful adviser ; and now we have advised you, that you might be happy, but you do not love faithful advisers."

And the affairs of men remained in discord, confusion, division, conflict and altercation ; some betook themselves to the Holy Land, some to Egypt ; others clung to the edges of inaccessible rocks ; others fortified themselves in hidden and distant places.

CHAPTER II

HOW SULTAN AL MALIK AL NASIR SET FORTH FROM CAIRO WITH TROOPS AND ARMIES OF ISLAM

THEN the Sultan moved without delay and with an army perfectly equipped marched into Syria ; and when this became known to men, their fear was calmed and their consternation ceased, and most of those who had departed, returned and their distress and anxiety was ended. None the less the more prudent and those who excelled in resolution and were of sound judgment, did not rate highly the coming of the Sultan, but sought their own safety, awaiting what new thing time would bring forth and it was as though the fingers of whirling time had written on the mirror of the heart the song which the poet recited :

" Truly the days are brothers and the nights all sisters ;
Therefore seek not from day or night aught but what has happened in the years before."

And I have said :
" If the future is hidden, yet you should guess it from the past."

SECTION

Then Timur, after completing the business of Haleb, collected baggage and the goods and booty, which he had taken there, which he placed in the fort and entrusted to an Amir that had valour and courage, namely Amir Musa son of Taghani, a resolute and wise man, and set out with that swelling sea of troops on the tenth of the second month Rabia to Syria and reached Hama, plundering whatever came to his hand, but he cared little about booty and prisoners and about advancing quickly, but marched slowly, for he was devising cunning.

STORY

I saw on a journey to the countries of Rum, in the beginning of the first month Rabia in the year 839, when we came to Hama, in its famous mosque on the east side over the south wall, a Persian inscription in marble, which I have translated.

" The reason for inscribing this memorial is this :

Allah Almighty opened to us the gate of countries and kingdoms, so that our conquest of kingdoms reached to Irak and Bagdad. But we spared the Sultan of Egypt, then sent to him a letter and envoys with various precious gifts and presents, but he slew our envoys without cause, though our purpose was to foster good will by these means between the two courts and to strengthen mutual friendship. Then a little afterwards certain Turkomans took some of our men, whom they sent to Barkuk, Sultan of Egypt, who committed them to prison and treated them ill ; therefore it was necessary that we should turn to snatch our men from the hands of our enemies, wherefore it happened that we pitched our camp at Hama on the twentieth of the second month Rabia in the year 803.*

Then he moved to Hamas,† but did not labour in wasting and desolating it, but gave it to Saidi Khalid, son of Valid, to whom Allah be merciful ! I have written on the spur of the moment :

" In life and death seek no neighbours unless good men.
  Have you not seen that Hamas with its citizens escaped
      safe from the raging seas of disaster ?
  Because they were neighbours of Khalid ; for he who is
      neighbour of the righteous shall not perish."

And there went out to him a singular man, by name Omar, son of Ravas, who gained his good will, offering him precious gifts, and he set him over the city and leaned upon him and appointed to rule that country a chief, by name Shamsuddin,

* A.D. 1401. † Homs.

son of Hadad, and proclaimed security to men far and near, and they accordingly carried on trade there and did not hesitate to enjoy the fruit of this security and peace.

Then the governor of Syria was seized with disease in his* company, and died in the tower Yalbagha, but the governor of Turabalas fled from him and looking to his own safety arrived at his own city, and remained in governorship of it.

Then Timur blazed and flamed with anger and the heat of his wrath was kindled and he slew all those to whom he had entrusted him for custody and gave them over to the pains of hell, sixteen in number.

But Tamardash, who was soothing him with flattery and making pretences, fled from him to the town Qara, but Alauddin Tunbagha Othmani, governor of Safad, and Zainuddin, governor of Gaza, and the rest remained with him in bondage. Then abandoning delay, he continued his march until he pitched his camp at Baalbeg and its people went out to him and entered his presence and threw themselves at his feet, begging peace; but taking no account of this request, he sent against them ravening beasts of plunder and slaughter.

And the Sultan approached. Then he moved camp, making that raging sea and rapid flood and boiling deluge flow until it threatened Damascus from the tower Siar.

And there came the armies of Egypt and forces of Islam, which filled the plains and made the earth glitter and shine; the arrows of that army were ready to split the kernel of the heart with the date-stone of dissension and the lightning of its swords smote the curled hair of every knave and the points of spears rent the solid sky of souls from the earth of bodies; and they assailed their assailants and pressed their hosts and arrayed the right wing and the left and formed the van and rearguard and drew up the centre and flanks and filled every space.

Then they advanced with squadrons compact, troops in array, columns in order, ranks of kindred and kindred in ranks and horses trained for leaping from and camels greedy to devour meat and in every host strong lions and old vultures.

I have said:

" That mighty army stood, like a mountain, in anger.
    As tho' it were a sea in the midst of forests of spears;

---

* Timur's.

Two seas in whose waves a lion plays with death, not
   seeking longer life :
Whoever saw its face and form before the battle and in
   the battle, would fall with fear.
When it advances, the sky revolving falls on the earth ;
   or if it charges, the earth is blocked in dust."

And they threw on their shoulders the bows of death and
hung from their necks swords of destruction and set thirsting
spears between legs and stirrups and they stood firm where
they sprang as though born from the backs of horses. I have
written :

" As tho' the air were adorned with a blue robe inwoven
   with gold, and its web were a garb of spears :
And if thick dust poured night thereon, its gleaming
   swords would show you the splendour of gold ;
And as tho' its arrows were stars, which smote opposing
   demons in battle."

Nor did the hosts of these waves cease to break on this
highway and the billows of this agitated sea to smite together
beneath the dust, each proclaiming his known valour (and
there is none of us but has his known place), and the demons of
war reached the tower Yalbagha, on the eleventh day of the
second month Rabia in the year 803* of the Hijrat, where all
the armies pitched camps on the right and left flank, the
armies and Amirs of Islam living in houses and huts.

And the forces of the Tatars occupied Daria and Haula and
the surrounding places on the west of Damascus. Some
baggage of the Sultan was placed in the city and the fort and
city were defended by arms and men. Then each army took
heed for itself and drew up for engagement and battle ; and
making trenches, each army made difficult its approaches
against the other and they began to engage and to advance
against each other and attack.

Then the Sultan ordered his armies to advance from the
city ; therefore, the chief men went forth from the city and
collected about their Sultan in battle. But the small children
in a loud voice prayed to the Almighty and all night ardently
cried in their trouble : " O Allah, O Merciful, help our Lord
the Sultan ! " and men in confusion and distress sought from

* A.D. 1401.

Heaven aid and blessings and day and night implored aid, saying, " O faithful warriors, be constant on the walls ! " And at that time there fell a martyr among the chief men of the city, the chief Qazi Burhanuddin Tadaki Maliki, Judge of Syria, and likewise the hand of the chief Qazi Sharafuddin Isa Maliki was maimed by the blow of a sword and they brought those of the enemy whom they captured and slew them and constantly they brought from them booty, either cattle or goods, which they showed publicly.

CHAPTER III

OF THE BATTLE THAT BEFELL AND THE BREAKING OF THE LINE, THO' NOT WITHOUT PROFIT

THEN one day about ten thousand of those barbarians advanced to the field of battle, and there confronted them of the armies of Syria about five hundred men, and the Amir Alsanbai ordered about three hundred to follow after them.

VERSES

" Lions, when they charge ; stags, when they stand erect ; mountains when they stand firm ; seas, when they advance ;
Suns, when they shine ; moons, when they appear ; winds, when they are roused ; clouds, when they move ;
Hawks, when they swoop ; leopards, when they leap ; thunders, when they crash ; thunderbolts, when they fall."

Each held a quivering spear, at whose shaking the fairest forms would fall, and a sharp sword whose glance was a sign of shedding of blood and a bow like his eyebrow and arrows like his eyes well directed and a shield light to handle with which when he was covered, you would see the moon over the sun, and above him a helmet, which seemed fashioned from the brightness of his cheeks or carved out of his flashing glance ; when the eye looked on it, it was smitten, so that the splendour of its lightning almost snatched away the sight ; and garments like the wearer, for the form of the outer garments was soft silk, like his skin ; but within it was iron like his heart in its hardness.

And they had mounted stallions of choice breed, and the crescents of those hosts with their spears gleaming at the points were like brides shining beneath tapers and they made for the field of battle and met in a valley behind the tower Yalbagha.

SECTION

Now when these lions saw those wolves and dogs, they were like the faithful seeing the hosts of confederates,* and they gave blows strong and weak, and said : " This is what Allah and His Prophet promised us." But the enemy surrounded them because of greater numbers and to cut these throats they drew around a drawn-out circle and becoming like a stake in the midst of this circle they strove to smite and cleave the circle by vehement combat. And above all they sought in that conflict to cut off heads, wound hearts and cut off hands ; and with long spears they smote their wisdom and shattered their semblance with great javelins and made havoc with broad swords among their hosts and pierced their mailed warriors with swift arrows ; then they cleft them, crushed, transfixed, scattered, separated, broke, routed, twisted, maimed and mutilated them. And they drove their front ranks upon the rear and shut off their way of escape and captured some of them, halved, maimed, mutilated, diminished, weakened and overthrown.

And the said Alsanbai returned, and they were cut by his piercing sword and their heavy and light and mail-clad troops were cloven by his continuously falling blows, he walking proudly because of victory and trailing the cloak of consummate pride, after he had made safe from ruin the tent of their harmonious circle and rescued its pole and frame from collapse and destruction.

* Who besieged Medina.

CHAPTER IV

OF THE DECEIT AND FRAUD PRACTISED BY SULTAN HUSSEIN,
SON OF THE SISTER OF TIMUR

THEN Sultan Hussein, son of the sister of Timur, showed his hidden purpose and came to the Sultan (of Egypt) and plotted secret things. And he was compounded of courage, levity and folly. And at his approach overcome with joy, they predicted victory and rejoicing for themselves ; and on his head was abundant hair which they cut off and they clothed him in a robe of honour and showed him in their array.

SECTION

Then Timur announced that he had become weary and weak and retired a little and moved back and displayed fear, all which was part of his cunning and like a hunter's net ; and the cause of this was that he had been informed that dissension had arisen among the armies of Egypt and that they were contemplating flight, whereby they might escape. Therefore he showed fear and spread a rumour that he was departing, so that he might recall them to steadfastness and draw them back from flight ; but after they clove to the counsel of flight, no steadfastness or calm came to them.

CHAPTER V

OF THE JEALOUSY AND DISCORD WHICH AROSE AMONG THE
ARMIES OF THE MUSLIMS

THE chief commander of the armies and protector of the Sultan, Al Malik Al Nasir, was the great Amir Bashbeg and in his hand was great and small. There were indeed abundant troops and an army seeming great in number, but each man behaved as commander and nothing among them was thought little except the head. Hence their counsels were divided, their purposes clashed and their harmony changed to discord, each persisting in his opinion as though he were a pillar, while carping at and reviling the opinions of others. And then became plain the signs of Allah the Merciful in the diversity of tongues and colours* and they fed the flock like the wolf and hyena and let loose to devour the lean thereof a ravening leopard and a lion, and in this discord the small imitated the great, the base the high, the first the last, and it befell them, as the poet said :

" On a certain day my herd was scattered and I said against it,
   O Lord ! Send against it a wolf and a hyena."

And their leaders made for Alqahira (Cairo), each abandoning his strength and his ally and they proved the truth of Timur when he denied that they knew how to rule and administer a state.

SECTION

And when those who were left knew that the others had gone, they had no choice but to gird themselves and follow them under the wing of night, but those among them who stayed behind or were overcome by drowsiness or sleep, fell into the net and perished headlong. But the citizens stood day and night on the walls, all glad and cheerful, convinced that now at last they were to be freed by the help of the Sultan ; but when one night they had climbed to a certain high place, lo ! they saw the Sultan's camp full of fires, no one understanding what was afoot, except that the world was full of evil and sparks ; but in the morning they saw the camp quite empty and none left in the tower Yalbagha to kindle a fire.

Therefore they ceased their clamour and stayed their movements and began to lose heart, and while they whispered among themselves, trouble flowed and raged and some said, " The Sultan has fled " ; whereby their strength was broken and they were assured of the misery which threatened them and their anguish grew, their fears increased, links were severed, various torments became common to all, their intelligence was crushed like their hearts and commands and counsels were confused.

---

* From the Koran, Sura xxx, 21. " And among His signs are the creation of the heavens and of the earth, and your variety of tongues and colour."

SECTION

Then Timur, after he had given thanks to his Lord, moved camp and occupied the tower, where he rested and slept soundly and announced as I have said, " Praise to Allah ! we have gained what we wished ; the enemy has turned his back and our prayers have been answered."

Then in his prudence he made trenches and distributed his infantry and cavalry on every side and sent men to pursue the fugitives from the rear and when anyone from the army was brought to him, he ordered him to be thrown between the feet of those elephants, who trampled on him in that desert, as beasts will trample on the day of resurrection on those who refused to give alms.

SECTION

But as for the Sultan, no one could injure him, since he rose like a cloud to a higher place and withdrew with the speed of a swift serpent and betook himself to the valley Al Tim. Then Timur's devils scattered over the earth, which they filled far and wide, their spies infested the country on every side and all the villages and their plains, and hastening from every hill through the east and west of the land which Allah blessed* they came to the city,‡ which as I have said was well fortified, furnished with every equipment, inaccessible, secluded. Therefore the citizens defended themselves against them and were unwilling to surrender the city, hoping that they might smell the odour of succour or that Allah would grant them release after distress, and they remained in this condition about two days, then knew the frustration of their hope and falsity of their opinion and the coming and going of the Sultan with his army was as the poet said :

" As if a cloud should make lightning over a thirsty nation,
But when they have seen it, it is driven by the wind and dispersed."

* Syria.   ‡ Damascus.   •

142

CHAPTER VI

HOW THE LEADERS WENT FORTH, AFTER THE SULTAN HAD DEPARTED, AND SOUGHT SECURITY FROM TIMUR

THEREFORE when their opinion had deceived them and they knew that fatal evil was descending upon them, the great men of the city assembled and the leaders that were present, namely the chief judge Muhiuddin Mahmud son of Al-Az Hanifi and his son the chief judge Shahabuddin and the chief judge Taqiuddin Ibrahim son of Muflah Hanbali and the chief judge Shamsuddin Mahomed Hanbali of Nablus and Qazi* Nasiruddin Mahomed son of Abiltib, who had charge of secret affairs, and Qazi Shahabuddin Ahmed son of Vazir Al Shahid, on whom at that time the dignity of vazir† conferred authority above the rest, and Qazi Shahabuddin Habani the Shafeite and Qazi Shahabuddin Ibrahim son of Qusha Hanifi, deputy judge—Allah have mercy upon them!—but the Shafeite Qazi that is Alauddin son of Abul Baqa fled with the Sultan ; and the Malikite chief judge Burhanuddin Shazali died a martyr as I have related. These leaders therefore went out and sought security from him, after they had taken counsel and consented among themselves, and their speech had been joined on the thread of agreement.

SECTION

But when the Sultan had committed to the winds the sails of the full ship of his armies, there fell into the sea of Timur's army the chief judge Valiuddin son of Khaldun, who was among the principal leaders, and one of those who had arrived with the Sultan, and who, when the Sultan was driven to flight, took no heed and so fell into the net. He was living in the college Al Adalia and those leaders approached him, concerning the direction of this crisis and by united judgment set him over this business, for they could not take him as an associate ; for he was by sect, as well as in respect of eloquence

---

* or Cadi, i.e., judge.   † i.e., vizier. The form " vazir " or " wazir " is more correct.

L

and poetry a Maliki, and in knowledge of tradition and history an Asmai.*

Therefore he set out with them, clad in a turban light and elegantly shaped and a robe long, like himself, with a narrow border, like the beginning of a dark night, and they wished him to go before them, approving whatever he might say or do for them or against them ; and when they went into Timur's presence, they stood before him and remained standing, trembling and afraid, until he mercifully bade them sit and be of good courage. Then with geniality and smiling pleasantly upon them, he marked their condition and with the probe of his mind tried their words and deeds. And when he saw that the dress of Ibn Khaldun was different from theirs he said :

" This man is not one of them " and the course was opened for speech and his tongue was loosened. And what he said, I will soon tell.

Then they folded up the carpet of speech and unfolded the rug of feasting and presently they brought heaps of boiled meat and set before each what was suitable and some abstained therefrom through zeal for restraint, some in that turn of affairs were through fear distracted from eating, but some ate with outstretched hand and were not slow in appetite and drew not back, but urged and roused the others to eat, reciting that verse : " Eat like one, who, if he lives, will be praised by his people, but if he dies, will come to Allah with full belly."

And among those who ate freely was the chief judge Valiuddin.

Meanwhile Timur glanced at them and with dull eye secretly observed them. But Ibn Khaldun also glanced towards Timur and when Timur looked at him, looked down ; then, when his glance turned from him, again lightly regarded him. Then he said in a loud voice : " O Lord and Amir ! Praise to Allah Almighty ! truly I have had the honour of admission to the kings of mankind and I have restored life to their memory by my chronicles. Of the kings of the Arabs I have seen that one and that ; to this Sultan and this I have been admitted ; I have visited East and West and everywhere talked with Amirs and governors, but thanks be to Allah ! that my life has been extended and by Allah ! that I have lived long

* The famous Ibn Khaldun, author of *Universal History* and other works, was born at Tunis in A.D. 1332, and lived successively at Fez, Granada, Tlemçen, Tunis and Egypt. He died in 1406.

enough to see this man, who is truly a king and knows rightly how to rule the Sultanate. But if the food of kings suffice to avert destruction, truly the food of our Lord Amir suffices for this, nay, suffices to gain glory and honour."

By this speech, Timur was more pleased, so that he almost leapt for joy and began a conversation with him, in which he relied on him above all and asked him concerning the kings of the West, their exploits, the days of their power, and memorable deeds. Then he expounded to him concerning it, things which charmed him and drew him almost beyond himself into admiration.

And Timur was very skilled in the history of kings and peoples and expert in the annals of East and West, of which I will give below excellent examples.

Section

Now while they were sitting one day in the presence of that keen observer, lo! they brought prisoner Sadaruddin Manavi, whom pursuers caught in Mislon, while he was following the Sultan in his flight, and put him in chains and brought him to Timur. He was clad in a turban like a tower and gauntlets like saddle-bags and passing those who already sat, without apology took a higher place, wherefore Timur blazed with anger and the assembly was filled with flame, his lungs swelled, he boiled with wrath, and he roared and snorted and anger flooded his body and overflowed and he ordered certain of his attendants to set an example of punishment on Qazi Sadaruddin and they dragged him over the ground like a dog, tore his clothes and heaped curses and abuse upon him and smote him excessively with their feet and fists. Then he ordered them to bind him with tighter bonds, sharpen his pain and vex him from time to time with constant torments and doubled afflictions. Therefore he was cast out, like a wicked man on the day of judgment driven away with back turned, who has no defender from Allah.

Then Timur returning to the contriving of his wonted evil and cunning, clothed each of those leaders with a robe of honour and set them in honour and dignity at his court. Then he sent them away cheered, having gained calm and joy, but in his heart evils and heavier matters were turning, which presently broke forth.

I have written :

" Like a victim which he who offers it adorns and honours, but soon gives it to eat to death as guest."

And he promised them and their followers security on condition that they should hand over to him the Sultan's goods and all his and his Amirs' utensils, means, riches, beasts of burden, cattle, slaves and domestics : and they performed these commands of his, bearing out to him all those things, whether hidden or open.

But the fort was equipped for sustaining a siege and its governor was called Azdar, who fortified it and rightly equipped it with every munition, expecting vigorous aid from the Sultan or some divine obstacle, whereby he might be freed from trouble.

But Timur in the beginning neglected it and did not consider it or attend thereto ; but when the goods had been brought and transferred to his treasury, he imposed on the city a tribute of security, for the exaction of which he wished to employ those leaders over whom he set his own masters of accounts and scribes and agents and the managers of his treasury. But the chief control of that business he entrusted to Allahdad, one of his ministers of state, whom he especially trusted, uterine brother of Seifuddin, who was mentioned at the beginning of the book, and added to them any and every unjust oppressor and men reared in the bosom of inhumanity and who had sucked the paps of oppression.

Then by the voice of a herald he proclaimed peace and security and that they should not vex one another. But when certain Jagatais after hearing this edict and its publication put forth their hands to plunder, Timur so soon as he learnt it, ordered them to be fixed to the cross in a public place. Therefore they crucified them in the silk market, where the vegetable market begins. This act of his was most pleasant to the people, who had good hopes of his goodness and justice and opened the small gate of the city ; and they began to inquire exactly about the state of the city to the very kernel and distributed this tribute between the wards, the ministers of oppression and insolence shouting to each other from near and far " Now for vengeance ! " and they made the court of gold* a place of robbery and they began to drive the people into that trap, among whom one attacked another and he hunted

* This it seems had been the residence of the governor.

the hares of that land with native hounds. And now autumn, like the army of Egypt, had retired and winter with its biting cold, like Timur's army, had descended on the world.

Then he made his way to the palace of Qasrablaq and thence to the house of Amir Butakhas, ordering that that palace should be laid waste and burnt. And entering the city with a great host through the Little Gate he performed the public prayers in the mosque of* the sons of Omayya and ordered the Hanifites to go before the Shafeites,† and there the chief Qazi Muhiuddin Mahmud, son of Alaz, the Hanifite, already mentioned, held discourse. Then affairs and evils befell, the tale of which would be tedious.

And between Abdul Jabar son of Abdul Jabar Rahman of Khwarizm the Mutazalite‡ and the doctors of Syria, especially the chief Qazi Taqiuddin Ibrahim son of Muflah the Hanbalite, there arose disputes, controversies, and arguments, in all which as though the interpreter of Timur he spoke with them in his name : especially about the battles of Ali and Muavia and what was done between them in that time in the past ; and also about the affairs of Yazid and other things and the killing of Husein, the blessed martyr, and that it was injustice and sin, which cannot be denied ; and that the man who thinks it lawful falls into unbelief ; and that without doubt that unlawful deed was committed by aid of the people of Syria ; that they if they approve it, must be held unbelievers ; if they disapprove, then rebels, evil and wicked ; and that those Syrians who live now are of the same sect as those of the past. To which they gave various answers, of which he rejected some and accepted others ; until Nasiruddin son of Abiltib, who was secretary of secret matters, replied well and aptly, if he sought advantage : " May Allah Almighty prolong the life of our lord and Amir ! as for me, I carry back my family to Umar and Othman and my first ancestor was one of the leaders of that time and was present at those battles and plunged into those combats and was a man of the right cause and a champion of truth, but among his wonderful deeds, whereby he showed himself zealous for the right, is this, that

---

* Or the Omayyads.

† The Sunni Moslems are divided into four sects : Hanifite, Shafeite, Malikitis and Hanbalites. They differ in ritual and law.

‡ The Mutazalites believe that man has free will, that the Koran was created and not eternal and they deny bodily resurrection. They are opposed to the orthodox Sunnis.

when he had found the head of our lord Husein, he removed it from the neglect and shame in which it lay, then cleansed and washed it, reverenced and kissed it, filled it with spices, treated it with reverence and buried it in a tomb, and so earned the highest rank of favour with Allah Almighty and hence,* O cloud pouring forth rain! received the name of Abiltib.† But, however that may be, those peoples have now passed and all those clouds of trouble have been dispersed. What had to be swallowed, is now finished and what had to be tasted, whether bitter or sweet. As for discords, Allah has given us ease, since he has freed us from them; and as for shedding of blood, Allah has made our swords clean from it. And now we profess the faith of those, who rely on tradition and accepted doctrine."

And when he heard this speech, Timur said:

"Ah, by Allah! this is wonderful! Is this the reason, why you are called sons of Abiltib?"

He replied: "Certainly; and my witnesses of this are both distant and near; for I am Mahomed, son of Umar, son of Mahomed, son of Abilkasim, son of Abdulmunaam, son of Mahomed, son of Abiltib Umari Othmani."

"Then he said: Pardon me, O noble seed! If I had not plain excuse, I would carry you on my neck and shoulders; nevertheless you shall enjoy honour and benevolence, with which I will treat you and your friends."

Then he dealt quietly with them and followed them with honour and reverence; further he put to them a cunning question, that contained harm and danger, saying:

"Which is more excellent, the rank of knowledge or the rank of birth?" And they grasped and perceived the aim of it, but for fear held themselves back from giving an answer, since they all knew that they were being led into danger. But Qazi Shamsuddin of Nablus, the Hanbalite, hastily replied, saying: "The rank of knowledge is more excellent than the rank of birth and its dignity is higher with the Creator as with men; and a learned man of low birth excels an ignorant of noble birth and a man base-born, but excellent, is better in the office of Imam than a noble Said, and the proof of this is clear, for the companions of the Prophet agreed in preferring Abu Bakr to Ali, knowing that Abu Bakr was more learned than they and firmer and prior in profession of the Faith.

* A respectful address to Timur.　　　† I.e., father of sweet odours.

And this proof is confirmed by the saying of the Prophet :
' My people will not agree concerning error.' "

Then he began to strip off his garment, listening to Timur,
whether he would reply, and he loosened its knots, and said to
his soul : " Thou art only a loan ; and the cup of death must
be drunk, which is the same, whether it happens soon or late.
And death with martyrdom is most excellent worship of
Allah and the good state of him who is convinced that he is
going to Allah is a word of truth before an unjust Sultan."

And Timur asked, " What is this madman doing ? "

Then he said " O illustrious lord ! Your armies are
scattered, like the tribes of Israel, and there are men in them
who fashion new religions and are drawn into diverse sects,
and are sundered and divided by religion ; and there is no
doubt that the meetings held in your presence are made public
and the excellent inquiries there held loosen and bind men's
breasts. Therefore when this speech is established against me
and someone hears it, who is not a Sunni, especially one who
defends the succession of Ali and being a heretic calls Abu Bakr
a schismatic, I am sure that death is prepared for me and that
there is no defender to save me, but that he will slay me publicly
and that my blood will be shed on that day. And since this is
so, I prepare myself for this felicity and I will seal with martyrdom the sentences of my judgeship."

And Timur said, " By Allah ! How ready and bold this
man is in speech and how shameless ! " Then looking at the
assembly he said : " Let not this man be admitted henceforth."

SECTION

Now Abdul Jabar was the doctor* of Timur and his
Imam and one of those who in his presence plunged in the
blood of Muslims. He was excellent in learning, a perfect
lawyer, a careful inquirer, precise and a subtle debater. His
father, Alnuman, was at Samarkand the head of the most
learned men of his time, so that he was called the second
Alnuman† and was among those who deny vision in the future
life ; therefore Allah blinded his eyes like his mind in this life.
Most of his learned contemporaries in Transoxiana counted
him as their head and consulted him in questions which they
raised. And the difference between the Sunnis and Mutazalis

---

* Man of learning.　　　　　† Founder of the Hanifites.

is not concerning the *branches*, but they differ about the roots of religion in many questions, in which the latter hold the path of error.

SECTION

Now there was employed to seize wealth from the people of Syria every wicked and cruel man and violent unbeliever and those who were in the greatest poverty, such as Sadaqa, son of Alharibi, and Ibn Almuhadit and Abdul Malik, son of Altukriti, who was surnamed Sumaqa, and other like men of the posterity of evil and their sons—and that, in the presence of the great men of the city and its leaders before mentioned and the chief citizens, who were not permitted to resist or even to withdraw for a moment or devise delays and in the presence of his secretaries, accountants, treasurers and clerks, among whom were Khwaja Masaud Samnani and Maulana Umar and Tajuddin Salmani, who were all in the court of gold, a famous place. And Allahdad was staying inside the Little Gate in the house of Ibn Mashkur. And everyone, who had in his heart hatred against anyone, or hidden malice or feud or envy or annoyance, handed over his own brothers to those wicked and harsh men, evil, violent, and fierce.

" They do not ask their brother, when he summons them
In misfortunes, to prove what he says."

Nay, on the slightest proof and least indication they built on the ground of the existence of that wretched man high towers out of the mountains of torture and raised over the gardens of his being out of the sky of punishments clouds of vengeance, which sounded over him bursting with thunder and sent forth upon him thunders of ruin and destruction.

SECTION

Then he began during this time the siege of the fort, for which he provided all the equipment he could and ordered a building to be raised in the opposite direction commanding it, whereby they might ascend and overthrow the fort ; and they gathered materials and timber, which they packed together and poured thereon stones and earth, which they levelled ; and this was on the Syrian and Arabian sides.

Then they climbed upon the building and stormed the fort hand to hand with lance and sword. And he entrusted the siege to the chief among his principal Amirs, by name Jahanshah, who took in hand the business entrusted to him and bringing up ballistas shattered its lower part and as it were suspended it.

In the fort among the warriors was a company lacking in numbers, and excellent among them were Shahabuddin Zardakash of Damascus and Shahabuddin Ahmad Zardakash of Haleb, who inflicted great loss on his army and whenever it approached their position, wrought destruction and slaughter, and dealt havoc among the army with fire and thunder and lightning more than could be counted or measured.

But when a violent flood from the swelling seas of that army had surrounded the fort and the cloud of its javelin-throwers was raining down javelins and the thunderstorms of its armed men raining down a direct onset, punishment came upon the fort from above and below and from right and left and the hands of the fighters were wearied with constant combat and strife.

Therefore they sought security and surrendered to him without delay.

And all these terrible things and prodigious destinies befell at the beginning of the second month of Rabia and in the months of Jumadi and Rajab ; nevertheless he did not accomplish his purpose concerning the fort until after a siege of forty-three days. Meanwhile he gave himself to seeking excellent men and masters of arts and crafts and men that had skill. And the silk-workers wove for him an all-silk tunic embroidered with gold without any seam, of wonderful workmanship. And he had built in the cemetery of the Little Gate two adjoining shrines over the grave of the wives of the Prophet, on whom be the Mercy of Allah ! and ordered slaves of Zinj* to be collected, of whom he sought to possess more and preferred them to others.

* Zanzibar.

CHAPTER VII

THE DEED OF ONE OF THE MORE PRUDENT WHO FEARED THE
THREATENING DISASTER AND BY MEANS OF HIS RESOURCES
PRESERVED MEN AND GOODS FROM HARM

THERE was a merchant at Safad among the townsmen,
chief among the magnates and merchants, by name
Alauddin, a kinsman of Davadar, who when he had served the
Sultan well, was appointed by him the Keeper of that place.
And when the Governor had gone to Haleb, according to the
custom that he who is Keeper should act as Governor of the
city in his absence, the Keeper of Safad, Alauddin Davadari,
held the place of the Governor Tunbagha Othmani.

Now in the clutch of that flood all the governors were
scattered, especially Othmani and Ibn Tahan, and some of them
were dead, some had fled ; and there remained in prison
Tunbagha and Umar. And when Timur had invaded Syria
and dealt with it as wicked judges do with the goods of orphans,
all the rulers of the country gave themselves to vigorous discharge of their duty ; some fortified their places, others
strengthened their ambushes ; one part took to flight and
another prepared for escape ; and others sought peace and
tranquillity, truce and quiet.

The said Alauddin therefore deliberated and thought and
reflected how he might set free his master and his city. And
there was a discreet man of tested wisdom, of whose sound
judgment he sought counsel concerning that matter and with
whom he spoke, who said : " Placate him with your wealth
and send a herd of cattle and pay him off." And he was not
mistaken when he told him that every propitiation on behalf
of one's people is a covering for them. And he had confidence
in him and since he was a rich man, said : " I have not stored
yellow and white coins except for black days."

Accordingly he sought to placate Timur and strove to try
the ford in the beginning by generosity and treated this
business as a skilled doctor treats a patient, and by placating
averted extreme calamity. And he sent to Timur various gifts
out of his ample wealth and strove to win his favour and sought
his commands. And he sent constantly new gifts in abundant

measure and Timur praised his action and so he advanced in esteem and position with Timur. And Timur sent to him a letter of security " that he and the inhabitants should behave towards each other calmly and kindly, and confidently lay aside their fear and should all be tranquil, that they might recover from their panic, throwing off their anxiety, so as to buy and sell among themselves and freely assemble for their trade with his army. And if anyone of his troops, even one of his brothers or sons, were guilty of excess, he should be treated with aversion, repudiation, flogging and public disgrace."

And when Timur sought from him whatever he desired, he sent him that and much more. And whenever he proceeded to demand money and goods from him with greater insistence, Alauddin always gave them more abundantly with promptness and goodwill. Among the rest also Timur demanded insistently from him on that occasion a load of white onions, though such were not available in all Syria, still less at Safad ; yet he immediately found three loads of them, which he sent to him, as they were, which happened by the favour of Allah, so that Timur loved him and wished to have him near himself. And he said about him, as I have written :

" You used flattery in season and served yourself by
    expenditure of your wealth !
If another like you had been in Syria, it would not have
    been exposed to harm."

And crowds came to them from the army, which bought from them and sold to them, and the bonds of mutual friendship held without a break, until the army raised its camp and left Damascus. But when the lizards of destruction had departed from Syria and the rope of travel was stretched in the hippodrome of the march, Alauddin Davadari came after, seeking that ravening lion, and brought precious gifts and royal presents and a letter full of fine sentiments, excellent professions and abject and humble language and expressions so tender as to make a man's flesh creep, and soften iron or the hardest rock or penetrate dry bodies, like water on wood, and in that letter sought his mercy on behalf of Othmani and Ibn Tahan, that he might cut the forelocks of their slavery with the shears of generous liberation and give thanks to fortune by pardoning them and pour on them a drop out of the seas of his clemency ; seeing that they were too weak to be counted among his slaves, when the kings of the earth wished to be infants in his bosom : further that Timur's noble judgment was the best and his chief aim was to conform to his mandates.

And when Timur had learnt the trend of this letter and understood its beginning and end and seen his valuable presents and gifts, reflecting what a web of slavery he had spun and woven around him from the beginning (and goodness is remembered and the man who pursues it is noble ; but evil is altogether diminished and the man who pursues it is unjust. I have written :

> " Expect the best reward, when you have done good ;
> And fear not evil, if you have done no evil."
> It is also said :
> " He who has done good, will not lose his reward ;
> Merit will not perish with Allah and among men.")

then his heart was softened, though it was of iron, and his roughness became smooth, though otherwise it ceased not to be vehement. Therefore he summoned both those men and received them honourably, and told them of Alauddin's intercession for them. Then he ordered them both to fear no harm and gave them three horses, two to Othmani and one to Umar, son of Tahan. Then he gave them men, who brought them to a place of safety, and each came to the seat of his dignity, the former remaining in his city Safad, the latter in his own Gaza.

SECTION

But after completing the capture of the fort, Timur ordered his affairs and resolved to return, after taking therefrom what he wished of precious things and goods by various tortures and pains and punishments.

CHAPTER VIII

OF THE SUBSTANCE OF THE LETTER, WHICH THE SULTAN OF
EGYPT SENT TO TIMUR BY THE HAND OF BISAQ, AFTER THEY
HAD FLED FROM HIM

THEY say that the Sultan after his flight sent a letter
to him, in which he declared war, and this was its
purport :

" Do not think that we were seized with fear of you and
fled from you ; but simply one of our slaves assumed lofty
airs and withdrew his head from the yoke of obedience, imagin-
ing that everyone who rebels, climbs higher ; and he did not
take an example from the man who takes a ladder to climb
and rises step by step. But he sought in that affair, like you,
to bring injury and destruction to men and countries. But
enough. To gain his end he has to strip the goat's thorn.

" The good man, when two diseases appear in the body,
heals the more dangerous and we thought you a slight and
mean affair ; therefore our august purpose turned to box the
ears of that refractory slave and bring him to the due order of
obedience. But by Allah ! we will leap upon you with the
charge of an angry lion and make our thirsty spears drink
from you and your army deep draughts from the springs of
hatred and mow you down like hay and trample upon you as
dry ground is trampled and the millstone of war will drive you
in every direction, vexed by dense stabbing of spears and close-
packed blows of swords, as milled flour is expelled ; and we will
block for you the ways of escape and you will cry out, but
there will be no time to escape."

—with further nonsense and folly of this sort, which was
like salt to wounds and air when breath fails. And if instead
of this, in which there was no profit, and mad speech, which
the ear spews forth and rejects, he had put forward something
which could have turned Timur's heart and calmed the blazing
fire of his wrath with gifts and presents, making bare his own
condition, like one who asks pardon and repents, perchance
he would have broken his rage and calmed and cooled him ;
but they asked pardon only after Damascus was burnt and
Basra laid waste, and they sent presents and gifts with ostriches
and giraffes, when the opportunity of a remedy had already
gone and slipped away ; and did, as is said in the poem :

" The fool does what the wise man does
In calamities ; but after he is ruined."

and in the verse :

" She is generous when generosity profits naught."

SECTION

This Bisaq reported, saying : " When I was admitted to his presence and had handed over the letter, and the writing had been read out to him, he said to me, ' Tell the truth ; what is your name ? ' I replied, ' Bisaq.' And he said, ' What is the meaning of this absurd word ? ' I replied, ' My Lord ! I do not know ! ' ' You,' he said, ' do not know the meaning of your own name, you fox ! How then can you be fit to undertake the task of an ambassador ? Were it not the custom of kings not to harm ambassadors, which custom they consistently observe and hold (and I am most worthy to follow the footprints of Sultans and restore the practices of past kings), certainly I would treat you as you deserve and deal with you according to your merits ; yet the fault is not so much with you, as with him who employed you as ambassador in this business ; nay, even he is not to be blamed, because in this affair it is plain that his skill does not stretch further nor are his mind and intellect more capable and in his base deed is plain the truth of the words :

" ' Choose, if you have to manage anything, a good ambassador ;
For on the ambassador depend the counsels of men.'

" Then he said to me : ' Go to your fort* and the place of your honour and strength ' ; therefore I departed and found it utterly destroyed and everything sacred in it overturned and violated. Then I went back and related to him what I had seen, and he said :

" ' The man who sent you is too feeble for me to show benevolence to him and too base for me to send an ambassador to him : but tell him, that I, treading in your footprints, will come to him ; and see, I will fix the claws of my lions in your tail ; therefore let him gird his loins either to stand or to flee and prepare for whichever course he has chosen, what force he can and strong squadrons.'

* Damascus,

" Then he dismissed me and I went out and did not believe that I should ever return to Egypt."

SECTION

When he had filled the bag of his cupidity with precious things and had gradually milked every drop clear or foul, until the place was wiped clean with a cloth, he ordered those great Amirs to be tortured and vexed them with water and salt and made them drink ashes and lime and singed them and squeezed hidden wealth from them, as oil is squeezed out of a press. Then he let his soldiers plunder at will, seize any they wished as prisoners, destroy suddenly and slaughter, burn and drag into bondage without restraint. And those evil unbelievers suddenly fell upon men, torturing, smiting and laying waste, as stars fall from the sky, and excited and swollen they slaughtered and smote and raged against Muslims and their allies, as ravening wolves rage against teeming flocks of sheep and did things, which to do is unseemly and which it is not meet to record and relate. And they took matrons prisoners, uncovered the veils of veiled women, made the unveiled suns descend from the orbits of palaces and the moons of beauty from the sky of dalliance, afflicting great and small alike with every kind of torture, men suffering things whose sum cannot be reckoned. By scorching at the fire the fine ore of mankind, they drew therefrom the purest gold and in exacting precious things from men by devising various tortures they achieved wonders ; and separated mothers from their children and souls from bodies and everyone that gave suck forgot her suckling and everyone received the reward of what he had done and had not done and men fled from their brothers, mothers, fathers, friends, and children. And then came to everyone a condition, in which he had what was enough for himself. And the powerful and noble became base and the famous and great became despised. And affliction was complete and judgment was shared by all.

Wisdom became fickle, sagacity was stunned and thick clouds of afflictions gathered, and I call Allah to witness that those days were a sign among the signs of the last day ; and that that hour showed the conditions of the last day. And this general plunder lasted about three days.

157

CHAPTER IX

HOW THEY SET FIRE TO THE CITY TO DESTROY ALL TRACES OF IT

THEN when they had completed the ruin and confusion and in their pilgrimage of destruction performed the ceremonies, which they discharged by crime, strife and impurity and fulfilled their circuit and course in iniquities and hurled fire on the houses and coals on men's hearts and caused rivers to flow with the blood of the Muslims slain in the fort, they hastened in circles of fire and sent flames of fire into the holy place of the city. And among them were Rafidites of Khorasan, who sent fire into the mosque of the Omayyads, and it clung by its own heat, with the help of the wind with its violent gusts, the wind and fire driving each other on in destroying traces of the city.

And this fire, by the will of Allah Almighty, lasted night and day and burned up what remained of precious things and souls ; and the tongue of fire wiped out what was written in the tablets of the city and towards evening in those pleasant mansions no more was heard vain conversation or whispering and in the morning the city appeared mown down as though yesterday it had not teemed, even after booty had been taken out and bundles put on beasts of burden.

CHAPTER X

HOW THOSE AFFLICTIONS WERE REMOVED AND THOSE CLOUDS OF CALAMITIES AND TROUBLES DISPERSED FROM SYRIA, ALONG WITH WHAT SHE HAD ENDURED FROM WRONGS AND SINS

THEN that tormentor departed and his cloud of calamities pouring forth constant storms withdrew on the Sabbath day, the third of Shaban, but since they had taken precious things beyond their strength and removed more than they could carry, they left them in narrow streets and houses and threw away one thing after another in the difficult places where they halted, because of the excessive abundance of bundles and lack of porters ; and wastes, plains, mountains and deserts seemed on account of precious things and goods like markets of liberality and the earth seemed as though it had opened its treasures and exposed its mines and minerals.

I have written on the spur of the moment :
" The tongue of their wickedness shouted on high mountains
and plains :
' Injury we know well and violence is custom with which
we are content.
This we have from our king and his rule in place of gain.' "

Nevertheless, even had twice so much been taken of the precious things of Damascus and a thousand times more cut from the heart of its treasuries, yet this would not have diminished the water in its spring or drained its abundant seas ; but the fire was a grievous affliction and deadly blow, for it devoured those within the city for want of help : think, therefore, how much perished of buildings, precious goods and chattels. The dogs also rushed to devour the flesh of dead citizens and none dared enter the mosque of the Omayyads.

CHAPTER XI

OF WHAT BEFELL IN EGYPT AND OTHER COUNTRIES AFTER
THESE NEWS WERE HEARD AND THESE EVENTS AND MISFORTUNES
KNOWN

AND Egypt and the adjacent countries were seized with consternation, their strength was dissolved, their hands were bound, resolution failed and they prepared for flight. And if you saw the men, they were confounded, drunk but not with wine, their bodies trembling, their hearts violently agitated, voices hushed, faces horror-stricken, lips dry, countenances wretched and looks gloomy, thinking that they must endure disaster.

And now all the citizens of the great cities and inhabitants of places high and low prepared for flight and listened to the awful news which they received, making every movement or inaction turn on that.

But Timur went forward on his tortuous way and returned to the path of his violence, which he had chosen instead of a straight and royal road ; and now his armies filled the countries on every side and fear of him seized the whole world.

CHAPTER XII

NOW one of the leaders of Syria, one of its famous men of learning, the chief judge Muhiuddin, son of Alaz Hanifi, after they had subjected him to various kinds of torture and branded him and made him drink water and salt and roasted him with lime and fire, he and his son, the chief judge, Shahabuddin Abu'l Abbas, came to Tabriz, where they stayed some time in misery and affliction, then returned to Syria, where their condition began to improve.

But Chief Judge Shamsuddin of Nablus, the Hanbalite, and Chief Judge Sadruddin Manavi, the Shafeite, were received to the mercy of Allah, the Giver, being drowned in the river Tarab.

And Shahabuddin Ahmad, son of Alshahid Almutabir, had also to undergo the punishment of sin, after they wished to torture and torment him ; and those who were associated with him having already been sent to distant places, he had remained at Damascus. Therefore, he told them his history and gave them the opportunity of removing his possessions ; then they took his hidden wealth and did not subject him to torture, but wished him to be their companion in wealth and poverty, and he came to Samarkand, where he had to endure many hardships through changes of fortune, to wit, exile, poverty and calamities. Then he returned to Damascus, where he passed to the mercy of Allah Almighty.

But of the chief Amirs, the great Amir Butakhas, who was a prisoner with Timur, died, when he had come to the Euphrates.

As for Qazi Nasiruddin, son of Abiltib, him also they tortured with every sort of affliction, but since he was of feeble body, and mild and melancholy temperament, he could not endure it, but by his death frustrated what they sought of him and carried off by sudden death, found rest and drank through martyrdom the cup of eternal glory and joy ; then at évening they buried him in the college Karusia.

But Chief Judge Taqiuddin, son of Mufalah, while the

tormentors were engaged in promiscuous destruction, was slain in error and Burhanuddin, son of Qusha, after an illness of ten days, died in the street Telaljaban and was added to the other dead.

And now they stalked through the live and dead and feared lest anyone by pretence of death might escape from their hands, and they kept each house of the city besieged and proclaimed that no one should go out alive or any dead be carried out.

Accordingly, when he, whom I have mentioned, died, great difficulty arose, for they were hindered in performing his funeral, until after much labour and effort they buried him in Salihia, after carrying out his body by the Little Gate.

And voluntarily there went from Syria with Timur Abdul Malik son of Tukriti, and he made him governor of Siram, where he remained a short time, this place lying beyond the Jaxartes. And another man, by name Yalbagha Almajnun, became a close friend of his, because he showed much zeal in advising him and pointed out hypocrites to him, as is said, and in this way he escaped from those dangerous places and precipices and gained his favour and frequent association and friendship, and that tyrant made him governor of a city, called Yanki Bilas, beyond the river Khajend,* about fifteen days' journey from Samarkand and four from Siram. The name of this traitor was Ahmed, but he was surnamed Yalbagha Majnun.

And he took from Damascus learned men and craftsmen and all who excelled in any art, the most skilled weavers, tailors, gem-cutters, carpenters, makers of head-coverings, farriers, painters, bow-makers, falconers, in short, craftsmen of every kind, and collected Ethiopians, as related above. And he divided these companies among the heads of the army and ordered them to lead them to Samarkand. He also took Jamaluddin, the chief physician, and Shahabuddin Ahmad Azzardakash, who in the fort, as related above, had overcome countless men of his army and was now ninety years old and bent. And as soon as he saw him, he received him with vehement anger and said to him : " Truly you have smitten my vassals, scattered my friends and driven out my followers ; but if by one blow I deprived you of life, my sickness would not be healed or my thirst quenched, but I will torture you despite your age and add affliction to your affliction and weakness to

* i.e., Jaxartes.

your weakness." Then he ordered a chain to be fastened to his knees, whose weight was seven-and-a-half Damascene pounds, and he sought thereby to afflict him, and he remained in bonds condemned to endless captivity, until the death of Timur, when hardships were removed and that prisoner escaped from his bonds, then passed to the mercy of Allah Almighty.

Perchance he also took others of the excellent and leaders and princes and eminent, whom I do not know, in the way I have related ; likewise all his Amirs and lords took an infinite multitude of lawyers, theologians, of men who knew the Koran from memory, and learned men, craftsmen, workmen, slaves, women, boys and girls, and in the same way acted each man of his army great and small, master and slave, since none was blamed, who seized anything and carried it off, but whatever anyone was first to take, went to him ; indeed, when he had given rein to general plunder, thereby the generals of the army and the rank and file were made equal, and if among them the plunderer were a slave or foreigner and the despoiler a stranger, yet that was permitted him, since, imitating their conduct and assuming their character, he enjoyed the same right as they. But, if anyone molested another before the granting of licence, though he might be to Timur in the position of father or son, or committed even the slightest excess or uttered a word of plunder or rapine, he punished him with loss of goods and life, violated his dignity and whatever he had inviolable nor could prayers and penitence save him or his family and dependants aid him ; nor was it said " Perchance he committed that fault through error." And this was an inviolable custom and a rule not to be destroyed.

CHAPTER XIII

OF THE DAMAGE, WHICH LOCUSTS DID AFTER HIM

WHEN the harvest of the wealth of Damascus had been completed and he was about to depart, there followed a plague of locusts, which advanced with him, until they reached Mardin and Bagdad, stripping every place, tilled or untilled, and utterly consuming whatever was found on the face of the earth. Then Timur reached Hamas,* which he did not plunder, but granted as described above, to Khalid, on whom be the favour of Allah! But they plundered its villages and laid waste its fields.

Then he moved to Hamat† and they plundered its precious things and dragged out hidden treasures, and carried away its maidens and brides. And on the seventeenth day of Shaban that flood poured into the mountains and sent men to Haleb and from its fort he took what had been stored there; then turned to the Euphrates, which he crossed in skiffs and otherwise. Then to Arruha,‡ which he plundered and milked its wealth. Then that traitor sent his envoy to Mardin, to summon Malik Azzahir; and his foul dispatch began, as is reported:

" Peace to you and may treaties be undisturbed!
For desires have been fully perfected."

But he scorned to go down to him and did not comply with his words or take account of him, for since he had been ill-treated the first time, as already related, he did not need a second trial, but trod with him the ground of safety and said that verse:

" Repentance comes too late to him, who tries one by
whom he has been tried."

Nevertheless he sent to him an envoy from among his ministers, by name Haj Mahomed, son of Khasibeg, and with him gifts and presents and excused himself from coming because of pressure of affairs and composed the beginning of his letter in the form of Timur's address to him, to wit:

" My longing for you also has grown more than can be
described,
But the soul fears concerning that which befell it."

But Timur took no account of these words and began to blame himself much, because of the first occasion he had escaped from his clutches in peace.

* Homs.　　　　† Hama.　　　　‡ Edessa, now Urfa.

CHAPTER XIV

OF HIS AWFUL APPROACH TO MARDIN AND DEPARTURE FROM
THERE AFTER A VAIN SIEGE

ON the second day of the week the tenth of the month
Ramzan, the enemy approached Mardin and pitched
their camp at Dunisir and in the morning approached to besiege
the place, but the citizens had left the city and retired to their
well-protected fort.

DESCRIPTION OF THE FORT

The summit of this fort standing forth like a griffin was
too proud to yield to a hunter and the nose of this virgin
scorned to receive the bridle of subjection of any suitor,
for it was set on the very top of the ridge of a mountain.
There was no difference between it and the vault of heaven,
but that moves while this rests firm without motion. Within
stretched a valley broader than the breasts of the free, and
in it were gardens, beneath which rivers flow, broad fields
and pastures for beasts and cattle. Its borders were precipices
whose edges even the effort of the boldest would not reach
and summits to link which the climber would weary himself in
vain. The path from or to the fort and the fort itself were
quite impassable and lofty. The city built around it clung
to its hem ; it ate of its abounding delicacies and drank of its
swelling stream. The citizens moved between their pleasures
and punishments and had their sustenance in heaven and that
which has been promised.*

And Timur relied on its difficult places to besiege it, wishing
straightway to reach ways and paths of falling upon it, but
there was no place round it for battle or plain for arraying
ballistas ; he therefore strove to undermine it with sharpened
mallets and axes and for this took to aid princes and leaders,
but the seam of the robe of its modesty and restraint kept
it from violation, since, like a virgin, it rendered impotent
its wooers, being impervious and by nature closed to assault.
And the hoes were constantly worn away and the hammers

* A quotation from the Koran. Probably the " sustenance " is rain.

blunted, and the edges of the axes bent and the hearts of the mallets broken like knives.

I have written :

" Their sharpened mallet in digging its soil is like the beak
    of a bird on the hardest rock,
  Or like the blame of the envious spoken to the deaf
  Or a glance of the eye for giving a sign to the blind."

And he continued the struggle and strife until the twentieth day of the month Ramzan, but in vain and without gaining his desire.

CHAPTER XV

ABANDONING THE SIEGE AND STRIFE AND HIS OBSTINACY HE
MARCHED FROM MARDIN TO BAGDAD ALONG WITH HIS FIERCE
RAIDERS

WHEN therefore he knew that he was smitten by that great misfortune (for truly to aim at what cannot be attained is useless labour and to oppose the truth is leaving the right road and eloquence out of place is mad futility) then he covered his disgrace and left behind him a certain awe and terror by laying waste the city and its walls, destroying its traces, overthrowing its buildings, mosques and towers and casting down its stones and foundations. Then he descended to Bagdad with troops countless like ants, moths and locusts, and sent a company to Samarkand with Allahdad and they reached the city of Sur, where there was no high-built house ; then came to Khalat and Abduljauz, which are populous cities of the Kurds, well built and first among those submitting to his authority in the provinces of Tabriz and Azerbaijan ; and the company kept that holy day of Ramzan at Abduljauz.

Then they entered the province of Tabriz, then Sultania and then the territories of Khorasan. And now the winter was ending and spring adorning herself and approaching and the broad face of the gardens was being coloured by divine Providence, as with the fingers of a skilled dyer and the bride of the meadows was putting on her golden ornament, with which she decked herself by Divine guidance, as from an expert goldsmith ; and birds among the flowers, hundreds of bulbuls and thousands of nightingales, were charming the ear and making harmonious melody and with their sweet voices soothing the heart, and the pity of Allah was renewing the earth's fertility, after it had seemed dead.

And that company continued its journey day and night, not like the pilgrims of Mecca, who daily complete the day's journey and rest each night; then they reached Nisabur, then Jam, then they crossed the deserts of Bavard and Makhan, then came to Andkhui, then to the river Oxus, which they crossed in skiffs, and proceeded on their journey like a piercing star and at length came to Samarkand on the thirteenth day of Muharram and the third day of the week in the year 804.* There were among them many Syrians, of whom the chief was Qazi Shahabuddin Ahmad son of the martyr Vazir, while the rest were farriers, dyers and silkworkers. And this was the first spoil which was brought from Syria and the firstfruits of prisoners and wealth, which he had plucked, to reach Samarkand. Then he sent other companies laden with spoil and burdens of wealth and prisoners.

Section

Then Timur set over Amid, Qara Iluk Othman and withdrew from Mardin on the fifth day of the week, the twentieth of the month of Ramzan, which is the fifth of Ayar,† and descended upon those parts; and he laid waste Nisibin and devoured its crops, then wiped it out of the volume of existence—chapter and verse—and it remained empty of inhabitants and destitute of dwellers in its houses.

Then he turned his greed to Mosul and destroyed it with his black army and after he had given it to ruin, presented it to Husein Beg, son of. Husein. Then with great noise he hastened to the bridge, spreading a rumour that he was ending his raids and seeking his own country; but Sultan Ahmad knew that he was making for Bagdad and disguising his intention, according to his habit in these things.

* A.D. 1402.   † A month in the Syrian calendar.

CHAPTER XVI

OF THE DEEDS OF SULTAN AHMAD, SON OF SHEIKH AVIS, WHEN
HE LEARNT THAT THAT PROFANE MAN WAS ATTACKING HIM

WHEN therefore Sultan Ahmad learnt that Timur after the storming of Damascus and Mardin, intended to storm Bagdad, he said : " It is best to return ; I will prepare myself, but for withdrawal," and he resolved not to remain in his place. Then he put in his own place a Governor by name Faraj, to whom, along with the son of Baliqi, he entrusted affairs, and, accompanied by Qara Yusuf, departed to Rum. But especially he enjoined him not to shut the gate against Timur, or draw a curtain before what he sought or unsheath the sword before him or oppose his will either by denial or by demanding explanation.

But when Timur perceived these things, that cunning deceiver sent twenty thousand soldiers to Bagdad, over whom he set, from among his Amirs and chief Vazirs and wicked rebels, Amirzada Rustam and Jalal Islami and Sheikh Nuruddin, and ordered that of those three the chief leader should be Amir Rustam and that when they had taken Bagdad, he should be governor of the country.

And when the sun of Sultan Ahmad had fallen from the sky of Bagdad upon his setting forth and the darkness of iniquity had spread the wing of Timur's armies over its horizon and hurled against it its flaming stars, the said Faraj refused to hand over the city willingly and prepared for battle and gathered what equipment he had for a siege, and collected supplies.

Therefore they announced this to Timur, awaiting what he might forbid or command. But he turned towards the city the reins of anger and destroyed, whatever his hand obtained, by flood and fire and overshadowed them with dense clouds of affliction, after he had thundered and lightened. And when he reached the city with that host, he sent on them calamities and gave them to taste terror and extreme hunger and consternation and smote them with mighty blows, and besieged them during the months of the Haj.* But their

* Pilgrimage to Mecca.

troops stood firm and slew and wounded many of his army ; therefore seized with fierce anger he attacked the city with his infantry and cavalry and took it by force on the day of sacrifice, and thus Timur kept the festival, as he had said, by slaying Muslims and performed his sacrifice on them. Then he ordered each of those who were enrolled in his register and reckoned among his soldiers and army to bring to him two heads from among the people of Bagdad. Accordingly they gave each of them to drink the wine of plundered life and plundered wealth, two cups. Then they brought them singly and in crowds and made the river Tigris flow with the torrent of their blood throwing their corpses on to the plains, and collected their heads and built towers of them ; but they slew violently of the people of Bagdad about ninety thousand. Some, when they could not have Bagdadis, cut the heads of Syrians who were with them and other prisoners ; others, when heads of men were wanting, cut off the heads of ladies of the marriage-bed ; others, when they had no captive, took those that came their way and in the heat of the moment slew their companion and friend, who redeemed the enemy with his life, taking no account of friend or brother, for they could not fail in obedience, nor would they accept ransom nor would entreaty avail anyone. And this number aforesaid was besides those, who perished in the siege or storming or were drowned in the Tigris ; for many are said to have hurled themselves into the water and died by drowning, and among their number Faraj, whom, when he was escaping by boat, they assailed from both banks with arrows and wounded ; and the boat was overturned and he was drowned. And there were built about a hundred and twenty towers, as I was told by Qazi Tajuddin Ahmad Namani, the Hanifite, Governor of Bagdad, who died at Damascus in the beginning of the month of Muharram in the year 834.* Allah Almighty have mercy upon him ! Then Timur laid waste the city, after he had taken thence the hidden wealth and made poor its people and desolated its habitations, and overturned the whole city from top to bottom, so that after it had been the city of peace, it became the house of surrender. And its feeble people that remained they took captive and the hands of the time tore them apart and scattered them utterly after they had lived in shade and luxury and dwelt in two gardens on the right side and the left, but now

* A.D. 1431.

in their homes the owl and crow made nests and in the morning only their houses appeared*; and this city is more famous than can be described and the aroma of its excellence and merits more fragrant than can be shown ; but let it suffice that it has the name and fame of City of Peace, and in it, as is said, the Imam does not die.

CHAPTER XVII

THAT TYRANT RETURNS AND HALTS AT QARABAGH

T HEN he marched with those Turks, each of whom would be truly called in Turkish an insolent tyrant, and resolved to make winter quarters in a place rightly called Qarabagh† among the Turks and Arabs in accordance with its qualities and nature. And he came there at evening, like a hovering hawk, nay rather an owl of ill omen, exploring the surrounding borders and especially the realms of Rum.

* i.e., empty houses.   † Black garden.

CHAPTER XVIII

OF THE LETTER WHICH THAT OBSTINATE ONE SENT TO THE SULTAN OF RUM, ILDARIM ABA YAZID*

THEN he sent a letter to the Sultan of Rum, Aba Yazid, that stalwart champion of the faith, and openly set forth what he sought concerning the country of Rum without circumlocution or enigmas, using Sultan Ahmad and Qara Yusuf as an excuse; saying that " they had both escaped the might of his swords and that they were the cause of havoc and destruction of cities and ruin of men and an omen of evil and ill fortune, and like Pharaoh and Haman in pride and insolence; and that if Pharaoh and Haman and their soldiers advanced and betook themselves with their men to the asylum of your protection, wherever they came, bringing with them ruin and disaster, yet truly they would not, like those two, suffer harm under the protection of the Lord of Rum. But beware of receiving them and repel them rather, seize them, throw them into prison and put them to death, wherever you find them; and beware of opposing our command, since all the grip of our power would fall upon you. For you have already heard the fate of our enemies and the examples displayed in their case and what has fallen upon them from us when they resisted and opposed and already it is clear to you how we dealt with them. And you do not need much talk between ourselves and you, much less combat and battle, when we have already given you plain arguments, and already set examples before you "—along with a mixture of diverse threats and intimidations and harangues designed to inspire fear and panic.

However, Aba Yazid was eager to fight and courageous and could not even restrain himself a little, since he was a just ruler, pious and brave in defence of religion, who when he had said and begun anything, did not rest until he had brought it to a conclusion. Because of his justice he enjoyed favourable fortune and his power had increased at home and he had subdued the whole kingdom of Karaman and put to death its King, Sultan Ala-uddin, whose two sons he kept prisoners.

* Bayezid I.

He had also subdued the kingdoms of Mantasha and Sarukhan, but Amir Yakub, son of Alishah, Governor of the province of Karaman, fled from him to Timur. And he had subdued all the realms of the Christians from the borders of the Balkan Mountains to the kingdoms of Erzinjan.

Therefore, as soon as he read Timur's letter, and understood the nature of his words, at one moment rising, the next lying down, he was seized with violent anger and indignation, now raising his voice, now lowering it, and was as though he had drunk hasheesh. Then he said, " Shall he frighten me by this folly or drive me to flight by these fables ? Does he suppose that I am like the kings of the barbarians or the savage Tatars of Dasht or that in collecting forces I am like the army of India ? Or that my army is in battle like the host of Iraq or my Muslim warriors like the armies of Syria or its mixed horde like my army ? Or does he not know that I know his affairs and how he has treacherously deceived kings and in what way he has always weakened one after another ? But I will lay bare this whole business and reveal his secrets. So far as concerns his original state, certainly he was a brigand, a shedder of blood, who violated all that is sacred, broke pacts and obligations, an eye turned from good to evil. And he charged and raged and conquered and presently lifted his head and was proud and gained for himself a wider field, while men paid no heed to him ; and he remained from the time he appeared a child, until his hair turned grey with vice and having acquired much, yet he did not come to maturity. However, his tribe was inflamed, after it had been a little spark, and the scattered seeds of his single grain became a full sack.

" As for the kings of Persia, truly he entertained them with deceit and cunning and then received them with horse and foot and hastened to kill them, after they had had an opportunity of killing him.

" As for Toqtamish Khan, truly the most part of his army betrayed him. But where could those base Tatars acquire the blow of a mighty sword and what have they but throwing of arrows against the lions of Rum ? As for the armies of Hind, truly he deceived them in their business and their stratagem returned to their own throats and their leaders were divided and their Sultan dead.

" As for the army of Syria, their condition is well known, and what befell them is a secret to none, for when their Sultan had died and their supports were shattered, their affairs were torn asunder and undermined, they attacked one another and their chief heads were cut off and only little heads remained among them ; therefore time scattered the pearls of their necklace and their kingdom with Damascus suffered dispersion ; further they have the appearance of spring but the reality of winter ; it is said of them : many and united they go to rest, but they rise divided and separate ; truly like the Sabæans, those hosts were scattered. Then his army did its business there without restraint and since the air was free to it, laid eggs and sang.* But if they had been at harmony among themselves, they would have ground him to pieces and scattered his whole army and overthrown him utterly, but though they might be thought to be united, yet their hearts were divided. But even if they had remained rightly united with arrows well aimed, strength of attack, warlike force, and firmness of spears, and shown themselves fine fighters and warlike lions, where had they the united order of our armies and that firm strength, with which we charge with united force and aid each other ? And what a difference between one who controls barefooted and naked men and one who controls the armed and warlike ! To fight is our habit, to join in combat our aim, to struggle for the faith our task. The law of waging war for the cause of Allah Almighty is our rule : one fights, like a dog, grasping at this world, but we wage war to establish the word of Allah which is the highest thing. Our soldiers spend their lives and wealth for Allah, that they may gain Paradise ; and how the ears of the infidels ring with their blows and the points of spears resound with their swords and how the nostrils of the sons of the Cross snort with the bending of their bows ! If we order them to hurl themselves into the sea, they do so ; if we urge them to shed blood of infidels, they obey. They threaten with their bent bows the defences of the infidels, and hasten towards them and seize the reins of their horses ; and whenever they hear the voice of battle, they fly thither and do not say to their king, when he sends them into the eddies of disaster and danger, ' We will sit here : you go, with your lord, and fight.' And we have warriors on foot stronger than mail-clad cavalry. Their battle-axes are sharp, their nails cling to their prey, like ravening lions or brave and fierce leopards. Their hearts are filled with love of us, and do not nurse within

* Like a lark.

hidden malice against us, but their faces shine beautifully in battle and look to their lord. In a word, our whole occupation and chief object and business is to destroy utterly the infidels, collect captives and gather spoils and we are fighters in the way of Allah, who do not fear the abuse of the abuser. I know that this speech will rouse you to invade our countries: but if you should not come, may your wives be condemned to triple divorce, but if I flee from you, when you invade my countries and decline to fight with you, then may my wives be utterly condemned to that triple divorce."

Then he ended his speech and replied in this manner. But as soon as Timur read this reply, he was excited and said: " The son of Othman is mad, for he was prolix and sealed the purpose of his letter with the mention of women." For among them the mention of women is a crime and grave offence, so much so that they do not even pronounce the word woman, and studiously avoid it, saying, if a daughter is born to one of them: " One who hides behind the veil has been born," or " a mistress of the bed," or " a veiled one," or something of that sort.

CHAPTER XIX

THAT OWL FLIES TO LAY WASTE THE REALMS OF RUM

TIMUR, therefore, found an opportunity of attacking Ibn Othman,* and sought a friend and a road and looked for a guide and reviewed his army: wild beasts seemed collected and scattered over the earth and stars dispersed, when his army flowed hither and thither, and mountains to walk, when it moved, and tombs to be overturned, when it marched, and the earth seemed shaken by violent movement, when the army marched hither and thither and the last day displayed its terrible signs.

And he ordered the appointed heir of his empire, his grandson, Mahomed Sultan, son of Jehangir, to come to him from Samarkand, with Saifuddin the Amir; then he moved towards Rum, fortune aiding him, not by the favour of Allah, and there that proud sea and dark night spread and after circling and wandering halted at the fort Kamakh.

* Bayezid.

DESCRIPTION OF THE FORT OF KAMAKH

Truly this fort is firm like the knowledge of God, and as fortified and invulnerable as the faith of the devout worshipper. The arrow of imagination would not cross the ditch of its inaccessible strength and the javelin-thrower of ingenuity would not find a way to reach it. Divine Providence like an architect set its strong foundations on inaccessible cliffs and the Creator built its towers geometrically like a builder. It is not too high or too low, besides excelling in its invulnerable defence. On one side the river Euphrates kisses its feet, on the other a wide valley guards its loftier parts, lest the feet should find a place to stand there, and through it water flows into the Euphrates. But on the other side is a cliff concerning which, when the sight fell upon it, the tongue of contemplation would say " Truly this thing is most wonderful."

But he took it without effort and entered its enclosure without perambulation or delay—and this after Mahomed Sultan had joined him, to whom he entrusted the whole business of besieging and storming it. The manner of it was in this wise : that valley behind the fort because of its slope frustrated those who might approach, for this reason, that the place was slippery and could not be filled because of its width or crossed because of the great space between. The arrow would not vie with its width nor would firm ground be found in it beneath the feet on the deepest scrutiny. But as soon as he had merely glanced at the fort, he saw its character, and ordered timber to be cut and logs brought. Forthwith as though in a moment they destroyed houses and cut down trees and bringing all that material and logs hurled them into the bottom of the valley, and thus made the ground of it flat and filled up its length and breadth. But as soon as the people of the fort saw this work, they threw fire and ashes on to those logs, and they burst into flame. But they cared not about the foundations of the fort, since they rested on the breasts of the hills. However, this did not foil his purpose or defeat his plan ; nay, he forthwith ordered each of his men to bring from those deserts as great quantity of stones, as formerly of timber. And scattering like ants and locusts over those deserts, hills, wastes and levels, they brought stones to the valley and at once filled that open space with stones and rocks. Then he ordered to be done with those stones in that wide space, what will be done with those men in Hell, on the day when it will be said to Hell : " Art thou filled ? ' and it will say ' Is there aught to be added ? ' Therefore they hurled some gathered heaps of those stones into that valley and filled it and there remained in the open spaces twice the amount of those stones that had been thrown down. But the valley being filled with stones, they crossed over them and approaching the walls, brought ladders and climbed and clung to the ramparts of the fort. Then the people of the fort ceased from battle and sought security, saying " Enter in peace." This siege and forced surrender happened in the month Shawal in the year 804.*

And when he was holding that fort, he ordered those stones to be removed from the valley ; therefore they carried them immediately and threw them in the place from which they had taken them.

Then he set over the fort one named Al Shams and departed thence after a stay of only one day. This fort is half a day's journey from Erzinjan, and was among those which are famous in the world for difficulty of capture and obstinacy in defence. Therefore so soon as he had gained it and done violence to it with his virile sword and after storming it handed it over for plunder, he dispatched couriers concerning that prize of victory to all that came and went in his kingdoms, with despatches, in which he related all his exploits, whether present or past. And the title of this account was in these words with translation : the poet said :

" With the edge of bloody swords, Praise be to Allah !
We stormed in war the fort of Kamakh."

And he mentioned therein Ibn Othman† and his own address to him, and the foolish reply received from him. And among other things he particularly set forth this, " We did not wrong him nor were we hostile to him, but using fair words we counselled him to expel from the sores of his realm the matter of corruption, to wit, Ahmad Jalairi and Qara Yusuf Turkoman, who laid waste provinces and destroyed men ; for to favour rebellion is rebellion, and to foster impiety is impiety. And a wicked man abandoned and resourceless is worse than an evil tyrant who dissembles. But those two became his vazirs in outrage ; he the Amir ; they are little enemies, he the great

* A.D. 1402.   † Bayezid.

one ; and in that thing they are his tax-gatherers and agents ; and as the lord is, so is his companion. And they brought him harm and no good ; loss, but no gain ; and it is as though he had spoken about them, who set forth their words and deeds, when he said :

" ' The nearness of the healthy helps not the scabious, but the healthy is infected with the disease.'

" Nor did he abandon his perverse way, and he became by protecting them like him who protected the lame hyena. We forbade him, but he did not refrain ; we advised him, but he paid no heed ; we showed him the examples of others, but he neglected them ; and the tongue of our revenge upon foes proclaimed to him : ' Beware, beware ! ' With our habit of courtesy and kindness we had put our name in our letters next to his, but he exceeded his bounds and showed his unreason, for in a letter of his he put his name under that of Tahartan, which befitted him and was well done ; and without doubt Tahartan compared with us is like one of our slaves and the least of our subjects. Then when he, Aba Yazid, received our letter and replied to us, he put his own name in gold above ours through folly and lack of culture."

Then he related that he was setting forth to conquer the realms of Rum. And in this writing and narrative he used full and diffuse style, for he was well-versed in books and histories, whence he sought aid in his speeches and replies.

CHAPTER XX

SETTING FORTH WHAT IBN OTHMAN RESOLVED AGAINST HIM, WHEN THAT FLOOD BURST UPON HIM

THEREFORE, when Ibn Othman understood his purpose and that he had resolved upon war, he turned his attention to conflict with him and prepared to confront him. And he was then engaged in besieging the wicked and infidel inhabitants of Stambul,* and was on the point of taking the city and war was about to remove the load of their crimes. But though he had his army with him, yet he ordered the leaders of his warriors and the bold eagles of his army and the

* Constantinople.

falcons and the finest of his braves and nobles of Karmian*
and the valiant horsemen of the seacoasts, the stallions of
Karaman, the soldiers of the provinces of Mantasha, the
cavalry of Sarukhan and all the Amirs of the tumans and
sanjaks† and lords of standards, leaders of divisions and all
the governors of posts and places under the sway of both the
capitals Brusa and Adrianople, and everyone that carrying his
white standard painted the green sea with the red blood of
blond Greeks and split the black heart of every blue-eyed
enemy with his black arrows, mounted on his piebald steed—
all these he ordered to carry out their business and take their
precautions and arms and he used as allies every noble and
unbeliever who had entered the Faith of the Muslims, that he
might attack every foe and usurper.

And he called to aid the Tatars, a people of strength and
wealth and true ; they have fertile flocks, with which they
fill countries and with their leaders and followers occupy high
mountains and plains. Often one of them possesses ten
thousand camels, none of which carries burdens and likewise
horses which are never saddled or bridled ; but the number of
sheep and cattle cannot be counted or reckoned, " and none
knoweth the armies of thy Lord but Himself : and this is
naught but a warning to men." They have in the realms of
Rum and Karaman up to the plains of Siwas winter and
summer resorts ; kings and sultans put trust in them ; they
have payments for diverse charities ; if any poor man comès to
them or rich stranger or student or man of learning, they collect
for him so much of sheep, cattle, wool, hair, curds, and smooth
skins, as to suffice him and his to the end of life. Because of
their multitude and that of the peoples which they have with
them, they are called the eighteen thousand worlds.

And each shouted with the echo of these mountains, so far
as he could make his voice carry, his ready compliance, and
hastened to execute his commands with obedience and fresh
vigour. And all the Tatars to a man readily joined him, and
there were drawn to him at once all the mountains of those
armies and the seas of troops and he mightily urged the armies
of soldiers fighting for the Faith to engage with Timur.

* Corresponding to the ancient Caria and part of Lydia.
† Districts.

CHAPTER XXI

WHAT THAT CUNNING DECEIVER DID AND SAID, THAT HE MIGHT
ENTICE THE ARMIES OF THE TATARS FROM IBN OTHMAN

BUT Timur, after waiting a little, kindled the tinder of his counsel and lit more of his fire to entice the Tatars from Ibn Othman, and for this purpose he wrote to their lords, chief Amirs and leaders and their Amir named Fazil (the excellent) ; and truly he excelled in virtues, but that he had no experience of affairs and possessed not the arts of the base :

" Your nobility " (he wrote) " is also mine, and your race joined with mine and our countries with yours : we have the same ancestors, we are all shoots and branches of the same tree ; our fathers long ago in the past grew up in one nest and gradually occupied countless others ; you are therefore truly a shoot from my stock, a branch of my branches, members of my members, my own marrow and my intimates. You are to me an inner garment ; other men are only an outer. Others may have acquired royal dignity, but˙ you hold it from the very beginning ; for your ancestors were of yore kings of the realms of Turan, of whom some were unwillingly transferred to these regions and inhabited them, and thereby they were superior in nobility and aptitude for rule and the means of lordship, and this vigour and force they maintained with zeal until they passed to the mercy of the Almighty ; and your last king was Artana who died in the Faith and the greatest king in the realms of Rum was your least servant : nor, praise be to Allah ! was the backbone of your power ever broken or your abundance diminished ; how then have you let this shame come to you, for you have become subjugated, so that you are bewitched, and after being greatest of all, how have you become least of all ? You are not in the house of contempt or perdition and the land of Allah is wide : and why should you be slaves of a man who is a son of slaves set free by Ali Saljuqi ?* And I know not what is the reason and cause of that and whence arises that fraternity and alliance, without dissent and discord. But in any case I am certainly the fittest and worthiest to

* The Seljuk Sultan, Alauddin, gave lands near Angora to Ertoghrul. Later Alauddin II conferred additional lands on Osman, who became independent on the death of his overlord.

manage your affairs and look to your interests. But if indeed you are to occupy these places and sell those wide realms for the mean kingdoms of Rum, yet at least you should be, like your fathers, rulers of these countries, holding the ramparts of the forts, and sitting on their hump, stretching your hands into them and holding their halter ; and this aim will be accomplished, when this war has been fought out by you and the racecourse made level for us by removing Ibn Othman from the midst ; but when the air is clear of the adversary and watering places made clear for me in these countries, and, after conquering these provinces, I take my own way therein, then I will give the bow to its maker and settle in the house its builder and give back waters to their beds and make you possessors of villages, forts, cities and their plains, and establish each of you there according to his merit : if then it seems good to you not to give aid against us and you have an opportunity of going over to us, take your chance as a prize and take your share of it and so you will be in appearance and truth on our side.

" But now outwardly you will be with Ibn Othman, inwardly with us, until at our invasion you separate and slide over to our army."

And the steed of his address did not cease to leap into the bosom of their minds or grow weary in making pretence, by the eloquence of which he would have brought contempt upon the speech of Aswad Bin Yafar, by penetrating like a diver into the vortex of their minds, that he might turn them from following Ibn Othman and treading in his footprints, like Satan when he calls men to wickedness, until he won their minds with this speech and they becoming ready to obey his words, were utterly demented by love of lordship, which even from a distance reduced to slavery the children of the free-born and enslaved the greatest of good men and true and hurled the heads of the wisest, who join action to knowledge, headlong into the fire of Hell. And so they agreed with him to desert, when it came to battle.

CHAPTER XXII

NOW Ibn Othman feared his invasion into the countries
of Rum, because the crops were now being cut and
fruits were swelling and the green things of the earth were
blackening and his subjects were sitting in the shade of security
and luxury; so fearing that the faithful might suffer harm
from Timur or that sparks might fly from the flame of his fire
to the families of his kingdom, he hastened to meet him,
driven by the prompters of destined ruin to drink his cup in his
own vineyard; and he wished that battle should be joined
outside his realm in the tracts of Siwas and so caused the
swelling torrents of his armies to flow and led them through
desert places, sparing his subjects that they might not be
trampled down by the beasts of burden; for he was merciful
to the weakest of his subjects and tender towards the poor of
his people. They say that it happened in one of his expeditions,
that one of his followers thirsting came into the house of a
certain woman and asked of her a drink of water; but she was
more ill-omened than Basus, who passed into a proverb for
greed and malice; and she said she had nothing to drink with
the words, " Be off, and do not waste your trouble," and when
he, overcome with thirst, saw in the house in a vessel a draught
of milk and drank it, she said, " This is the food of the children,"
and complained about it to Ibn Othman, who sent for the man
and questioned him; but he, fearing the severity of his
punishment, denied the deed; therefore Ibn Othman said to
the woman, " I will slit his belly to find whether he spoke true
things or false, but if milk appears in his belly, I will pay you
the price; but if I find that he has spoken the truth, I will
show in you an example of like punishment." Then she
replied, " By Allah! He certainly drank; and from the truth
of that which I have said, I perceive his falsehood; yet I
would wish him freed from distress, and I pardon his fault;"
but Ibn Othman said, " It must be that justice be done, and
this judgment will settle the case." Then he sent for a sword
and cut him in the midst and did in his belly what he had

promised ; and his belly being slit poured itself forth, and milk flowed out, which appeared mingled with his blood. Then he ordered him to be carried through the camp and that it should be proclaimed over him : " This is the reward of him, who under the rule of the just king, Ibn Othman, takes aught that is not due to him." Then Ibn Othman continued his march and proceeded thereon night and day.

CHAPTER XXIII

SHOWING HOW THAT LAME ONE OUTWITTED IBN OTHMAN AND HIS ARMY

BUT when Timur understood that Ibn Othman had taken the way of the desert, he cast him off, as the Jews cast the book of God behind their backs, and took the high road of well-tilled country and with his army approached shades, springs and choice fruits, where on every hand the eloquent tongue of their condition recited and proclaimed :

" I care naught whence I attain eminence,
Whether by inheritance or gain."

And they ceased not to delight in crops and pastures and udders, amid sidras without thorns and tall trees set in order and spreading shade and flowing water and gentle breezes and health-giving delights, in security, tranquillity, abundance and amplitude, without fear, journeying at their convenience, confident of prosperity and victory, promising themselves wealth and spoils, bending Fate and Providence to their will.

No lukewarmness cooled the fervour of their zeal to bring tears to the eye of the enemy and gain an easy prize, and in the well-ordered diadem of the stars of his armies was no loosening nor amid the lions of his host was there panic or fear nor in receiving the enemy to the banquet did the spears weaken in their strokes or break ; but Ibn Othman did not rise from his sleep, until Timur had laid waste his countries and he was seized with panic as though it were the day of resurrection and bit his hands with grief and remorse and roared and howled and burning with the fire of anger was almost suffocated and abandoned rest and sleep and resolved forthwith to return ;

then rolling together the waves of the sea of his armies and massing the piles of his mountains and towers, he returned, whence he had come, and marched without pause, and hastily; and the march wearied them with its speed, the place by its solitude, the season by its heat, the Sultan by his roaring, nor did they come to him, until every one of them was already weary with sickness and the tongue of their condition read: " This trouble we have endured because of our march."

SECTION

Now Timur had already reached the city of Angora, and his cavalry and infantry were resting, trained, waiting for battle, and ready to engage, nay they anxiously sought that with one mind, and already went in front to the water, like the leaders of the Koreish,* and like the Muslims of Badar, they left his† army in a thirsty place ; and they were perishing with distress and violent thirst and being murdered by thirst for want of water, and it was as though he himself had shown them this place and invited them by reciting these verses :

" O guest, if you visit us, you will find that we are the guests,
And you are the master of hospitality."

And Angora is the place mentioned by Aswad Bin Yafar in his poem *Al Tanana*.

" They dwell at Angora ; the water of the river‡ flows over them, falling from the mountains ;
O delight ! But whenever time is cheated by delight, it ends in grief and calamity."

But when the armies had approached each other and those wild beasts were mutually raging, the plains and deserts being filled with them, and when the left wing engaged with the right and the right with the left, the Tatars withdrew from the army of Ibn Othman and joined Timur's army, according to the arrangement and plan ; and they were the strength of the army and a numerous part among the host of Ibn Othman, so many that the multitude of the Tatars was about a third of that great and warlike army, nay, it is said that the whole host of the Tatars nearly equalled the army of Timur.

* The tribe of Mahomed.   † Bayezid's.
‡ The Engari Su, a tributary of the Sakaria.

And Ibn Othman had with him his eldest son, Amir Suliman, who, when he saw the deed of the Tatars, certain of the calamity, which threatened his father, took the rest of the flower of the army and withdrew from the battlefield and turning his back abandoned his father in the fierce stress of battle and made his way with his men towards Brusa, and none remained with Ibn Othman except footmen, and those inferior, and a few mail-clad troops. None the less, with his remaining companions he sustained the battle, fearing that if he fled, he would encounter that divorce, and it was in that battle and confusion as is said in the poem of *Antara :*

> " Truly I remember you, while the spears quench their
>   thirst upon me,
> And the white swords of Hind are washed in my blood,
> And I desired the kisses of the swords, because they shone
> Like your flashing, gleaming mouth."

And he was patient of the turn of fortune and wished according to the rule of Imam Malik to perform what he had undertaken. Then he was surrounded by cavalry like arms by bracelets. And when the kindred of Ibn Othman were certain of defeat and knew that they had fallen into the army of calamity, the infantry stood firm against mail-clad cavalry, skilfully using axes and all the sharpest swords. And in those ranks were about five thousand who scattered their enemies and routed many of them ; yet they were like a man who sweeps away dust with a comb or drains the sea with a sieve or weighs mountains with a scruple. And out of the clouds of thick dust they poured out upon those mountains and the fields filled with those lions continuous storms of bloody darts and showers of black arrows and the tracker of Destiny and hunter of Fate set dogs upon cattle and they ceased not to be overthrown and overthrow and to be smitten by the sentence of the sharp arrow with effective decree, until they became like hedgehogs, and the zeal of battle lasted between those hordes, from sunrise to evening, when the hosts of iron gained the victory and there was read against the men of Rum the chapter of " Victory."*

Then their arms being exhausted and the front line and reserves alike decimated, even the most distant of the enemy advanced upon them at will and strangers crushed them with

* A reference to the Koran.

swords and spears and filled pools with their blood and marshes with their limbs and Ibn Othman was taken and bound with fetters like a bird in a cage. This battle occurred about one mile from the city of Angora on the fourth day of the week, the 27th of Zulhaj, in the year 804* and most of the army was destroyed by thirst and heat, for it was the 18th of Tamuz.

SECTION

And Amir Suliman reached Brusa, the place of refuge of Ibn Othman, and collecting what was there of treasure, wealth, women, children and precious things, he sought to transfer them to the mainland of Adrianople, visiting many places beyond the sea,† whose arm is drawn into the Black Sea, which as though gaining courage stretches up to the country of Dasht and Karj (Georgia), between which and the Caspian Sea lie the Caucasus Mountains.

CHAPTER XXIV

OF THE PANIC WHICH HAPPENED. AFTER IBN OTHMAN FELL INTO DISTRESS AND BONDAGE

AFTER the head of the kingdom of Rum had suffered this disaster and those great bodies of its army had been crushed by a violent blow and the ill-omened army had destroyed them and the magpie had croaked at dawn and the owl screeched at evening and the Imam of Fate and Providence in the mihrab of its people had read to the assembly‡ " A.L.M. The Greeks are defeated," then the heads of the kingdom submitted and the leaders and the forts and castles were seized with a tremor, men near and far were shaken and the obedient and refractory alike were troubled ; therefore they took to flight like fleeing asses, despairing of household, country, wealth and life, their head being removed and none remaining to rouse martial valour.

But when they heard that Amir Suliman, drawing men to himself, had resolved to cross the sea and go over to the mainland of Adrianople, men flowed to him out of the valleys

* A.D. 1402   † i.e., The Sea of Marmara.
‡ A Quotation from the Koran, in which the Greeks are denoted by the word " Rum."

184

and passes, hoping through him to emerge from that flood of swelling calamity.

Therefore he made peace with the people of Stamboul and conciliated them and making a pact with them lest they should deceive each other, he allowed them time, then requested them to bring him help from the two straits of Gallipoli and Stamboul, since these two seas have no nearer way or crossing between the two continents than these two straits. For the sea of Alexandria extends to Antioch and Alaya; then it turns towards the countries of Rum, and is shut off by mountains before it reaches the northern regions, and thus is continuously diminished and the distance between the two shores is lessened, until one is visible from the other and the two sides are almost joined, the length of this conjunction covering a journey of about three days. Then it grows wider and expands with a bold sweep: then the masses of its waves bend in a circle and are tightly compressed and it runs towards the countries of Dasht and Karj (Georgia), until it washes as I have said the country of Caucasus, nor could the subtlest philosopher or most cunning geometer add in this narrow space a third crossing to these two.

Now the strait of Gallipoli was in the power of Muslim sailors; but the strait of Stamboul was in the power of the Christians, enemies of the Faith; and the part of this double strait and crossing which is widest and greatest also had Christian sailors. Therefore most of the men betook themselves and collected there. Then the Franks swiftly rushing up with shameless outrage plunged in the blood of Muslims and seized their women and their goods, and ranged hither and thither. For Ibn Othman, while he was besieging this city, had afflicted it and destroyed its country-houses and laid waste its plains and brought its people to extreme distress. In this situation, when the flood had come to the heights and inevitable disaster was threatening them, behold, Timur brings them liberation after distress, and Ibn Othman is reluctantly driven away from them! Whereupon they became bold and confident, all the more because the Muslims needed their help and seeking escape from the enemy threw themselves at their feet; and they as soon as they were freed from their own distress, seized as a prize the opportunity of taking revenge on the Muslims. Then they began to fill the ships with men and baggage, and crossed in them to Stamboul.

Now Stamboul is behind the summit of a mountain and peak of hills, and is one of the greatest cities of the world, so that it is commonly called Constantinia the Great. But when they had landed their ships behind that summit and were hiding beneath that strong mountain from the sight of those who were on the shore, they seemed like dead men, who fell into pits, hurled to the bottom of tombs, uncertain whither they were turning and where they were arriving, in the land of peace and Islam or the place of war and the bondage of base infidels ; then some of them disembarked, but they could not make their last testament or return to their families. But when the ships had come to land and were empty, all this crowd with the utmost eagerness and haste climbed upon them, without knowing what was coming to them and what was to be the issue of their affairs and with their vision blunted and their concerns confused they were like the stork and the fish mentioned in the book *Kalilah*. And the end was that, of that great multitude in all the ships only the white crows* escaped, and the enemies of the Faith raged at will against the Muslims ; but Amir Suliman, crossing the sea, gained command of that mainland, whose provinces he occupied and set affairs in order. And it is wider than this side, having more spacious pastures, more abundant crops, larger revenues and tributes and strong forts and posts. And the capital is Adrianople. And men joined Suliman and affairs in general were a little eased and improved.

CHAPTER XXV

OF THE SONS OF IBN OTHMAN AND HOW TIME SCATTERED AND DESTROYED THEM

THE said Sultan Bayezid † had these sons : Amir Suliman, the eldest, Isa, Mustafa, Mahomed and Musa, the youngest, each of whom sought a refuge and to each some of the better sort came from his father. Of these sons Mahomed and Musa were in the fort of Amasia, that is Kharshana, lofty, inacessible, of which Abil Tib wrote :

* That is, few.　　　　　　　　　† Ibn Othman.

186

" As long as he shall stand on the walls of Kharshana,
Through him will fall Greeks, crosses and churches.
Their brides shall be taken prisoners, their children
carried into bondage,
Crops shall be burned, the wealth they have gathered
shall be plundered."

The top of this fort is very high, as though it were hung from the dome of the sky : it is more difficult to descend than others to climb ; they call it the Bagdad of Rum, since its plain is crossed by a great river ; it is one day's journey from Tokat, if the journey be quickly completed.

As for Isa, he made his way to a certain fort, where he remained until he was murdered by his brother, Amir Suliman ; then Musa killed Amir Suliman to avenge Isa ; then after the rest Mahomed slew Musa and the commands of Mahomed repealed the institutes of the law of Musa and Isa, until he gave up his breath, at the beginning of the year 824,* dying of poison secretly given to him by Kujakar among the presents of Al Malik Muidi, and the kingdom passed from his hands to his son Murad, who held it in our time, that is in the year 840.†

As for Mustafa, he was lost, and nearly thirty men of that name were killed on his account.

CHAPTER XXVI

RETURNS TO THE AFFAIRS OF TIMUR AND HIS EVIL ATTEMPTS

THEN Timur, having captured Ibn Othman, pushed towards Brusa his host of soldiers and auxiliaries, and appointed as their commander Sheikh Nuruddin ; then following them, he arrived there with mighty dignity and tranquil breast and descended on the place, like an inevitable destiny, seizing whatever came to his hands of the whole resources of Ibn Othman, wives, riches, treasures, followers and slaves. And he presented the Amirs of the Tatars and their leaders with precious robes and gained their good will by courtesy and distributed their Amirs among his own and joined

* A.D. 1420. † A.D. 1436.

all their strength to his own leaders, and greatly commended them to these and ordered them to treat them with the utmost kindness. But he maintained his old habit in plundering precious things, hunting mankind and carrying off prisoners. Ibn Othman he ordered to be brought to him every day, and received him with kind and cheerful speech and marks of pity, then derided and mocked him.

CHAPTER XXVII

HOW HE GRIEVOUSLY AFFLICTED IBN OTHMAN, WITH EVIL TALES OF A PAST TIME

THEN he one day held a public banquet and when the wing of hilarity was loosened for gentle and simple, he rolled up the carpet of prohibition and command and unrolled the carpet of wine and music and when the place was full of men he ordered that Ibn Othman should be brought in ; and he came with trembling heart and hampered by his fetters, but he ordered him to be of good courage and put aside his fear and seating him comfortably and treating him with courtesy, he removed his sadness.

Then he ordered circles of merrymaking to be formed and they were formed ; and he ordered that the sun of wine should move from the east of the goblet to the west of the lips and it was done : but as soon as the clouds of veils were scattered from the sun of the cupbearers and stars were circling in the sky of society, rising quickly at the command of Timur like new moons, Ibn Othman saw that the cupbearers were his consorts and that all of them were his wives and concubines ; then the world seemed black to him and he thought the likeness of the agonies of death sweet and his breast was torn and his heart burned, his distress increased, his liver was crushed, groans came from the bottom of his heart and his sighs were redoubled, his wound broke out again and his sore was newly inflamed and the butcher of calamity scattered salt on the wound of his affliction.

This calamity befell Ibn Othman, because in his letter he had sworn an oath mentioning women, for it was remarked before that among the Jagatais—nay all tribes of Turks—the mention of women is regarded as the greatest offence and crime against them ; this besides was the retribution for the crime, which Ibn Othman had committed against the wives of Tahartan at Erzinjan. But the crown of Ibn Othman's affliction came from the kindness which Timur showed to the sons of the Prince of Karaman ; for Ibn Othman had formerly subdued the kingdom of Karaman and put to death its ruler Sultan Alauddin after besieging him and taking him prisoner and had cast his sons, Mahomed and Ali, into the prison of Brusa, both of whom he kept in perpetual misery and distress, until Tamerlane brought them relief—throwing Ibn Othman into prison and then presenting them when released with robes of honour and after showing them much kindness, setting them over their original capital. I have written :

" He did not reject Muavia, because he loved Ali, but to hurt Yazid."

and it is said :

" Not from love for him he favours him, but he hates the tribe of others."

And I have written on the spur of the moment :

" I cultivate friendship with the foes of my foes, tho' there
    is no bond between them and me.
And I hate him who harasses my friend, tho' he abun-
    dantly satisfy my desires.
For let my enemy be afflicted and let my slaves prosper ;
    thereby I gain friends."

And Amir Mahomed is he, whom Amir Nasiruddin Mahomed, son of Dalfar, Amir of the ravaging Turkomans, took prisoner, and killed his son Mustafa in battle and sent him bound to Al Malik Al Muid—which happened in the month of Rajab in the year 840.*

*.A.D. 1436.

CHAPTER XXVIII

AT that time Amir Isfandiar, son of Aba Yazid and one of the kings of Rum, who had a firm seat of dominion, which he had inherited from his father, was an absolute ruler, between whom and the Othman kings lay hereditary enmity and hostility and he had under his sway certain cities, valleys and plains ; among them the city of Sinope, commonly called the island of lovers, whose beauty passed into a proverb throughout the world. Set near the sea on a great island it offers a difficult approach ; it has a mountain more beautiful than the buttocks of the houris of Paradise, and adjoining it is a pass more graceful than the slenderest loin ; and it was a fort for Isfandiar and his place of refuge, where he kept his treasures, and his stronghold—more rebellious than Satan, more tenacious than the hand of a miser, who fears poverty. He also possessed Kastamuni, his capital, and sea for his ships ; also Samsun, a fort on the shore of the sea of the Mussulmans, set opposite a like fort of the wicked Christians, which two are less than a stone's throw apart and each fears the other ; and he had also other forts, villages and towns in valleys and mountain-tops.

But when Isfandiar learned what that traitor, Timur, had done with the sons of the Prince of Karaman and the Tatars and Qara Iluk and Tahartan, lord of Erzinjan, and Amir Yaqub, son of Alishah, Governor of Karmian, and those of the lords of Mantasha and Sarukhan who had gone to him, and that he did no violence to those who submitted to him and complied with his orders, he hastened to present himself to him and prepared to approach him and brought excellent presents and gifts of great price and Timur received him courteously and dealt familiarly with him and confirmed him in his dignity, that he might annoy Ibn Othman ; then he instructed him and the Princes of Karaman and Amirs of those countries, who had shown themselves ready to obey and submit to him, to have public prayers recited and money coined in the name of Mahmud Khan and the Great Amir Timur Kurkan. And they obeyed his orders and shunned what he forbade and so were safe from plunder and havoc. This Isfandiar died during the year 843,* in old age, and was the last of the kings who visited Timur ; he was succeeded in his kingdom by his son Ibrahim Beg, between whom and his brother Qasim Beg disputes arose and Qasim betook himself to King Murad bin Othman. But Allah rules for ever.

SECTION

Then Timur carried off whatever treasures Ibn Othman and the rest had and scraped into his treasury everything valuable and excellent belonging to the kings of Rum, whether by inheritance or acquisition, and wintered in the provinces of Mantasha and used as he wished the means of investigation of his whole power for surveying its districts and came to their furthest borders and accurately and diligently exacted a fifth part of their resources.

His forces were scattered there in every direction and plunged like divers into the sea of the provinces of Mantasha from the eminences of its mountains to the very bottom of its valleys. Some climbed its mountain peaks and the tops of its forts ; some hanging from the ears of its summits, climbed its overhanging ramparts ; some rode on the shoulders of its slopes, descending to its shores, trampling with the feet of their onset the cheeks of its well-watered gardens, sitting on the withers of its people ; some took out the brain from skulls for the sake of wealth, seeking thence without hindrance whatever they wished, with one hand or both hands ; some lay on the prominence of its chest, the heads and faces of the submissive being bent over its back and some stretched the fingers of their oppression without check to its wrists and elbows, attacking its belly and hips from the west and east with the feet of rapine. They shaved heads, amputated necks, crushed arms, cut off shoulder-blades, burnt livers, scorched faces, gouged out eyes, split open bellies, blinded the sight, made tongues mute, blocked the hearing, crushed noses to the earth and brought low the lofty noses, lacerated mouths, shattered chests, crushed backs, pounded the ribs, split navels, melted hearts, severed sinews, shed blood, injured private parts, did violence to souls, destroyed men, poured out bodies like molten images, destroyed lives, and not a third or fourth part

* A.D. 1439.

of the subjects of Rum escaped the havoc which they dealt, but most of them were either strangled or struck down or hurled headlong or destroyed by goring or devoured by wild beasts.

CHAPTER XXIX

OF THE STORMING OF THE FORT OF IZMIR (SMYRNA) AND ITS DESTRUCTION, AND DESCRIBING BRIEFLY ITS WONDERFUL POSITION AND QUALITY

THEN he besieged the fort of Izmir, which is a stronghold in the midst of the sea : its spelling is difficult : *hamza*, with short i, z with a dot above, m with i and *ye* and r without any distinguishing mark ; the fort projected into the sea and by the difficulty of storming it and its powerful defence could burn the hearts of its suitors, with castles on mountains too inaccessible and remote to be won by horse and foot. But arranging matters rightly for besieging it he took it on the fourth day of the week, the 10th of the second month of Jumadi in the year 805,* the 6th of the first month of Kanon according to the calendar of Rum ; and he slew the grown men and cast in bonds the women and children and from the corpses of the slain built mosques and from the skulls raised towers ; then he despoiled that fort of its wealth and robbed it of its treasure and emptied it and desolated and plundered it and utterly drained its silver and gold and made the wings of glad news fly with these exploits, which news according to his presumption he sent through the world with propitious augury and swift flight.

* A.D. 1403.

CHAPTER XXX

OF THE FURTHERING OF HIS PURPOSE, WHILE HE WAS IN THE
COUNTRIES OF RUM, OF ATTACKING THE COUNTRIES OF THE
KHATAS AND CONQUERING THE KINGDOMS OF THE TURKS AND
JATAS AND HIS PLAN, WHILE HE WAS ENGAGED IN THE WEST,
TO DRAIN THE REMAINING PROVINCES OF THE EAST AND OF
THE MOGULS ; AND HOW THE OVERWHELMING DESTINY, WHICH
DESCENDED UPON HIM, CHECKED HIM, INFLAMING AND BURNING
HIS HEART, FORTUNE BETRAYING HIM AND UTTERLY OVER-
TURNING HIS CONDITION AND THAT QUITE SUDDENLY

THEN Timur had summoned from Samarkand his
grandson, Mahomed Sultan, and Amir Saifuddin, with
his family, as related before ; and this Mahomed Sultan was a
refuge for excellent men and haven for the learned ; the signs
of felicity appeared in the lines of his brow and the glad news
of nobility shone from his features :

" In the cradle the gleaming mark of prosperity
Spoke of the nobility of his grandsire with clear proof."

But Saifuddin was one of the companions of Timur in his
beginning and one of his chief counsellors, when he had reached
his goal; and these two had caused Ashbara to be built,
laying foundations therein of plunder and brigandage. It lies
near the countries of the Moguls and Jatas in the furthest limit
of the authority of Timur, where the countries of the Khatas
begin. And they set over that town an Amir by name Argun
Shah, giving him some divisions of the armies, that he might
keep watch on the borders of the Moguls, all which was done
under the orders of Timur. But when they had undertaken
it, this black deed quite displeased the Moguls, since they well
knew that if that viper stayed in their neighbourhood, he
would certainly give himself to destruction and they would
not be safe from his malice or be a match for his propinquity.
Therefore, troubled in mind and their inmost thoughts agitated,
they prepared to flee and leave their homes. But, therefore,
the Jagatais attacked them the more eagerly and all the worst
of both sides put forth the hand of insolence to inflict injury
and on every hand excess prevailed, drinking the cup of

brigandage, and devouring what fell into its hands, untouched by any religion or scruple of moderation. And this pleased the Jagatais and enmity arose between the two sides ; one lay in ambush for the other and the Jagatais began to fit out squadrons against them and to smite any of them who fell into their hands ; the Moguls also dealt in the same way with the Jagatais and expecting that Timur at such a distance from them would encounter fatal misfortune, they kept themselves to dangerous country, but this greatly rejoiced Timur, when it was reported to him. Then those two* fortified that place with every equipment and with troops, partly from the armies of Indians and of Multan, partly from the forces of Arabian Iraq and Azerbaijan, partly from the cavalry of Fars and Khorasan, partly from those who are called Jani-Karman, which troops with a *tuman*† of the army of the Jagatais they entrusted to the Amir Argun Shah and they came to Khajend, when they crossed the Jaxartes and proceeded to Samarkand, over which they set an Amir, by name Khwaja Yusuf, who walked in the fetters of obedience and sincerity. Then, leaving Samarkand, they both proceeded to that tyrant (Timur) ; then both died at the same time, Saifuddin in Khorasan and Mahomed Sultan in the territory of Rum.

And at the death of his grandson, Mahomed Sultan, Timur fell into great grief and clothed his army in black garments, and they observed the laws of public mourning, though they needed not black signs, since they were themselves a black horde. Then he sent his bones in a coffin to Samarkand with pomp and magnificence and an order that the people of the city should receive his body with lamentation and weeping and pay him due funeral rites and none should not be clad from head to feet in a black garment ; therefore at his approach the people of Samarkand went out and they had covered themselves to meet him with black garments and in black walked noble and humble, base and illustrious, as though the face of the world were covered with a fog of deepest night. Then they buried him in his fortified college, called Anshaya, within the city, in the year 805,‡ and when Allah Almighty gave his grandfather to destruction, they buried him beside him as will be related hereafter.

* Mahomed Sultan and Saifuddin.   † Ten thousand men.   ‡ A.D. 1403·

CHAPTER XXXI

HOW THE ANGER OF THAT HUNTER FELL ON ALLAHDAD WHOM HE BANISHED TO THE FURTHEST BORDERS

AFTER that horde, which Timur had sent away, had set out with their baggage, with Allahdad as leader, proceeding to attack Bagdad (and Allahdad had jealous companions, enemies and rivals; and envy is a collar of slavery on the neck of him who cherishes it and jealousy of companions is a wound, which does not easily heal); his enemies found a way free to pierce him with the spears of calumny and an opening to rend his fame with abuse, and this opportunity they took in his absence and ate his food without salt and using the abuse of the absent as a relish, accused him before Timur, to whom they related his deeds in Syria, namely that he had sought out endless treasures, and taken therefrom the more precious things for himself and that countless spoils of the more excellent sort had clung to him. And it was as they said and most of their charges were not unfounded and so they undermined his position and filled the mind of Timur with the heat of anger against him, especially as his wings had been cut by the death of his brother Saifuddin, whose power and authority were so great, that Timur himself dreaded and feared him, and his exploits had been displayed in the realms of Transoxiana and he left behind known results of his wisdom.

When therefore Allahdad came to Samarkand, Timur sent after him a command in his own name, that he should betake himself to Ashbara and there be ready for brigandage and forays and this was like perpetual exile, whereby he banished him to the borders of the realm and handed him over into the throat of the enemy and the mouth of the adversary, but he summoned thence to Samarkand Argun Shah, and Allahdad remained there, until Timur had been given over to the malediction of Allah.

Then the Moguls sending forth divisions against Ashbara began to plunder whatever wealth came to their hand whether mute or animate, seizing the chance while Timur was far from them. Meanwhile Allahdad defended himself bravely and moreover sent raids against them and by cunning dug pitfalls and snares for them, killing, capturing, stabbing and shattering, until he left Ashbara empty after Timur's death and these deeds will be told later.

CHAPTER XXXII

AN EXAMPLE SHOWING THE WAY THROUGH THE DEPTHS OF THAT SURROUNDING SEA, AND WHAT THE KEEN DIVER OF ITS EXPLORATION OBTAINED

THEN Timur, pitching his camp in the territories of Rum, sent a letter to Allahdad with orders in full and diffuse terms, to make a map of those regions and describe their condition in his reply, that he might explain to Timur the situations of those realms and show the nature of the way through them and the paths and explain to him the nature of their cities and villages, valleys and mountains, castles and forts, the nearer parts and the remote, the deserts and hills, wastes and deserts, landmarks and towers, waters and rivers, tribes and families, passes and broad roads, places marked and those without signs of the way, dwelling-places and houses for travellers, its empty places and its people, weaving the path of a diffuse style and avoiding abridgment and omission ; and explaining the distances between all the stages and the manner of the journey between all the dwelling-places, so far as he could and so far as his knowledge and information reached, from the Eastern region and the kingdoms of the Khatas and those places on the boundary up to those in the direction of Samarkand, which Timur himself knew ; and to take care that the greatest fullness of expression should be employed in the contents of the reply, that he might include therein according to his power abundance of facts and full exposition and in his account keep to the road of plain direction and avoid the hidden road in this writing, that he might also direct his industry to describing the remaining traces of places and defining things which had disappeared and showing the remains even to a mouthful of wormwood and southern wood.

Accordingly Allahdad composed a description in that manner and expressed it in the most elegant forms and finest style ; for he used many leaves of glistening papyrus, which he bound together and reduced to a square shape and set that delineation on them, drawing the shape of all those places and what things were there, movable and immovable, and in them showed everything according to Timur's command, towards east and west, distant and near, to right and left, villages and mountains, lengthwise and across, sky and earth, places barren and covered with trees, places abandoned and green, watering places and houses for travellers and added the names of all places and a delineation of them and the course of the road and a delineation thereof, its excellence and defects and presented what was absent, as though he had seen it and were the guide of that road and the explorer. And he sent it to Timur, according to his sudden demand for all those things from him, while he was moving hither and thither in the territories of Rum.

CHAPTER XXXIII

OF THE TREACHERY WHICH THAT DECEIVER COMMITTED AGAINST THE TATARS AFTER FINISHING THE AFFAIRS OF RUM

WHEN therefore Timur had got a clear draught of the provinces of Rum after muddy disturbance and the world had been seized with the greatest admiration for his exploits, and the people of Rum had been plundered and his soldiers had fully satisfied the lust of brigandage and the stream of that raging flood was filled with booty and the boy of spring had grown up and the old man of winter was infirm, then the Sultan, the blessed warrior and martyr, Ildarim Aba Yazid, was translated to the mercy of Allah the Glorious ; he had been shut in an iron cage at the camp of Timur, which Timur did only for revenge, as Caesar* did with Shapur ; and he had intended to take the Sultan with him to Transoxiana, but he died in his camp in the territory of Rum at Akshehr, where also Timur's grandson Mahomed Sultan died.

Then after resolving to depart and collecting baggage he called together the leaders of the Tatars, for whom he secretly intended injury, and said : " Now the time has come when

* Maximian.

I shall give you the fruit of your diligence and reward your deserts, but this place is unfavourable for us and we are weary of long delay in the narrow places of Rum, come then, let us go to a wider field and refresh ourselves by leaving narrow limits of time and space for the broad tracts of the fields of Siwas, that pleasant retreat of men and home of the wise. Therefore after arranging the affairs of this great region, we will establish every one of you there, according as our noble judgment finds fitting ; for it is necessary that the whole manner of it should be rightly discussed and the direction and execution thoroughly planned ; how its cities and forts are to be held in check and its villages and plains administered ; the total of its tumans and fiefs must be reckoned and its boundaries singly and as a whole.

"But as soon as we have ascertained what things are included in one total and what there appears tangled has become plain to us, we shall enquire into your heads and tribes, gain knowledge of your affairs, assemble your leaders, gather together your lords, compute your numbers, accurately ascertain your fathers and ancestors, consider your brothers and children, note your relatives and kinsmen, obtain knowledge of the resources of Rum and make you heirs of their land and country, then settle this question according to the number of heads and distribute among all the precious things of these realms and send you away generously treated and we shall suffice to relieve the want of yourselves and your families, since you have put faith in us. In any event we shall treat each of you according to his merits and use such clemency towards you, that its memory will be kept for ever in books and annals."

This speech they all accepted and replied unanimously to this enquiry, not knowing what fatal disasters were hidden in it and after they had calmly agreed to this journey, in spite of their numbers no dispute arose among them and so he continued the march until he reached Siwas.

SECTION

But when the dense cloud of his cavalry packed in the expanses of Siwas had given out lightning and thunder, and the time had now come for him to discharge the promise made to the Tatars, he proclaimed a public assembly, and drew up a great company of guards of the army, then he called all the leaders of the Tatars and those who formed the strength of their force and whom he feared as dangerous to himself and whose revenge he dreaded and the rebellious devils among them and obstinate leaders and received them with an open face and a tongue pouring forth the sweetest favour and honourably made them sit according to their dignity, nay, attributed to them greater dignity and power, then said:

" Now the countries of Rum lie open and their tracts and all their villages and plains have become known and how Allah having destroyed your enemy has made you successors there. And I also will hand it over to you to possess by equal right, before I leave you and hand you over to the care of Allah in place of my own ; but the sons of Aba Yazid will not leave you undisturbed or be pleased with your fellowship there ; but your action against their fathers has blocked the way of conciliating them and no crossing is given you to the way of true friendship ; and there is no doubt that after restoring their damaged strength, they will rouse to war their collected forces and incite against you the people of town and tent and all who are summoned by them will obey, since, in their opinion, we are considered traitors, and will put on the leopard-skin against you and singe you along with every leader and soldier, and attack you from every side and rend you from every quarter, all the more because most of the fortified places and castles are in their power and the remaining parts of the armies and posts are under their command ; but if you are equal among yourselves, without a leader, they will plunge in your blood at their pleasure ; therefore stand and hear, if you have not yet understood and heard :

" 'There is no prosperity for men, who are equal among themselves, except through princes ; and not even through princes, if the foolish among them rule ! '

" But I am not always with you nor have I two right hands to defend you, therefore to strengthen your condition there is need of order and to guide your assembly laws and statutes are needed, whose keeping would yield the best result and safety ; and the first law should be : to set up an Imam, who would bring leaders and people to imitate his actions ; then to arrange the whole society in suitable order and assign to each his place of obedience, and next, to administer justice, hand the reins of office and administration to those who are fit for them, advance every worthy man to that of which he is worthy and transact every affair with harmonious counsel, and when your counsels agree and your aims are united, then your sons will be powerful and your enemies will be over-thrown, and with one hand resisting your foes, you will rise superior to your enemies and opponents.

" And that is best, lest any force be used against you and that the plots and efforts of your enemy may not reach you. And that this may be accomplished, the state of your affairs must be thoroughly learned and the conditions of your infantry and cavalry thoroughly studied and care had for warlike equipment and arms. For these are the instruments of victory and prosperity. Therefore let each of you show his sons and people and present his horsemen and infantry and bring his forces and weapons, soldiers, and sons and lay bare his need, if any, and not think it difficult, for it is now easy ; for if any-one needs anything by way of supplement, we will supply him fully and if any want anything, we will help him and we will distribute to each what he seeks, that he may be secure and that his fear may abate. But above everything show us your arms, that we may complete them and equip you perfectly."

Accordingly each of them brought his arms, and showed Timur his equipment and piled them in that parade and they were heaped up like a great hill, as he did in the beginning with the people of the city of Seistan. So when in this way he had deprived these lions of talons and teeth and snatched not only the beaks but the claws of those brave eagles and fixed the manly sword of his brain in the entrails of their minds and the star of their power had changed from armed to unarmed, and over against it was now rising the star of the " Slayer," he ordered all whom he had with him to lay hands on the Tatars and fasten them with the fetters of captivity ; then he ordered that those arms should be brought into the armoury and he burned the tribes of the Tatars with the coal of destruction, whose smoke ascended to the star Capella, and this broke their arms, split their livers and broke their backs, and having kindled a fire of them, he quenched their light. Then he placated them with deceitful promises and wished to conciliate them with a vain hope of security and sought to gain their friendship by coloured words and malicious deeds, and having changed their condition, he ordered that the camp should at once be moved.

They say that Sultan Aba Yazid said to that evil one, " I have fallen into your talons and know that I shall not escape from the dangers you threaten and that you will not stay long in this country ; therefore I think you should be warned concerning the tribes whose usefulness will be plain in this life and also the future life. The first thing is : Do not kill the people of Rum, for they are the mantle of Islam and it especially behoves you to defend the faith, since you declare yourself a Muslim ; and now you are in control of human affairs and have become head of the body of the world ; if then by the passing of your hand the concord which obtains among them is shattered and broken, there will be in the earth much sedition and destruction. The second thing is this : Do not leave the Tatars in this country, for they are material for wickedness and crime. Do not neglect their affairs or be secure about their cunning. The evil which proceeds from them is not equalled by their virtues. And do not scatter their settlements over the country of Rum ; for if you do so, they will fill the whole country with the fire of their tribes and make seas run with the tears and blood of the people ; and they are more harmful to the Muslims and their countries than the Christians themselves. But since you seduced them from me, you have pretended that they are your nephews by a brother, your cousins and kinsmen ; it will therefore be best that your horde and your men should follow you and that each of those sons of your brother should say to you : ' Uncle, take me with you.' You should therefore devote all the power of your mind to taking them hence and when you have driven them into some enclosure, do not raise a hope of their ever escaping. The third thing is : Do not stretch forth your hand to lay waste the castles and forts of the Muslims, or drive them from their homes ; for they are havens of religion and places of refuge for warriors fighting for the Faith ; and this is the will, which I entrust to you and the duty which I allot you."

And that wicked fool received it gladly from him and betook himself to this will and valued it according to the intention of Ibn Othman and executed it with the force of his strength and power.

CHAPTER XXXIV

HOW THAT CLOUD WITH ITS THUNDERSTORMS OF CALAMITY LIFTED FROM THE COUNTRIES OF RUM

AND a heavy cloud of dust went forth, from which a mist covered the eye of the sun, and the sea of the Tatars raged like that which God swelled into seven seas; and it advanced entering no town without laying it waste nor did it descend upon a city without destroying and removing it; and it crossed no place without damage and no neck submitted to its bond but was broken, nor did the top of a high fort resist it without being overthrown.

Then he gave to Othman Qara Iluk a robe of honour, when he came to Erzinjan and confirmed him in his province, adding to him several places and pleasant resorts and he commended to him Shamsuddin, whom he appointed governor of the fort of Kamakh, wishing that they should strengthen and support each other.

CHAPTER XXXV

HOW THAT PUNISHMENT POURED WATER AND FIRE INTO THE KINGDOM OF GEORGIA AND THE COUNTRIES OF THE CHRISTIANS

THEN he ceased not riding more stormily on that deep sea, until he halted at the country of the Karj, which people inhabits Masiah; their kingdom is not large, but well fortified with castles, forts, caves, caverns, mountains, precipices, hills and cliffs; and all these are difficult to capture because of a noble spirit joined to a base nature.

And among their cities are Tiflis, which that Satan had already taken and Trebizond and Abkhas, which properly is the capital. But when these places resisted him and did not submit, he stood to besiege them and sat down to take them by storm. There is among them a cave with an opening in the midst of a high precipice, safe from misfortune and immune from calamities. Its roof is secure against the thunder-bolts

of engines of war and its skirt too high for ladders to be moved
up to it. The approach to it is more hidden than the night of
Qadr.* It is clearer than the full moon that it cannot be
approached. But eagerly seeking to besiege it and adhering
to the plan of wearing it down by exhaustion, he used the
geometrical skill of his mind and neglected no thought or
prompting. Then his solid judgment and firm reflections
decided that he would attack it from above and catch that
dove climbing aloft on its feet by the collar and therefore he
ordered boxes to be made in the shape of mantelets† as though
they were female devils, stronger than men, and bound them
with strong chains and put on them daring soldiers; then
he let them down from those heights and from the summit of
the mountain. And they were let down through the air, like
a fate firmly fashioned and filling the spaces between they
caused the extremities of mountains and men to tremble, and
those hawks and falcons were as though shouting in their own
tongue to all who saw them. "Dost thou not observe the
birds moving in the air, whom nothing but God upholds?"‡
But when they had come opposite the gate of that cavern,
they smote them with arrows which bewitched, drove them
off with flying balls, discharged upon them in a mass every sort
of weapon and spreading hooked snares attacked them nor did
those eagles cease to wheel in the air and swoop and approach
the very nest, threatening it, yet they dared not pierce with
sharp beaks the navel of its people or fix in them their crooked
talons, for this unconsenting virgin denied every approach and
used the aid of the infidels whom she had with her in repelling
them; but one of those eagles did not cease to fix his wounding
claw in the gate, then urging victory the ally to be with him
and relying on Allah, leapt from the mantelet into that nest;
but the arm of felicity carried him in its bosom, and the arm
of help protected him and the hand of safety seized his claw;
then the Christians turned their backs to him and single-
handed he ceased not to destroy them, until he had slain their
rank and file and leaders, then he caused his comrades to
enter, who dragged forth what was hidden there. The name
of this man was Luhrasb having six letters, of which only two
are vocal: *lam* with the vowel *dhammah, he, re* with the vowel

---

* On which the Koran is believed to have come down from heaven.
† Military engines in which men are moved up to walls.
‡ A quotation from the Koran.

fethah, alif, sin and *be*, three letters without vowels joined in a way frequent among the Persians and found also among the Turks, but more rarely.

Of these forts another especially is very high, and its precipices, as well as the letters of its name, proclaim its inaccessibility, and in storming them, because of their height, neither accident nor prayer has served ; its name, they say, is Kalkurkit, that is : " Come, see, return," since to one who approaches it, it grants only a view. Its three sides are set on the top of hills, which rise above all the surrounding heights and are like landmarks to the mountains themselves ; but the way to it is on the fourth side, which is itself narrow and it goes out by a difficult path after various difficulties to a steep precipice between it and the gate of the fort ; as for the bridge, when it is raised, no chance of approaching the fort is left to cunning and one who has escaped to its middle summit is in safety, so that it can truly be called " Refuge, child of the mountain."

But when Timur had explored its true character and its hidden condition was clear to him, he was loth to leave it without gaining his object of seizing it. But there was no place near where he could pitch a camp, or mainland to carry or hold that overflowing sea, but round it were only precipices, and rocks were the wrinkles on its brow, like the face of an old woman shrinking from her husband, beloved by eagles.*

But eagerly desiring to take it, though he could not hope to do so, he pitched his tent where the fort could be observed by sight and hearing and the strong lions of his army besieged it, approaching and withdrawing by turns. Besieged daily, with the bridge removed, they were secure from the traps of conflict and siege, for it has already been said that there was no place for fighting round the fort or nest of the *kata*† suited for throwing darts.

Therefore they daily aimed at the fort, because of distance, only the darts of their eyes, satisfied to cast their eyes at it from afar, like lovers content with little, but when night covered them, they withdrew to their tents, since round the fort they had no place to spend the night or take midday sleep ; then the Christians let down the bridge and returned to their business. When therefore Timur saw the standards driven

---

* An obscure phrase which may refer to the preference of eagles for rocks.
† Perhaps " sandgrouse."

back from the fort and knew that the hope he had conceived of storming it was false, as I have said :

" Most hard to find is the fruit of desire in a barren season."
—he decided on departure, but fearing disgrace he sought reason and excuse for this withdrawal.

CHAPTER XXXVI

OF THE MEANS WHEREBY HE GAINED THIS IMPREGNABLE FORT AND THE NEW AND WONDERFUL DEED WHICH THEN HAPPENED

TIMUR had in his army two young men, rivals, alert lions, alike in character and appearance, between whom was little difference in manly courage and vigour ; these two strove every time in the stadium of virtue to gain the fort of excellence and were like the two scales of a balance and like two horses in a race on whom a stake is placed. Now it had happened that one of them came upon an infidel among the Karj (Georgians), brave like a lion, and tall like a tower, whom he slew in battle and carried his head to Timur. He therefore praised him and gave him rank above his comrades, which impressed his rival, as though he had cut the vein in his throat. Then he turned over in his mind by what deed he could depress his rival and himself become more honoured. His name was Bir Mahomed, and his surname Qumbar. But he thought nothing greater or more glorious than to make a secret attack on the bridge and so relying on the help of Allah Almighty and taking with him his whole equipment of weapons, he waited his time one night and hid in a desert place and continued to watch the stars and observe from them the omens of dissolution and irruption and having measured those dangerous places with the palms of his hands and his forearms, he crawled alternately on his belly, then on hands and feet, until the light had thrown aside its veil and the air shed its skin ; then, when the Christians were returning to their tent and helping each other in raising their bridge, Bir Mahomed leapt on to it and cut its ropes and shot arrows into them from his quiver and they could not dislodge him nor was his position changed ; therefore gathering together, they attacked him with arrows and stones, which they threw upon him from above as from the sky when it pours forth plenteous rain, but he, unwilling to abandon his purpose, and reckless of his own danger, received what befell from the inscription of arrows and stones on his head and eyes and ceased not to hurl himself at the foe, to protect himself, engage and struggle fiercely, until, when day came, the world bit the fingers of admiration at his deed and the eye of the place was blinded. And the men who were besieging the fort had refrained from battle, and Timur, as I said, had decided on withdrawal and set up his tent on a high place, when the tongue of victory called him and the herald of success addressed him :

"Do not despair of the thing that you seek, whose handle men have cut off ;
If they have shut their gates, yet God will open His gate."

Therefore looking at the gate of the fort, he thought he saw from the distance men rushing on each other and a vision of some charging on each other and struggling together and he said to his tribe (that is to his chief helpers), "I see what is hidden from you ; therefore give attention rightly with me, then hasten towards that mêlée and bring me true news." And they hastened to see the thing more closely and removing the curtain, uncover its mysteries, and one went across fiercer than a leopard, another ran more swiftly than a lion and every man of them in his movement and pugnacity was another Tabat Shara and they ceased not to rush thither in companies and reinforcements, like devils, impetuous, bold, insolent and more, until the foremost reached Bir Mahomed, who was being consumed with his own fire in the eddies of death and exposed to the arrows of the enemy was near destruction ; but as soon as he perceived them from a distance, he gained new life and revived and fear left him ; and when the brave heroes reached the enemy, those cowards and unwarlike ones were repulsed by them and when they could not raise the bridge and retreated, they wished to withdraw into the fort and shut the gate ; but Bir Mahomed mingling with them and entering the fort prevented them from shutting it ; then they pierced him with swords and bruised him with death-dealing stones ; but he wished only to hold out and strove to avert opposition, caring nothing, what befell him from the pounding of stone, nor heeding the wounds dealt by the sword, like one who when death overtakes him stands erect in the hall of the house in the profession of faith in one God—until those lions overwhelmed them and poured over them like torrents of rain with lightnings of anger from a sky of courage ; then the lions of death seized their garments about their throats and snatched Bir Mahomed from their clutches ; then they took the Christians prisoners, seized their wealth as booty, led their wives captive and their children bound and carried Bir Mahomed to Timur, to whom they related his exertions and efforts in that business and examined his dark wounds and lo ! he had received eighteen, and each of them deadly. But Timur after praising his deed promised him abundant reward and sent him with great honour to Tabriz and ordered the chief Nawabs and leaders to consult concerning him the most skilled doctors and expert surgeons, so that they might use all their industry and diligence in healing him, and employ every theory and practice in curing him, and they obeyed these mandates received from him and laboured their utmost in curing him and repelled his sicknesses so that his wounds healed and his sores were remedied as best might be.

Then after he was healed and came to Timur, he made him a leader and head of a regiment of his army and promoted him over many after he had been of lower rank and set him over a thousand men, who had been leader of a hundred.

CHAPTER XXXVII

CONCLUDING THE HISTORY OF THE DOINGS OF TIMUR, THE LAME SHEIKH, IN GEORGIA

NOW this fort and cave were the two eyes of the forts of the Georgians and the fires of their mountains, the rest only candles ; and these eyes being now plucked from their face, they knew that their affliction was now certainly coming upon them, that they must mourn for themselves, that their strength was dissolved, their bonds broken, their skill ended, and that the horror of the last judgment was rising against them and demons with gloomy face leading them to Gehenna, no hope of salvation being left them ; but Timur taking therefrom an omen of victory, strengthened afresh his purpose of winning the realms of Georgia and soon his devils scattered over them and vehemently smote the people, and rent utterly the garment of their life, and shaved their hair and sewed their funeral shrouds with weapons of war and burdened them with stitches and hems and seams and over them the tongue of vengeance read these words :

" Hast thou not seen that we have sent devils against the unbelievers to smite them vehemently ? "

CHAPTER XXXVIII

HOW THE GEORGIANS SOUGHT PEACE AND IMPLORED THE INTERCESSION OF THEIR NEIGHBOUR, SHEIKH IBRAHIM, GOVERNOR OF SHIRWAN, WITH THAT TYRANT

WISHING therefore to recover from their weakness and stir up their governance, they repaired their rent before it became too wide and joined together the rope of their life before it was quite broken and eagerly begged for peace and for their safety sought the aid of Sheikh Ibrahim, Governor of Shirwan, to whose will they committed themselves, hoping, though he was of a different religion, that he would be Imam of their assembly and appointed him pleader in this cause, holding sweet whatever fruit they might reap from his management, whether ripe or dry.

And now the armies of summer, like the host of the Georgians, turned their backs and the armies of autumn and winter, like the forces of Timur, threatened and the Sultan of winter polished his black sword and stripped off and removed from the branches the royal standards and on the tops of the mountains pitched tents of crystal and on the loins of the lake put breastplates of David solidly woven by strong wind ; and everything in the world, whether frozen or growing, was safe from the whole army of Timur or held him in check. I have written :

" When God wishes to help his servant, his enemies are his
　　allies ;
And when He wishes to snatch him from perdition, He
　　draws rivers for him from the fire thereof ;
And if the mind appears baffled, soon flowers appear for
　　him among thorns."

Then Sheikh Ibrahim was admitted to him and kissed the earth in his presence and saluted him with the salutation with which royal Khosrus are saluted and stood in a humbler position than a slave and asked permission to speak and a gracious reply, which favour granted, he said :

" The general clemency of our Lord and Amir and his exceeding affection towards the wretched and poor and his generous kindness, which embraces all, and his excellent pity impelled a slave to offer what came to him for his lord's august judgment. And truly desires have prospered well—praise be to Allah !—and prayers have gained their purpose ; nay, the fear of our lord and Amir has sufficed to him through East and West without the need of sword and battle ; also the victorious armies are too abundant to be numbered and in them are so many prisoners and men enslaved that their total cannot be reckoned, especially the hosts of the Tatars, whose fortune has turned round and who have descended into the house of destruction. Now cold has them in its grip and the breath of their felicity moves between indrawing and expulsion. But if affairs abide in this state, the illustrious will be brought low, the base will perish, the great will become an exile and the weak will be crushed ; and this country like the rest cannot but render constant fealty to your sway ; and its unbelieving and wicked leaders knowing the clemency and pity of our lord and Amir towards his slave have entrusted themselves to him because of neighbourhood, hoping from his august favour, what the poor beggar hopes from the rich and noble, and whenever royal commands reach them, all those slaves will readily submit to them and all that people will obediently and reverently accept his august commands ; and if gathering of wealth be required, somehow your slave will provide it, for whence has your slave wealth but by the charity of our lord and Amir ? And your slave has no other purpose thereby, but to remove trouble from both sides and make easy a hard matter and observe the law of neighbourliness, by the performance thereof according to the Prophet, on whom be the blessing of God and Peace !—' Gabriel ceased not to commend neighbours to me.'

" But your august counsel is highest and will be best and most excellent, if your slave fail not of his hope."

And Timur consented to his request and sought from him a great sum of wealth, to be paid either from their resources

or his ; therefore Sheikh Ibrahim said : " I go surety for it "
and with the greatest diligence he brought it into his treasury.

Then he marched and finished his winter halt in Qarabagh,
which happened in the year 806.*

CHAPTER XXXIX

HOW HE RETURNED TO HIS HOME AND SOUGHT HIS OWN COUNTRY
AFTER CONCLUDING HIS DESTRUCTION

AND when nature, like a tire-woman, had decked the
place like a bride and the adorner of the dry earth had
raised the season to its height and the growing strength of
things was roused and the high peaks had decked themselves
and the dust was kindled and reptiles crept, that viper roused
himself to movement and spat poison at the dead serpents
of winter with his live armies ; and lo ! when this viper moved,
the drum was beaten, and its echo gave back a mighty thunder
and corslets shone like mirrors, from which rays were reflected,
blinding the sight like lightning, and the flash striking the
shields threw a rainbow round the hills. And his cavalry
advanced in corslets, and squadrons of horsemen, like hills
of sand, riding through tracts of roses and fragrant herbs,
circled in that distant country. Camels strode and mountains
passed like clouds ; squadrons marched and clouds ascended
from the cloudy dust and spears were stretched forward.
And fresh branches were hanging down and swords were
rustling and when the trickle of streams poured into the seed,
the points of swords and spears quivered ; and when the tops
of stalks sprouted, the flags of the squadrons were unfolded ;
and now the glitter of flowers spread abroad and spring with
its thunderbolts recalled his lightnings and with its thunders
his thunderstorms ; with its smooth groves and hills his couches
and divans ; with its thick clouds his cloud of dust ; with
its anemones his banners ; with its flowering trees his tents ;
with its branches his spears ; and with the storms of his commands and interdicts were its winds and with his black squadrons its green sandhills and with its blue flowers his glistening
spears and with its sweeping torrents the rush of his army

* A.D. 1404.

and with the commotion of the sea of his forces, the fields were shaken, while the wind of destruction raged. And steadily marching amid those fragrant herbs and laurels, with mind free from care, he returned to Samarkand and on the march had joy for his familiar, gladness for servant, mirth for boon companion, hilarity for nightly gossip and went with negligence and haste, until having crossed the provinces of Azerbaijan, he halted in the kingdom of Khorasan, the kings of regions and wearers of the diadem doing him homage.

CHAPTER XL

HOW THE KINGS OF THE BORDERS ROSE TO MEET HIM AND WENT TO FELICITATE HIM ON THE SUCCESS THAT HE HAD GAINED

AND when the rumour reached the limits of the provinces that he was returning to his own country, kings came to him from their borders and satraps from their territories and the chiefs of the people and leaders hastened to meet him and chief men and nobles hurried from Transoxiana and other parts and magnates flew to him from countries and Kings and Sultans from provinces and frontiers; and those who kept guard on the frontiers and who remained in charge of weighty business sent to him their deputy or envoy or chamberlain or forager, to show their joy at his coming and felicitate him on the victories, that he had gained in India, Iraq, Rum, Georgia and Syria and offering to him presents and loads on beasts of burden and providing splendid feasts and supplies. After them came lords, learned men, elders, great men and the chiefs of the magi and the magi of the chiefs, and to each of them he enjoined a way and advised them to humble themselves in obedience and loyalty by reverence and silence, and he laid down to them in those things, that concerned him, foundations and principles in which no hollows or jutting hills would be seen.* Then he let each go as seemed fit to him and dismissed them and came to the Oxus, where skiffs and boats were already prepared for him, with the help of which he crossed; and the people of the city all went forth to meet him, with hearts overflowing with joy and well-ordered condition.

* From the Koran : here metaphorically.

And he entered Samarkand, in the beginning of the year 807,* having with him of different nations† seventy-two sects and mostly Qadaris‡ and Murjites§ ; then he dismissed whom he wished from his army and they departed hither and thither and dismissed also the armies of Transoxiana which were dissolved.

CHAPTER XLI

HOW THE TATARS WERE DISPERSED, BEING SENT EAST AND WEST, NORTH AND SOUTH

NOW when he had rested at home, he began to disperse the Tatars, a people well-furnished with arms, numerous, warlike and active, whose back and strength he broke, when he deprived them of their arms, but God had left many of them surviving, wherefore, fearing their spirit, he scattered their society and emptied their home of their assemblage and dispersed them in deserts and marshy valleys and distributed them in wastes and plains and separated them in regions of labour and trouble and spread them in borders of tears and lamentation, and set against their heads the mouths of frontier-posts and shut behind their backs the gates of approaches.

One part he banished to Kashgar, which is one of the frontier-posts between the limits of the Khatas and the Indians; another he sent to Duwira in the midst of a lake called Issykkul, which is a border-post between the kingdoms of Timur and the Moguls. And these gained some good fortune and withdrew from their host,¶ as what is further removed is easily separated from that to which it belongs.

Then combining they took flight by a straight road and going North betook themselves through Dasht‖ to Idaku.

But the rest Timur with their tribes and families from every place of their settlement handed over to Arghun Shah and with set purpose and diligence sent them to the frontiers of the desert and the borders of Khwarizm. And this was according to his custom and the principles of his rule and government, for he was a devil addicted to transportation

* A.D. 1405. † Considered as the number of the sects of Islam.
‡ This sect believes in free will.
§ This sect relied on faith alone apart from works.
¶ i.e., Timur. ‖ i.e., Kipchak.

and in deceiving and making sport of men like Dalla, the cunning. Whenever he had built a fort on the boundaries or gained a corner in an approach to hostile country, he posted there as garrison those from his armies, who were furthest removed, men from the most opposite forts and villages, and transferred thither in turn soldiers of the North to the South and of the South to the North. And when he had gained the kingdom of Tabriz and its territories, he set over it his son Amiran Shah, to whom he gave some rough and hard Jagatais, among whom was Khudaidad, brother of Allahdad.

And to the borders of the Khatas and of Turkistan he transferred hosts from the army of both Iraqs, of India and Khorasan, and gave to Samaka, son of Tukriti, whom he had brought from Syria, the governorship of the city of Siram, which is about ten days' journey from Samarkand on the East, and to Yalbagha Majnun the governorship of Yanki Talas about four days' journey beyond Siram, and these two states, shut in by narrow boundaries, are beyond the Jaxartes n the territory of Turkistan. And these two men were unworthy of mention and still more of becoming governors and Amirs, but he did that, only that a report might spread through the borders of the kingdom that he had with him an assembly of the chief magnates among the leaders of Syria and that in his realms among the ministers were heads of nations, governors of the Arabs and of the strangers, and that his eye ranged and lorded and ruled everything between Syria and the Khatas.

SECTION

Then he began to inquire into those things which during his absence had befallen his realms and subjects and to examine the affairs of the kingdoms, for whose kings he appointed just ways of action and set in order the business of the borders and frontier-posts and approaches and looked to the affairs of great and small and applied himself to arranging the business of rich and poor and maintained equity and handed the reins of offices and dignities to worthy men and anticipated the words of the poet :

" By Allah ! how excellent a man is Anushirwan !
How well he distinguishes slaves and the base !
He forbids them to handle the pen in his realm
And permits not the noble to grow base by servile toil."

He respected princes, honoured the leaders, magnified those worthy of honour, extolled learning and the learned, fostered the excellent and their dignity, removed the double-dealers, subdued schismatics, strangled adulterers and crucified thieves, until by his care the condition of the empire was well ordered and the foundations of government were made completely to conform to the law of Jenghizkhan.

CHAPTER XLII

OF THE PRODIGIES THAT HE PLANNED AND THE SEAL OF HIS FINAL CRIMES, WHICH WERE FULLY DISCHARGED BY THE SHEPHERD OF DEATH

THEN he resolved to settle in marriage his grandson Ulugh Beg, son of the famous Shah Rukh, who in our time, that is the year 840,* governed Samarkand in his father's stead ; and he ordered the people of the city to deck themselves finely, and that grievance and oppression should be lifted from them, taxes and debts remitted, a carpet of security spread for them and that great and small, high and low among them should deal rightly and kindly among themselves and the sword not be unsheathed in his dominions, and no violence and injustice admitted therein ; and he wished them to go forth in their festive attire to a place about a mile from the outskirts of Samarkand, called Kanikul, whose air is more fragrant than musk and the water sweeter than sugar, as though it were a part of the gardens of Paradise, which its watchman Razwan had left unguarded. I have written :

> " The gazelle freely roaming there crops the wormwood
> and part of its blood turns to musk."

The breath of its air is softer than the breath of morning and the draught of its water sweeter than the water of life, clear with no muddy impurity, the strains of its birds delight the ear more than the tongue of the pipe heard above the string. I have written :

> " A carpet of emerald, on which are sprinkled diverse gems
> of hyacinth."

* A.D. 1436.

It is also written :

" As though it were a circle of flowers in whose fair face
   roses are set in graceful order—
Plates of silver or onyx and pearl and jacinth and gold—
Full of powdered musk and gilded within.
Gardens desire to show them to us and they fashion things
   like them."

The dyer of imagination learns the mixture of colours from
the secrets of its flowers and the tirewomen of fair brides adorn
perfect beauties according to those choice forms. I have
written :

" Its hills especially at dawn appear like a sword adorned
   with jewels and gold."

It is wider than the hope of the greedy, who craves dignity,
rich, splendid and profitable, and pleasanter to the eyes and
sight than the fresh vigour of blooming, gleaming youth, which
fortune blesses with cheerful face, perfect charm, long life and
abundant wealth. And it is one of the most famous places and
retreats, known through the world for pleasantness and
abundance of all delights.

There begins Sod,* whose faces abound in delights.

I have written :
" Its sides are blooming cheeks decked with the black
   of eyes."

The army of Timur, though a surging sea, yet in that place
was like the children of Israel in a part of the wilderness.
Then he ordered kings, sultans and princes wearing diadems to
make their way to that place and disperse over it and he
assigned a place to each in those meadows and disposed them
on the right and left, rear and front, and ordered each to
display what he could elegant and beautiful and erect all his
tents and tabernacles painted with different colours and
decorated. Then below them in those sweet gardens and
meadows lengthwise and breadthwise he disposed magnates,
leaders, chiefs, amirs and ministers, each of whom showed what
he possessed and roused his equals to a contest, that they might
mark what his hands had produced, and strove and exerted
himself for fame with the more famous among them and kindled

* Or, The Hill.

that rivalry to the utmost limit. They unfolded from the contents of all the pages of their life and even the volumes of their crimes, rarities of distant countries and cities and valuables from mines and seas and precious things whereby souls were ravished and spirits roused and beauties of wealth in whose honour goblets were drained and at which wise men were astounded—which would put to shame the flowers of those verdant meadows or even the bright stars themselves ; and the fair scene made the joyful hosts reach the heart of secrets, and so the fresh beauty of that place grew and increased and the power of its charm rose and soared above the whole earth.

Then he ordered that his tents should be made the centre of that circle and a point in the ambit of those orbs ; and a fence surrounded all his tents and tabernacles, furnished with a wide entrance, which gave admission from a great hall into his inner dwelling and had two lofty horns, on which heads could be broken and at whose sight the soul would shudder, whence clung to it the name " Horned." And in that plain they had pitched for him many tents of different sort, of which one had the upper and lower border inwoven with gold and was adorned within and without with the finest feathers ; another was all woven of silk and decorated with various figures and flowers of diverse hues interwoven ; a third was girt on every side, as by a crown, by great pearls, whose price is known to the Knower of secrets alone ; and another was decked with gems of various sort, which, set in broad curtains broidered with gold, dazzled the eye. In the midst also they set roofs of silver and stairs to ascend and doors for their houses and couches, on which they might recline ; also painted leaves and tent-curtains broidered with gold and marvellous tents and buildings, and in them fans of cloth of fine texture for coolness and other contrivances and cushions and keys and bolts. They also showed rare treasures and hung there curtains of marvellous beauty and among them a curtain of cloth, taken from the treasury of Sultan Aba Yazid, of which each part was about ten cubits of the new measure in breadth, decorated with various pictures of herbs, buildings and leaves, also of reptiles, and with figures of birds, wild beasts and forms of old men, young men, women and children and painted inscriptions and rarities of distant countries and joyous instruments of music and rare animals exactly portrayed with different hues, of perfect beauty with limbs firmly jointed : with their mobile faces they seemed to hold secret converse with you and the fruits seemed to approach as though bending to be plucked ; and this curtain was one of the wonders of the world, yet its fame is naught to the sight of it.

And they set in front of his tents, at the distance which a horse covers in one gallop, a royal tent in which might assemble attendants and courtiers ; and this stood high and its fence reached the sky, furnished with about forty columns and pillars and with walls on which they raised high its supports and made strong its structure ; the chamberlains climbed to its top like apes as though they were devils and reprobates who listen secretly and upon its roof they strove among themselves, when they had raised it, previously low, to a height.

SECTION

The people of Samarkand also brought forth what they had gathered of their furniture and ornament and put it opposite those tents so far as the eye could see ; and each of the citizens gave his mind to what he could make ; and each of the craftsmen laboured with might and main to show a sample of his art and the workmen in what concerned their work, so that a weaver of linen cloth displayed a horseman fitted with all his equipment and perfectly formed even to the nails and eyelids and showed fully even the niceties of his whole armour, as the bow, the sword and the rest of his equipment and that all out of cloth of fine linen and brought it out from the place without trouble. The cotton weavers made of cotton a tower built high, constructed in a new way, raised like a mountain, stable and beautiful in appearance with a whiteness of body excelling the houris of Paradise and perfect height overtopping forts ; and when they had set it up, by its beauty it held the beholders and by its height, visible far and wide in that plain, men crossing were guided, so that it became a raised landmark for travellers and served as a tower over the courts of those buildings.

Likewise did the goldsmiths, ironworkers, makers of greaves and of bows and other craftsmen and those who dealt in shows and jests. And truly Samarkand is a place, where men of excellence collect together and a resort of those who excel in every art. Then every company placed, what it had made, each thing separately in its place before the tents of Timur and the tent of his court, behind which they set all the market places. In the midst of the crowd trumpets sounded, decorated elephants marched and fine horses with splendid trappings and he loosed for men the reins of indulgence and pleasure in various delights and enjoyments ; then every suitor hastened to his desire and every lover met his beloved, without one harassing another or superior dealing proudly with inferior, whether in the army or among the citizens or the mean suffering injury from the noble.

SECTION

Now when everything had been prepared according to the wish which he had conceived and the earth had received its adornment and had been decked out by his army and the people of the city, he betook himself to that pasture with his majesty and calm and went forth to his people in his array ; then he ordered the jacinths of red wine to be poured on the emerald of that verdant meadow and made it flow to all, so that nobles and people alike swam in its waves ; and orbs of hilarity were formed in that firmament and on its horizon angels descended with inspiration of pleasure from the orbs of beauty and those lions became tame and these gazelles like calves and from the Hell of combat they went to the Paradise of loving converse and that roughness and wildness were exchanged for charm and beauty and now after oppression they practised courtesy and friendship and talked as I have said in these verses :

" Our justice has destroyed tyranny among men ;
  No longer is the oppressed fastened to the oppressor,
  Except the fond heart which the dark eye chases,
  And the graceful thigh, the gentle lover presses."

Nor was the sword drawn except the sword of contemplation and that defeated, nor was the spear brandished except the lance of love and that bent by embraces ; and you would have seen nothing moved or struck save the lyre or cups thick or clear ; or singers warbling or young gazelles drinking, or maidens bringing drink, or flowing streams, or cheeks fragrant with roses or the roses of cheeks burning with love, or goblets sipped by the lips or branching trunks bent to embrace or the capture of delight or the moment chanting and singing :

" When swift gazelles grow to their prime,
    Through rose-strewn meads blow zephyrs fair
Brooks flow and in the glad springtime
    Boughs bend to earth as though in prayer,
We meet in gardens of such grace
    As charms the world and evening showers
Pour plenteous rain and on our face
    Gems sparkle from the crystal towers.
Before us plates and goblets set
    With rubies, at whose beauteous sheen
Men smile, and eyes even forget
    To sleep, such silver here is seen.
Trees shade us with their varied dusk.
    Birds flutter and out-sing the lyre.
The branches scatter fragrant musk,
    Among the hills soft winds suspire.
'Tis Paradise ! The full moon shines.
    In Eden what could rival this
Eternal spring ?   All joy combines—
    Our only care to drink and kiss !
The wine revolves 'mid wealth and song.
    Seeing this garden, a fakir
Would shun its fragrance ; not for long
    Could he preserve his virtue here.
Come, fellow drinker, hand to me
    (This moment grief will not allow)
The cup of pleasure, which will free
    From all misfortune ; wine and thou,
Water and verdure and fair face,
    A mixture sweet. And listen not
If treacherous heart impute disgrace.
    Say not a friend has love forgot."

There was security, tranquillity, leisure and comfort ;
grain was cheap, necessities satisfied ; evenness of fortune ;
justice of the Sultan, health of body, fair weather, ceasing of
enmity, attainment of desire, and company of the beloved.

" And if one said much, length of speech would still miss
    the mark."

And in that marriage there was such magnificence, pomp,
splendour and magnitude of power, as I do not think any of the

ancient Khalifs or more recent enjoyed; Almamun* indeed on his nuptial night had beneath him a carpet of gold and scattered upon his head the choicest pearls, of which he thought nothing, and did not fasten them behind him or in front, so that he said : " May God slay Abu Nawas ! " as if he had been present when the poet said :

"As though the least and greatest of his jewels
Were the litter of pearls on a floor of gold."

But Timur at that marriage had for maid-servants the daughters of kings and for menservants their sons, all of whom rendered service and there came to him ambassadors of Al Malik Al Nasir Faraj from Egypt and Syria, bringing with them various gifts and among them giraffes and ostriches ; also there came envoys of the Khatas, of India, Irak, Dasht and Sind and messengers of the Franks† and others and of all countries, alike remote and near, and of all, whether enemies or allies, foes or friends. All these he kept to be witnesses of his magnificence and to see his power and pride in that nuptial feast, which he ordered in that manner, fearing no punishment or harm. I have said :

"Who yields to pleasure, easily forgets the fear of God ;
Free of care he fears not the outcome."

He ate and drank things forbidden and permitted them and under him those foul and base things had free course ; whenever he invited his company to those things, they presently complied, glorying in rivalry over all their base deeds and not forbidding to each other the iniquity which they wrought. I have said :

"He recklessly shed blood, and violated what was forbidden
And allowed what the Law of God forbids."

Then he summoned Kings, Amirs, Sultans of countries, great men, leaders of tumans, generals of armies and headmen, to whom he held out goblets with his own hand, treating each of them as brothers and sons and clothing them in robes of honour, presented them with generous gifts and put each of them near him on his right hand, for the left is allotted to women and princesses and the women do not hide themselves from the men, especially in the public assembly.

* Son of Harun al Rashid. † From Castile.

And he remained in this condition amid zithers, harps, lyres, organs and pipes ; amid dances, zither-players, singers and things wonderful and rare and the Tempter urged him and death came upon him, and the follower made plans and the listener commanded and the sun revolved above the stars and moon and goblets were filled, but minds were drained of their sagacity ; everything succeeded according to desire and wishes were satisfied, until pleasure and bounding joy made him light and agile and he linked his arm with another's and stretched out his hand to one who rose before him and they helped each other with arms joined. And when he was in the midst of dancing, he tottered among them because of his age and lameness. I have said :

" Among the wonders of the world are a maimed man applauding, a dumb man speaking and a lame man dancing."

And kings and great men and wives of Sultans and Amirs scattered pearls over him and great pearls and silver and gold and all precious things and the end was not made, until he had taken his fill of joy, when the bridegroom betook himself to his marriage-chamber and that desire was accomplished and the assembly departed.

This life is naught but drunkenness ; its pleasures recede, and intoxication comes.

SECTION

And when he had fully gained his desire in this world and his might had reached completion and he had climbed to the peak of his desire and the ladder raising him ever and anon, he had scaled the very summit and his moon was near its setting and the sun of his life about to fail, fortune assailed him with an arrow, which smote him where he was and he did not survive and it cried out to him with eloquent tongue, if any heard.

" The marriage is ended, O house of relatives ! " I have said :

" Truly time is naught but a ladder, whereon,
When one has climbed, he may descend as much.
What then of his suffering decline ?
For the condition to him who climbs is that he should fall.

And the higher he reaches, the heavier his fall
And when the conditions of decline are complete, he turns
   to decline."

Then he slept away his drunkenness and presently returned to his own vomit and went astray and did not regain wisdom and knew that he had led his people into error and not guided them aright and saw that he had not observed restraint in governing the state and had fallen from the threshold of princedom and empire and brought the kingdom to harm and that the ruler of an empire has a hundred, nay a thousand ways of punishing himself for failure ; therefore he began to cure his vices and sought a way out of the danger, into which he had hurled himself.

CHAPTER XLIII

SOME NEW ADDITIONS TO THE CIRCUMSTANCES OF THAT VAINGLORIOUS ONE

TIMUR had seen in India a mosque pleasant to the sight and sweet to the eye ; its vault was beautifully built and adorned with white marble and the pavement likewise ; and being greatly pleased with its beauty, he wished that one like it should be built for him at Samarkand, and for this purpose chose a place on level ground and ordered a mosque to be built for himself in that fashion and stones to be cut out of solid marble and entrusted the business to a man called Mahomed Jalad, one of his helpers and superintendents of the court. This man accordingly used all diligence in building it and raising its columns, and completed it in such a manner that its construction was most elegant in foundation, structure, arrangement and ornament, and raised on it four towers, in which the architects and skilled builders reached the zenith, and he thought that if anyone else were in charge of that business, he could not achieve and rival this skill, nay that he himself would be praised by Timur for his work and consequently be had in great honour at his court ; but when Timur returned from his journey and inquired into those things which had happened during his absence, he betook himself to that mosque to behold it ; but merely casting an eye upon it, he pronounced against Mahomed Jalad sentence of death and forthwith they drew him on his face and bound his feet and ceased not dragging him and drawing him over the ground on his face, until in this manner they had torn him to pieces ; and Timur took for himself all his servants, children and property.

Now he had diverse reasons for that deed, of which this was the chief ; the queen, the chief wife of Timur, ordered to be built a college and the architects and geometers judging by unanimous consent that it should be built opposite that mosque, raised its columns high and elevated its structure and lifted its stories and walls above that mosque, wherefore it became stronger than it and stood higher, but since Timur was by nature like a leopard and of the temper of a lion, no head was raised above him but he brought it low and no back grew stronger than his but he broke it and he was thus in all things which concerned or touched him. Therefore when he saw the great height of that college and that it bore itself more proudly than the slighter structure of his own mosque, his breast was bitter with anger and he blazed forth and dealt as he did with that superintendent, who did not find the fortune which he had hoped. And this story foreshadows that whose narration will presently follow.

A Pointed Saying

Around the sides of this mosque were loads of stone, as his sins surrounded its owner, weighing down its back and shoulders and by their weight crushing and weakening the neck of its strength so that its roof seemed to say,* " When the heavens were shattered " nor could Timur exert himself for its destruction and rebuilding afterwards or complete anew its fabric once dissolved, and so he left it shattered and kept its mass, as it was, weak and broken ; but he ordered his courtiers and servants to assemble in it and be present at the Friday prayers, and it remained in this condition while he lived and after his death.

When therefore they had assembled there to perform prayers, they expected for fear of God that some stones would fall and the angel of the mountains seemed in that place to read (from the Koran) " When we shook the mount over them, as if it had been a roof." And once, when that place was filled

* Taken from the Koran.

Q

with men, and fear of it had seized each of them, there fell from its very top a piece of its stones ; therefore they all fled who had bowed themselves in prayer and poured out towards the doors and left the Imam standing and one of them was Allahdad ; but as soon as they knew the real situation, their panic ceased and they at once returned. But when the service was ended and they had dispersed over the earth, Allahdad, a wise man, clever and of keen judgment, who made a hundred courses and a thousand circuits round the Kaaba of jest said to me :

" This mosque should be called Haram and prayer in it the prayer of fear ! " Further Allahdad said, when the meaning of this saying was understood, " It is plain that the saying of the poet is used of the state of this mosque and as a writing on its tapestry and inscription on its front and porch :

" I hear that thou buildest a mosque out of rapine
But, praise be to Allah ! thou pleasest not ;
Like him who maintains orphans by harlotry,
Woe to thee ! mayest thou not enjoy love or gain alms ! "

SECTION

After Timur had ravaged the countries of Rum, in his ever-wandering thought was the conquest of the kingdoms of the East and he had ordered, as said above, that Allahdad should describe for him the situations of those countries and when their state was known and their towns with the surrounding countries familiar, so that the eye of his attention saw them openly and their character was held in his heart, he sent thither the governors of those outer regions, among whom were Birdibeg and Tankari Birdi and Sadat and Elias Khwaja and Daulat Timur and others, with military forces, which he entrusted to them and ordered that all should proceed to Allahdad and that Allahdad should speed on his business and that going further they should build a fort, called Bash Khamra, about ten days' journey from Ashbara, in the possessions of the base Moguls, whose condition was confused ; and since there was a quarrel between the two kingdoms, that place was being laid waste.

Setting forth therefore to that region with a large army they exerted themselves, besides their habit of plunder, to build. Now this host set out about the end of the year

806 and the beginning of the year 807.* And the aim of this plan was that they should have an asylum and in their march against the Khatas and their return a refuge and safe harbour. But when they had made strong its foundations and had marked out the several plans of its houses and set in stone the feet of its foundations and had raised its standards on the tops of the walls, he sent them an order to abandon this work and forget it, thereby enjoining them to return and exert themselves to fill the country with crops, like farmers, and that those skilled in corn-growing among the inhabitants of the villages and cities and those of the husbandmen in places high and low, who attended to tilling of fields and vineyards, and the villagers and farmers from the borders of Samarkand to Ashbara should cease business and trade and in word and deed give themselves to tilling the soil and farming and he announced in the assembly of them that every man should give his whole care to sowing the fields and if anyone were compelled by necessity, he should rather omit his regular prayers than tillage ; whereby he wished to make provision for supplies for them during the march and concerning food if stores failed on the way.

Accordingly, abandoning the work of building, all the leaders sought their homes and strove to increase the produce of cattle and crops and laboured to recall to life what was dead according to his instruction and mandate and they did not rest from that care, until the summer had folded up its carpet and autumn, the forager, had unfolded over the world its banners and coverings.

CHAPTER XLIV

OF HIS PROJECT AGAINST THE KHATAS, WHEN THE STUPOR OF
DEATH TRULY CAME UPON HIM AND THE VEIL WAS TAKEN FROM
HIM AND HE WAS REMOVED FROM THE MARCH TO HELL

NOW when he had recovered from his drunkenness, he attacked his plan of going to the ends of the earth and seeking its coasts and borders that he might despoil kingdoms and countries, and turned the reins of his march towards the Khatas, according to his wont taking the straightest way ;

* A.D. 1404-5.

therefore he sent to the tribes of his armies an order to be ready and to take equipment for four years or more and prepare for the march. And every tribe obeyed the summons of his envoy, receiving his orders, like ear-rings to adorn their ears and every lion brought the twins* of his provender and every Capricorn showed his vigour and every Bull made ready the Virgo of his supplies and Aquarius his liquor and every Scorpion among them crept forward like a Crab and they poured forth, like Fishes, into seas of hostility, carrying oppression of the human race without measure or balance ; and the sign ot the Archer sent forth an arrow of his cold with an order announcing to all ears, that winter had led forth his army against the world and that rapine was resting and that the rich should be ready for his coming and the bare-footed and naked beware and not be content with their accustomed crop, for all of it was not enough, since this time there would be one of God's signs and God's signs must not be taken in jest and that he (winter) intended by his coming that breath should freeze, noses and ears be frost-bitten, legs fall off and heads be plucked off ; but that autumn was the forager of his army, the leader of his forces, the flatterer of his countenance, the image of his thirst, the inscription of his letter and the preface of his command.

Soon (winter) with his storm-winds roared and raised over the world the tents of his clouds which went to and fro, and with his roaring shoulders trembled and all reptiles for fear of that cold fled to the depths of their Gehenna, fires ceased to blaze and subsided, lakes froze, leaves shaken fell from the branches and running rivers fell headlong from a height to lower places,† lions hid in their dens and gazelles sheltered in their lairs. The world fled to God the Averter because of the winter's prodigious vehemence ; the face of the earth grew pale for fear of it, the cheeks of gardens and the graceful figures of the woods became dusty, all their beauty and vigour departed and the sprout of the earth dried up to be scattered by the winds.

But Timur, hating the foul voices of these spirits and thinking cold the breaths of these winds, ordered coverings of tents to be prepared and tunics to be kept ready covered on both sides with thick cloth and defended himself against the broad swords of ice and sharp spears of cold with cloaks

---

* The Arabic word also means " sheep."   † Refers to avalanches.

for shields and thick shirts for breastplates ; then for a covering against the onset of winter he fitted double breastplates and forged them to the measure of his burning project and from his abundant supply provided shields abundantly and caring naught, what was said or blamed, he thought himself enough defended against the injuries of winter by garments and all the equipment which he had got made and said to his men " Do not be anxious about the injuries of winter : truly this is refreshment and safety."

Then collecting his armies and arranging everything according to his command, he ordered to be made five hundred wagons armoured with iron, on which his baggage might be set.

But winter, by its approach anticipating his departure, brought from the court of perdition a sentence of the breaking short of the course of his life, but he set out in the month of Rajab, when the cold was prodigiously violent, and marched, not sparing the weak nor pitying the bodies which cold had scorched and came in his course to the frozen Jaxartes, on which the light wind had built a level palace. I have said formerly :

" I saw over the sea a bridge extended
 Which God Almighty built like a level palace.
 I wept and forthwith with cold the tear
 Became clear wine on the side of a glass."

So he crossed the river and stubbornly continued and pushed on his march ; but winter dealt damage to him, breaking on him from the flanks with every wind kindled and raging against his army with all winds blowing aslant, most violent, and smote the shoot of the army with its cold, intense and so more lasting. He none the less advanced with that great host, feeling no pity for prisoners nor caring that the weakness of the injured should recover, desiring to outpace the winter with his runners and making its December run along with his cavalry and stalwart soldiers ; but the winter poured round them with its violent storms and scattered against them its whirlwinds sprinkling hail and roused above them the lamentations of its tempests and discharged against them with full force the storms of its cold and descended with its herald, proclaiming to Timur, " Why yield to delay, caitiff, and why act slowly, fierce tyrant ? How long shall hearts be burned by your fire and breasts consumed by your heat and ardour ? If you are one of the infernal spirits, I am the other ; we are

227

both old and have grown weak while destroying countries and men ; you should take therefore an ill omen for yourself from the conjunction of two unfavourable planets ; if you have slain souls and frozen men's breath, truly the breaths of my frost are far colder than yours ; or if among your horsemen are men who have stripped the hair of Muslims by torments and pierced them with arrows and deafened them, truly in my time by the help of God there was that was made more deaf and naked. Nor by Allah ! will I use pretence with you ; therefore mark my warning and by Allah ! the heat of piled coals shall not defend you from the frost of death nor shall fire blazing in the brazier."

Then he measured over him from his store of snow what could split breastplates of iron and dissolve the joints of iron rings and sent down upon him and his army from the sky of frost some mountains of hail and in their wake discharged typhoons of his scraping winds, which filled therewith their ears and the corners of their eyes and drove hail into their nostrils and thus drew out their breath to their gullets by discharging that barren wind, which touched nothing that it reached without making it putrid and crushed ; and on all sides the whole earth became with the snow that fell from above like the plain of the last judgment or a sea which God forged out of silver. When the sun rose and the frost glittered, the sight was wonderful, the sky of Turkish gems and the earth of crystal, specks of gold filling the space between.

When the breath of the wind blew on the breath of man (which God forbid!) it quenched his spirit and froze him on his horse and so also the camels, until it destroyed all of softer constitution and this condition went on till fire seemed to exhale a sweet odour of roses and give safety and refreshment to him that approached it. As for the sun, it also trembled and its eye froze with cold and it dried up and became as in the poem :

> " A day when the sun because of cold would desire that fire should approach its disk."

When any breathed, his breath congealed on his moustache and beard and he became like Pharaoh, who adorned his beard with necklaces ; or if a man spat sticky phlegm, it did not reach the ground, warm though it might be, without congealing like a ball ; and the covering of life was removed from them and the condition of all said :

" O Lord ! if in the morning harsh frost fall,
Thou knowest what will befall me, which is unknown.
And, if to-day thou shouldst wish to send me to Hell,
Hell compared with this day will be sweet."

Therefore many perished of his army, noble and base alike and winter destroyed great and small among them and their noses and ears fell off scorched by cold and their necklace of pearls was loosened and confounded* and winter ceased not to attack and pour against them wind and seas, until it had submerged them, while they wandered in weakness ; and of them it is said : " Because of their sins they were drowned and thrown into hell and they found no helper save God."

Yet Timur cared not for the dying and grieved not for those that perished.

CHAPTER XLV

OF THE COMMAND SENT BY TIMUR TO ALLAHDAD, WHEREBY HE
SPLIT LIVERS AND BROKE HEARTS AND ARMS AND HIS
DISTRACTION WAS INCREASED BY ANXIETY BECAUSE OF
TROUBLES

TIMUR, before he left Samarkand, had sent an order to Allahdad in Ashbara, which took away and routed his rest and made sleep fly like a bird from the nest of his eyelids, for he understood from its substance that Timur wished his ruin and to make his children orphans and lay waste his home, through it throwing him into the greatest difficulty and blocking all ways for him, while he demanded from him things, compared to which it was easy to break through mountains and transport cliffs and compared with the least of which a draught of sea-water would be sweet. The least of those things was that against the time of his arrival he should have supplies ready for him only ; on that very day food, which he might then eat, and barley to feed his horses, whereby he indirectly demanded a hundred camel-loads of the best meal and that

* Or, their order was confounded.

for himself only for a single day, even if he did not stay with his army except for a single night in Ashbara ; and so with the rest. Therefore as soon as Allahdad read this letter and understood the substance of the despatch, he knew that punishment was descending upon him, and spent his resources and exerted his efforts and devoted himself diligently to collecting meal and driving the water-mills, but these were even less active than the state of a cultured man in this time of portents, and the canals from which they got their water were drier than the hand of a miser forced in time of want to scatter flour to the winds ; the blood of rivers, sunken in the veins of the mountains, was hidden and the tears of fountains had receded far in the crevices of springs ; so he spent treasures which he had stored for every turn of fortune and calamity and held cheap the precious resources which he called to his aid, that he might make water flow ; and he besought the help of strong men and strove to get aid from all water perennial or standing and summoned as leaders friends from among his associates, that by their help he might avert what was befalling him from the talon of recurrent affliction ; and he knocked at every door, that to him might be opened that which he could not himself attain for want of strength ; and they gave a kind response to his summons and appeal and were pained at his grief and sought a remedy for his sorrow and collected lions and wolves among the craftsmen and workers, who laboured to drive the water-wheels in the place where rivers met, fighting the frost and breaking the ice in the path of the water, but they were like one who beats cold iron or strives to smooth the heart of the impious by silvery admonitions and they did not break the ice with iron to a distance of a cubit, before, its hardness softening and it grieving, as it were, over their obstinate labour, its eyes began to weep, when presently over its sad face a dry wind blew fiercely ; but as soon as the cold wind blew, which the water received with smiling face, its breath was chilled by their fire and its heart grew cold with their heat and what was over the water froze. Therefore, reduced to despair, they withdrew and recoiled. Allahdad none the less expended resources and called for help " O water ! O men ! give aid ! " I have written :

" Each of them was like an ass, that runs over the plains
    while it can.

Flowing water checks it ; but
When frost bids it stand, it runs."

It was agreed among the associates that by this effort a thing impossible to do was put upon them ; but when he saw their work and his eyes perceived their plea, black fortune came upon him and he knew for certain that he must inevitably perish and that he had fallen into a calamity, broad and long, and that his master had not asked flour of him at that moment except for a great cause. He had marked also the calumnies of his rivals and what his adversaries and enemies had carried to Timur concerning him and he knew that Timur's mind was changed towards him and what Timur had done with Mahomed Jalad, the architect of his mosque, and already it had been reported to him, how Timur had killed him by a cruel death, plundered his wealth and claimed his children and family as slaves. While therefore he looked for the double of these misfortunes from Timur, he found no rest or calm by night or day and now despairing of his life, he said goodbye to his life, family, wealth and children.

And the month of fasting was now near, when Timur was about ten days' march distant : and now affairs halted and* weak was the suppliant and the supplicated.

" When thou art brought to extreme peril expect escape ;
For the greatest peril is nighest to escape."

CHAPTER XLVI

HOW THAT PROUD TYRANT WAS BROKEN AND BORNE TO THE
HOUSE OF DESTRUCTION, WHERE HE HAD HIS CONSTANT SEAT
IN THE LOWEST PIT OF HELL

NOW Timur advanced up to the town called Atrar and since he was enough protected from cold without, he wished something to be made for him, which would drive the cold from him within and so he ordered to be distilled for him arrack blended with hot drugs and several health-giving spices which were not harmful ; and God did not will that such an impure soul should go forth, save in that manner of which he by his wickedness had been the cause.

* A quotation from the Koran.

Therefore Timur took of that arrack and drank it again and again without pause, not asking about affairs and news of his army or caring concerning them or hearing their petitions, until the hand of death gave him the cup to drink.* " And they shall be made to drink boiling water which will rend their bowels."

But he ceased not to oppose fate and wage war with fortune and obstinately resist the grace of God Almighty, wherefore he could not but fail and endure the greater punishments for wickedness. But that arrack, as though making footprints, injured his bowels and heart, whereby the structure of his body tottered and his supports grew weak. Then he summoned doctors and expounded his sickness to them, who in that cold treated him by putting ice on his belly and chest. Therefore he was restrained from the march for three days and prepared himself to be carried to the house of retribution and punishment. And his liver† was crushed and‡ neither his wealth nor children availed him aught and he began to vomit blood and bite his hands with grief and penitence.

> " When death has fastened his talons
> I have marked that every charm is in vain."

And the butler of death gave him to drink a bitter cup and soon he believed that which he had resolutely denied, but his faith availed him naught, after he had seen punishment ; and he implored aid, but no helper was found for him ; and it was said to him : " Depart, O impure soul, who wert in an impure body, depart vile, wicked sinner and delight in boiling water, fetid blood and the company of sinners." But if one saw him, he coughed like a camel which is strangled, his colour was nigh quenched and his cheeks foamed like a camel dragged backwards with the rein ; and if one saw the angels that tormented him, they showed their joy, with which they threaten the wicked to lay waste their houses and utterly destroy the whole memory of them ; and if one saw, when they hand over to death those who were infidels, the angels smite their faces and backs ; and if one beheld his wives and servants and those who continually clung groaning to his side and his attendants and soldiers, already what they had feigned fled from them and if one saw, when the wicked are in the sharpness of death, angels stretch forth their hands and say,

* Koran.   † Engl. idiom " heart."   ‡ Koran.

" Cast out your souls ; to-day you shall receive the punishment of shame, because you spoke concerning God without truth and proudly scorned His signs."

Then they brought garments of hair from Hell and drew forth his soul like a spit from a soaked fleece and he was carried to the cursing and punishment of God, remaining in torment and God's infernal punishment.

That happened on the night of the fourth day of the week which was the 17th of Shaban, the month of fires, in the plains of Atrar and God Almighty in His mercy took from men the punishment of shame and the stock of the race which had done wickedly was cut off ; praise be to God, Lord of the ages !

I have said :

" The earth is a water-wheel turning joy and adversity.
    A man reaches the topmost peak ; soon thou mayest see
        him crushed beneath the stones of the tomb.
    How many suns that have climbed in the sky to the
        zenith, each with its moons,
    When they have touched the zenith of their glory, have
        failed and waning light has brought them eclipse !
    The kings of the world have burned seas with the fire of
        their injustice ;
    They rule countries and their peoples ; their sway spreads
        far and wide.
    The deceitful world drives them, kindled by greed, and
        the Deceiver fills them with vain hope concerning
        God.
    Fortune regards them with smiling mouth and they hold
        strong places on the frontiers.
    Soon like wolves they go forth to ravage and prowl like
        lions.
    They abound in wealth and dance like black shadows
        without knowledge.
    They present in their courts the ghost of fancy when it
        wanders.
    They picture Fortune ever complaisant to them, so that
        it would never flee away,
    Or their share of this world overflowing, so that it would
        never decrease.
    They rush one on the other, they fight, they leap like
        panthers,

They struggle, and provoke one another and smite like
    lions.

They stab each other, they rend, they pierce like eagles ;

Madness ! Oh that they had fostered mutual peace and
    forgiven each other lies and cunning !

But like moths they have flown into the fire, thinking the
    fire a light.

While they hold the peak of their glory, Fortune deceitful,
    jealous,

Swoops on them from above like a hawk on petty birds.

They become unfortunate and each of them is thrown like
    food to the hawks.

No king or kingdom or house has repelled from them the
    hand of destruction—

Nothing, neither army nor children nor armies of allies.

Then their footprints are destroyed, as rain destroys lines
    of tracks.

Their time leaves naught of them but a blurred memory.

Like them all are the calamities of Timur, like dark seas,

That lame impostor, who broke skulls and backs,

Subdued countries and homes therein, in the revolving
    fortunes of this world.

God the Merciful prolonged his life, but he added iniquity
    to iniquity.

And He gave him aid, permitting to him progress in things
    that pass and perish,

That He might see whether in his rule he would follow
    justice or tyranny.

He rooted out all men among Arabs and barbarians,

He destroyed right custom and went forth wicked with
    insolent sword that moved hither and thither.

He destroyed kings and all the noble and learned,

And strove to put out the light of Allah and the pure
    Faith,

With the tenets of Jengizkhan, that wicked tyrant and
    unbeliever ;

He permitted the shedding of blood of all the constant and
    grateful,

He made it a free right to take captive chaste believers
    from the harem ;

He threw children upon the fire as if burning incense,

He added to fornication the drinking of wine.

Now he saw treaties violated, now vows broken ;
And against noble matrons among the chaste and grave
They let loose every ravening wolf and fierce dog ;
They rushed in and sundered hearts, after rending the curtains.
They branded their brows while they prostrated them-selves before God the Forgiver ;
They dragged men from pleasant beds and branded their sides and backs ;
They violently snatched wealth from men's hands
And gave them to drink a draught of the simoom and to suck a draught of scorching wind ;
They took for slaves the people of the Prophet, the elect, the purest one ;
They sold them to Turks in the country of unbelievers
And so also the only son of every mother of one son alone.
And in these crimes they continued and went forward constantly
Crossing through the countries between Iran and Turan ;
And he advanced further, penetrating from the Khatas to the furthest regions.
When his raids reached their height and that evil-doing was completed,
The onset of Fate seized him ; for in every consummation is decrease ;
The hands of death snatched him from those sins to the tomb ;
His nobility was exchanged for contempt and hatred ;
He departed to the house of punishment with a heavy load of crimes ;
Those hosts were scattered and oblivion destroyed what he had built.
His deeds brought on him curses, so long as the ages revolve,
And the monuments of his evil-doing are committed to perpetual memory.
Look therefore, brother ! and consider this evening and this dawn !
Death distinguishes not between the grateful pious and the infidel.
Where are they whose faces shone, like the star Zubur ?

The fortunate, the clever, famed for dominion and
 majesty,
Who obscured the moon in the sky and put to shame
 the abundant seas ?
They were great among leaders and leaders among
 warriors ;
Trampling ground down those great ones and shattered
 those leaders ;
And the wind of destruction scraped them as the hand
 of the storm scrapes the sands.
Where are the sons and those who brought the heart joy
 and light ?
When the curtain was parted and the hangings removed
 from them,
Thou wouldst see a new splendour, like the sun, rise from
 the darkness of the curtains,
Beyond any buck or doe with beautiful eyes, that sur-
 passes the houris.
Elegance clad them with the robe of comfort over
 coloured tunics.
Everyone would have wished with his last heart's blood
 to redeem them from the evil of calamities.
The place in which they rested they altered because of joy ;
They were eyes in the face of this world and a light to
 the eyes
And gardens for its pleasaunces and in its pleasaunces
 flowers.
And while they are drunk with their sweet fortune, pride
 the wanton mixing them drink,
And their life is blooming and fortune favouring,
Lo ! the cupbearer of death, who brings them cups of
 destruction.
Then the cup, which comes to every evil one, waters the
 gardens of their life.
Reluctant they leave their noble palaces for the narrow tomb,
And perforce drink the cups of their departure to every
 sad and jealous one,
Who rends his bosom with grief and beats his breast for
 desire of them.
If bribery availed aught or gifts according to vows profited,
The careful shepherd would redeem, defend and guard
 them.

They dwell in the tomb, their splendours and joys altered,
And the consuming worm devours them and rends like
　　a butcher ;
They rot in the tomb and abide there till the day of
　　resurrection.
The friend dutifully visits their tombs and addresses
　　them,
And wails, and lamenting, asks of the tomb what it easily
　　forgets
And stains with dust his cheeks, which stream with tears.
They call, but they answer them not, except the echo
　　of the dumb rocks.
He who visits now is soon himself visited—
By the will and providence of God which works slowly.
The world is a bridge, whence take an example by which
　　to be warned ; seek money for the journey
And seek the sound kernel ; all the rest is shell.
Were not the world with its goods a smoke, which easily
　　vanishes,
Its plain would not be withdrawn from every constant
　　and faithful one.
This one and most of those who go proudly on the earth,
　　are lame and blind ;
Yet they suffer not themselves to be guided, but bear
　　themselves too proudly :
They fight against the truth and turn from it to lying
　　and iniquity.
O Lord, make us constant in those things that please
　　Thee !
Forgive us the sins well known to Thee, O Forgiver !
Confer blessedness upon us, with which we may match
　　the malice of Satan
And give us from the gate of Thy bounty the merchandise
　　that will never perish.

CHAPTER XLVII

OF THE EVENTS AND HAPPENINGS THAT OCCURRED AFTER THE
DEATH OF TIMUR AND THINGS JOYOUS AND EVIL THAT BEFELL

ONE of the friends of Allahdad was named Sadak, governor of Andakan, a noble and famous man and one of the Amirs who had set out to build Bash Khamra ; this man, sending a messenger, informed Allahdad that the cause of trouble was removed and that Timur had ceased to strive for kingdoms and because of his crimes had gone to the infernal abode of Malik.*

And Allahdad received that glad news on the fourteenth day of the month Ramzan in the year mentioned above,† which freed him from his solicitude and removed his anxiety from him ; and it was as though it had begun a new life for him or restored to him a beast by which food and drink are carried, after he had lost it in the desert. But the story of Allahdad and his affairs and subsequent fortunes to the end of his life will be told later.

CHAPTER XLVIII

SHOWING WHO WITH THE HELP OF FORTUNE OBTAINED THE
THRONE AFTER THE DEATH OF TIMUR

WHEN Timur finished his journey and his oppression was removed from the world, he had with him in his army none of his kinsmen and sons except Khalil Sultan, his grandson, son of Amiranshah, and his sister's son, Sultan Hussein, who fled to the Sultan (of Egypt) in Syria, on his approach. And they wished to hide this fact, lest it should reach the knowledge of any of the people, but it was published and spread and against their will became manifest. For when they were in the greatest confusion and panic, every man sought the cause thereof and learned and knew that the remnant of those who had done wickedly was cut off.

* Guardian of Gehenna.   † 807. (A.D. 1405.)

Then the armies in fear turned and taking his bones returned to Samarkand; but Khalil Sultan, fortune aiding him, seized his chance and obtained the throne. And his father, Amiranshah, was governor of the kingdom of Azerbaijan with its territories, and had with him his two sons, Umar and Abu Bakr, between whom and Transoxiana were obstacles and bars, a hundred enclosures and a thousand barricades. This Abu Bakr was, among the Jagatais, one of the cavalry and one of those who with the sword severed heads and helmets together, of whom it is said that he set up an ox or made a camel kneel before him and with one blow of the sword cut it in the midst. As for Amiranshah, Qara Yusuf slew him after the death of Timur and snatched from him the kingdoms of Azerbaijan; but his son Umar was slain by his own brother, Abu Bakr, and Abu Bakr was killed by Idaku, governor of Kerman. But their battles and histories are well known.

And Shahrukh was in Herat and the country of Khorasan and Bir Umar in the province of Fars and those parts. Timur had appointed Mahomed Sultan his successor, whom, though a grandson, he preferred to his own sons, since he noted in him signs of good fortune and conspicuous proofs of piety and probity, but fate opposed his purpose and Mahomed Sultan died, as related above, at Aq-Shahr in the country of Rum. But he had a brother by name Bir Mahomed, whom Timur appointed after him as his successor. But when the shepherd of death attacked him and reproved his foul spirit with awful clamour, he was plunged in the seas of his recklessness, acting carelessly in his sloth; then he slew him with joy and scattered his army. And he was then far removed from his sons and grandsons, resting calmly in his own place, fearing no danger, free of every care of destruction. They, like Timur himself, were acting carelessly and Bir Mahomed was at Kandahar, which is situated between the borders of Khorasan and India, and between it and Transoxiana lie deserts and wastes and none was nearer to the capital, which he had established, to wit Samarkand, than Khalil Sultan, son of Amiranshah, and moreover the spinner and carder of winter had spread his carpet over the floor of the earth and shaken over it threads of snow, which covered the face and sides of the earth and filled its back and shoulders; and none of those serpents was so secure as to put his head out of his hood or to show the end of a finger hiding in its sleeve for fear of the rude air, lest it be plucked the sooner thereby, still less to stretch himself on the couch of preparation for the march or extend his hand to attack or his foot for movement.

Therefore Khalil Sultan became master of this easy prize without any opponent or rival and the kingdom, nay, the world, exchanged Gehenna for the waters of Paradise and the Sultanate announced in his realm : " O noble successor ! I have set a beloved in place of a hated and a Khalil* in place of an enemy."

And he had in his power armies and Amirs and an excellent soldiery and able leaders, and he joined to himself those peoples and hosts of the best of the Arabs and barbarians and placed the necks of all in the rope of obedience and opened to them taverns of gifts in the markets of liberality, where they made with him compacts of fidelity, nor could any withdraw from entering into obedience or oppose even for a moment the completion of his installation with all speed on the same day. And he opened his face to them and spoke graciously to them and was a second Yusuf (Joseph) in goodness, an Abraham in kindness, an Ismael in sincerity. He joined the signs of grace to various forms of beauty. The writer of creation with the pen of K and N (omnipotence) wrote his graceful qualities in the charm of his movements and rest. And first on the tablet of beauty he wrote the Alif of erect stature and all who returned from beholding him sold themselves to his service, bowing like Dal and Jim (D and J). His grace pleased all who saw him and he debased not the beauty of his mouth when he opened it by falsehood or lying. He refreshed all his followers with the rain (of munificence) and with his liberality contented all the needy and made gold rain from his hand as from a cloud and with it all his soldiers were enriched beyond all his enemies. Therefore they devoted themselves to guarding his life and diligently defended his excellence from the eye of the accidents of fortune, using as it were a charm, and warded off rivals from him with the mountain and the sandhills† and zealously defended the curve‡ of his eyebrow, mouth, eye, hair and back with the letters H.M.A.S.K.§ ; and kings with open mouth prayed everything favourable for him and bent

* Dear friend.   † Titles of chapters of the Koran.
‡ Lit. N, a curved letter in Arabic.
§ These letters whose meaning is doubtful stand at the beginning of Sura xlii of the Koran, entitled *Counsel*.

before him their faces accustomed to his elevation, saying the words Ya Sin and Ta Ha.*

CHAPTER XLIX

THE ARMIES RELEASED FROM THE STANDARD RETURN TO SAMARKAND WITH HIS BONES

WHEN the butcher of death slew Timur and cut his throat like that of a camel destined for slaughter, he roared like a bull or cow ; then he wished to roast him in the oven of the fire of hell ; but he begged the aid of his Khalil, who protected him and checked the butcher, saying : " Deal not overhastily with him," and had him slowly carried in a litter behind his chariot and began to return to Samarkand. And now the River Jaxartes was free (of ice), and winter, the avenger, had taken his revenge, whereby his breast was cooled and his rage abated. I have said :

"The heart of the zephyr was moved with pity towards the world,
And the season turned a calm face."

Then the victorious army of spring advanced and the defeated army of cold took to flight and turned its back.

CHAPTER L

OF THE SECRET DESIGNS WHICH ALL THE VIZIERS OF TIMUR FOSTERED IN THEIR BREASTS

IN the spheres of that army were planets, by whose aid its sky shone, by whose counsels it was led and to whose experience it owed its light. I have said :

" From all chosen for exploits he is chosen,
Like the sun in counsel, like the lion in courage."

Truly, difficult tasks had trained them, and they had been fashioned by the efforts of Timur, who by their aid had opened

* The headings of Suras xxxvi and xx of the Koran.

closed doors and by their onslaughts widened narrow places and by their attacks escaped from the stress of every mêlée and by their constancy obtained what he needed and by their counsel reached the hidden treasures of his desires. He had been the moon, they its halo ; he the craftsman, they the instruments ; he the spirit, they the senses ; they had been members, he the head.

But when the sun of their hosts was darkened and their planets were scattered and their Saturn retired and they fell from their hope, I have said :

> " The world exchanged bright day for dark night
> And Jupiter for Mars."

Each of them shook the prophetic arrows of his thought and from that event looked for the end of his business and Khalil Sultan became of small account and knew that he must be buffeted on every side by the waves of contention and that the waters of the kingdom would not be clear of trouble or its air free from dust and that it was a small thing that the messenger of his eminent kinsmen said to him : " Call, O call God to aid."

Therefore he made ready his strength against every attack and his remedy against every disease and his defence against every injury and his agility against every mutilation and a covering against every evil and a shield against every arrow and a dog-tooth against every accident of fortune ; a speech against every speech, a reply against every address, against every war, orders to meet every transaction and horses against every treason and watchfulness against every calamity and against every enemy removal and against every disaster opposition and destruction.

But the bitter cold, like wolves, checked the courage of the insolent and the frost, like a broadsword, cut the wings of every swimmer and so every man of them could not but submit with obedience and homage and let himself be led by the command of Khalil and they remained with him in the return, inwardly nursing against Khalil a plan, such as Abdullah, son of Abi, son of Salul, nursed against the Beloved Prophet. One of them was by name Barnadaq, who wished to defend himself in a fortified citadel and said to Khalil Sultan, " If it seems fit that I should go before and arrange affairs for you until your coming, I shall be the forager of your rule and the leader of your sultanate and shall raise foundations and cheer all that I meet with glad news; then all will be ready to meet you and have prepared those things which are fit for your reception." And he gave him permission and sent him in advance. Then he came to the Jaxartes (Sihun), over which a bridge of boats had already been made and means arranged for all the cavalry and infantry to cross it. So he crossed it with his men; then forthwith ordered it to be cut and broke into open rebellion and made for Samarkand, openly proclaiming mutiny.

SEQUEL

But the walls of Samarkand set their teeth against him, and the city, like a maid guarding her modesty, let down over the gate its curtain and dropped its veil over its unapproachable face, and so Barnadaq was mocked of his hopes and gained not his aim. But when Khalil Sultan reached the bridge, he found its ropes already broken and its fastening disturbed, but caring naught for Barnadaq and what he did, he renewed the bridge and crossed it and set over the country beyond the Jaxartes the former governor, by name Khudaidad, who was the greatest of his enemies and had wished to be like and equal to Timur, tracing his family to Sultan Hussein, and in that country was held as head and eye.

But Khalil Sultan could not but make peace with him and confirm him in his country and make a truce with him, since his affairs were still in their beginnings; therefore he entrusted affairs to him in spite of jealousy.

CHAPTER LI

HOW KHALIL SULTAN CAME WITH THE POWER, WHICH HE HAD GAINED, TO HIS OWN COUNTRY

WHEN he came to Samarkand, the chief men went to meet him and the Governor of the city went out to him and its head men and the Governors of the country went forth to him in black and clad in dark garments. Leaders and magnates came to pay honour to those bones and felicitate

Khalil Sultan on his safe return and because he had gained the throne of empire. I have said :

" The faces of all who approached were like the coming of spring,
Clouds weeping, while the flower's face smiles."

They brought splendid gifts and precious burdens of beasts and he received each of them according to his rank and placed each in his proper station and said to Barnadaq : " Let there be no reproach," and received him like a dear friend and laid for him a carpet of pleasant converse and deceived him ; but when his supports were strengthened, he uprooted him and threw him unawares into the mouth of the lion of death, who devoured him ; then loosened into his abode the dogs of plunder and flames of fire and overturned it utterly and broke through its harem and destroyed everything in it new and old.

CHAPTER LII

OF THE BURIAL OF THAT EVIL ONE, WHO WAS CAST INTO THE PIT OF POLLUTION

THEN first he gave heed to the burying of his grandfather and performing his obsequies and placing him in the tomb. Therefore he had him laid in a coffin of ebony, which the chief men bore on their heads. Kings followed his body and soldiers with faces cast down, clad in black, and with them many Amirs and ministers, and they buried him in the same place in which they had buried Mahomed Sultan, his grandson, in the college of his grandson mentioned above, near the place called Ruh-Abad, which is well known, where he lay on supports in an open vault ; and he paid him due funeral rites, ordering readings of the Koran from beginning to end and in portions and prayer and giving of alms, food and sweet-meats, and set a dome over the tomb and discharged his debt to him and scattered over his tomb his garments of silk and hung from the walls his weapons and equipment, which were all adorned with gems and gold and embroidered and decked with so much art that even the meanest of them equalled the income of a country and one grain from the heap of those gems was beyond price.

He also hung star-candles of gold and silver in the sky of the ceilings and spread over the couch of the tomb a coverlet of silk and embroidery up to its sides and borders. Of the candles one was of gold, weighing four thousand sesquidrachms,* which make according to the weights of Samarkand one pound and ten according to those of Damascus.

Then he appointed for his tomb readers of the Koran and servants and placed at the college janitors and managers, to whom he generously assigned pay for each day, year and month. A little later he transferred his body to a coffin of steel made by a man of Shiraz, a most skilled master of his art, and buried him in the well-known tomb, where vows are made to him and petitions offered and prayers said. And when kings pass it, they prostrate themselves to show honour and often dismount from their beasts to honour him and do reverence.

CHAPTER LIII

OF THE CHANGE OF SEASONS AND THE DEEDS OF KHALIL SULTAN

AFTER just punishment had removed Timur and he became like dust and Khalil Sultan sat on the throne and the winter after kneeling, arose, poets dipped their pens to celebrate the time and felicitate Khalil Sultan and eulogize Timur. And when the winter heard these things, it uttered its voice and departed and rising lifted from the world its breast and buttocks. Then the world was cheered by the coming of spring and gardens gave thanks to the clouds for the beautiful web, which they had woven for them, and raised their standards on the hills with verdant places and set up their tents of the beautiful workmanship of flowering trees and eyes were lit by the splendours of orchards and the birds like preachers discoursed in praise of the Creator on the branches of the gardens, as though on the pulpits of mosques ; and all endowed with reason and speech, who were admirable in the council of eloquence and excelled in splendid marks of rhetoric, confirmed this by their opinion. Then the trees danced to the songs of birds and rivers flowed clear and it was the equinox

* Or, *matkals.*

and the earth put on a flowered silk mantle and the branches instead of their cotton garb of snow put on with the fingers of divine power garments all flowered and woven of flowers like damask and all the ground in every grassy place was bright with birds of every sort and their young and the earth unfolded over the place where Khalil Sultan approached long robes of rose and sweet basil.

SECTION

When Khalil Sultan finished those things, he strove to compose the state and bring it to order ; and knowing that none would follow him, unless he used the rope of liberality and that hearts would not be joined to him except by the distribution of wealth, he strengthened his heart against the magic seals of his treasury and solved their mystic signs and drove forth the demons of custodians from those desired and hidden treasures and strengthened his resolve to open his coffers and catch men like sparrows by scattering gifts like grain under the net of munificence ; and so he spent the wealth, which his grandfather had gathered, in bringing all men together, and he weighed down men's backs by pouring forth, that which had crushed the back of Timur with a heavy burden of crimes and wrongs, and filled the packs of desire and the purses of pay with riches and made his right hand rain with a plentiful shower of largesse and overflowed on the left side with abundance of liberality ; and the mouths, ears and eyes of men were filled when the maw of treasures and chests was emptied alike on the mean and noble of his army. Then also at the approach of spring the branches of trees put forth their various flowers and his fingers were joined in scattering darhams and dinars and the clouds gave plenteous rain of pearls and showers of his generosity. All men therefore let themselves be led by this rope and from distant quarters, moved by his gentleness, rendered obedience to him, abandoning other leaders.

CHAPTER LIV

OF THOSE AMIRS AND VAZIRS WHO MADE OPEN OPPOSITION AND
STRIFE AND CLUNG TO THE TRAIN OF SEDITION AND REBELLION

BUT some of those governors and princes and vazirs and
soldiers made open what had been hidden and openly
proclaimed the rebellion which they had secretly conceived.

And the first who unsheathed the sword of rebellion and
aimed the arrow of hostility and hurled the spear of sedition,
was Khudaidad Husseini, governor of the country beyond the
River Jaxartes and of the parts of Turkistan. Therefore whoever strove to free his hand from the knot of obedience found
an Imam to imitate, going before in stirring up sedition and
division, and all the more, because spring like a goldsmith had
now melted with his coals the sheets of ice and snow and
adorned as though with threads of gold drawn therefrom, the
cheeks of the earth and the pleasure gardens and the couches
of meadows ; and the reptiles heard, as though they were
dead men, the shout of thunder truly saying : " This is the
day of coming forth."

But in the footsteps of Khudaidad in rebellion and defiance
followed Sheikh Nuruddin, one of those who were held in high
position with Timur and were mighty in counsel and authority.
And he rebelled openly and journeyed night and day and came
to Khudaidad, whose power was thereby strengthened, and
joined with him in obstinacy and sedition.

Then after him Shah Malik broke the pearlstring of
obedience, who likewise with great diligence entered the way
of rebellion and left Samarkand imploring assistance, and
crossed the Oxus and came to Shah Rukh. He was, like
Sheikh Nuruddin, marked by firm purpose and sound judgment.
But Khalil Sultan, neglecting the rebels, honoured the loyal
and surrounded every head with the tiara of his beneficence
and kept naught for himself.

CHAPTER LV

OF THE DEEDS OF ALLAHDAD, LORD OF ASHBARA, AND HIS
LEAVING IT AND COMING TO HIS OWN COUNTRY AND HIS ACTS
IN THE GOVERNMENT OF THE REALM AND WHAT HE EFFECTED
BY WORD AND DEED, AND OF HIS PLANS UNTIL HIS RUIN AND
DEATH

THEN Allahdad, on the night on which he received that news, summoned his more powerful friends and consulted them concerning that which he should do and the manner of action which he should now adopt. But with one consent they advised that he should leave Ashbara and return to his own country. For in that place they were like an impious man in the month of Ramzan or an unbeliever among followers of the Koran.

Therefore as soon as the air had folded up its cloak of musk and spread over the earth its mantle of camphor and the dawn like a serpent had thrown its shining pebble into the high roof of the sky, the Amirs of the army according to their wont and the heads of the forces of the Turks and Khorasanis and Indians and Iraqis were ready to render service to Allahdad. Then he withdrew to a secret place with the more eminent and principal leaders among them, to whom he unfolded the matter and sought from their counsel the right way and the wrong and asked them to hide this business, lest the Moghuls should smell the report of it ; but how can aught be hid in a clear sky from the eye of the sun ? and how can the day be hidden from him that hath two eyes ? Then each of them entrusted the business to his direction and committed the cause to his secret bosom and he sought alliance from them, that they might do along with him in the affair what seemed fit to him and they consented to this request and bound their acts to his words. And to confirm it, he demanded an oath from them, that their inner thoughts in that matter were according to their open professions. Then all swore that there should be no dissent in their agreement and that they would follow all the plans of Allahdad and do whatever he ordered.

And when he was sure of their rebellion and revolt, and had gained an advantage by binding their necks with his oath, he said :

" O best of allies ! You have provided against evil and repelled disaster ; I will see that in the service of this business I act as your Imam. I will go before you with my men to Samarkand and make affairs ready for you and send others to this country of yours and by Allah ! I will not rest and will not leave you as prey in the mouth of the enemy. And if you see to it that you govern your affairs by the best consent and defend the oasis of your fort and your walls from the lips of the enemy, I certainly will not delay you longer than needs be in crossing the River Khajand* and coming to Samarkand. Therefore wait for me, until I arrive and go to Khalil Sultan."

Then, following his wish and approving what he desired, they promised him that they would not disagree on any account or break the rope of their pact after his departure from their company. Then he set over them the head of the army of Iraq, who was the greatest by consent of all the allies, and put each division of the troops in a separate part of the walls and the leader of those troops became like a prophet in his own country, though he boasted himself innocent.

SECTION

Then Allahdad ordered his affairs to be speeded and went forth on the seventeenth day of the month of Ramzan already mentioned, recking naught of cold or heat ; and he had already made Ashbara his own country, and had fixed his home there and had transferred to it his harem and children and also his followers and troops. Therefore all went out with him, great and small, and he left not there of his possessions even the vilest and most worthless. And they journeyed, now creeping, now hastening, now step by step moving forward ; now the earth with its snow forced them to fast, now the heaven sent down morsels of food upon them and the Id, albeit meagre, came to them in a place called Qulatajuf, coldest of all places, like the burst of wind, whereby the people of Ad perished.† I have said :

" When Gehenna needs violent cold,
   It draws breaths therefrom with its nostrils, which cool
      its midday heat."

---

* i.e., the Jaxartes or Syr-Darya. The town is now called Khojend.
† Koran lxix. 6.

CHAPTER LVI

ALLAHDAD RECEIVES TWO LETTERS FROM KHALIL SULTAN AND
KHUDAIDAD, WHOSE SUBSTANCE AND SENSE ARE AT VARIANCE
AND OPPOSITE ONE TO THE OTHER

THERE was brought to him a despatch of Khalil Sultan,
whereby he showed the turn of fate which had come to his
grandfather and that he had taken his throne and that all
kings, great and small, were obedient to him ; that the state,
praise be to Allah ! was well-ordered and that the laws of the
kingdom continued according to received custom ; and
therefore he should make no change and not assail the mainland
from the sea of his city and should remain in his place and
cling to Ashbara with his troops and conciliate each and all by
benefits.

Then Allahdad hesitated and meditated and argued with
himself whether in that journey he would make profit or loss ;
and thought and decided, but perished according to his decision.
But while in weighing his business he turned this way and that
and wove warp and woof in the web of his thoughts, lo ! there
came to him a messenger of Khudaidad, who urged him to leave
Ashbara and forthwith come to him, and he found ample
ground with Khalil Sultan for his departure from Ashbara and
regained life and slept free of care and when he had had his
eyes closed as though in death, now had them open ; therefore
he folded up the carpet of his hesitation and went forth with
fuller hope towards his goal.   But between him and his purpose
were hedges of goat's thorn and obstacles, such as he described
who desired to reach Soad,* especially because the river Jaxartes and Khudaidad were alike swollen. Therefore he continued
his march day and night, until he came to Khudaidad, who rejoiced at seeing him and thought his desires accomplished by the
sight of him.   Then both crossed the river Jaxartes and sought
the plains of Samarkand and came at a time of sloth and languor
to a place called Tizak and shook the sword of enmity and
brandished the spear of violence.   Then they came on a horse-
master of Timur and plundered him and took from him whatever they found of coin and goods and stripped him and they

* The name of the poet's mistress in a well-known poem.

both continually did greater evil and violence, and in their boldness were like the tribes of Thamud and Ad. And this was the first spark of evil and the first flame from the tinder and its force spread with tumults, after the death of Timur, through the kingdoms of Samarkand; for while Timur was alive, its people had been safe from calamity and hostile invasion, but when those evil ones overwhelmed them with hostile incursions, trouble crushed them, even whence they looked not for it. And that happened in the month Shawal of the seventh year, that is the year in which Timur met his end*; and Sultan Khalil could not remedy this grievous matter.

CHAPTER LVII

OF THOSE WHOM ALLAHDAD LEFT BEHIND AT ASHBARA AND THE STRIFES AND CONTENTIONS WHICH AFTERWARDS AROSE AMONG THEM

THE troops which Allahdad left at Ashbara, fearing that the Moghuls might harm them, assembled, but the parties were at issue one with another, of whom there was a section among whom one and another said: " I will cling firmly to my pact and not break my plighted word or tell a lie and henceforth will hold to the treaty firmly established and will be constrained by the bond of my oath and will not be of those who shall be set on the left hand because of a broken oath and at least we should wait until a messenger comes from Allahdad or a letter and see what way is then enjoined and therein discern by proper attention deviation from the mark. But if it accords with our intention, we will obey his opinion and follow the letter and the messenger and forthwith exert ourselves as disciples of tradition with the congregation.

" But if he opposes us in his talk with repulsive speech, we will turn to heresy and each of us in managing his affairs will obey the precept that in need self-interest is best."

But the other sect among them inclined towards leaving that outpost and setting forth from Ashbara and they passed from repetition of this dispute to fighting; and the head of one of the leaders of the Khorasanis was cut off in the very

* A.D. 1405.

place of the fight. But some of them, greatly anxious for themselves, delayed not but for an evening or morning ; then, taking their baggage, they went forth from the city and left a house which proclaimed the death of its builder. The rest therefore could not but follow them in their departure, for their assembly in that place from the beginning was like a fort built upon snow.

Therefore all to a man moved and went forth with their hale and sick and left the city, taking with them what was there of grain and fruit, chattels and goods and wealth and furniture and things of great price and naught remained there of that multitude that had been as though imprisoned, except that which they could not carry away of heavier goods and one mad woman ; and they came to Allahdad, who was with Khudaidad, and he did no hurt to any of them for what they had done, nay, he asked their pardon, because Khudaidad had hindered him from going to Samarkand and making an exchange for them and he bade them remain with him ready to set out and to be prepared to seize the chance of making for Samarkand when it offered itself.

CHAPTER LVIII

WHAT ALLAHDAD DID WITH KHUDAIDAD AND HOW BY HIS ARTS HE STOLE HIS MIND AND DECEIVED HIM

THEN Khudaidad convinced by this estrangement between Khalil Sultan and Allahdad, that firm hostility was established, placed some trust in him and began to consult him concerning the issue of his own business. But Khudaidad had with him a host of slaves of soldiers, left in that country by the armies, whom he had held in custody and he wished to transfer them from malik to Malik.* But therein dissenting from him Allahdad said:

" The habit of wise men is, especially in the beginning of their plans and the first onset of misfortune, to conciliate men's minds ; do not therefore drive men from yourself, but first conciliate them by kindness and caresses ; and what profit is there in slaying and utterly destroying them except

* Malik = owner, lord, and also the guardian of Gehenna.

the alienation of true friendship and strengthening of enmity between us and their masters ? Perchance in the mind of one of their masters will be aversion from Khalil Sultan, and he may therefore seek a high place and refuge, to which he may fly from his ally and need will then drive him to betake himself to the kingdoms of Turkistan, but if you have injured those who depend on him, how will he have left any confidence and security in you ? And the least you should do with them is to keep them comfortably or let them go with kindness ; thus their masters, who are friends of Khalil Sultan, will become our allies. But if you scatter benefits among them, you will gain for yourself all the slaves and masters and stir up enmity between friends and intimates who hate you."

And after hearing this speech, he entrusted to him the decision of that business. Then Allahdad advised him to let them go and to do good to them in all their affairs. Therefore he generously granted them a happy departure and relieved their want and sent them away with honour upon the road of their convenience and their orbs revolved in a fortunate constellation and they went to their lords and masters.

CHAPTER LIX

A LETTER ARRIVES FROM KHALIL IN SOFT WORDS TO SETTLE A HARD MATTER

THEN an envoy of Khalil Sultan came to Allahdad asking him to strive to heal the discord, which had come between Khalil and Khudaidad and to win the good will of Khudaidad and to cause him straightway to be friendly and forgive the past and begging him to undertake and promise on behalf of Khudaidad whenever required, that Khalil would be excellently received and that Allahdad himself would be an arbiter between the two and that both would approve an agreement.

Allahdad therefore approached Khudaidad and informed him of this letter and unfolded to him its whole purport. But the cause of the enmity, which as I have said existed between Khalil Sultan and Khudaidad, was this : when Khalil Sultan in the beginning was a neighbour to Khudaidad in that country, his grandfather had made him his guardian and entrusted to him the task of directing him, and he was hard, rigid, severe and rough and treated him with inhumanity and handled him hardly and rudely. But Khalil Sultan was of a gentle nature and elegant character and the calm air of his mind could not bear the storms of Khudaidad nor could the delicate garb of his temperament because of its thin texture resist the pull of discord and strife and so from that harshness enmity arose between the two and informers went to and fro, until he secretly gave poison to him, which he drank, but soon perceiving it, he took precautions and used a remedy, but his constitution was hurt; yet fortune willed that he should escape this peril; and he came out of it—would that it had brought death to him!—and there remained in him an odour thereof and it caused lameness to him; then this private enmity became public and this affair became a sufficient cause to this sick man for sedition.

Section

Then Allahdad swore a great and mighty oath to Khudaidad and confirmed it by taking the Koran, which he showed and placed his hand on it, and he strengthened it more by an oath of divorce and by obligations and vows, that he would not withdraw from obedience to him or ever change his mind towards him and that he would proceed to Samarkand with zeal to join what had been severed and restore what had been taken away and sew together that which was rent on both sides and repair what had burst in their minds because of hatred and enmity, and that he would win for him in marriage Tuman, one of the wives of Timur; and in short, he promised to cut away the causes of evil and arrange affairs and that if he failed in removing hatred and destroying the signs of enmity, yet he would neither secretly nor openly fall away from cherishing friendship with Khudaidad; and constantly using adulation and flattery, by the cunning dye of his speech he thoroughly crept into the mind of Khudaidad and made and confirmed an oath, at which hearts would tremble and break, by the one God, and repeated it, swearing by triple divorce from his four wives; and they had their camp pitched on the bank of the Jaxartes, about two stages* from the city Shah Rukhia.

* " barids " = each probably about four leagues.

Then his guile like an arrow craftily pierced and penetrated the other's heart and with him he carefully sifted and separated the portion of grain, which with his right hand he had sown in that field, until he was easy in letting him go after he had confirmed the pledge and promise which he had given ; then Allahdad returned to his camp and met his followers and allies who were at Shah Rukhia and expounded this matter to them ; and he had already prepared what he needed before undertaking that business and taken arms and precautions from every side.

Then girding his loins, he crossed the Jaxartes in boats under the wing of night.

CHAPTER LX

ALLAHDAD COMES TO KHALIL SULTAN AND ABIDES WITH GREAT HONOUR IN HIS OWN COUNTRY

WHEN he reached this bank and none of his men was missing on the further side, he forthwith ordered that packs and baggage and arms should be taken before any act of plunder and they poured forth upon them abundance of arms and he caused the prayer of departure to be said before the morning meal and sent in front the weak among his people and the baggage and forbade any delay in that ceremony and made a messenger fly to Khalil Sultan to unfold these news and the transactions between himself and Khudaidad and to ask that help and troops should be sent to him, if the evil Khudaidad, marking the danger of this action, should think of repelling them and should send men from the rear to hinder them.

Then they advanced like an arrow which moves straight towards the mark and flew like a meteor and so soon as the dawn shone upon them, salvation appeared to them from a favouring star and they traversed all the dusty, wide-extending wastes and speeding the movement of their beasts they passed over varied tracts, like many-coloured webs of gardens, as though cutting them on the loom, and they continued their march by night and all day, so that evening came on, and when riders and beasts alike were worn with fatigue and darkness like an eagle spread its wing over them, he turned aside with them to a certain valley and withdrawing took rest and ordered that no fire should be kindled and that none should seek to taste the lightest sleep and the edge of the sword should not be set in the sheath ; then they hastily swallowed enough lightly to sustain life and performed the prayer of fear and worshipped God for the sake of gain and delayed long enough to gather hay ; then he ordered them and taking up the baggage, they moved camp, riding upon the road.

CHAPTER LXI

HOW KHUDAIDAD AWOKE WHILE ALLAHDAD STOLE AWAY HIS INTELLECT BY TROUBLES AND AFFLICTIONS

THEN Khudaidad awoke from his sleep and dismissed the night and knew that Allahdad had stolen that day from him and beguiled him and eclipsed the sun of his intellect and made play with him by his oath and conquered him ; then he bit his hands as the wicked shall on the last day and forthwith gathered a great army which he sent against him ; and they pursued him with much diligence and they sought to meet him, but neither saw him nor his footprint nor got any news of him and in seeking him they ceased not to wander this way and that ; then they were defeated and departed with shame ; and Allahdad came to the place whither he was tending and found the office of Vazir not yet filled, which he alone obtained, since before his coming Nuruddin had withdrawn and Shah Malik and all who intended rebellion had gradually departed.

And Khalil Sultan rejoiced at his coming and put him, as he had been, above the other vazirs and ministers.

Then Allahdad, having gained the power of acting as he willed, engaged with skill in expounding the affairs of the realm according to his excellent eloquence and ordering them and forthwith applied himself to directing things well and equipping troops and guarding the posts on the borders. Thus the realm again came to itself and was brought to a firmer state and the knot of the pearl-string of the realm after being snatched away was rightly joined and the condition of the people established and pillars set firmly on their bases and he and Barnadaq and Arghunshah and another by name Kajuk directed the affairs of the realm and ordered everything, but Allahdad was Dastur* and Azam and the fount of power and favour—like the string of knots, whereby pearls are held, which loosens or binds.

But Sheikh Nuruddin and Khudaidad continued to raid countries and overflow in wickedness and destruction, and they gained the borders of ·Turkistan and the dominions of those cities, among which were Siram, Nashkand, Andakan, Khajand, Shah-Rukhia, Atrar, Saghanaq and many others which lie in those parts and regions. But when they crossed the Jaxartes and made towards the realms of Transoxiana, Khalil Sultan himself moved against them and equipped bands of soldiers and auxiliaries against them in every crisis and those two persisted not, but were driven to flight, and how this was done will be told hereafter.

CHAPTER LXII

OF THE TURNS OF FORTUNE WHICH BEFELL IN TURAN AFTER THE DEATH OF TIMUR

WHEN news reached the Moghuls of the death of that evil one,† they thought that he was aiming the stones of his cunning to shatter those posts on the borders and fitting the arrows of his purpose to pierce bellies and throats and they doubted not that it was a net of his fraud and a snare of his hunting ; therefore since they had no place to rest, they proclaimed that resort should be had forthwith to flight and scattering over the country, seized the mantles of forts and tops of mountains and fled to castles and steep places and pretended death in the depths of caves and caverns ; likewise did all the people of Dasht‡ both of the South and the North and dispersed over sandy deserts ; and the people of the East and of Khata§ and so far as the borders of Sin¶ and those who roamed in that part for pasture did as in the Koran, " If they find a place of refuge or caves or a hiding-place, verily they will turn thither and quickly flee to it " and truly he had climbed so far in his reign of terror and excess that he destroyed the

---

* Chief minister.   † Timur.   ‡ i.e., The Steppes.
§ Or, Cathay.   ¶ Or, China.

world east and west by the odour of his repute and it befell as is written :

> " Almost his bows without an archer would fix arrows in their hearts.
> Almost his swords undrawn would cut by creeping to their necks.
> Almost his swift horses that carry him could start content without rations on their course."

But when one message came after another and these sweet tidings were repeated and the report spread so that from single rumours it grew to a continuous succession of statements and this truth was confirmed among all, so that it could no longer be doubted or disguised, every heart returned to its cavity and gained security in place of its former fear and they proclaimed "Attack!" Then they began to make raids on every side and everyone to whom aught was due demanded his debt and every slave sought liberation from his master. But the first who moved from the East were the Moghuls who invaded Ashbara and Issyk Kul and spread through those parts until they became neighbours of Khudaidad, who made peace with them and appeased them and promised them restitution of their homes, which Timur had taken away, and agreed that with united hand they should oppose their enemies ; and each observed good neighbourliness with the other and by this peace those parts gained tranquillity.

CHAPTER LXIII

HOW IDAKU ROSE WITH THE TATARS AND INVADED TRANSOXIANA AND THOSE PARTS

THEN Idaku rose from the north with armies like the sands and marched with a will and resolved to invade the domains of Khwarizm, whose governor was called Musika ; who, as soon as he perceived the Tatars, feared harm for himself and taking with him his household and those who belonged to him, departed; and that after the Tatars of Rum, who followed Arghunshah, had made an incursion and crossed the frozen Jaxartes ; and Arghunshah returned to his home

and Idaku came to Khwarizm, which he gained, and he wished
to advance with his cavalry to Bokhara, whose surrounding
country he plundered, then returned to Khwarizm ; and now
the fire blazed more fiercely among the Jagatais and hurt them.
But in his name there governed Khwarizm with its vilayets a
man called Anka ; but the country remained calm and
travellers and inhabitants alike enjoyed tranquillity, because
Khalil Sultan received with kindness all who wished him ill,
striving to appease everyone that was angered and by his
generosity to win over all who were opposed to him ; and he
hunted men's minds with precious gifts and strove to catch
lions by throwing food before them. Therefore strangers and
those from far off held him dear and one and all desired him,
except Sheikh Nuruddin and Khudaidad, who continued in
insolence and persisted in rebellion, laying waste the country
between the two borders.

CHAPTER LXIV

OF BIR MAHOMED, GRANDSON OF TIMUR, AND HIS APPOINTED
HEIR, AND WHAT PASSED BETWEEN HIM AND KHALIL, HIS
KINSMAN

THEN Bir Mahomed, son of the uncle of Khalil Sultan,
whom Timur had appointed as successor, after the death
of his brother, Mahomed Sultan, led forth from Kandahar
towards Samarkand a numerous army and wrote to Khalil
Sultan and all the chief Vazirs and ministers, that since he
was the designated heir and successor of his grandfather Timur
after his death, the throne was rightly due to him ; why therefore should it be snatched from him ? and that the kingdom
was his kingdom ; how then should he be robbed of it ?

Then all of them gave a reply that agreed with his speech,
but Khalil Sultan turned to contradict and received the whole
question with denial and refutation, whereby he might repel
it, and said :

" It is not so much a question between us of the kingdom
at this time, O you, whoever you may be, but whether it is
gained by right of inheritance or by right of possession. If the
former, then certainly there are some to whom it is due by

greater right than to me and you, namely, my father Amiran Shah and my uncle Shah Rukh, his brother, and in that case the shares of both will be equal and you will have naught to say to them. But I am too noble to be a companion to him, and protect his side and act as his attendant. On the other hand, if each of them should abstain from the contest, verily he will leave to me his share of the province which is claimed and be satisfied with his own domain and guard his own flank; but if each should appoint me his deputy in government, I will guard his share and fortune; but if it be a matter of possession, your speech will avail naught, since a kingdom, it is said, has no children and before my time and yours it was said in maxims:

'Equip your noblest horses and polish your arms and gird your loins, for on this victory depends.'

"You boast that your grandfather appointed you successor or in his will made you his heir; but how did he gain power, unless by the path of victory, and how will kingdoms come to you unless by forcible conquest? Nay, even if it be granted that the affair of his will is in order, certainly, while he was still alive, he had divided his realms and distributed them among his sons and grandsons; and he set my father over the territory of Azerbaijan and gave my uncle to possess the vilayets of Khorasan and to the son of my uncle, Bir Umar, Persian Iraq and those parts and among them he set you over Kandahar and made you his successor according to his expressed wish and he himself had to carry the load of his iniquities and met his end.

"But where is my share of this gift? Therefore appoint my share from that which I have gotten and let each of you be content with the part in the possession of which he is established and which is allotted to him. None the less, if my father and uncle obey you, I also will obey you or if both deal with you according to the will and recognize you as ruler, then I too will so recognize you; but if in this matter we follow the way of truth, truly the kingdom is a chase, in which the best man is he who, going in front, seizes the quarry. But God removed the excuses thereof, when He furnished me with strong defences in possessing it and He granted me that as a matter of common justice; but that which belongs to none goes to him who first takes it; certainly all the doctors of the law of government take my side, and those who shared in the compacts of the sultanate, abandoning dispute, pay their duty to me and count the compact of my governance as gain and having learned my ways, have submitted to me and acknowledged me as ruler."

But the Vazirs and ministers sent him a reply, in which there was nothing good, nay, which the ears of the hearers might reject, except Khwaja Abdulawal, who held first place among the doctors and was pre-eminent among the lords and chief men of Transoxiana and whose thoughts penetrated like an arrow all the Amirs and Chiefs. He with his good answer hit the mark straight and in sound, brief and terse words rejected Bir Mahomed and sided with Khalil Sultan and said in his answer what conformed with the words of Khalil: "Certainly you are lawful heir and successor of Amir Timur, but fortune does not favour you, for if it did, you would be near the capital. But in your condition the best course is to be content with what you possess and with your means and to spare your horse and foot and keep the part of the realm which you hold; but if you greatly strive to get increase and are not content with the lot which God has given and assigned to you and advance from your domain into this plain, truly you will fall into trouble and lose the authority which you now hold and will not gain one object or the other."

CHAPTER LXV

HOW KHALIL SULTAN SENT BIN HUSSEIN* TO DEFEND HIM AND
HE DESERTED KHALIL SULTAN AND LAID HANDS ON THE AMIRS
AND OPPOSED KHALIL

THEN Khalil Sultan, not content with the subtleties of these opinions, soon sent after them truths of deeds and ordered the army that was gathered to be fitted to receive Bir Mahomed, and over it he set Sultan Hussein, the son of his father's aunt, and added all the best of the Amirs of the Jagatais along with the stoutest of them, among whom were Kajuk and Arghunshah and Allahdad. And they set out with a great host and perfectly equipped with arms in the seventh year† in the middle of the month Zulkaada and crossed the

* This refers to Sultan Hussein.   † A.D. 1405.

Jaxartes to Balkh in whose plains they pitched camp and spread through its parts and districts; and while they lived softly, free of care and joyful, Sultan Hussein pretended sickness, then called to him the Amirs to deliberate with them concerning that matter about which he desired to take counsel and first he set an ambush for them, placing soldiers to their left and right, and when they had entered his lair and gone into his trap, he fell upon them like a lion on its prey, and roused against them his lions, who rushed on them, like hungry men upon meat; then one of his companions shouted: "Smite their necks, until you have made great slaughter of them, then cast the rest into bonds." But there was, as already said, a man active, spirited, bold, eager, impetuous and fierce, whose deed anticipated that one's word and forthwith was shed the blood of one of that company called Khawja Yusuf, who in Timur's life had been Deputy at Samarkand during his absence and was a famous Amir; yet he was slain forthwith and carried to the other life. Then Sultan Hussein lifted himself higher, claiming the sultanate, and called men from every side to acknowledge him. And astonished by this matter the chief men knew that truly punishment and affliction had descended upon them.

CHAPTER LXVI

ALLAHDAD OUTWITS SULTAN HUSSEIN, USING CRAFT AND GUILE
AS REMEDY FOR HIS RUIN

BUT Allahdad, strengthening his purpose, as though filling his wallet with supplies, and forthwith recalling his absent intelligence, ran with a loud voice to Sultan Hussein and secretly conferred with him about their affairs and said openly to him, " I have a sincere warning to offer you "; then withdrew with him to a lonely place and said : " I had divined this thing concerning you and expected of you a manifestation of your purpose. But why should Khalil Sultan claim the whole kingdom for himself alone ? But the fear of my Lord and Sultan is great and between him and his servant is no place for free speech ; but if I had had the least sign of that matter, I would have ordered affairs as your gracious commands and position required ; nay your gracious mind will bear witness to the truth of this saying and truly I am your slave from of old ; and ask of the slaves and soldiers, whom Khudaidad held captive, ' Who freed them from the nets of that captivity and snatched them from the sword of that injury and put out what had been kindled from the sparks of that malice ? ' Had I not been present, he would have destroyed them and made their children orphans and deprived them of all their means. Certainly if you ask them, they will inform you and expound it to you according to the truth and plainly and perchance they informed you thereof when they came to you ; and also consult your heart and if they teach and instruct you, they will teach what is certain."

And he ceased not with the water of his chatter to quench the fire of the other's ferocity, as though he were a second Pharaoh, and to put out his flame and to burn the ambergris of his deceit in the nostrils of Hussein's madness, imbued with the odour and fragrance of his musk, and from the bow of his deception to shoot into his inmost imagination the arrows of his cunning and thither penetrated the spears of fate and destiny because they hit the mark.

So he imbibed his deceit and following his opinion made him his helper and in his affairs was eager to take counsel from his sagacity ; then after favouring him by sparing his life, he consulted him about the killing of his friends, and Allahdad said to him : " It cannot be doubted, that Khalil Sultan holds men in his power by clemency and liberality, for though in strength he is lacking and profits little, yet he gains stronger men by goodness of heart and profusion of wealth ; but wealth easily vanishes and fails. But your famous endowments are celebrated by all and your banquets of war are attended by the bravest warriors and the standards with which you break the horns of rivals are unfolded on the front of your leaders and the heads with which you ram the bulls of war are famous for victories for all time." I have said :

> ' How many brave men you have pressed in the field of
> battle,
> Who seeing your face, turn their backs and flee ! '

" Truly, since you have been the head and eye in battles, I have seen victory in your head and a talon in your eye and I am certain that every soldier will rejoice at the sight of you and that because of the rest prepared for them their hearts will exult with joy at your movements ; for they want a leader to rule them and a great-hearted commander to guard their wealth and lives by his management and a master like a strong lion and overflowing river, nay, eddying sea, famed for his victories, whether he challenges or is challenged, and a protector as the poet said :

> " ' With the art of rule he joins courage in war
> And desires only to govern the brave.'

or as another wrote :

> " ' Only the brave man drives away sorrow,
> Who sees the eddies of death and leaps therein.'

" Where is one found in this age marked by these gifts, but you ? And none is more spirited, braver and nobler or would be a companion to you wherever you went and stand wherever you stood and if it had been told to Shah Malik and Sheikh Nuruddin that your favour was an impregnable fortress in their rear, I would have confirmed that true saying by your authority and certainly they would resort to the strong pillar of your lofty court. In short, you are truly master of all and all are your slaves, and since this is so and you have them in your power, it is yours to protect them or destroy them, but to spare them is best nor will slaves cease to hope for the mercies of their lord and if your august judgment requires that we should all be held by iron chains with the bond of a strong oath, that judgment is the supreme law and to obey its decree is fit and right."

And he followed his counsel and adopted him as banner and standard in his affairs and sought to follow him immediately and said : " I will follow him."

CHAPTER LXVII

SULTAN HUSSEIN MAKES AN AGREEMENT WITH THE AMIRS WHO WERE HELD IN BONDAGE BY HIM AND MOVES AGAINST KHALIL SULTAN

THEN he ordered the Amirs who were prisoners in his power to be brought and the laments of all their kinsmen filled the country and news came to every house and they were lamented like dead men, and he bound them with iron fetters and by an oath that they would side with him in prosperity and adversity against Khalil Sultan, and each of them reached forward his foot to the fetters and his hand to the oath and promised whatever the Sultan wished and that he would offer to him his life and his servants, his wealth and his children. Accordingly being confident about them, he gave them a promise of security and so warded off misfortune from them, but he kept them in bondage and returned towards Samarkand and sent to Khalil Sultan a messenger to announce to him the end of his business and to advise him to prepare for battle with himself when he had crossed the Jaxartes and that he should advance and stating that he yet demanded a share of the kingdom of his uncle and agreed with Khalil Sultan in seeking a throne of higher power.

CHAPTER LXVIII

KHALIL SULTAN LEADS HIS ARMY FROM SAMARKAND TO MEET
SULTAN HUSSEIN, WHO WAS DISAPPOINTED IN HIS HOPES

BUT Khalil Sultan, equipping an army against him, went forth from Samarkand to oppose him with all speed ; then summoned Allahdad and his friends among the devils who were bound in fetters and renewed agreements with them and bound them more firmly with the knots of a compact and setting each of them in his own place, cut off and loosened his bonds and presented him with precious raiment and gifts and treated with honour and respect whatever belonged to him and was kind and gracious towards those who belonged to him and journeyed with them, until he came to the city of Kesh. However, before that time Allahdad had sent a messenger to Khalil Sultan to announce to him the occurrence of this trouble and the misfortunes which had befallen them and which had reached their issue. Then he said to him, " Certainly your omens are favourable and your object is worthy of praise ; therefore arise with proper counsel and an armed force, for certainly your enemy has been caught in a net and God Almighty will be your ally ; therefore fear not ; though you are young, yet because of your youth men's hearts burn with affection for you and all the old men of the kingdom and all people have become your supporters."

Therefore Khalil Sultan came to that place, and Sultan Hussein prepared his army and used his military ardour and vigour and put Allahdad in command of the right wing and his two friends in command of the left ; but when those two armies came in sight one of another and the two lines of battle had approached and the moment of engagement had come and the battlefield had become narrow and those lions had charged one on another and the armies and every man had rushed from his place, all those who were with Allahdad and his friends made for the camp of Khalil Sultan ; thus the armies of Sultan Hussein were scattered and the garment of his power was taken from him and leaving it he put on the double garment of frustration and destruction ; and affliction came upon him which made him forget his aim. He therefore returned disappointed in his hopes and departed alone, going through the desert, until he came to Shah Rukh, the son of his uncle, lord of Herat, with whom he lived, but not for long, whether poison was given to him in drink or he met a natural death. This was the end of the treaty with Sultan Hussein and Khalil Sultan returned joyous and tranquil to his capital.

CHAPTER LXIX

OF THE OTHER ACCIDENTS WHICH BEFELL BIR MAHOMED, WHETHER FORTUNATE OR ADVERSE, AND HOW HE CAME TO CALAMITY AND SORROW AND FAILURE

THEN Bir Mahomed, continuing in his rebellion, went forward to take his pleasure in the fields and pastures of desire and letters were exchanged between the two and after long discourse their arguments at length reached this issue, that they abandoned the abode of war* and entered the fortresses of strife and conflict. And there was a Controller of Affairs at his Court and supporter of the pillars of his kingdom and rule, by name Bir Ali Taz, who was protector of the gate of the kingdom and guardian of the innermost valleys of his realm, the zenith of his orbit, pattern of the doctors and

* The sense here seems to require " peace."

strength of the wings of his army, and he prepared every mighty host of the armies of Kandahar and leaned upon a broken mass, and he set out with a plan keener than a sharp sword and more penetrating than a quivering spear, leading that great host and rushing torrent and swelling cloud of his army, until he reached the Jaxartes, where that flood halted ; then he ordered that stormy sea to ride over the Jaxartes, whose waves smote one against the other ; and God parted two seas, one sweet and pleasant to drink, the other salt and bitter. Therefore they crossed the river with their boats and went over, as the Israelites passed over the Red Sea, and he advanced with that army like a great mountain until he halted in the plains of Nakhshab.

CHAPTER LXX

THE ARMIES OF KHALIL ENGAGE WITH THE FORCES OF KANDAHAR IN STRENUOUS COMBAT AND INFLICT ON THEM IN THEIR FLIGHT GRIEVOUS SLAUGHTER

KHALIL SULTAN had now completed his business and scattered the fragrant odours of his kindness and given command to summon kings to pluck the fruit of his revenues and largesse, with which they might equip themselves to confront the devils of Kandahar ; and this summons was obeyed by nobles and commons and every builder and diver* among the demons of the armies, and there assembled all those who were obedient among the leaders of those allies and they gathered the fruit of that garden from men and jinns and the waves of the army flowed from every side to that sea of generosity and among them were the leaders of the Jagatais and Jatas and every despot from the country of Turkistan and horsemen of Persia, Iraq and Rustamdar and the demons of Khorasan and India and of the Tatars and those whom Timur had kept ready when he was in extremity, who left him neither abroad nor at home, but guarded him in every vicissitude, fortunate or adverse :

>" Horsemen unwearied by slaughter,
>When the grindstone of furious war is turning."

* i.e., everyone. A phrase from the Koran.

And he put before them afresh omens of victory and chose from them for weightier matters every true friend and gave to them generous defences from his store and clothed their hopes with royal mantles of his kindness, more excellent than double breast-plates ; and the earth opened its treasures to them and poured upon them from its mines and veins of metal open and hidden wealth, so that every foot-soldier and horse-man who advanced gloriously with that precious adornment far surpassed the fairest maidens in beauty. When they advanced, the fragrant breath of prosperity was wafted from their spirits and lightnings of victory flashed from their gleam-ing standards and their faces foretold the opening of the gates of success and victory ; and the leader continued the march from stage to stage, until he pitched his camp in the plains of Karshi, the city mentioned above ; and those victorious armies halted on the first day of the beginning of the month of Ramzan in the year 808,* and both those great armies passed the night and girded their loins and checked their floods from dispersion and diffusion and he kept with him his infantry and cavalry and sat all night awaiting the dawn. I have said :

" Until the splendour of light rises from the darkness,
    And gleams like a wave of water from the curtain of the
    reeds."

But when the dawn drew its silver sword and held forth its golden shield and wiped away from the tablet of the air the blackened picture, which night had painted anew after day had blotted it out, all those mountains of armies made ready to engage and in the hearts of those tribes was kindled a fire of noble ardour to endure the furious onset of battle and overthrow. And each army drew up its right and left wing and van and rear guard ; then approaching each other they exchanged pleasantries and promised mutual aid and gave encouragement one to the other and kindled battle by song and with their hands embraced each other's necks and provoked each other to courage and seizing each other's throats strove to destroy one the other, and foot-soldier engaged with foot-soldier, horseman with horseman, and impenetrable dust rose to the points of their spears, so that the stars of night appeared at noon, and in the billowing dust there flowed from every spear torrents of blood. Then about noon the dust lifted and it was

* A.D. 1406.

seen that the mountain of the army of Kandahar was shattered and the fortune of those giants was ended and that they were cut to pieces and were departing defeated ; but the zephyr of victory of Khalil Sultan moved everywhere ; so Bir Mahomed turned his back and the sea of destruction flowed over his head, and in his heart the flints gave out fire as though live coals were burning within him or a fire kindled by flint and tinder were blazing in his bosom, and his soldiers were overwhelmed and his mighty warriors smitten, his baggage plundered, his power overthrown, his women and slaves carried into bondage and all his wealth despoiled ; and he girded his loins for flight, knowing well that a safe return was equal in worth to plunder, as it is said :

" Your safe return is equal to the spoils of victory,
And a mind secure is equal to any prize."

And Khalil Sultan returned and the whole world was eager to be illumined by his rays and his power was strengthened and fear of him spread afar and he gave thanks to God the King and kept the fast of Ramzan in a place called Jakdalik.

CHAPTER LXXI

OF THE MUTINY OF THE ARMY OF IRAQ FROM KHALIL SULTAN
AND THE ENERGY WHICH THEY SHOWED IN THEIR DEFECTION
AND OF THEIR RETURN TO THEIR COUNTRY

THEN on the day of the new moon at the beginning of the month of Shawal, the leaders and brave soldiers of Iraq mutinied, taking with them their womenfolk, households, offspring and followers ; chief among them was one by name Haji Basha, according to whose will they ordered themselves in everything and they were fierce and eager warriors ; in their company they had Sultan Alauddaulat, son of Sultan Ahmed of Bagdad, whom Timur had held in bondage and worn out and tested with affliction and trouble, but Khalil Sultan had loosed him from prison and given him a station of authority and dignity in his realm. But while men were engaged in the feast of Id, those leaders took their squadrons, as though some promise had been made to them and departed under the wing of night and girding their loins, sought for themselves brides of Iraq, divorcing the wives of Transoxiana, from whom they turned with great eagerness, because they had heard that the house of Iraq is receiving its owner and the waters of the rivers of that kingdom are returning to their channels.

But no one opposed or pursued them or could hinder them or restrained them in their march, and they crossed the Oxus and came into Khorasan. Then all who heard about them met them from every side, but their links were broken for want of mutual agreement and they were scattered through the country before they came to Iraq. Iran is far from Turan and Tigris from Oxus! But Khalil Sultan having celebrated Id in that place returned to his home.

CHAPTER LXXII

CONCERNING THE DEEDS OF BIR MAHOMED AFTER HIS DEFEAT AND HIS COMING TO HIS OWN CITY OF KANDAHAR

AFTER Bir Mahomed came to Kandahar and established himself and his affairs were restored and his soldiers flitted about his palace like thirsty hawks and men from the hosts of his army revolved like the full moon, the poisonous wind of the simoom blew more fiercely day and night and the sparks of his malice leapt forth and his heart blazed with anger and he was torn and rent with wrath and was foolish and of little wisdom. Then he made his commands fly to his subjects and roused against Khalil Sultan all his true friends and familiars, and asked all who had been wounded by spear and sword and whose heart was sore, and also those that were sound, to bring a remedy to his wounded heart and they obeyed his summons and received his command with obedience and compliance. Soon the valleys and hills flowed with horsemen and infantry and he sent an envoy to Khalil with a letter in these words : '' Truly our first conflict was unforeseen and so came to an end and was like a spark which we neglected to put out and so it blazed forth ; but if I had foreseen what I now know and had taken heed against that which I despised and had thought a great matter, that which I considered small, truly I should have taken back victory instead of disaster and gained my purpose and not failed therein. But I neglected to look forward and so success was forbidden me and because I handled your affairs only with the tips of my fingers, therefore I have bitten my hand for remorse, although the strength of your army and power of your might and the arrows that you hurl and the arm of your good fortune and the sword of your anger and the spear of your rectitude and the edge of your sword and the force of your vigour depend only on the leaders of Iraq, who nevertheless have not agreed well with you ; but now when their quarrel has come upon you and their discord has befallen you with open mutiny and defection, by this your heart is diminished, your wisdom weakened and your army broken. I truly have brought against you fresh zeal, strength and steel ; therefore be ready to meet me and look for certain harm, for war as you know brings turns of fortune and as yesterday it was granted to you to enjoy fortune against us, so to-morrow we shall be granted the same against you."

CHAPTER LXXIII

OF THE SECOND EXPEDITION OF BIR MAHOMED AGAINST KHALIL
SULTAN AND WHAT CAME TO HIM FROM HIS PRIDE AND HOW AS
AT FIRST HE WAS TURNED TO FLIGHT

THEN he led forth his armies and allies and crossed the Oxus and came to a place called Hisar Shadiman ; and Khalil Sultan came against him and with him infantry and horsemen and the locusts, insects and frogs of his army to shed a deluge of blood and with them he crossed mountains and seas and marched, now halting, now advancing, until he came to the forces of Kandahar ; and already, as I said, arrows had like flints kindled in the breasts of the armies of Kandahar the fear of the fury of Khalil and they were pierced by the sting of the arrows, for the beast wounded by the scorpion fears the rings of the halter ; therefore before the trumpet sounded or the drum was beaten, part of every host among them was affrighted and fled and they cried : " The last day has come, which only God can ward off." Therefore Bir Mahomed put on the cloak of flight, but he had not the means thereof, and so hastened to the fort, whose gates he shut and fortified the walls ; and he prepared himself for a siege in the fort of Hisar Shadi-man ; then he was surrounded by every vulture and eagle of his army and girded by every son of Japhet and every one of them who fought with spear, sword and arrow gave himself eagerly to the business of the siege ; then Bir Mahomed was overcome by remorse for what he had done zealously in that matter and recalled to memory what Khwaja Abdulawal had said to him in the beginning, but he used the excuse of fate and destiny and so fate smote him with its answer keen and striking the mark like an arrow and said :

" He who is weak in counsel ruins his chance,
Until, foiled, he disputes with destiny."

Then all his prudence and fortune was overthrown and his whole state was altered and what he had possessed of the kingdom and of wealth left him and there fled from him every brave lion of war, after leaping fiercely on every bold defender ; and every man of his household left him because of his evil government, since the falseness of every appearance and mirage was plain, and his rule was rent asunder like a web on its frame.   Therefore no refuge was left to him except God.

CHAPTER LXXIV

OF THE DEVICE EMPLOYED BY BIR MAHOMED, THE PLANNING
OF WHICH HARMED HIM, FOR IT WAS OF LITTLE USE

ACCORDINGLY devoid of strength he gave himself to the employment of a stratagem and sent for a large supply of skins grooved, properly fitted together and dyed with various colours ; then from them he made defences against every danger and fixed to them polished mirrors and divided sheets of metal, which he gilded and strengthened with nails, and gathered the chief men among the subjects of his city and prepared many squadrons of the unwarlike and common people, then ordered that those shining breastplates and defences should be brought, and distributed these leather coverings among the leaders and followers and when the sun rose, they used to climb the walls and those lions advanced outside the city covered with those long and wide corselets, so that anyone who saw them from a distance thought they were soldiers, not knowing that they were like fireworks; but when those vanishing spectres appeared, they filled the plain like a mirage, which a thirsty man mistakes for water, and in this way for a time he withstood the might of the enemy and opposed their violence.

The man who planned this device was the first Vazir of his kingdom, by name Bir Ali, but nonetheless this stratagem profited him nothing, nay, his evil counsels and unsound proposals injured himself and his secret was uncovered and the curtain rent; then he was powerless and could no longer resist and his weapons and forces failed and time added to his affliction.

CHAPTER LXXV

BIR MAHOMED SEES THE INJUSTICE OF HIS USURPATION AND SEEKS PEACE AND SUBMITS TO KHALIL SULTAN

THEREFORE he spread the carpet of submission and entreaty. He sought pardon and came to know that none is defended from the command of Allah, except him on whom He has pity and so he entreated Khalil Sultan in the name of God and of their kinship and said in the words of the poet:

" The noble man is wont to forgive and his temper
  Turns not from giving and forgiving, when a fault is
  committed."

And Khalil Sultan consented to his prayers and on both sides mutual friendship was strengthened and a treaty made, that one should not seek the country of the other and since God Almighty had lifted him up, he would not leave his side and would hand over to him what he possessed and now and in future would maintain sincere friendship. Then the two made an oath, that they would not attack each other, and confirmed a pact to maintain concord and agreed in promising mutual sincere friendship and they departed one from the other on condition that they should become comrades, and they agreed not to act with hypocrisy, but to maintain the treaty and alliance and protect their kindred and households, and they departed one from the other with their retinues, and this happened in the year 809.*

CHAPTER LXXVI

OF THE STRIFE AND ENMITY THAT AROSE BETWEEN BIR MAHOMED AND BIR ALI TAZ, WHEREBY THE GARMENT OF LIFE WAS TAKEN FROM BOTH AND THE ENEMIES OF BOTH HAD REST FROM THEM

AFTER Bir Mahomed came to his home and rested among his slaves and servants, Bir Ali Taz rebelled against him and claimed for himself the title of king and pre-eminence ; then he seized him and put him in bondage and then slew him ; and wandering and scattering terror, he began to say : " The things of the world are troubled and signs of the last hour have come nigh ; now is the kingdom of antichrists and the time in which false teachers and impostors have prevailed ; Timur, who was a lame antichrist, is no more ; now is the time of a bald antichrist ; after him will follow a blind antichrist. Nay, if anyone fears to knock at the doors of the kingdom, I will knock at them."

But none of the leaders or commons consented to his question or answered that which would content him and his heart was oppressed with grief, since in undertaking this business which he had planned nothing was found to make it lawful and in the lottery of the realm naught was promised to him but a blank number.

Therefore he summoned the great men humbly and timidly, but all set their teeth before him and rent this corpse between them and no rest or steadfastness was any more left to him, and therefore withdrawing his hand he stretched his foot towards the Lord of Herat, who, as soon as he fell into his hunting-net, set hands on him and uttered against him a judgment of just retribution and the realms of Kandahar yielded to him with easy obedience without opposition or struggle ; nay, even Khalil Sultan rested from trouble and attack.

* A.D. 1407.

CHAPTER LXXVII

OF THE NEW EVENTS WHICH HAPPENED IN THE ABSENCE OF
KHALIL SULTAN

IN the same year the Tatars of Rum broke forth impetuously
and set out on a march and crossed the frozen Oxus on foot
from Khwarizm and sought their own country, but men
opposed them on every side and scattered and routed them and
this happened to them for lack of concord, as had befallen
the armies of Iraq ; so also while Khalil Sultan was absent and
detained on a long journey, Khudaidad and Sheikh Nuruddin
seized the occasion and without fear made for Samarkand and
threatened it and despoiled its surrounding fields, but it was
impregnable to them and looked down proudly upon them ;
then after despoiling its suburbs they returned and went back
to their own country.

CHAPTER LXXVIII

KHALIL SULTAN SENDS FOR HIS ARMIES AND FIGHTS AGAINST
SHEIKH NURUDDIN AND KHUDAIDAD

AFTER Khalil Sultan returned to Samarkand, he gave
rest to the hosts of his army and then, summoning the
soldiers, he marched against them and began to follow those
two and set out with great diligence with those tribes kindled
with fury and strong lions and lusty stallions ; and that
mountain of his army continued moving and resting, until it
reached the Jaxartes, and when that mountain and gleaming
fire crossed the Jaxartes, it seemed like a full sea.

Then Shahrukhia and Khajend submitted to him, but
Tashkend resisted him ; therefore he turned to besiege it and
strove to overthrow the stones thereof and after he had
besieged it some time and smitten it with great hunger and
misery, it sought peace and handed to him the keys of submission and he consented to its prayer and by this peace its
condition was made prosperous ; then he followed the tracks
of Khudaidad and Sheikh Nuruddin, seeking their death.

CHAPTER LXXIX

SHEIKH NURUDDIN AND KHUDAIDAD KINDLE A FIRE AGAINST
KHALIL, WHEREBY THEY MIGHT CONSUME HIM, BUT GOD
ALMIGHTY QUENCHED THAT FIRE AND PROTECTED HIM

NOW Khudaidad and Sheikh Nuruddin wandered about
the camp watching an opportunity of plunder and spoil
and the turn of events ; therefore he made after them and
sought to confront them, but presently they departed, when
they saw and heard him, and descended to a place where he
eagerly hoped to follow them and he pursued them at every
stage and when they moved, followed in their rear and pitched
his camp ; and Khalil Sultan put confidence in his army,
certain that he would have good fortune and victory ; but
one night, when he had neglected to take precaution and they
had a diligent spy in his army, he was mistaken and deceived
and moved his camp to a place called Sharbakhana and he
had gone in front of the baggage ; then their spy brought news
to them of what had been done and soon they hastened to
attack like a torrent and fell on him by night ; then a host
went forth from his army, as though in that hour the last day
was upon them. Then they left him and went back and fled
from him and were divided and scattered in deserts and waste
places. But how should a Sultan pursue bandits ? Therefore
he abstained from pursuing them and returned safe to his
home.

CHAPTER LXXX

NURUDDIN AND KHUDAIDAD DEPART ONE FROM THE OTHER
AND DIVIDE THAT COUNTRY BETWEEN THEM

BUT since the friendship of Khudaidad and Nuruddin
was like an earthen vessel and the foundations of their
mutual sincerity were like one who has built his house on the
edge of land eaten away by the waters, they fell into discord
and did not remain joined together and they drew between
them a web of strife and the merchandise of enmity was sold

between them and one knew not who would bring a charm to avert evil and it seemed that the time of separation was come. Then Sheikh Nuruddin withdrew towards Saganaq and took possession of those parts.

CHAPTER LXXXI

SHEIKH NURUDDIN RETURNS TO EXCUSE HIMSELF AND IS RELEASED BY KHALIL SULTAN FROM HIS FORMER FAULT

THEN Sheikh Nuruddin sent a letter to Khalil Sultan and excused himself for the rebellion, which he had committed, and prayed that he would receive his fault with favour and restore to him the former enjoyment of his kindness; and he consented to his prayer and spread over the baseness of his crime the long cloak of oblivion and sent to him Tuman, the wife of his grandfather.

SECTION

And Sheikh Nuruddin ceased not to draw the thread of friendship over the rent of the web of strife, until Khalil Sultan fell into bonds and Samarkand remained open to Shah Rukh. And Shah Malik came, offering peace but inwardly fostering enmity, and by cunning enticed him from his fort of Saganaq, after the two had established a treaty of alliance and had agreed to meet each other on horseback and after salutation, kisses and embraces, to open their desires to each other; and there was a man in the company of Shah Malik by name Argudaq; then Shah Malik approached with his company and Nuruddin came down from his fort and Shah Malik came alone without soldiers or arms and they embraced each other, being both deceived, and he unfolded to him the events, which had happened in his absence both fortunate and adverse, and made a treaty and pact with him and each advised the other what he should afterwards do. Then he let him go and turned and joined his own company and halted and every man of his company hastened, one after the other, to take the hand of Sheikh Nuruddin and kiss it, until the turn came to Argudaq, who came with hidden cunning and enmity; but he was a lion in courage, and in strength and size like an elephant. And he came near to him and kissing his hand clung to his neck and firmly holding his neck dragged him from his saddle and over-threw him like a star from its height and cut off his head ; and his death grievously afflicted his people. But when Shah Rukh heard it, he began to mourn for the one who was dead and pray for help and curse Shah Malik and blame him and he scourged Argudaq and exposed him publicly to reproach, but he could not join what those two had cut or plant what they had plucked, as the saying is, and after death there is none to give back life. And for some time he would see neither, but at length received both into his favour.

But Khudaidad continued to cling to the garment of rebellion, unfaithful between exorbitance and sedition, un-willing to submit to treaties of peace, until fate destroyed him and gave him to ruin ; but hereafter it will be told how in his destruction he was generous and conferred benefit.

CHAPTER LXXXII

KHALIL SULTAN GIVES ORDERS TO BUILD TARMID, WHICH JENGHIZKHAN HAD LAID WASTE, AND PREPARES HIS ARMY FOR THAT WORK

THEN in the month of Safar in the year 810* Khalil Sultan sent a host from his army, over whom he placed Allahdad, and added to them leaders and followers, to wit, Elias Khwaja and Ibn Qamari Mansur and Tukal Qarqara and Daulat Timur, and sent them to Tarmid with others to build it and they continued the march until they came to Tarmid and forthwith they collected stones and timber and gypsum that they needed ; then those leaders divided portions among themselves and after climbing raised the top of the walls of the city and houses and forwarded the work without delay and built towers on every height to mock at those that passed and omitted to take food by day or sleep by night and com-pleted their building in the space of about fifteen days ; and they divided its quarters and distributed its streets and high-ways and raised the standards of its mosques and minarets and

* A.D. 1407.

marked off the places of markets and houses; then they ordered the remnant of the offspring of its people who had fled far off and all who had gone from its rugged and wasted places to the cultivated plains, to return to it and complete it; and those poor men who had dwelt in its gardens had built there their markets and houses and collected their food and crops and this continued from the time of Jenghizkhan to the time of Timur Kurkan. Therefore they lived secure in their minds and rested from the movement of oppression and disturbance; but when after the death of Timur new evils and affairs befell, Khalil Sultan wished to defend them and sent word to strengthen their fortifications.

And the new city was distant from the old by the space of about one league, which old city became better fortified and stronger than the new, especially because its tower was covered with rubble and the River Oxus touched the foot of the mountain which carried its walls, but the case of the new city was opposite, for its buildings were not built high and the city was far from the river. But when the proclamation was made, " Enter the abode of your rest," they were as though the order had been given to them that either they should destroy themselves or leave their homes. But Allahdad was not troublesome to them or anxious about that matter nor did he make effort concerning them or openly oppose them for that reason, but he assembled them, proclaiming by the voice of a herald " He who first of the people occupies any place of the city and new building, it shall go to him and none shall oppose him or forbid or remove him." Then he ordered millers, butchers, cooks and sellers of butter to go to that place, to whom he gave dwellings and houses and did not labour much about winning over the rest. And they began to deal with the soldiers and sell and do business and did not suffer loss; and thereby the remaining multitude was diminished, for man is by nature social and they were compelled by need to follow them and every one among them great and small desired means to arrange his affairs and he established well by his commands the foundations of their condition. Then collecting his army he returned to Samarkand.

CHAPTER LXXXIII

OF THAT WHICH SHAH RUKH DID TOWARDS KHORASAN OPPOSITE
TO THE WORK OF KHALIL SULTAN

WHEN Shah Rukh heard of that which was done by
Khalil Sultan, he prepared a host from the armies of
Khorasan and assisted the feeble force from the sea of the realm
of the Amir by name Marzab, brother of Jahanshah, whom
Timur had set in command of the siege of Damascus, and
ordered the leaders of those armies to build a fort, called the
fort of the Indians, in the furthest borders of the country of
Khorasan which was separated from Tarmid by the River
Oxus ; and the builders and armies of Khorasan established it
near a place far removed from the armies of Khalil Sultan and
during the building Allahdad and Marzab sent envoys one to
the other and were of open and sincere mind one to the other
and met in pomp and magnificence and kept peace one with
the other.

CHAPTER LXXXIV

OF NEW EVENTS IN THE PARTS OF IRAQ AND THE TORRENTS OF
BLOOD WHICH FLOWED WHEN THAT STORM BURST

THEN Sultan Ahmad and Qara Yusuf returned to Iraq
and made a pact about the government of the realm and
Sultan Ahmad remained at Bagdad and Qara Yusuf with the
worshippers of Allah attacked the Jagatais to take away
the country from them which they had subdued and victory
wrote over his banners the words, " Help is from God," and
so he obtained all the provinces of Azerbaijan, after he had
defeated their army and slain Amiranshah ; but to give rein
to speech in completing this matter would take us far from our
aim, but discord came between them, whereby Azerbaijan
and Iraq were confounded. Then Qara Yusuf slew Sultan
Ahmad by the advice of Bustam in the year 813* from the
flight of the Prophet, on whom be peace !

* A.D. 1410.

As for Persian Iraq, since it was a fortified stronghold, its Governor, Bir Umar, claimed the title of King, but there rose against him his kinsman by name Iskandar, who engaged with him and defeated him and taking him prisoner removed him and took his title for himself ; then Shah Rukh, Lord of Herat, set out against him and took him and slew him and his death grievously afflicted his household and children and he took his whole country and all the Persian provinces went to Shah Rukh and showers of wealth from them were poured into his treasury, without any opposing him therein, nor in gaining it did he suffer harm or trouble, although his kingdom was placed in the midst of others, yet none put evil in his way, since he was a good neighbour, loving tranquillity ; and his father by slaying the Persian kings had already cut off the material of any bloodshed and he stood firm in his place among proud lions and increased and with the help of his friends overthrew his enemies and he stood and the lands of his realm were swollen with the sea of strength and the eyes of fortune were upon him and the brides of the kingdom spoke to him and sought his favour with these words :

" Stay thy mind from our despoiling and ravishment, for
    our threshold is open to all that are pure,
And patience is a talisman to open the treasure of our
    enjoyment ; he who comes with that talisman, gains
    that hidden treasure."

CHAPTER LXXXV

MEN LEAVING THE CITY OF SAMARKAND SEEK THEIR HOMES IN TRANSOXIANA

WHILE these things were being done they bethought themselves to leave Samarkand and scatter hither and thither and every stranger sought his own country and went seeking his home and household either with permission and warning or by flight and secret withdrawal ; the first of the people of Syria to ask permission to go and to wish to depart was Shahabuddin Ahmed, son of Shahid Vazir ; then companies departed to the Persians and Arabs and they scattered through the countries towards east and west and at Samarkand there arose want and excessive cost of goods and nothing was cheaper among them than gold and silver ; but then came plenty and that which they desired and needed came in good supply to men's use ; there was good fortune, and security ; hatred departed and the time was prosperous.

But in fair and clear season often murky storms arise.

CHAPTER LXXXVI

OF THE DESTRUCTION WROUGHT BY DECEITFUL FORTUNE, WHEREBY KHALIL WAS CAST INTO THE FIRE

K HALIL SULTAN had espoused Shadi Mulk, wife of Amir Saifuddin, and the power of his love of her conquered him and like a prisoner he bowed to her nod, so that his eye was fixed upon her and his love of her grew stronger and the story of it committed to oblivion the love of Kais* and Laila or Shirin and Farhad ; as the poet says :

> " I embrace her ; and my soul still burns with love of her,
> And after embraces is still devoted.
> I kiss her mouth to assuage my desire
> But thereby I thirst the more
> As though my heart would not rest
> Until our spirits were united."

And it continued until his love of her maddened him and beguiled his heart, bound his limbs and loosened his ribs and they were as though clad in one garment and he spoke with her tongue and she with his and they seemed to repeat and apply truly to their condition these verses :

> " I, who love and am loved, am one ;
> We are two spirits dwelling in one body."

Nay, rather it was the opposite. I have written :

> " Truly they possess one spirit, which God has created in
> two bodies."

He wrought nothing except in accord with her opinion and in governing the realm sought light only from her counsel and

* Often called Majnun.

282

let himself be guided by her judgment and made his will
subject to her will, and this was the height of folly and madness,
for how could he be happy, who suffers his wife to rule him ?

Now she had a servant, old, not noble or generous, but
from the lowest rank, who sold cotton and linen, by name Baba
Tarmis, blear-eyed, his face marked with sores, ugly in appearance, unpleasing in disposition, who used to perform menial
offices for her before Khalil Sultan entered her presence ; but
when his mistress reached a rank, which none had attained
before, the rank of her servants was exalted and the magnificence of her household increased and Baba Tarmis gained
honour because he belonged to her, for the servant is honoured
according to the nobility of the master ; and he became master
of the household and ruled her and made himself noticed in her
assemblies, wearing a precious cloak ; so he advanced until
he was the pivot of affairs ; then his foot stepped beyond the
bounds to discussion of affairs of state and other matters ;
then he gradually came to intervene in the judgments of the
Court and give out the decisions of the Sultanate ; then he
gained the power of appointing to offices and removing therefrom and engaged therein in jest and earnest and advanced,
until he became chief minister of the realms, whose authority
none could resist because of the strength of his power drawn
from the power of his mistress and he put forth his hand and
tongue as he wished and every man obeyed his commands and
counsels ; and he insulted Allahdad and Argunshah, con-
firming what they had dissolved and dissolving what they had
confirmed, and so disregarded courtesy, that he stepped forward in their presence, and did not observe in the least what
was due to their dignity ; then ordered that nothing should be
completed without his advice and that, if absent, he should
be awaited or they should come to him : and from the time
that he came forward until he reached the highest point was a
space of about three years, the Jagatais like demons and jinns
remaining in shameful punishment, and from his advance there
came to Allahdad and Argunshah the greatest affliction and
trouble and they reached the peak of shame and distress and
their sickness was grievous and their remedy in vain and they
thought death pleasant rather than longer life in this condition.

CHAPTER LXXXVII

SHOWING THE PLAN OF ALLAHDAD AND HIS DEVICE IN SENDING
NEWS TO KHUDAIDAD

THEN Allahdad deliberated, but his malice was in vain, and he cooked a dish which was overturned upon himself and wove the net of his death with his own hand. I have written :

" When the fortune of a brave man is overturned,
His mind thinks fair those things that are foul,
He labours in everything to no purpose
And spoils what men think good."

And they found nothing suited to calm their hearts but to send news to Khudaidad, and they revealed to him the condition of affairs and showed it to him openly and plainly and proposed to him, that he should come with full confidence and aim at Samarkand with his army with tranquil mind ; and he rose forthwith and led forth his army and followers and crept forward like a flight of locusts and came to a place called Aurataba.

But when Khalil Sultan heard this, he summoned his armies and allies, wondering at the arrogance of Khudaidad and invoking vengeance on his hostility and he sent against him Allahdad and Argunshah with great armies, who stood opposite to him but attacked him not. Then they sent to Khalil Sultan, seeking aid and saying, " This man is perfect in stubbornness and in the vehemence of his wickedness and in his recklessness, so that he does not move from his camp and the breath of fear of us has not reached his ears."

Therefore he sent them aid with the rest of his army, awaiting news. Then again they told him : " This man truly brings harm and goes forth to plunder and in his enmity is like the tribes of Themud and Ad ; therefore you should yourself come to our aid and help us by your wisdom and counsel, for fear of you has the greatest effect and your presence is most august and he has not boldly undertaken this matter or come to this perfidy without already conceiving in his mind much evil and enfolding much pitch in his bosom. Therefore help us with your remaining forces ; for this affair will be decisive."

Therefore Khalil Sultan went forth with heart and mind secure concerning the turns of fortune, with ample hope and joyous breast, rejoicing in the vigour of his youth, utterly devoted to his intimates, prancing among his friends, walking delicately among his contemporaries, with a small company and elegant retinue. Remote from him the onset of care and strange to him the coming of trouble and affliction ; and he was confident in his perfection and his condition proclaimed these verses :

" O Leader, fortune is with you, for you are worthy ;
Use the power which charm has given you."

And he came with that Sultan's retinue to Sultania and Allahdad informed Khudaidad that the equipage of the Sultan on such a day had gone forth from Samarkand and at such an hour would halt in the town of Sultania.

CHAPTER LXXXVIII

OF THE STRATAGEM OF KHUDAIDAD, BY WHICH KHALIL SULTAN FELL INTO THE HUNTER'S NET

ACCORDINGLY Khudaidad exerted himself to set an ambush and leaving his baggage opposite the army and his troops behind him, like another Tabat Shara, he hid under his arm the evil of his sparks and the staff of his defence and took with him a bold and intrepid force of brave warriors and fierce soldiers.

" They are heavy when they charge the foe ; light and
    alert when they are called to aid ;
Many when they attack ; few when they are counted."

And he covered himself with the cloak of night and mounted on horseback, betook himself by night by a crooked way to him whom he desired and for guide to the one that he sought he had the darkness of night, like a procurer, as is written :

" Seek not him to whom you are devoted except by night,
Truly the sun is an informer ; but the night is a procurer."

So he came to Sultania, a town founded by Timur, and none observed him nor did Khalil Sultan detect him until the floods of calamity beset him on every side ; then all his companions rose and began to struggle vehemently, fighting a fight of death and knowing for certain the onset of sudden slaughter ; and devouring war bit them and overthrew them broken, beaten to death and crushed, and mean and great alike among them were destroyed and friends and loved ones fell into the fire of the enemy ; then Khudaidad returned to his army, his purpose accomplished, rejoicing in his victory.

SECTION

Then Khudaidad gave his pledge to Khalil Sultan by the strongest and mightiest oath which could be given, that he would do him no harm or cast even the phantom of a straw into the eye of his life or injure him by words or deed or send against him any who by cunning and fraud might do him harm and that he should see the result of his oath ; truly God Almighty pardons what is past.

SECTION

Then he begged him to inform Allahdad and the forces that he commanded that they should submit to the orders of Khudaidad and besides he informed men : " I have your leader in my power ; if you bow to my wishes, I will obey him, but if you refuse to join me, I will slay him." But after Khalil Sultan fell into this affliction, he thought, " This is the arrow which is thrown whence one knows not," but afterwards the ambush was plain to him and he came to know how he had been caught in a place of security and knew whence that misfortune fell upon him and how he had been caught on the side that he trusted and his condition spoke in these words :

" God gives us good from him with whom we had no friendship or acquaintance.
And shame and trouble have come to us only from our friend and familiar."

Then he ordered all the other Amirs and heads of the army and Vazirs to submit to Khudaidad and not oppose him or prevent him in the things that he wished or hinder him ; all therefore gave themselves to him and went to his camp and submitted to his command, whereby he had in his power those equipped armies and was safe from deceitful evils by the help of straight spears and Indian swords ; and placing in the front line the soldiers of Jand and Khajend and the infidels of Turkistan and the worse troops, and the others in the rear, he moved to Samarkand, caring naught for Allahdad, and those who were subject to him, and Allahdad knew for certain that his hope of gain had now become fruitless and that fortune had taken and withdrawn from him the garment of power with which he had been clad and had fled from his hands and that he had cast away his former glory and wealth and this change like the resurrection of the dead happened in the year 812.*

CHAPTER LXXXIX

OF THE EVILS WHICH SAMARKAND ENDURED WHEN KHUDAIDAD CAME

WHEN Khudaidad came to Samarkand and entered it, laws and fortunes were utterly changed, and it was as though there befell the discord of sects or of bees. Now he had a son, by name Allahdad, upon whom before witnesses he conferred the title of Sultan and he searched for hidden treasures and sought in mountains their deposits and veins of gold and mined the hiding-places of wealth and searched secret and hidden things ; and manners were changed and clemency of temper exchanged for harshness and they became as the verse has it :

" The tents are as their tents, but I see women of the tribe
     different."

And accidents† were so transformed that the substance of things was altered or the earth and sky changed to another earth and sky :

" The earth of the cave has become unknown and no longer
     is it this cave,
Nor is this the same heap of sand."

* A.D. 1409.   † i.e., external qualities.

CHAPTER XC

WHEN this news reached Shah Rukh, his face was stern and sad, he frowned and looked aghast and his face was darkened and altered and his colour changed because of wrath and he implored help and was astonished and lamented and entrusted himself to God and was kindled with anger and grieved heavily and groaned and said these words (on the calamity of his house) :

" Truly it is consumed by wasting until its reins protrude and every poor man makes a bid for it."

Then he caused to fly to every side to the borders of his kingdom written mandates to assemble the army and he bade Shah Malik march without delay or rest and with the swift speed of his horses excel even the nobler birds and repair the broken pearl-string and drive from the comfort of the kingdom the base infidels and not permit their forager to descend or him that prepared their pot to take from the flock a beast that he might cook ; accordingly Shah Malik set forth immediately with his army extended like the hills and numerous like the sands ; then after him came Shah Rukh with the other horsemen and victorious royal eagles and marched without delay or resting in his movement to observe the constellation of the heavens or explore the road and when they came to the Oxus and crossed it, they covered its face as though with a curtain and that torrent spread over the face of the water and that sea was covered with thick clouds and drowned in the sea of abundance.

SECTION

When that sea went over those mountains and news came to Khudaidad, he was certain that his flies and apes were unequal to the wolves and lions of the army of Shah Rukh and that the greater part of his army would flee from him and betray him or take him and hand him over to Shah Rukh.

Therefore he gave himself forthwith to completing his needful business and hastened to prepare that which he required and took what came to his hand of wealth and set on beasts of burden what he could obtain of precious things and baggage and taking with him Khalil Sultan he departed to Andakan and shut in the fort Allahdad, Argunshah and Baba Tarmis and deigned not to take any of them with him and he left also Shadi Mulk in the city deprived of her Khalil and given as a pledge and exposed to contempt, her former glory taken from her.

CHAPTER XCI

OF THOSE THINGS WHICH HAPPENED AT SAMARKAND AFTER THE DEPARTURE OF THE ARMY OF JAND AND BEFORE THE COMING OF THE HAWKS OF SHAH RUKH

THEN after Khudaidad departed and withdrew, when as yet none of the party of Shah Rukh had come and the people had no leader or support, Allahdad and Argunshah wished to depart to Shah Rukh and receive him, but Khwaja Abdulawal opposed them and placing his guards, prevented them from leaving the fort and called to aid against them the rogues of the city, for formerly Allahdad had done him a grievous injury, which aroused hatred in him according to the proverb :

" He who sows thorns will not reap grapes."

Nor were two found to disagree concerning his government or two goats to attack one another with their horns because of his commands and his nod stood for command and forbidding and the streams of his commands flowed freely among men and in that past time his orders were observed.

Knowledge raises the house that has no pillars.

And Khawja Abdulawal ceased not to rule the people according to his will and to hold fast Allahdad and his companions and those who acted with them and to tighten the strings of government, until the front line of Shah Malik advanced, followed by the armies of Shah Rukh.

CHAPTER XCII

THE FULL MOONS OF THE PROSPERITY AND RULE OF SHAH
RUKH REVOLVE IN THE SKY OF THE KINGDOMS OF TRANSOXIANA
AFTER THE SETTING OF THE SUN OF THE FORTUNE OF KHALIL

THEN the townsmen went forth to receive him, rejoicing at the sight of his face like a new moon, and after setting everyone in his place and order, he laid hands on Allahdad and his companions, whom he visited with torture of every kind, and in torturing them and extorting wealth from them he used diverse kinds of torments, then slew them by violent death and sent them from this life to the other. And they scorched Baba Tarmis with various torments, but on a certain day, when he had endured grievous torments, he led his guards to show them the truth or go with them to a hidden treasure and they went with him and being bound with strong fetters he was near a tank wide and deep, then he withdrew his hand which was ready, like a sword, from the sheath of their hands and suddenly hurled himself into the water and was drowned.

SECTION

Then Shah Rukh visited the tomb of his father and paid his dues to his body and renewed the order of reading the Koran over his tomb and the military guard and restored the pay of those who were appointed thereto and the servants and transferred into his own treasury most of the furniture and utensils and his weapons, which had been on his tomb, and dug the floors of the treasuries and searched the limits of those hidden places and strove to set the state in order and fix the rank of his kinsmen and those distant from him.

SECTION

Also they seized Shadi Mulk, whom they put to shame and abused, prostituting her to her guards, and tortured her with thongs and led her hither and thither to produce her wealth, as do the servants of tyrants ; and after that abasement and when diverse wealth had been drawn from her, they bound her tightly and led her through the market-place, proclaiming her infamy by the voice of a herald. And the rule of Shah Rukh was established and the chief men gained higher place and the rest were broken, one was raised, the other brought low. But praise be to God, whose majesty is eternal and whose supreme dominion changes fortune and alters condition, but itself knows no change or alteration !

CHAPTER XCIII

OF THE MALICE AND INSOLENCE WHICH KHUDAIDAD STROVE TO ACCOMPLISH, AND HOW THAT EVIL AT LENGTH REACHED SO FAR THAT HE SUFFERED PUNISHMENT

BUT Khudaidad, when he stood in his own country and had withdrawn with Khalil Sultan to Andakan, the city of his own government, renewed with him his promises and pacts and bade him not to fear his cunning and treachery and said that that affliction and trouble had been stirred up against him only by Argunshah and Allahdad in return for the benefits which he had conferred on them and the generosity with which like a long robe he had clothed them and that they had repaid to him evil for good and rewarded his kindness with their malice ; and he said : " Remember how you dealt with me at first and openly and turn your mind to that which I did with you secretly and lastly ; nay, I will still do with you that whereby the refined purity of counsel and sincerity of intention shall be confirmed, so that filth may be removed and only purity remain and trouble being abolished, the faith of promises may stand firm and for the rest of our lives we may remain sincere friends and meet in fullest concord in the gardens of pleasure ; nay, if God Almighty so wills, I will lead you to the abode of your glory and will spend all my zeal in doing that which shall lead you to your former joy and vigour."

Then he caused his name to be recited in the sacred assemblies at Andakan and likewise in all Turkistan.

CHAPTER XCIV

ADDING HOW KHALIL AND KHUDAIDAD MADE AND CONFIRMED
MUTUAL PROMISES, PACTS AND FRIENDSHIP, UNTIL THE DES-
TROYER OF PLEASURE SEIZED THEM BOTH

THEN when the bonds of an oath had been strengthened between those two, Khudaidad departed to seek the aid of the Moguls for Khalil Sultan and he left Khalil Sultan at Andakan. But when the Moguls had heard of the death of the base Timur, their place of abode having been taken from them and having left their homes, they betook themselves to forts and clung to the hem of every strong place of refuge, as was said already, but as soon as they became certain of his death and thoroughly assured themselves of his end, they proclaimed security and peace and observed the law of neighbourhood with Khudaidad in that region and sent envoys to felicitate Khalil Sultan and sent to him precious gifts and excellent royal presents among which was a throne of gold fashioned with wondrous skill by a goldsmith. And Khalil Sultan received these their envoys generously and with great honour and accepted their friendship and returned to them tenfold in every sort. I have written :

" He preserves longest what is good, for thereby time is
    prolonged ;
But he destroys what is evil, which lasts only for a
    season."

Nor did the gold-embroidered garments of friendship cease to be woven between them and mutual faces of reverence and respect to be gladdened daily, until there came upon him that which came and over him flowed from the sea of Fate and Providence that which flowed. Therefore as soon as Khudaidad came to them, they seized him and by an envoy told Khalil Sultan the manner thereof, saying : " Know what true friendship there is between us and you ; we know well what happened between you and Khudaidad and that he was author of your overthrow and caused the kingdom to leave your hand. But now he has come to seek our aid for you. Therefore write to us what seems fit to you ; if you order, we will slay him and if you desire, we will spare his life and in short whatever you bid us, we will do."

Then he sent an answer saying, " You know truly how he hurt me and rent my dignity and dishonoured me and drove me from my kingdom and rule and drove me into exile remote from my people and friends and when I was ground down afflicted me with separation from my love and my country. But now he makes me a shield whereby he may ward off grievous happenings and misfortune ; but you know his purpose if he can do according to his will and whatever it be, a word to the wise is enough. Therefore whatever seems good to you concerning that matter, so do."

Presently therefore they cut off his head which they sent to him.

CHAPTER XCV

KHALIL SULTAN RETURNS FROM THE KINGDOMS OF ANDAKAN AND SEEKS HIS UNCLE SHAH RUKH AND PLAYS WITH THAT ROOK*

AND Khalil Sultan remained in that place and in the parts of Turkistan, writing in Persian poems concerning his parting from his beloved and inditing verses to her surpassing the songs of Zeidun and therein he told of his travel and what had befallen him from desire of the absent one and affliction, so that with violent affection it broke his heart and sundered his reins, until weariness of longer sojourn in that country pierced him ; therefore he shook the hem of his robe and gathering his footmen and horse betook him to his uncle, marching by the high road.

Then his uncle received him kindly and reminded him not of the past or of things forgotten and joined to him his beloved and gave to Khalil his *khalil*† and established and raised the pillar of that realm, over which he set his son Ulugh Beg and returned to Khorasan, taking with him Khalil Sultan, whom he then set over the Kingdoms of Rai, but he governed them only for a little, passing to the mercy of Allah, for his uncle had given poison to him, which he drank and he was buried in the

* A play on words, taken from the game of chess.
† Meaning " dear one."

city of Rai and his life was ended ; and when Shadi Mulk heard this thing, her heart burned with the fire of Khalil and she said : " I will not endure desire or live after you," and amid groans and laments she recited and sang :

> " Thou wert the pupil of my eye and the eye weeps for you
> Which wished for your death ; and blaming your deeds,
> I was always in fear."

Then taking a dagger, she plunged it into her throat and leant upon it with such force that it pierced her head and she burnt with her fire all that beheld her ; then both were buried in one tomb and their fate said :

> " We are protected, for we are both strangers here
> And every stranger is akin."

And submissive to Shah Rukh were the Kingdoms of Transoxiana and Khorasan and Khwarizm and Jorjan and Persian Iraq and Mazanderan and Kandahar and Hind (India) and Kerman and all the countries of Persia and so far as the borders of Azerbaijan, until our time, that is the year 840,* and we seek from God Almighty a good end through his grace and favour. Praise be to God, Lord of the worlds !

* A.D. 1436.

294

CHAPTER XCVI

OF THE WONDERFUL GIFTS OF TIMUR AND HIS NATURE AND CHARACTER

TIMUR was tall and of lofty stature as though he belonged to the remnants of the Amalekites, big in brow and head, mighty in strength and courage, wonderful in nature, white in colour, mixed with red, but not dark, stout of limb, with broad shoulders, thick fingers, long legs, perfect build, long beard, dry hands, lame on the right side, with eyes like candles, without brilliance, powerful in voice; he did not fear death; and though he was near his eightieth* year, yet he was firm in mind, strong and robust in body, brave and fearless, like a hard rock. He did not love jest and falsehood; wit and sport pleased him not; truth, though troublesome to him, pleased him; he was not sad in adversity or joyful in prosperity.

The inscription of his seal was: *Rasti, Rusti*—that is, " Truth is safety "—and for a brand on his beasts and centre-mark on his coins he used three rings placed in this way ∴ He did not allow in his company any obscene talk or talk of bloodshed or captivity, rapine, plunder and violation of the harem. He was spirited and brave and inspired awe and obedience. He loved bold and brave soldiers, by whose aid he opened the locks of terror and tore in pieces men like lions and through them and their battles overturned the heights of mountains. He excelled in plans that struck the mark and in the wonders of physiognomy; was excellent in fortune, of apt diligence, firm of purpose and truthful in business. I have said:

" How often his plans kindled the fuel of trouble,
And blazed for the author of disasters and inflamed peoples."

A debater, who by one look and glance comprehended the matter aright, trained, watchful for the slightest sign; he was not deceived by intricate fallacy nor did hidden flattery pass him; he discerned keenly between truth and fiction, and caught the sincere counsellor and the pretender by the skill of his

* In fact, seventieth.

cunning, like a hawk trained for the chase, so that for his thoughts he was judged a shining star, and the arrow of every star, making straight for the mark, imitated the sagacity of his judgment. I have said:

" In his judgment he saw openly the vicissitudes of things,
As one sees with keen eye a thing perceived by the senses."

When he had ordered anything or given a sign that it should be done, he never recalled it or turned thence the reins of his purpose, that he might not be found in inconstancy and weakness of plan and deed. I have said:

" When he has spoken his opinion or indicated his will,
Presently his command is counted as an oracle."

He was called the unconquered lord of the seven climes and ruler by land and sea and conqueror of Kings and Sultans. It is said concerning the supreme judge, Waliuddin Abdurrahman, son of Khaldun Maliki,* supreme judge in Egypt, who was author of a wonderful chronicle, in which he used a new method, as I was told by a wise doctor and true man of learning, who saw it and marked its diction and substance, though I myself saw it not—this Waliuddin had come with the armies of the Muslims into Syria and when they had turned their backs, fate seized him in the claws of Timur ; it is said of him, that he said to Timur, in an assembly when he was familiar and clement : " By Allah ! O Lord and Amir, give me your hand, which is the key to conquer the world, that I may glory in the honour of kissing it." He also said to him (when he wished to go with him and had recited to him a part of the annals of the kings of the west—and Timur was greatly given to reading and hearing histories—and this had delighted him greatly, wherefore he eagerly wished to keep him with himself) " O Lord and Amir ! Egypt refuses to be ruled by any ruler but yourself or to admit any empire but yours. But I for your sake have left my wealth, ancestral and new, my family, children, fatherland, country, friends, kindred, relatives, intimates and the kings of mankind and every helper and leader, nay, all men, since the wild ass is worth every trophy, and I have no regret or grief except for the time which has passed of my life and my age which has gone, because it has

---

* The famous historian, Ibn Khaldun, who was grand cadi of the Malikite rite for Cairo.

been passed in a service other than yours nor has my eye been anointed with the light of your presence, as with antimony, but fate fulfils what could not be accomplished before and I shall gain the truth instead of the appearance and how rightly shall I repeat the verses :

' May God give you good in return for diligence !
But I have come in the time of accomplishment.'

" Now therefore I will begin another life in your protection, will consider wicked the time of absence from your side and will pay for the loss of my past life by spending my remaining years in your service and clinging to your stirrup and will count it the most precious of times and highest of places and most eminent of my states ; but nothing breaks my back except my books, in which I have spent my life and paid out the pearls of my learning in composing them and extinguished my day and made sleepless my night in writing them. I have set forth in them the annals of the world from its very beginning and the life of the kings of east and west, but I have made you the centre pearl of the necklace and the finest part of their wealth and have embroidered the golden robes of their age with your deeds, and your empire has become a crescent moon on the forehead of their time ; but those books are in the city of Cairo and if I recover them, I will never depart from your stirrup or exchange your threshold for another. And may God be praised who has given me one who knows my worth and guards my service and does not destroy my dignity ! "—And with this he added eloquent words, fluent, wonderful, and polished, by which he might easily carry a man beyond himself and deceive him ; so Timur was marvellously pleased thereby and his desire for books of annals and customs roused and he was maddened by love of knowledge of the condition of the kings that he had mentioned, so that he did not mark that he was deceived and carried away by the magic of this wonderful eloquence. Then he sought that he would describe to him the countries and kingdoms of the west and clearly set forth to him their position, extent, cities, roads, tribes and peoples, as his custom and habit led him, and in this he sought to test him, for he did not need instruction, since he had hidden in the treasures of his imagination the forms of all kingdoms, but he wished only to know the quantity of his learning and how he would prove his sincerity or dissimulation. Then he said

297

all those things by word of mouth, as though they were before his eyes and he was sitting in their very place, and he set forth those things as they were in the mind of Timur.

Then he said to him : " How have you mentioned me and Nebuchadnezzar among the greatest kings ? For we are not of such descent as that glorious one or sprung from the kings of the hive ; why then do you compare us with that prince ? " Waliuddin replied : " Your wonderful deeds have brought you to that high rank of honour." And much pleased with these words he said to his assembly : " Let us follow this man for he is the Imam." And Timur began to tell to the Qazi the events in his country and deeds done among the kings of the west and his armies and ceased not to tell to him the history of men until continuously he showed him the affairs of his kinsmen and children, so that the Qazi was astonished at his speech and said : " Truly the devil reveals things to his friends ! " Then Timur agreed with the Qazi that he should go to Cairo and take his family and children and his plentiful books and should not delay longer than to accomplish the journey and return to him with ample hope, certain that he would gain his wish. So he departed to Safad and rested from this affliction.

SECTION

Timur loved learned men, and admitted to his inner reception nobles of the family of Mahomed ; he gave the highest honour to the learned and doctors and preferred them to all others and received each of them according to his rank and granted them honour and respect ; he used towards them familiarity and an abatement of his majesty ; in his arguments with them he mingled moderation with splendour, clemency with rigour and covered his severity with kindness ; he was devoted to artists and craftsmen and to works of every sort if they had dignity and nobility ; by nature he spurned actors and poets. To his inner circle he admitted soothsayers and physicians, and was attracted by their talk and gave ear to their discourse ; he was constant in the game of chess, that with it he might sharpen his intellect ; but his mind was too lofty to play at the lesser game of chess and therefore he played only the greater game, in which the chess board is of ten squares by eleven, that is increased by two camels, two giraffes, two sentinels, two mantelets,* a vazir, and other pieces and the description of it will be added hereafter. But the lesser game of chess is as nothing compared with the greater.

He was constant in reading annals and histories of the prophets of blessed memory and the exploits of kings and accounts of those things which had formerly happened to men abroad and at home and all this in the Persian tongue. And when readings were repeated before him and those accounts filled his ears, he seized hold of that matter and so possessed it that it turned to habit, so that if the reader slipped, he would correct his error, for repetition makes even an ass wise. But he was illiterate, reading, writing and understanding nothing in the Arabic tongue, but of Persian, Turkish and the Mogul language he understood enough but no more.

He clung to the laws of Jenghizkhan, which are like branches of law from the faith of Islam, and he observed them in preference to the law of Islam. Thus it is also with all the Jagatais, the people of Dasht,† Cathay and Turkistan, all which infidels observe the laws of Jenghizkhan, on whom be the curse of Allah! rather then the laws of Islam and accordingly our Maulana and doctor, Hafizuddin Mahomed Bazazi, on whom be the favour of Allah! and our Maulana, Seidna and doctor, Alauddin Mahomed Bokhari, whom Allah preserve! and other doctors and banners and leaders of Islam have given an answer to all, that Timur must be accounted an infidel and those also who prefer the laws of Jenghizkhan to the faith of Islam, and also for other reasons. It is said however that Shah Rukh repealed the law and customs of Jenghizkhan and ordained that they should make his rule flow along the streams of the law of Islam, but this I do not consider true, since it is considered among them as the purest religion and true faith and if it happened that he should summon his chief men and doctors to his palace and closing the doors look upon them from his throne and propose to them anything of this sort, truly they would flee like asses to the gates.

SECTION

He was of rare temper and depth so deep that in the sea of his plans the bottom could not be touched nor could one reach the high peak of his government by a smooth or rough

---

* An engine of war holding soldiers.   † i.e., Kipchak.

path. He had placed through his realms his informers and in other kingdoms had appointed his spies and these either Amirs like Atlamis, one of his allies, and learned fakirs, like Masaud Kahajani, his chief minister, of whom the former was at Cairo Moizzia* and the latter at Damascus among the Sufis† in the college of Shamisatia, or traders seeking a living by some craft, ill-minded wrestlers, criminal athletes, labourers, craftsmen, soothsayers, physicians, wandering hermits, chatterers, strolling vagabonds, sailors, wanderers by land, elegant drunkards, witty singers, aged procuresses and crafty old women, like the deceiver Dalla, and men who had won much experience and journeyed through east and west ; whereby in accordance with his aim he reached from cunning and intrigue to the highest consummation and by the subtlety of his fraud and cunning joined water to fire and truth to error and in cunning and craft excelled Sasan‡ and Abuzeid and by his wisdom and argument surpassed Ibn Sina (Avicenna)§ and by his logic reduced the Greeks to silence, when he overturned propositions against them and conciliated deadly foes and made the bitterest enemies into friends. I have said :

" He is mightier, who leads every army against the enemy
  by words, who joins near and distant ;
Mingling smoothness with severity he rules the lover and
  leads the beloved."

They brought to him events and news from the furthest borders, described to him what things excelled there and were remarkable, made known to him the weights received there and the prices of things, marked their posts¶ and cities, mapped their roads, rough and smooth, showed their houses and settlements, set forth distances, long and short, and the defiles and wide spaces and borders and bounds to east and west and the names of cities and villages and titles of caravanserais and clans and the people of every place and their leaders, Amirs, magnates, excellent men, nobles, rich and poor, and the name, surname, title, and family of everyone and the craft which they practised and tools which they used. And in this

---

* The city is called after the caliph El-Moizz, for whom it was founded.
† Moslem ascetics and mystics, so called because they wore wool, *suf*.
‡ The ancestor of the Sassanid Emperors of Persia.
§ Avicenna, the great physician and philosopher, born A.D. 979, in the province of Bukhara, died 1037. His authority in medicine lasted in Europe until the seventeenth century A.D.
¶ i.e., halting-places.

way he marked those things with his attention and by his prudence had all the kingdoms in his power.

When he stayed in a city and any of its chief men met him, he used to ask him about this person and that, and what happened to such a one at such a time, whether good or bad, and how far that matter went and how so-and-so behaved in their controversy, whereupon the man would stand like an astonished spectator and think that Timur had been present at that time ; often he put to them some questions liable to error and related to them disputes and discussions held on those matters, whence they imagined that he excelled in that science or had been a servant of learned men and therefore some thought that that devil had resided secretly in the college of Salaria, while others went so far as to say that they had seen him among the fakirs of the college of Shamisatia.

SECTION

As an example of his sagacity it is said, that when he had besieged Siwas, which brave and stout soldiers were defending against him, he said to his army : " Devise cunning : we will storm this city on the twelfth day," which was proved by the event and it could not be doubted that that lame one was inspired or borne up to the heavens.

He excelled in various arts of leading others into error and in a profundity of actions which could scarcely be penetrated ; when any business came upon him, which he strove to remove, he pretended as if he greatly desired it ; often on the other hand he would pretend to shun that which he was seized with a great desire of obtaining, examples of all which have been shown above.

An example of his dissimulations is this : when he was making for any place or wished to descend into any plain and intended to hide his purpose and involve it in an enigma and sought to inspire error and doubt (but the sea of his army was not without a spy like a crocodile or seizer of news like a crab, nay, even if there had been no spy in his army, yet the rising of the sun cannot be hidden from those who have eyes), he used to summon great men and leaders of his kingdom and his counsellors, so that none of them was left out or a son admitted in the place of the father or father instead of the son ; then he expounded to them the secret of his affairs and sought from them advice about the regions against which he

should move and gave them a full permission to speak, saying :
" By no means shall he be blamed who discusses it, whether
noble or simple, observing future events from day to day and
year to year, but let each one debate freely and it shall not be
counted to him for a fault, whether he falls into the bottom-
most pit of error or climbs to the peak of right judgment ;
if he has missed the mark, he shall not suffer loss, but if he
has put his point on the fact, he shall win reward ; therefore
let each one exert his strength and employ his zeal and labour
and show his diligence in that which lies upon him and convince
himself that it will be agreeable to his desire and so let opinions
conspire to mark out a place." Then dismissing that assembly,
he would collect and consult his intimate friends, such as
Suliman Shah, Qamari, Seifuddin, Allahdad, Shah Malik and
Sheikh Nuruddin, who would discuss that question afresh
zealously and dispute subtly thereon and when at length they
agreed about attacking a certain country, at once he summoned
the forager and the driver and guide of the beasts and ordered
them to march in that direction and they at once scattered in
different directions according to that which had been entrusted
to them. And when the darkness of night struck its tents and
the dawn unfolded its banners as though going forth to pasture
and the drum sounded for the march and men by common
consent packing their baggage turned to that side towards
which he had ordered them to proceed, he summoned his
followers after they had packed their baggage and started upon
the road and he ordered them to scatter and move in another
direction, which he would show to none of his army until that
very hour and but for necessity would not have revealed it or
repeated his secret to anyone or even shown it for the first time.
So men moved this way and that and the armies marched now
east, now west, and the mountains of those armies were shaken
and scattered and the knots of pearl-strings loosened and
scarcely held together and the feet of the beasts could scarcely
be set free from the march and again bound and men dashed
one against the other like raging waves and overturned the
heavens upon the earth far and wide and everyone was troubled
at heart and no longer knew himself or could tell whither he
was going ; and when there was a spy in his army or one who
watched its going and coming, as soon as he saw their vessels
collected and perceived that they were moving camp and
marching, he flew to his master and told him what he had seen

of the army's march towards the side that they had agreed and that he had seen them with his own eye marching in that direction ; accordingly the people of that country would take care for themselves, while the rest were free from fear of danger and did not observe until he was already invading the country he had proposed to himself and was hurling it broken from the fire of torture into hell and Gehenna.

But how great was his cunning, deceit, dissimulation and subtlety ! of which let this be an instance : when he was in Syria and opposite the army of the Muslims, he ordered a rumour to be spread that the links of his army were broken ; and he withdrew a little and retired and announced that his cavalry and infantry were in trouble for provisions and that he was making for Bagdad ; but it appeared that the armies of Egypt had taken to flight and his object therein was to strengthen their minds and make their leaders and confused rabble stand and that each of them should return to his place and remain there and not take to flight, so that this way he might surround them all with his ambush and all at once might become his prey.

As an instance of his strength of purpose and constancy in that which he intended and resolved and of the heavy punishment which came upon those who resisted and opposed him and contradicted his will, it is said : when he led his army into India, he reached a high fort, from the ears of whose heights there hung earrings of stars and the javelin-throwers of the stars learnt the art of throwing from its straight-aimed javelins ; Mars in his orbit seemed to be one of its satellites and Saturn in his nightly path an attendant of its sentinels and the sun at midday a white mark on its brow and the drops which poured from the clouds seemed to have flowed from the depths of its spring and the expanse of red dusk above the ears of its heights and prominences of its battlements seemed like a cauldron and the orbs of the stars of the green vault of heaven were like the mouths of its ballistas and like the balls and shells* thrown by its slings.† Its guard was a company of Indians, resolute and intrepid spirits, who had sent their families and things dear to them to places which could not be taken and bravely persevered in defending and guarding that fort, though they were a small band and wretched crowd, among which

---

* Or bombs.
† The use of " Greek fire " in India at this time seems probable.

nothing could be gained but damage and loss ; and there was no way of storming the fort nor could anyone find in its circuit a place to rest by night or day, rather from above it threatened the besiegers, safe from attack. But Timur would not pass it by because of pride, unless he had first besieged and beset it ; truly a wise man of spirit withdraws not in face of the enemy. Therefore the troops began to attack it from a distance and all the people in the fort began to assail them at will with every sort of deadly weapon, whereby countless men of his army perished daily and the fort thereby became prouder and more obstinate ; but he was unwilling to leave it unless he had gained his object concerning it ; but on a certain day, when abundant rain held them back from the siege, he urged them to battle riding up to see what they were doing in that condition, but their deeds displeased him, since fear had overturned their fortune ; so he summoned the chief leaders of them and the captains and lacerated the skin of their shame with the edge of his abuse and rent the curtain of their honour with the talons of his cursing and condemnation and Satan filled his nostrils and he discharged against them the fires of his wrath and malice, saying : " O cowards and unworthy of your food ! You enjoy my benefits at will, but delay against my enemies. May God turn my benefits towards you to evil and give you in return for ingratitude ill-success and punishment ! O faithless and ungrateful and fearful and worthy of punishment ! Have you not crushed the necks of kings with the courage of my feet and flown to the ends of the world on the wings of my favour and kindness and opened the closed doors of victory with the sword of my terror and let your fancy batten on the pleasant places of the earth under the protection of my sway ? Through me you possess the eastern and western parts of the earth and have melted their solid parts and made solid that which flows.

' Have I not entered the fire of war, whereby your enemy
    was burned,
  And defended you, when you would have been forced to
    flee from the high places ?
  And with my right hand poured good things upon you,
  And with my left hand averted evil from you ? ' "

And he ceased not to roar and bellow and babble and stutter with anger, while they with eyes fixed on the ground answered

nothing and heeded not his words, wherefore his anger grew
and he was almost choked and he drew his sword with his
left hand and brandished it over the heads of those slaves and
wished to use their necks as a sheath and to drench the edge of
his sword with their blood and in this condition submissively
and humbly they offered themselves up to death with heads
bent. Then he withdrew and checked himself and held himself
back a little or so pretended and put his sword in its sheath,
that he might not slay them, not knowing what he did with it,
and put back and hid its blade in the sheath. Then he came
down from his horse and ordered to be brought to him the
greater game of chess that he might play it ; and he had with
him one named Mahomed Kawjin, who had with him a firm
place and trusted position, being preferred to all the Vazirs
and highly esteemed before all the Amirs, whose speech was
welcome and his counsel accepted, endowed with a fortunate
and lovable temper ; therefore they sought his intercession
and entrusted to him the solution of this doubt, saying :
" Help us by a word and look upon us with but the glance of
an eye and mark the words of the poet :

> Help with your worth the stranger who seeks you,
> reduced to poverty.
> For wealth of lofty worth is better than wealth of riches.

And as it is written :

> The least thing that a friend should give to a friend
> Is to speak for him.

And these words :

> If anyone grudges to speak for me,
> Even a miser will thereby lighten my poverty."

And he consented and undertook to draw Timur from the
plan to which he clung obstinately and looked for an opportune
place to speak and seized the chance, and the mind of Timur
began to boil and rage because of that fort and to seek light
from the light of their counsel and take fire from their opinions,
but none of them could do aught but approve what Timur
thought right and said.

But it happened that Mahomed Kawjin, when fate was
coming upon him and destined evil threatened him, said :

" May God preserve our Maulana and Amir and with the keys of his plans and banners open the citadel of every difficult enterprise ! Suppose that we at length storm this fort after losing some of our brave and stalwart warriors, will this be worth the cost, so that the gain will balance the loss ? "

But Timur, paying no heed to his words, counted it vain to reply ; rather he summoned one of his cooks, ugly of aspect and of base condition, by name Hara Malik, stinking with sweat and black of visage, fouler than the workers in a kitchen and more putrid than those in the shambles ; a dog's spittle was clean compared to his sweat and the dregs of pitch like fresh milk beside his fetid skin ; but as soon as he came into his presence, Timur ordered the clothes of Mahomed Kawjin to be stripped and the rags of Hara Malik to be dragged off, then clad each in the other's clothes and girt each with the other's belt and sent for the account books of Mahomed and his managers and the stewards of his property, both movable and immovable, and his scribes and marked his wealth, movable and immovable, his possessions both live and dead stock, furniture, household, houses, dependants and slaves, both Arabs and infidels, his farms, lands, gardens, estates, domains, followers, horses, camels, baggage and chattels, even to his wives, concubines, sons and daughters, all which he granted to that base one and the day of the fortunes of Mahomed was turned to evening and ended by that night of punishment. Then Timur said : " I swear by Allah and His signs and words and attributes, His earth and sky, and every prophet and his miracles and every saint and his wonders and by His very essence ! If anyone gives food or drink to Mahomed Kawjin or makes him a comrade or friend or cares for him or turns to him or receives him as guest or treats with me about his affairs or pleads with me for him and strives to excuse him, I will deal likewise with him and make an example of him." Then he drove him forth and cast him out and threw him stripped of his fortune into misery.

And he was despoiled of his goods and, visiting on him the vicissitudes of punishment, they dragged him hither and thither and he saw his fortunes handed over to the basest of men and when the change of his fortune was published, men sundered intercourse with him and the core of his heart was tormented with grievous torment and he continued thus in bitter life and dark estate, and feared that his fate would be like that of Kaab, the son of Malik*; so he thought sweet the bitterness of death and accounted slow the signal of dissolution and every moment of this misery was heavier to him than a thousand sword-blows; but after the death of Timur, Khalil Sultan recalled him to life and restored to him the wealth that his grandfather had taken.

SECTION

And this is a sample of his pomp and magnificence and vehement pride and arrogance and majesty: the kings and sultans of surrounding countries, though they had full right that sacred meeting should be held in their names and were alone entitled to coin money and alone exercised rule and government, as Sheikh Ibrahim, king of the realms of Shirvan and Khwaja Ali, son of Muid Tusi, Sultan of the province of Khorasan, and Isfandiar of Rum and the Chief of Karaman and Yakub, son of Ali Shah, Lord of Kerman and Mantasha, and Tahartan, Amir of Erzinjan, and the Sultans of Fars and Azerbaijan and the Kings of Dasht,† Khata (Cathay) and Turkistan and the princes of Balkhshan and governors of Mazanderan and in short those that obeyed him of the kings of Iran and Turan, when they came to him and offered him gifts and presents, stayed on the thresholds of servitude and slavery, as far removed almost from his tents as the eye can see, observing the laws of courtesy and reverence, and when he wanted one of them, he sent to him one of his chamberlains or messengers, who called him and hastening like a courier summoned that one from a distance, calling by his name " Ho, such a one ! " and he forthwith rose from the place, where he had sat with knees bent, answering, " What do you wish ? Lo ! I am ready to obey his summons," and hastened to Timur, cumbered by his robe, readily and eagerly receiving his commands and humbly and abjectly bowing his head, bending his ear reverently and submissively, proud that Timur thought him worthy to summon and notice.

They say also that some of his army played at backgammon, and there arose among them a dispute and argument concerning the marks on the dice and one of the two players said : " By the head of Amir Timur ! so-and-so is the mark of the two

---

* Kaab is said to have died of thirst after giving away water which he had taken for himself.
† i.e., Kipchak.

dice." Then his opponent, raising his hand, slapped him and abused him and rent him with curses, as though he had slain John, the son of Zachariah, or denied Mahomed or set Moses above the human race and said, " O son of baseness and foulness ! Your impious insolence has reached the peak, when with lip or mouth you took the name of Amir Timur and how can you have such daring as to offer your cheek to be crushed by his shoe ; much less to swear by his head ? Truly he is too great for anyone like me or you to pronounce his name or mention anything which concerns him and certainly he is greater than Kai Khosrau and Kai Kaus and Kai Kobad,* who held empire over east and west, greater even than Nebuchadnezzar and Shadad."

They also say that once, when he wished to go hunting, according to his custom he sent to right and left columns of his army and forces with an order that the travellers of that region and footmen of that tract should advance and extend through the valleys and hills and when all the wild beasts were shut in the ring of ambush and it was certain that the moment had come for killing their prey, none of them should advance to strike their quarry with sword, spear or javelin, but they should merely drive the wild beasts of that desert into the midst of those plains. Then all followed his orders and when the line of those troops and bands became like a compact fabric and the columns of those hunters encircled the beasts like vultures, as stars encircle the moon, then the beasts flowed hither and thither through that continent like a storm-tossed sea and from the vortex of those swelling rivers found no exit or crossing and so they wandered and ran this way and that astonished and confounded, and after bellowing sought for help and after groaning submitted and the earth became too narrow for them and they were scattered over it and when the gold-embroidered garments of its mountains were adorned with signs of impending judgment, the beasts were gathered together and while they moved in this state in violent fear, he ordered drums to be beaten on every side and pipes and trumpets to be blown ; then when the drum was beaten and the trumpet blared, the world was filled with groaning and moaning and the earth quaked vehemently and the borders were shaken with the great convulsion, and when the wild beasts heard the sound of

---

* Seljuk emperors of Rum. Kai Khosrau I, A.D. 1192-1211 ; Kai Kaus I, A.D. 1211-1219 ; Kai Kobad I, A.D. 1219-1234.

drums and saw these terrors, their strength failed them and their reins were sundered and they sank on their knees and rose not again ; then they approached nearer one to the other and collected in herds, thinking that the day of judgment was at hand and one held the neck of the other and rested and among them the bull embraced the lioness and the lion lying between them embraced the deer and the wolf hid among gazelles and the fox betook himself to the young of the hare and the ostrich fled to the chamois and the hare to the eagle and the Libyan lizard joined the fish and the field-mouse the stag.

Then he ordered his sons and the sons of his Amirs and grandsons to hurl darts and they accordingly did to death their prey and destroyed them at will and without hesitation and he watched them and rejoiced and burst into laughter and guffaws at their actions and he accustomed them to courage and javelin-throwing and so made them brave to pursue gallant warriors ; and the followers of the army collected the game that they had wounded, so that that bandit seemed to sing and declaim these verses :

> " Kings hunt hare and foxes,
> But I, when I ride, hunt stout warriors."

SECTION

The hyacinth* was brought to him from Balkhshan and the turquoise from Nisabur, Kazarun and the mines of Khorasan and the ruby from India, and from India and Sind the diamond and the pearl from Hormuz and silk and down and agate and musk and other things from Cathay and from other countries refined silver and pure gold.

SECTION

And he planted at Samarkand several gardens and built splendid palaces, which were all firmly constructed in a new style with marvellous beauty and on the trees he engrafted excellent fruits. One of these gardens he called " Aram,' another " The Glory of the World," another " Paradise," another " The Garden of the North," and another " The Sublime Garden."

When he had laid waste a great city, in all its gardens he

* Or jacinth, an orange-coloured sort of zircon.

built a palace and in some of these palaces he had depicted his assemblies and his own likeness, now smiling, now austere, and representations of his battles and sieges and his conversation with kings, amirs, lords, wise men, and magnates, and Sultans offering homage to him and bringing gifts to him from every side and his hunting-nets and ambushes and battles in India, Dasht* and Persia and how he gained victory and how his enemy was scattered and driven to flight ; and the likeness of his sons and grandsons, amirs and soldiers and his public feasts and the goblets of wine and cup-bearers and the zither-players of his mirth and his love-meetings and the concubines of his majesty and the royal wives and many other things which happened in his realms during his life which were shown in series, all that was new that happened, and he omitted or exaggerated none of those things ; and therein he intended, that those who knew not his affairs, should see them as though present.

When he had gone abroad and the oppressors had left Samarkand and the sentinels of Satan had abandoned those gardens, the citizens, rich and poor, went to walk therein and found no retreat more wonderful or beautiful than those and no resting place more agreeable and secure ; and its sweetest fruits were common to all, so that even a hundred pounds' weight thereof would not sell for a grain of mustard.

Also he founded in the country and domains of Samarkand towns, to which he gave the names of great cities and capitals, such as Misar, Damascus, Bagdad, Sultania and Shiraz, which are the brides of countries. Also he planted in the fields of Samarkand towards Kesh a garden, in which he built a palace which he called Takht Qaraja. They say that one of its builders lost his horse, which grazed for six months in that garden until it was found.

SECTION

He had as wives the greater queen, who was noble and excellent, and the lesser queen, who was beautiful and charming, both daughters of the kings of Cathay ; and Tuman, daughter of Amir Musa, Amir of Nakhshab, who was mentioned in the beginning of this book ; and Jalban, who was like a moon when it is full and the sun before its setting. While he was alive, he had her put to death for some fault

* Kipchak.

which was told him concerning her ; but it was false ; but he
dealt with her according to the opinion of him who said :
" Whether it is true or false, it is a fault that she is suspected."

His courtesans and concubines were more than can be
numbered ; but Shadi Mulk removed by poison both the
queens that I have named, fearing them because of Khalil.
As for Tuman, Khalil Sultan sent her to Saghanaq to Sheikh
Nuruddin as is related above ; then she returned to Samarkand : I have heard also that she in this our time, that is, the
year 840,* has proposed to herself the pilgrimage to Mecca
and God Almighty knows.

Section

His own sons, surviving him, were Amiranshah, whom
Qara Yusuf killed, and Shah Rukh, who now reigns, and his
daughter by name Sultan Bakht, wife of Suliman Shah, a
virago, who did not love men, having been corrupted by women
of Bagdad, who were brought to Samarkand, and base things
are related concerning her. As for his grandsons most of them
were cut off, except the sons of Shah Rukh, of whom the chief
is Ulughbeg, the governor of Samarkand, and Ibrahim Sultan,
governor of Shiraz, and Baisanqar, governor of Kerman, who
both died in the year 839,† and Juki, who undertook an
expedition against Iskandar, son of Qara Yusuf, and defeated
him after the death of Qara Iluk, which happened in the year
839† ; then about the end of that year he also died.

Section

He had countless Amirs and Vazirs, of whom the more
famous have been mentioned in this book. His Diwans were
Khwaja Mahmud, son of Shahab Haroi, and Masaud Samnani
and Mahomed Shagharji and Tajuddin Salmani and Alaud-
daulah and Ahmed Tusi and others. The munshi of the diwan,
which is a title of the secretary, was Maulana Shamsuddin,
judge of his time and most skilled of his day in the Persian and
Arabic tongues, who engaged at will in chronicles of elegant
style ; his pen in describing those countries pierced deeper
than the spears of his master. After the death of Timur he
withdrew from business and folded up the carpet of learning.
When they said to him : " Men laugh, come then, join them

---

* A.D. 1436.   † A.D. 1435.

and now that all troubles are calmed, joyous conversation prevails; come then, enter into society," he replied, "He is dead who knew my worth and I will not waste my venerable age in serving younger masters."

His Imam was Abduljabar, son of Naman the Mu'tazilite. His chief ministers were Maulana Qutbuddin and Khwaja Abdulmalik and Khwaja Abdulawal, the son of his uncle, and others.

The reader of histories and annals was Maulana Abid.

His physicians were Fazalallah and Jamaluddin, chief of the physicians in Syria, and many others. He used always electuaries of stones, and in old age was wont to deflower virgins.

The names of his astronomers do not come to my mind.

SECTION

During his reign the judges at Samarkand were Maulana Abdul Malik, son of the author of *The Hidaya*, who could at one time train the studious and follow a game of chess and dice and compose a poem, and Namanuddin of Khwarizm, father of Abduljabar, mentioned above, who was called a second Naman and was blind, and Khwaja Abdul Awal, son of the uncle of Maulana Abdul Malik, who gained the governorship of Transoxiana after his cousin, and Maulana Asamuddin, son of Abdul Malik, to whom that governorship has now come after his cousin Abdul Awal.

The declarers of the truth of the Koran were Maulana Saduddin Taftazani, who died in the month of Muharram in the year 791* at Samarkand, and Said Sharif Mahomed Jorjani, who died at Shiraz.

The teachers of tradition were Sheikh Shamsuddin Mahomed, son of Jazri, whom he had carried away from Rum, whither he had fled from Egypt after his arrival from Syria before the warlike commotions, who died at Shiraz, and Khwaja Mahomed Zahid of Bokhara, the great interpreter who retained the traditions in memory, who expounded the sacred Koran in a hundred volumes, who died in the city of the Prophet, on whom be the blessing and favour of Allah, in the year 822.†

The readers were these two and Maulana Fakhiruddin and among those who knew the Koran by heart and read and

* A.D. 1389.   † A.D. 1419.

recited with knowledge Abdul Latif Damgani and Maulana
Asad Sharif Hafiz Husseini and Mahomed Muhriq of Khwarizm
and Jamaluddin Ahmed of Khwarizm and Abdul Qadir
Maragi, who excelled in skill in music.

The orators and public speakers were Maulana Ahmed, son
of Shamsalaima Serai, who was called the king of eloquence
in Arabic, Persian, and Turkish, and was the wonder of the
age, and Maulana Ahmed Tarmidi and Maulana Mansur
Qagani.

Those who excelled in beauty of writing were Said Khatat,
son of Bandakir, and Abdul Qadir, mentioned above, and
Tajuddin Salmani and others.

Of astronomers some flourished, whose names escape me,
except Maulana Ahmed Tabib Alnahas Mustakhrij, who said
to me : " I have drawn up astronomical tables up to 200
years." He said this in the year 808.*

The goldsmiths were Alhaj Ali of Shiraz and Alhaj Mahomed
Hafiz of Shiraz and others. The polishers of gems were many,
of whom the most excellent was Altun, a marvel of the art,
who adorned gems with various figures and carved jasper and
onyx with the letters of Yezd more beautifully than Yaqut.

The players of chess were Mahomed, son of Aqil Alkhimi
and Zainal Yazdi and others ; but the most skilled in that
game was Alauddin of Tabriz, a lawyer learned in tradition,
who could give a pawn to Zainal Yazdi and beat him or a knight
to Ibn Aqil and defeat him.

Timur, who subdued the countries of east and west and
conquered every Sultan in the field of battle, who checkmated
every king equally in war and in play, said to him, " You have
no one second to you in the realm of chess, as I have none in
empire and I have performed wonders, as Maulana Ali Sheikh
has in his own sphere ; to whom no equal is found." He is the
author of the commentary on " Chess and the theory of play."
No one could divine his intention in playing with him, before
he moved. He was also a lawyer of the Shafeite sect, learned in
tradition, handsome and cultivated in speech. He said to me :
" That he saw the leader of the faithful, Ali, whose face may
Allah make glorious ! in a dream and that he handed to him the
game of chess in a wallet and that since that time he had not
been defeated by any man." One of his gifts in playing was
that he did not reflect and as soon as his opponent after

* A.D. 1406.

reflecting and long delay played, he would move without deliberation ; he used to play with two opponents at once and show when he moved his skill single-handed against two adversaries. He used to play the greater game of chess with the Amir,* and I saw in his possession the round game and the long game of chess.

The greater game of chess already mentioned is enlarged and the rules are best learned by practice and their explanation in words would not have much value.

The musicians were Abdul Qadir Maragi, already mentioned, and his son Safiuddin and his son-in-law Nashrin and Qutb of Mosul and Ardeshir Janki and others. He had many painters, of whom Abdul Hi, of Bagdad, was considered the chief. Among the planters of trees was Shahabuddin Ahmed Zardakashi and there were innumerable sculptors of glass, bronze and other things, each of whom was the most skilful of his age and the equal of all in his craft and a marvel of his time. But if the necklaces of speech were adorned with the pearls of the gifts of these excellent men, truly they would be filled with pearls of great price and with chains of pure gold.

These are the men who are known to me and come to my mind, but those that I know not or that I know but cannot remember now, are far more than can be counted and too numerous for all to be reckoned. In short Timur gathered from all sides and collected at Samarkand the fruits of everything ; and that place accordingly had in every wonderful craft and rare art someone who excelled in wonderful skill and was famous beyond his rivals in his craft.

SECTION

There was a man at Samarkand by name Sheikh Alarian, a fakir of the Adhami sect, of handsome figure and lofty mind, whose age according to common repute obtaining among great and small was said to be 350 years, though he was of upright stature and beautiful face ; feeble old men and those most advanced in years used to say : " Truly, when we were still small, we saw this man in this same condition and we have heard the same from our honoured fathers and noblest old men, who had the same tale from their fathers and elder contemporaries." He was black and of such strength and vigour that anyone who saw him thought he had not yet reached manhood.

* Timur.

He had no wrinkles or marks impressed on his face through age. The Amirs, great men, leaders, good men, the learned and eminent often visited him in his cell and uttered blessings at sight of him and sought the happiness of his blessing.

There was also at Samarkand a mosque called the Mosque Alribat, which refreshed those who entered with cheerfulness and gave their minds fresh vigour. One of its builders is said to have been a saint called Sheikh Zakaria, an oracle of those parts, whose monument is in a well-known place on a hill and prayer at his tomb is thought to be heard. Samarkand is distant about a day's journey and the fame of miracles is spread abroad and the place is known as the scene of these assemblies. It stands on a strong hill, on which are gardens and beneath them streams flow and is open on the right and left as if it were a fragment of the chief place of Paradise. They say that when he was engaged in that building, a drop of mud fell on his face, which one of the managers saw and that it remained in that state for three days; but when they wished to set up the mihrab,* a dispute arose about the right place and much clamour and tumult was roused for that cause and Sheikh Zakaria said: "Put the mihrab on this side and do not turn it thence to right or left." Then that manager said to those who were present: "Oh! prodigy and marvel! that a man who has not washed his face for three days should show men the way to the know-ledge of the Faith!" And that worshipper of God replied: "Does anyone live who does not wash himself even once in three days? But come near, O wicked one, wait a little and calm your mind and be not among those who deny and turn themselves away; and behold the Kaaba, how, like a bride, it shows itself." Then that unbelieving one attended and behold! the sacred Kaaba seemed to move from its place hither and thither; and presently when they looked for the sheikh, they found him not and sought him through heaven and earth but did not find him. There is in this mosque a wonderful thing, to wit several pillars of wood, of which one is about 15 cubits higher than the rest and so wide that its circumference cannot be grasped by anyone; but the others can be grasped in the arms. It is said to have been a cotton tree and to it is attributed the wonderful, excellent and rare virtue, that even the smallest particle of the wood of that cotton tree applied to an aching tooth effects a cure and its

* i.e., pulpit.

pain at once ceases, which I have tried and proved. If a man says that he has seen Samarkand, he is asked concerning the wonderful things, which he saw there, and what miracles of elegance and rare things he beheld, if he says that he saw this wonderful pillar, his story is true and he is believed ; if not, what he has seen is only a confused dream.

SECTION

At Samarkand they measure nothing but weigh everything with a balance and the pound of Samarkand equals 40 ounces, each of which is a hundred sesquidrachms ; so their pound makes 4,000 sesquidrachms, each of which equals a drachm and a half, neither more nor less ; and so their pound equals ten pounds of Damascus.

Maulana Mahmud Hafiz Almuhraq of Khwarizm, who was called Almuhraq because the arrows of his speech penetrated men's inmost hearts, when they were hurled, and their sound filled men's hearts and smote them like a bird which falls in the very place, where it has been struck, and the stone of their hearts was shattered and by its shattering which gave out fire he made sparks fly into their spirits and so kindled their spirits by his sound and inflamed their bodies by the modulations of his voice—he said : " Timur wished me to be his companion on a certain journey and I was his constant slave day and night, but when his armies had encamped to besiege a certain fort and he had pitched his tent in a higher place, from which he could watch the battle and was enjoying this spectacle, at a certain time I was with him with two others, when he had fever which smote him and pained him and the struggle was like the heavens strongly fastened together and the spears of combat were caught one by the other and mingled. But when he wished to see their condition and look upon their deeds and his desire in that mighty wish could not be restrained, he said : " Carry me to the door of the tent." Then those two men supported him with their arms and held him in the door of the tent and I was with him. Then he began to look upon the battle and perceive the blows that they gave with spear and sword and wishing to give them some command, he said : " O Mahmud ! come to me," and forthwith I went to him and supported him ; presently he sent one of those two to his men, to convey to them whatever he had ordered him. But he had not yet recovered from his malady or satisfied his thirst ; so

316

he said to us: "Let me go and place me on the ground;"
and we did so and he fell like a piece of worn rope or a piece of
flesh upon the floor. Then he sent that second man to them
and ordered them according to his thoughts and spurred them
on. Then, when we were left alone, I and he, and no one was
left with us, he said to me: "O Maulana Mahmud! behold
the weakness of my body and feebleness of my strength; I
have no hand to grasp or foot to run; if men should cast me
away, I perish and should they abandon me and my condition,
I cannot help myself or do good or ill for myself or obtain any
good or avoid harm; therefore think how God Almighty has
subjected men to me and made easy for me the opening of
closed gates of kingdoms and filled both horizons with fear of
me and caused my terror to fly through east and west and
subjected to me kings and mighty despots and humbled before
me Khosrus and Cæsars. And whose deeds are these but
His? And whose these exploits but His? For who am I but
a weak, poor man, who had no opening or strength to accomplish these things?" Then he wept and drew tears also from
me, so that my sleeves were filled with tears. See therefore
how this base one in his speech followed the opinion of the sect
of Jabaris* and concerning him are said these Persian verses,
which I have translated into double verses:

"Truly Providence by His hidden command has brought
    forth
  One who should possess the furthest bounds of the earth,
    though by nature rough and unfit.
He has lost a hand and yet by his seal he holds the
    kingdom;
  He lacks a foot and yet the throne lies under his foot."

SECTION

As for his soldiers and their manner of advancing, they
according to the custom of their kings moved forward gradually,
whence they expected not, and received pay, whence they
thought not to receive it; hidden treasures came to them,
secret stores of wealth were open to them; the hiding places
of what they desired and mines opened easily to them; all
their eyes roamed and ranged and on the road of avarice were
better guides than the bird called *sandgrouse†*. They were

* Those who believe all acts to be controlled by God.
† This bird finds water from a distance.

317

sharpened by experience, knew changes of fortune and had endured calamities, sustained ambushes, struggled with adversity, dealt with affairs, explored men and the world and knew the approach of every field of battle and the way from it and had passed through all its vicissitudes ; no evil affrighted them too much nor did insolence lead them into error ; when they crossed a desert or wide solitude,

" Whose terrors the hare would not approach
And where you would not see the lizard fleeing to its lair,"

one of them halted a little and carefully looked at the earth of that place and then said : " This earth is not from this place." Then dismounting from his beast he took some of that earth and smelt it, then turning to the four points of the compass he deliberately proceeded towards one of them and continued on his way with his companions, until they arrived at a place which they explored and took from it hidden treasures and all the wealth that it contained. In the same way, when they came to public buildings or passed through burial-grounds, they searched for hidden wealth, as if they had placed it there with their own hands or their spirits had revealed it to them.

Sometimes they came to a place which the inhabitants had held long and where they had passed months and years and something had been hidden underground, which neither the governor of the place nor the inhabitants had observed ; as soon as they entered the place, that thing was opened to them and explored and when the inhabitants saw this, they bit their hands with remorse and grief. And in their time they had marvellous cunning and wonderful acuteness which struck the mark. They put loads upon cattle and rode upon them and fitted asses with saddles and bits and with them outstripped those who rode on Arab horses, going to despoil the towns, and they took the spoil ; they fed their camels on the flesh of dogs and rams ; instead of barley they gave their horses wheat, rice, millet, dry grapes and beans and if perchance those were lacking on the march, they fed their beasts with the bark of trees.

I was told by Qazi Burhanuddin Ibrahim Alqusha, the Hanifite, mentioned above, on whom be the mercy of God Almighty ! that when Ghazan* and the Tatars came into those

---

* Mongol ruler of Persia (A.D. 1295-1304), who for a time held Damascus.

parts, whoever could, fled from misfortunes, as they did in the time of Timur. Among others a merchant in the village of Salahia, who led a pleasant life and abounded in much wealth, gathered his gold and silver and hid it in a jar of beans, then dived into a pond which he emptied and under it placed the jar and hid it, then restored the pond to its former state and let the water into it again. But when he had to start on his journey and his beasts were ready for riding, he said to his wife : " We have forgotten my earrings and I fear lest they be lost on the way ; seek a place for them and make us safe in that matter ; " and she said : " But there is no place ; " then he took them and put them in the roof of the bed-chamber, which rested on a thin beam ; then mounting their beasts and leaving their house they fled. But when the Tatars came to Damascus, some of them occupied that house and began to eat and drink, passing the time in jest ; but one day, when they were merry, a mouse gnawed one of the earrings, from which a pearl rolled and fell to the ground and they all hastened towards it one against the other, running as if they strove for the earrings of Miriam. So running they entered the pond and removing from the face of the earth the curtain of its inner part, they found the wealth as it was in the jar and took it and the pearl, which they took out, and sought the rest of the earrings, which they divided among them.

Thus also were the soldiers of Timur, to whom every difficult thing, which befell them, was easy and each of them following the example of his king reached the highest peak in his own kind and if you wished to tell their histories and achievements, it would be as easy as to tell of the ocean.

SECTION

They say that one of them who had a keen and shrewd mind, wished in winter-time to take his pleasure in the country and so took out his beast to go to hunt, which was a cow, and fastened a saddle upon it, the wood of which was fragile ; he had for a stirrup a branch bent in a circle, for girths a torn rope and he was dressed in his finery, that is the leather garb of a beggar, and his tiara, which was a cap of painted wool, and he fastened his quiver, which was bound with cord made of torn skins, the rents of which were joined, his arrows were bent, his bow was straight. He had with him a falcon, which had lost its feathers in moulting, and from its body as from a field the crop and herbage of feathers had been plucked out ; then mounted on his noble beast and carrying his falcon, he went to hunt and saw a flock of geese, resting near the bank of a lake, then he lifted his hand with the falcon that it might see the flock, then lowering his hand he set the falcon on the ground and it hopping slowly hid its cunning from the geese, since it had no strength to fly or wings to use ; so it came slowly to the reckless birds who looked for no harm to fall upon them but from the sky and mingled with them ; and they did not flee from it in fear nor was it seen, until it fell upon one and rent it, when its master soon came and took the bird.

And when the soldiers of Timur had departed from Damascus, after they had plucked the leaves of its abounding fortune from the branches of its wealth with vehement plucking, one of them had with him a cow, which he had carried off, and placing on it his plunder and his slave, he journeyed with it some time, but after a march of two or three days the beast became angry and seemed to declare, that it was not made for such use, but when none was found to receive its complaint and comfort it, it committed itself to God and fell on its knees ; then they took down what was laid upon it and shouted at it, but it rose not and so, loosening its baggage, they smote it but it moved not ; then they tortured it with whips and covered it with curses and reviling, but when with bended knees it seemed to pray, they wounded it and whipped it, so that it was almost slain ; one dragged it from the front, another from the rear, one clung to its horns, another to its ears, but it lay motionless like the elephant of Abraha* and so, unable to move it, they despaired concerning it ; but while they were in this state and reduced to extremity, lo ! they came upon an old man with a thin beard, like the *ausah* tree, who had travelled through east and west and experienced many things, who had endured cold and heat and tasted sweet and bitter and known good and evil ; he passed them while they were in their trouble ; but when he saw them as if bound with fetters, powerless, astounded, drunken but not with wine, he said : " Withdraw from it, O demons ! " Then he went nearer to the cow, like an enchanter to one possessed of a devil and took a

---

* The Axumite king who gave asylum to persecuted followers of Mahomed. According to the story, the elephant refused to move forward in an attack on Mecca.

handful of soft dust, which is the life of youth and holding its horn he poured it into its ear, then shook its head while it lay until the dust reached the entrance of its ear, then at once it leapt forward and rose, moved by the power of that dust and began to shake its head and to be more and more agitated and made itself restive and longed for the journey and was almost about to fly; then they put baggage upon it afresh and increased its load and it became mad and ran even beyond its power.

He had in his army Turks that worshipped idols and men who worshipped fire, Persian Magi, soothsayers and wicked enchanters and unbelievers. The idolaters carried their idols; the soothsayers spoke in verses and devoured that which had died and distinguished not between the strangled and the beasts slain with a knife. Diviners and augurs, who observe times and seasons, examined the entrails of sheep and from what they saw therein judged concerning the fortune of every place and what would befall in every region of the seven climes, whether security or fear, justice or injustice, abundance of crops or want, sickness or health and every other event nor did they easily err.

They have their days, months and years; each year is named after some animal and in this way they reckon the years that are past and nothing more or less is taken into the reckoning.

The writing, which the Khatas use, is called Dalbarjin, of which I have seen the forty-one letters; and the reason why they have more letters is that they count as different letters the same letters pronounced strongly or softly; and thus *Bin* and *Bainat* differ in pronounciation and so more letters arise, each of which is redundant.

But the Jagatais have another kind of writing called Uighur, well known in Mongol writings, which manner of writing uses only fourteen letters, and this small and compact number arises because they express guttural letters by one and the same form and pronounce them alike. They do likewise with letters of which the pronunciation is nearly alike, as B and F, Z and Sin and Sad, and also Te, Dal and Ta. In this character they write their despatches, orders, open letters, epistles, catalogues, measurements, annals, poems, histories, reports, public acts, the prices of corn fixed by public authority and all that concerns their civil law and even the laws of Jenghizkhan. He who knows this writing does not perish among them, for among them it is the key of gain.

Section

As there were among them men fitted by nature for inhumanity, hardness and cruelty, of little mercy, nay, without religion, impious, criminal, slaves, base men, savages, who held him as leader and patron beside God and gloried in this and were greatly proud ; their impiety and love for him drew them so far that if he claimed either the rank of prophet or divinity, they put faith in him ; all of them approached God Almighty, relying on his merits ; they made vows to him when they fell into danger and honoured these vows and persisted in their vain and impious religion, so long as he was alive, and after his death they sent votive offerings and offered *korban* at his tomb and went so far in attributing to him a share of divinity that he was believed to observe and know everything.

They say that when on the march he saw one of his army bending forward his neck in sleep or while marching bending to one side or in some other way, for which he did not deserve blame or reproof, still less flogging or abuse, Timur said : " Is there no one here to cut off the head of this scoundrel ? " and he said no more and when one of those wicked and base men named Daulat Timur, a great amir and noble, whom God had clothed with the garb of cruelty and not imbued with the least odour of mercy, forthwith cut off his head between his shoulders and carried it to Timur and laid it before him and Timur said : " Woe to thee ! What is this but murder ? " and he replied : " This is the head that you ordered to be cut off." And this reply caused him to wonder and on his knees he praised God because his command was carried out at the lightest sign.

There were among them also men of intellect and learning and ability, poets and those excellent, doctors, and among them defenders of the truth and students of the sciences and subtle explorers thereof and men who in every sort of science and its full investigation combined the double path of enquiry, logic and perception, approving the principle of the Sufis and the " Ihya ul Ulum "* and indeed some of them observed what their teaching demanded and were of the number of the faithful

* " Revival of sciences." The religious encyclopedia of Ghazali A.D. 1058-1111.

and commended equally patience and mercy, but some of them along with poverty of estate and subtlety of the faculties and abundant learning and elegance of such beauty as to excite affection and wondrous eloquence, had a heart harder than rock and by their deeds wounded more vehemently than the blows of the sharpest sword, speaking with the words of the most excellent of creatures,* but bending away from religion as the arrow bends from the bow. When any Muslim fell into their talons or a stranger was afflicted by their torture, that wise searcher of truth and subtle doctor in extorting wealth devised tortures and torments of divers sorts and employed books and questions as means of torture and composed speeches and dissertations in the science of accusation, but when that wretched one was scorched with pain and lamented and with impatient wrath implored the aid of God and of His miracles and besought the intercession of all those in earth and sky, angels, prophets, friends and helpers, that elegant one would smile and show his skill and turn proudly this way and that, flatter, recite witty verses and employ the refinement of rare sentiments and histories ; sometimes he would be kindled with anger and would weep and groan at the torture which he inflicted and grieve vehemently and do as some judges of Islam, who having seized the goods of orphans wail and lament, while by their deeds they wound the hearts of Muslims.

When they were at Damascus, they entered the house of one of the magnates in the street called Ajam, which was full of precious things,

> " A palace of blessing and safety which the days adorned
> with their beauty,"

then laying hands on the master of that house, they bound him and visited him with various torments and tortures and binding his feet strongly, they suspended him and extracted precious things and dragged forth their greatest beauties, set out the choicest food and drink, so much as they needed, took for themselves of those delicacies, ate and drank, enjoyed jest and merriment and when one of them became hot with wickedness or pride and grew foolish in his drunkenness, he seized that wretched one, who had been afflicted with vehement torture, and gave him water to drink and the dust of chalk and ashes to taste.

* Mahomed.

323

There was also among them a learned man, passing his life on meagre sustenance and with vile raiment, abstaining from strong drink, as the poet says :

" I marvel at my sheikh and his abstinence and because so
    often he remembers Hell and its terrors ;
He dreads to drink out of silver and would drink silver
    itself, could he take it."

When they carried into the circle the cup red with wine, they offered to him spiced sugar, in Chinese cups, to which they added pure water, and made themselves drunk with shameful potions and that unhappy one became drunk with the odour of wine ; then he turned to the master of the house and smiled upon him, while he endured grievous pain, and greeted him with mirth and jests and bent this way and that to the sound of strings and took of those foods and drink, saying : " Wealth rejoices the miser, whether he gains it by toil or inheritance."

There were also in his army many women who mingled in the mêlée of battle and in fierce conflicts and strove with men and fought with brave warriors and overcame mighty heroes in combat with the thrust of the spear, the blow of the sword and shooting of arrows ; when one of them was heavy with child and birthpangs seized her, while they were on the march, she turned from the way and withdrawing apart and descending from her beast, gave birth to the child and wrapping it in bandages, soon mounted her beast and taking the child with her, followed her company ; and there were in his army men born on the march and grown to full age who married and begot children and yet never had a fixed home.

In his army were also good men, worshippers of God, religious, continent, generous, and ennobled by the glory of good works, always engaged in the study thereof, who were wont to set free captives or restore that which was broken or quench fires or rescue the submerged or practise kindness or succour the afflicted, so far as they could in any way, whether by force and might or artifice and guile or generosity and intercession or exchange and purchase and they followed him under compulsion or freely wandered for these ends.

I was told by Maulana Jamaluddin Ahmed of Khwarizm, a famous and eloquent reader of the Koran, who was the Imam of Mahomed Sultan*, while he lived, and Imam of his college

* Grandson of Timur.

after his death, then preacher at Brusa, where he died in the
year 831,* may God Almighty be merciful to him! " I was
teaching the Koran at Samarkand in the college of Mahomed
Sultan to his slaves and the children of the Amirs, when his
wicked grandfather wrote to him, when he was beginning his
march into Syria, to come to him and meet him with Amir
Seifuddin, and he obeying the command made ready those
things, which he needed for the journey, and he said, ' Prepare
yourself as a companion of the journey and cut off your
impediments and take the equipment of the journey and see to
the affairs of your household and estate and agree with us in
accompanying us, for the best companionship is that which
comes of agreement ; ' then I sought from him pardon concerning the journey and tried every means with him to close
the window thereof and said to him ' Maulana ! I am a teacher
of the Koran and a soothsayer ; I am unequal to undertaking
the journey, for 1 am weak in bodily frame and feeble of limb,
I am not strong enough to march, though in the companionship
of our master and Amir there be every happiness and blessing,
especially on this long expedition, joined to many hardships,
and while I live so feeble, I have not in my stable a camel male
or female. As for you the journey comes to you of necessity
and is a debt not to be avoided ; you cannot make excuse or
delay therein, nor is postponement open to you.' But he
excused me not and set before me reasons whereby he wished
to soothe and persuade me ; but succeeded not ; and I saw
no escape from preparation for the journey and making ready
my retinue and provisions. Then we journeyed until we
reached his grandsire, who was advancing on the highway with
zeal and diligence and we saw the sea of that army, to which
there was no beginning or end. If anyone had fallen from the
ranks of his host or withdrawn from the straight path of his
way, even with lamps and tapers he could not find his comrades
or return to his own people except on the day of resurrection.
And while I journeyed with them, I was weakened, broken
and crushed by the footprints of weariness and 1 fell sick and
was wearied with marching by night and prevented from sleep
and left my companion and departed on a wide road, where,
when I was alone, in a low voice I read the august Koran,
and was charmed with the savour of it and love of it and with
my throat I threw aloft the reading and its sound was sweeter

* A.D. 1428.

than a delicate song on the pipe and more delightful than the company of the wine cup, tempered by the cool air of the north and mixed with the breath of a lover."

Moreover he said : " Lo ! two men, weak like timber rotted with age, lean, unkempt, pallid, clothed in torn rags, and dusty, who had seen me from the side of the road and remained fixed to me like a rope to a stake, marking my actions and listening to my words ; after I had finished my intoning and completed my murmurs and hidden in the treasury of my breast the gems of my speech and sealed the flowers of my verses with the ring of prayer, they shed tears at my petition and said ' Amen ' to my prayers. Then they came nearer to me and saluted me, exulting and rejoicing at my reading, which they had heard, and said : ' May God refresh your heart as you have refreshed ours and wiped away our sins with the charm of your reading engraved on the tablets of our breasts ! ' Then they began familiar speech with me and dealt with me by question and answer. And they were both of the refined flower of the Jagatais and of the picked army of Timur and of the stock of the Tatars and of the root of calamities and evils. Then they asked me about my family and home and my companion on this journey ; then I unfolded to them my descent and origin and place of birth in my province and that I was among the people of the Koran and a companion of Mahomed Sultan. And they said to me : ' O reverend doctor ! We have only come to you that you may do us good and to consult you about something and let it not anger you against us.' I replied freely : ' We will speak so long as you please and you will not find me at all proud.' Then they said : ' Maulana ! this thing troubles us and has troubled us : whoever truly applies himself to a business that touches him not and leaves what concerns him, falls into a cause of affliction.

" ' And he who discerns not good from evil falls into evil. Say, therefore, by Allah ! O doctor, whence do you take food ? ' I replied : ' From the table of Mahomed Sultan.' Then they said : ' Is the food of this army permitted or forbidden and unclean ? ' and I replied : ' Most of it is forbidden, nay, by Allah ! it is all oppression and sin, since it is gathered by spoil, plunder, raiding and rapine.' Then they said : ' By Allah ! O Imam, truly we were discourteous and importunate, when we proposed this talk to you ; but you are lovers of learning ; your nature and habit is to pardon the sinner ; it is yours above all to restore what is broken, set free captives and make easy that which is hard. Therefore receive our inquiry with pardon and do not reward this importunity with anger.' And I said : ' Ask and do not be verbose.' And they said : ' We ask from you in the name of Allah, who chose you as guardian of His Word, which he gave to be observed by His servants and wherein He declared the signs of that which is permitted and forbidden, blame us not for addressing you, for the doctor and spiritual guide is like a kind and merciful father, who is not angry with his son for the meagreness of his learning.' Then I said : ' No, ask what you will and continue your speech as pleases you.' And they said : ' Is not a wide road open to you to leave the company of those evil men and cannot steadfastness in permitted things suffice instead of that which is forbidden ? ' And I replied : ' Truly I came to them, but perforce, and went forth with them, but shunning it and unwilling, and Mahomed Sultan, who by the kindness with which he received me reduced me to shame, compelled me against my will and I went with them, but the eye of my being was spoiled for lack of the salve of quiet and my horse bore me with pain on my journey and set me down with pain.' Then they said : ' Do you think, if you had refused to go forth, they would have shed your blood and carried your children into slavery and your wives into captivity ? ' I replied : ' No, by Allah ! God forbid !' ' Or,' they said, ' would they have cast you into bonds or scourged you or treated you ill ? ' And I replied : ' I am too noble and worthy that they should disgrace or torture me, for I am a guardian of the Koran and the Koran guards me from this harm.' They said : ' The most then that they would have done to you, when they saw that you were bold and unapproachable, was to receive you with abuse and take away your office and cast you off and reprove you and abandon their kindness which you experienced.' I replied : ' They would not have done even this and my firmness and courage would not have descended from that rank of honour, in which I excel before them, to this injury, but by smooth words they soothed me and put me to shame and enticed me and I suffered myself to be enticed ; would that I had refused it ! ' Then they said : ' This is not enough to remove your guilt nor will it bring you by a straight road to a good excuse before Almighty God. Why then did you not sit in your place engaged in reading your Koran and in your pursuit of learning and argument with your brothers, whereby you would have been free from toil and have filled your belly with lawful things and have been safe in the haven of your religion from those wicked men and have rested from that compulsion of taking forbidden things, besides what we have heard about men like unto you, which is commonly spoken of them : the doctors of the Koran and those who recite it are the family of God and His intimates and most excellent among His creatures and by their blessings it is brought about that the cloud of His bounty pours forth rain ; there are indeed Sultans, Kings of all men, but you are Kings of Kings and Sultans and since God has given you liberty, men also hold you immune and to the men of this world you are in place of heart and liver and head and no one has power over you, but you hurl yourself against this precipice and fly into harm, like moths into the fire. When you could be free, you grasp the hem of necessity and compulsion. And how will this plea suffice and in what way will it free you from the Almighty King ? And those words befit you :

> ' O assembly of readers of the Koran ! Salt of the earth !
>> If the salt has been corrupted, wherewith shall it
>> be salted ? '

"Then I said : ' When you express this opinion, are we not all touched thereby ?

>> ' I am pointed at equally with thee, O dove !
>> And that fits me, which fits thee.
>> I am the trunk : you are the branches.'

Then they both wept and uttered groans and sighs and drew breath from the bottom of their chest with indignation and said : ' How will not our case and yours differ by a great interval ? Truly, by the Lord of East and West ! The difference of the two cases is as East differs from West ; but it is not the place to speak nor can what is known be spoken, and secrecy is better than divulging, for the walls themselves have ears.' I replied : ' This is not proof ; do not then turn from the right way.' Then they said : ' We were compelled by force and carried off quite unwilling and enrolled in the register of the army, compelled by the command of one of the leaders. When the command comes to us, for example, to go forth on a feast day or the first day of the year, and that we should go forth at midday, and one of us delays until evening, he has no reward for his offence but the cross or the cutting of his neck ; so far is it from the fact that scourging and reproof suffice or giving of compensation and offering of intercession ! And wherein is your state like ours ? If we sit still or resist or hide beneath the skirts of secrecy or delay, we look for a similar fate, and by the example of our comrades we guard ourselves from this evil, always attentive to his nod and doing what he commands, as is required by the mercy of Allah concerning observing and taking example from another. Would that we could leave his kingdom and migrate from the country subject to his sway ! But how could we do that, since it is our country and the home of our race and the place of our familiarity, where we have been wont to journey, the fields sown with things for our sustenance, the way by which our fathers went and our children go forth, the seat of our tribes and families, the dwelling-place of our citizens and strangers ? But if of the beasts of our tribes even a cricket, to say naught of a bulbul or hoopoe, lies hidden, the rest are snatched by a flood of injustice and violence and the tyrant of death rages with sword brandished at will against the necks of the rest. But when we have to march forth and it has been decided that we should proceed with him, we ask : ' How many years must we wander and whither turns that perverse and obstinate one ? Then we take necessaries for that space and each of us is the other's cousin and neighbour and has his own wallet, in which he has his barley and rations with him, and his horse and fodder ; for the most part hungry and content with what suffices the needs of life and clad in torn garments, which suffice to cover nakedness ; and all this comes from the sowing of our hands and our labour and from the sweat of our faces ; and our great zeal is lawful in waging holy war ; we attack the goods and wealth of none ; we do not demand them with importunity ; none of us has immovable estate ; we have no relationship with any or link of kinship, but, O Maulana ! the same evil involves all and the same affliction is common to all.'

" Then they moved their heads to right and left and their shoulders trembled with fear and awe and their lips grew pale and their brows blackened and they began to weep and wail and lamented without ceasing. And truly, by Allah ! my soul melted because of them and thinking of them I made small account of great saints and considered the difficulty in which they laboured and knew that they had taken the coals with their own hands ; then I uttered groan after groan and said : ' In the name of Allah, O brothers ! what is this mighty evil and common affliction of which you speak ? ' They replied : ' As for our horses and beasts carrying rugs and coverings, we spared them in loading nor did we ride upon them beyond the time of fatigue on the march ; their condition is of such concern to us as to break our backs and reduce us to extremity ; and we are compelled to hurl ourselves upon the blood and the goods of Muslims and are led to devour their crops and endure their hatred and we do not know an escape or how we should avoid this snare. Therefore in the name of Allah, O venerable doctor ! can you find for us in this thing some indulgence of great price or cool drop, whereby this fire may be quenched and the suffocation of this anguish may be assuaged ? ' I replied : ' No, by Allah ! except the grace of God. Truly, by God's right hand ! you have surfeited me with evil and given me bitter aloes to drink and afforded me abundance of grief and affliction : I had enough of cares to afflict me and cause me grief up to the day of my burial, but now you add affliction to my affliction and trouble to my trouble. But, by Allah ! who are you ? How are you called and where is your country and sky and whose companions are you ? Thus may you be safe so long as you live ! Tell me that and do not leave me uncertain, that I may be able at any time to come to you and salute you.'

" Then they said : ' Maulana, praise be to Allah, who has blessed us with the sight of you ! Acquaintance with us will be of no use to you or avail you aught and not to know us will bring you no loss or harm and it seems to us most probable that after this day you will never behold us ; but if perchance it shall be granted that we should gather in one place, we will come to you ; meanwhile in place of us, God and peace be with you ! '

" Then without further delay they left me, and went back, leaving to me the pain of separation."

This is a drop from the sea and a particle of dust from the mountain.

And we pray God Holy and Almighty to guard our speech from error and our deeds and condition from levity and vice ! God suffices us and He is the best advocate.

APPENDIX

THE Muslim era begins with the first day of the month preceding Mahomed's flight to Medina, that day being in our era July 15th, A.D. 622.

The years consist of twelve lunar months, namely :—

Muharram
Safar
Rabia 1
Rabia 2
Jumadi 1
Jumadi 2
Rajab
Shaban
Ramzan (Ramadan)
Shawal
Zulkada (Dulkaada)
Zulhajia (Dulheggia),

each month having either 29 or 30 days.

So in about 32½ solar years the Muslim calendar loses a year : also all the months pass through all the seasons.

I have shown the years A.D. in footnotes, but have not thought it necessary to give precise days and months according to the Christian era.

THE LAWS OF JENGHIZKHAN

are referred to in several places in the text. Gibbon gives a brief account of them in *The Decline and Fall of the Roman Empire* (Ch. lxiv). " The code of laws which Zingis dictated to his subjects was adapted to the preservation of domestic peace and the exercise of foreign hostility. The punishment of death was inflicted on the crimes of adultery, murder, perjury, and the capital thefts of a horse or ox ; and the fiercest of men were mild and just in their intercourse with each other. The

331

future election of the great Khan was vested in the princes of his family and the heads of the tribes ; and the regulations of the chase were essential to the pleasures and plenty of a Tartar camp. The victorious nation was held sacred from all servile labours, which were abandoned to slaves and strangers ; and every labour was servile except the profession of arms. The service and discipline of the troops, who were armed with bows, scimitars and iron maces, and divided by hundreds, thousands and ten thousands, were the institutions of a veteran commander. Each officer and soldier was made responsible, under pain of death, for the safety and honour of his companions ; and the spirit of conquest breathed in the law that peace should never be granted unless to a vanquished and suppliant enemy. But it is the religion of Zingis that best deserves our wonder and applause. . . . His first and only article of faith was the existence of one God, the Author of all good, who fills by his presence the heavens and earth, which he has created by his power. The Tartars and Moguls were addicted to the idols of their peculiar tribes ; and many of them had been converted by the foreign missionaries to the religions of Moses, of Mohammed and of Christ. These various systems in freedom and concord were taught and practised within the precincts of the same camp . . . in the mosque of Bochara the insolent victor might trample the Koran under his horse's feet, but the calm legislator respected the prophets and pontiffs of the most hostile sects.''

TRIBAL NAMES

Moguls (Moghuls, Moghals) and Mongols are the same.

Tatars is a more correct form of the familiar Tartars. It appears that the Tatars were a Mongolian tribe, whose name was often used for all Mongols. The Tatars of the present day are of various origin.

Turks are speakers of Turkic languages.

Khitans, whom Ibn Arabshah calls Khatas, were a Tatar tribe inhabiting Manchuria in the tenth and eleventh centuries A.D. Their country was called Khitai, in English, Cathay. Sometimes they held parts of North China. Yenking, now Peking, became their capital. In Timur's time, they, or their name at least, reached westwards into Central Asia.

APPENDIX

Jagatais are people of the dominions, including Transoxiana, inherited by Jagatai, one of the sons of Jenghizkhan.

Jats are by some writers connected with the Getae of Herodotus. Ibn Arabshah mentions " Jata " in Central Asia and also in India. The modern Jats of India are presumably the same people.

I do not think we can altogether identify Jats and Jagatais. In the Baluch country, however, we find Jagdals, whose name might be supposed to be derived from Jagatai, but who seem to be Jats. Among the Mahrattas we find the surnames Jagdev and Jagdale, which may perhaps come from " Jagatai." The origin of the Mahrattas is unknown.

INDEX

(*n* means footnote ; numbers refer to pages)

INDEX